Billy the Kid on Film,
1911–2012

ALSO BY JOHNNY D. BOGGS

Jesse James and the Movies (McFarland, 2011)

Billy the Kid on Film, 1911–2012

Johnny D. Boggs

McFarland & Company, Inc., Publishers
Jefferson, North Carolina, and London

All photos from the author's collection unless otherwise noted.

LIBRARY OF CONGRESS CATALOGUING-IN-PUBLICATION DATA

Boggs, Johnny D.
Billy the Kid on film, 1911–2012 / Johnny D. Boggs.
pages cm
Includes bibliographical references and index.

ISBN 978-0-7864-6555-2
softcover : acid free paper ∞

1. Billy, the Kid—In motion pictures.
2. Motion pictures—United States—20th century—Catalogs.
I. Title.
PN1995.9.B54B65 2013   791.43'75—dc23   2013028640

BRITISH LIBRARY CATALOGUING DATA ARE AVAILABLE

© 2013 Johnny D. Boggs. All rights reserved

No part of this book may be reproduced or transmitted in any form or by any means, electronic or mechanical, including photocopying or recording, or by any information storage and retrieval system, without permission in writing from the publisher.

On the cover: Emilio Estevez as William H. Bonney in *Young Guns*, 1988 (20th Century Fox/Photofest)

Manufactured in the United States of America

*McFarland & Company, Inc., Publishers
Box 611, Jefferson, North Carolina 28640
www.mcfarlandpub.com*

For Paul and Tracy Hutton

Acknowledgments

This book could not have been written without help from Max and Pat Evans of Albuquerque, New Mexico; Bob Boze Bell of Cave Creek, Arizona; Johnny Fusilier of Hammond, Louisiana; Mark Lee Gardner of Cascade, Colorado; Tommy and Kathy Hildreth of Franklin, North Carolina; Dennis Hogan of Santa Fe, New Mexico; Paul Andrew Hutton of the University of New Mexico, Albuquerque, New Mexico; C. Courtney Joyner of Sherman Oaks, California; Boyd Magers of Albuquerque, New Mexico; Robert G. McCubbin of Santa Fe, New Mexico; Tomas Jaehn of the Palace of the Governors/New Mexico History Museum, Santa Fe, New Mexico; Robert Nott of Santa Fe, New Mexico; film historian Tom Weaver; and the staffs at the Library of Congress, Lincoln (New Mexico) State Monument, the Santa Fe Public Library, and the Vista Grande Public Library.

I should also thank my wife and son, for putting up with me, and even sitting through some truly awful movies, while I researched this book.

Table of Contents

Acknowledgments — vi
Introduction — 1

One. Billy the Kid, 1859–1881 — 3
Two. Billy the Kid in Pop Culture — 12
Three. The Silent Era, 1911–1916 — 15
Four. Early Billy, 1930–1938 — 22
Five. The PRC Programmers, 1940–1943 — 38
Six. The 1940s: Bs, As and *The Outlaw* — 64
Seven. The 1950s: The Kid Moves Forward — 98
Eight. Pat Garrett Rides Alone, 1948–1958 — 151
Nine. The 1960s: The Decline of Billy the Kid — 167
Ten. Billy Turns Violent, 1970–1973 — 182
Eleven. The 1980s and Beyond: Young Actors, *Young Guns* — 211
Twelve. Billy in Foreign Films — 231
Thirteen. Billy in Made-for-TV Movies — 238
Fourteen. Billy in Continuing Television Series — 242
Fifteen. Direct-to-Video Billies — 249

Appendix: Forgotten Billies — 253
Chapter Notes — 255
Bibliography — 269
Index — 277

Introduction

My first introduction to Billy the Kid came ... I'm not really sure. Back in 2007, I tried to figure that out after being asked to participate in a symposium at the Albuquerque Museum of Art and History as part of an exhibit, "Dreamscape Desperado: Billy the Kid and the Outlaw in America." Having written *Law of the Land: The Trial of Billy the Kid* a few years earlier, I was there as a novelist, joining collector Robert G. McCubbin; historians Michael Wallis and Frederick Nolan; and curator Paul Andrew Hutton. Over the course of our respective careers, we had become intrigued by, and perhaps even obsessed with, a bucktoothed outlaw who had lived violently, and died violently, more than 125 years ago.

I remembered reading a comic book, Charlton perhaps, in which Billy dropped cartridges into a chimney to scare off bad guys. That could have been my first Billy sighting, or he could have easily popped into my existence on a *Bronco, Cheyenne,* or *Death Valley Days* rerun. Or maybe one Saturday morning watching *The Monkees.*

Eventually, I would watch him on television in the movies *Chisum* and *The Left Handed Gun.* On May 25, 1986 — I remember the date because it was "Hands Across America" — I visited Billy's grave (for the first of many times) on a stormy evening in Fort Sumner, New Mexico. I would see him on the big screen in *Young Guns* and *Young Guns II.* I delved into his story, writing magazine articles as well as that novel. I researched his life, his career, his legacy.

While preparing this book, I rode — immediately after fracturing two ribs, courtesy of a bucking mare — to the spot where Billy's employer, John Tunstall, was killed. That murder was the pivotal moment in the life of Billy the Kid, launching him into a career of vengeance, maybe justice, perhaps a homicidal lust. It really depends on your take on Billy, and there are myriad takes on Billy the Kid.

As late as December 2010, Billy the Kid was attracting media attention across the world when then-governor of New Mexico Bill Richardson debated granting the long-dead killer a pardon. Eventually, Richardson decided not to grant that posthumous pardon.[1]

Billy the Kid died — sorry, conspiracy buffs — on July 14, 1881, but his legend has endured. Yet that legend is often wrong, thanks, in a good part, to motion pictures.

In January 2012, I emailed David DeCoteau, who had just directed a direct-to-DVD movie about Billy the Kid. "I just found out yesterday from my dear friend C. Courtney Joyner that Billy the Kid was not left-handed," DeCoteau emailed me back. "Interesting."[2]

Like novels, feature films are not meant to be historically accurate. They are meant to entertain. Yet far too often, the general public accepts film depictions as the truth. Thus Billy the Kid remains a left-handed gun when, in fact, he was right-handed. At least, he wears a right-handed holster in the one documented photograph of him. That photo was a tintype, taken in Fort Sumner in 1880. Tintype images are reversed, however, thus leading to the myth that Billy was left-handed.[3]

My ten-year-old son once asked me, "Weren't Billy the Kid and Pat Garrett friends?"

Well, maybe. Maybe not. They definitely knew each other, but it's unlikely they were bosom pals. But that's the image Hollywood has almost always painted. After all, it makes good theater.

In this book, I examine the known feature films about Billy the Kid, comparing the film versions of history to the historical fact. Two movies eluded me. *A Bullet for Billy the Kid* (1963) is presumed lost. The other, *The 1st Notch* (1977), I simply could not track down. Those two movies are mentioned in an appendix. As for the others, good (well, mediocre) and bad (sometimes really awful) are chronicled, as well as brief looks at TV movies, TV series, direct-to-video releases, and foreign films. I've even included three feature films that don't feature the Kid, but his slayer, Pat Garrett.

Fair warning: I spoil the plot, including the endings. Because unlike movies about the Alamo or the Battle of the Little Big Horn, the ending to a movie about Billy the Kid is not preordained. In that regard, he's a lot like Jesse James.

Billy can be evil. He can be good. He can be a good boy gone bad, or a bad boy turned worse. He's intelligent; he's stupid. He's psychotic; he's heroic. But he's always Billy the Kid.

Billy has turned up everywhere.

The very first *Gunsmoke* radio show was about Billy the Kid. In that April 26, 1952, broadcast, Billy was a "12-year-old runaway from Cottonwood, Kansas, always hanging around Marshal Matt Dillon."[4]

His most recent appearance, in a direct-to-DVD 2012 release, had him fighting some sort of vampire-zombie cross.

Gunsmoke to zombies? Billy's everywhere.

As Paul Andrew Hutton wrote in *New Mexico Magazine*: "Billy the Kid just keeps riding across the dreamscape of our minds — silhouetted against a starlit Western sky, handsome, laughing, deadly. Shrewd as the coyote. Free as the hawk. The outlaw of our dreams, forever free, forever free, forever riding."[5]

CHAPTER ONE

Billy the Kid, 1859–1881

The moon shone full on the evening of July 14, 1881, when Lincoln County Sheriff Pat Garrett and two of his deputies, Kip McKinney and John W. Poe, rode into Fort Sumner, New Mexico Territory. They were looking for an outlaw known as Billy the Kid.[1]

Less than three months earlier, the Kid, who had been awaiting execution after being convicted of murdering Sheriff William Brady in 1878, had escaped from authorities in Lincoln, killing two guards in the process. That event had helped catapult Billy the Kid, a relatively minor figure except in New Mexico, into the national spotlight. Periodicals across the country, from the *National Police Gazette* to daily and weekly newspapers, had carried articles about the "Remarkable Career of this Border Bandit" and "New Mexican Marauder."[2]

Waiting in a peach orchard, Garrett saw a figure rise from the ground, leap a fence, and walk into the compound of the former military post near the Pecos River. The lawmen headed for the home of Pete Maxwell where Garrett left McKinney and Poe outside as he slipped inside to question Maxwell. The Kid was said to be sweet on Maxwell's sister, Paulita.

While Garrett was waking up Maxwell, a man began walking toward McKinney and Poe. They paid little attention to the stranger since he was hatless, wearing stockings and no boots, and appeared to be buttoning his pants. When the figure stepped onto the porch and spotted the two deputies, he called out in Spanish, "*¿Quién es?*" (Who is it?)

Thinking he must be Maxwell, one of Maxwell's Mexican hands, or a guest, Poe rose and tried to calm him. "Don't be afraid," Poe said. "There is no one here to hurt you." But the figure asked again, "*¿Quién es?*," and quickly backed into Maxwell's room.

Reports vary on if Billy the Kid was armed at the time. Garrett would later say that the Kid carried a revolver, a .41-caliber Colt Thunder, and butcher's knife. Others said the Kid had gone to Maxwell's carrying only a butcher's knife. A friend, Celsa Gutiérrez,

Pat Garrett, the slayer of Billy the Kid (Robert G. McCubbin Collection).

The one documented photograph of Billy the Kid was taken in 1880 in Fort Sumner as a tintype, which were reversed images. This photograph has been changed to show how Billy would have appeared, i.e., right-handed (Library of Congress).

had sent him to cut meat from a freshly butchered yearling (hanging over Maxwell's porch) which she planned to fix for his supper.

Inside Maxwell's room, the figure called out, "*¿Pedro, quiénes son esos hombres afuera?*" (Pete, who are those men outside?) Realizing there was someone else in the room, he asked again, "*¿Quién es?*" Then, in English. "Who is it?"

"*El es*" (It's him), Maxwell told Garrett, who drew his revolver and fired twice.

Maxwell bolted out of the room, startling the two deputies outside so much that they almost shot him. "Don't shoot!" Maxwell cried. "Don't shoot." Garrett had to knock down Poe's gun, saying, "Don't shoot Maxwell."

Breathless, Garrett stayed near the outside wall. "That was the Kid that came in there onto me, and I think I have got him," he told Poe.

Poe didn't believe it. "Pat," he said, "the Kid would not come to this place; you have shot the wrong man."

After thinking it over, Garrett said, "I am sure that was him; for I know his voice too well to be mistaken."

Carefully stepping inside, they found the body of the man Garrett had killed. The first bullet had struck his left breast above the heart. The second had ricocheted off the wall and lodged in Maxwell's headboard.

A crowd gathered. From the reaction of Billy's friends, the body was definitely that of the Kid. Deluvina Maxwell, the Maxwells' Navajo servant, pounded Garrett's chest, screaming at him: "You pisspot. You son of a bitch!" Other women comforted Paulita.

The next morning, a coroner's jury was convened and found the shooting justifiable. Women washed the corpse, combed his hair, dressed him in a shroud (one of Pete Maxwell's shirts), and laid him in a coffin. That afternoon, Billy the Kid was buried in the old fort cemetery alongside his pals Tom O'Folliard (whose surname probably was really Folliard) and Charles Bowdre. Garrett's posse had killed those two back in December. Now the Kid had joined them.

Billy the Kid was dead.

But his story had really not even begun.

* * *

For such an iconic figure in the history of the American West, little is known about Billy the Kid, alias Kid Antrim, alias the Kid, alias *El Chivato*, alias Henry Antrim, alias Billy Bonney, alias William H. Bonney. Actually, his name was Henry McCarty.

He was born in New York City on November 23, 1859. Maybe. When Pat Garrett wrote a biography of the Kid, published in 1882, he gave that city and date, but November 23 happened to be the birthday of his ghostwriter, Ash Upson. Naysayers insist that Upson conveniently picked his own birthday for the Kid. Disciples argue that made it easier for Upson to recall.

New York City? It's as good a place as any. Others suggest that McCarty was born in Indiana. According to an 1880 New Mexico census, the Kid was born in Missouri and was 25 years old. One can argue that the Kid had no reason to lie to the census taker. On the other hand, he did lie, giving his name as William H. Bonney instead of Henry McCarty. Besides, census takers and individuals providing information to census takers aren't infallible.

In any case, the Kid reportedly first showed up, in history, in the 1868 census in Anderson, Indiana, where he was listed as the son of Catherine McCarty (widow of Michael) and brother of Joseph.

Some time in the mid- to late 1860s, Catherine McCarty met a Civil War veteran named William H. Antrim. In 1870, the McCarty family and Antrim left Indiana and settled in Wichita, Kansas, where Catherine ran a laundry. They moved again, possibly to Denver, Colorado, but on March 1, 1873, they were in Santa Fe, New Mexico. On that day, Antrim married Catherine at the First Presbyterian Church. The new family then departed for the rough New Mexico mountain mining town of Georgetown and eventually Silver City.

In Silver City, Catherine did laundry, baked pies and sweetcakes, and took in boarders at their home. Antrim tried working as a butcher and carpenter before turning to prospecting and gambling. He succeeded at nothing.

Young Henry McCarty attended school, starring in a minstrel show. Apparently he was a good student, if somewhat mischievous.

His life changed, however, after his mother died of tuberculosis on September 16, 1874. His stepfather farmed out Henry and Joseph to butcher and blacksmith shops, but Henry, and likely his brother, also hung out in gambling halls and saloons. The boy that history would remember as Billy the Kid was learning to be a fair hand at cards.

He also began getting into trouble.

In April 1875, he stole butter from a rancher and sold it to a merchant. Sheriff Harvey Whitehill caught the culprit but let him go after Henry promised he would stay out of trouble. He didn't.

He began associating with a grafter called Sombrero Jack, and on the night of September

4, 1875, helped him break into a Chinese laundry and steal clothes, blankets, and two revolvers. When some of those items were discovered in Henry McCarty's room, Sheriff Whitehill locked him up. Sombrero Jack conveniently left town. The young McCarty escaped up a chimney and fled to Arizona Territory.

There, the former butter and clothes thief moved on to stealing livestock. On August 17, 1877, Henry McCarty, now calling himself Kid Antrim, entered a Camp Grant, Arizona, saloon. Thirty-two-year-old "Windy" Cahill decided to bully the Kid, throwing him to the floor, pinning him down, and slapping the boy's face. The Kid freed his right hand, grabbed his revolver, and shot Cahill in the stomach. He fled, and Cahill died.

By the fall of 1877, the Kid was working for John Tunstall in Lincoln County. Tunstall was a young Englishman — probably not much older than the Kid — who had settled in New Mexico to make his fortune. He acquired a ranch about thirty miles south of Lincoln and then, allied with Scottish lawyer Alexander McSween and cattle baron John Chisum, opened a store in Lincoln.

This was in direct competition with The House, a mercantile operated by Lawrence G. Murphy and his protégé James Dolan. The House charged exorbitant prices. The House controlled government contracts. The House, in short, controlled Lincoln County. The House had the backing of the powerful Santa Fe Ring, the "political powerhouse of New Mexico and the most lawless machine in that territory's history."[3] Even the county sheriff, William Brady, was loyal to The House.

The Lincoln County War, pitting the Irish-controlled House against the Tunstall-McSween-Chisum faction, which was supported by many area Hispanics, was about to begin.

The ruins of John Tunstall's dugout at his ranch.

Markers near Glencoe, New Mexico, mark the site where John Tunstall was murdered, setting off the Lincoln County War in 1878.

Even today, the Lincoln County War is a complicated subject that would require hundreds of pages to sort out. Suffice to say that things came to a head in February 1878. Sheriff Brady began attaching Tunstall's property as part of a judgment against his partner, McSween. Trying to keep his livestock out of Brady's grasp, Tunstall and several of his hands drove a herd of horses from his ranch. Brady sent a posse.

On February 18, the posse caught up with Tunstall and his men in the rugged country near present-day Glencoe. Tunstall's riders had picked an inopportune time to go chasing wild turkeys. The posse found Tunstall alone, and murdered him.

McSween had persuaded Justice of the Peace John B. "Squire" Wilson to swear in Tunstall supporters as constables, so the Lincoln County War became a case of McSween's law vs. Brady's law.

Brady wasn't about to arrest his own men. On the other hand, he arrested the Kid and Fred Waite when they attempted to serve arrest warrants on Brady. (Brady's action would cause the Kid to miss Tunstall's funeral, and probably led directly to Brady's death.)

Two members of the posse that killed Tunstall, William "Buck" Morton and Frank Baker, were captured by the pro–McSween lawmen known as the Regulators. They didn't make it to Lincoln, but were shot dead — along with a Regulator named William McCloskey — and their bodies left to rot.

On April 1, 1878, Brady was walking down Lincoln's main (actually, the town's *only*) street, when the Regulators opened fire, killing Brady and Deputy George Hindman. A few days later, the Regulators met another member of the posse that killed Tunstall. This time, things didn't go quite as well.

Andrew "Buckshot" Roberts and the Regulators fought it out at Blazer's Mill. Roberts was mortally wounded, but he managed to kill the leader of the Regulators, Dick Brewer, and wound several others.

Lincoln County continued to spin out of control.

By mid–July, Alexander McSween was tired of running. He returned to Lincoln with plenty of men, and they took up defensive positions in McSween's home, the Tunstall store, the Baca house, the Torreón (a tower built for defense against Apaches), the Montaño store and the Ellis store. What became known as the "Five-Day War" began on July 15.

It ended on July 19, when the Murphy-Dolan faction had fired the McSween home. The Kid led Tom O'Folliard/Folliard, Jim French, José Chávez y Chávez and Harvey Morris out of the inferno, hoping to draw fire and allow McSween and others to escape. Morris was killed, but the other four made it. McSween and his group, however, waited too long, and were pinned down.

Deputy Robert Beckwith announced that he had a warrant for McSween's arrest. As Beckwith approached, someone — probably McSween — shouted, "I shall never surrender." A bullet killed Beckwith, and the Murphy-Dolan men opened fire.

McSween, Francisco Zamora, Vicente Romero, and Yginio Salazar fell beside the bodies of Beckwith and Morris. The posse celebrated, forcing servants-handymen George Washington and Sebrian Bates to play their fiddles, and looting the Tunstall store. Andy Boyle was about to put a bullet into Salazar only to be told by Milo Pierce: "Don't waste your shot on that greaser, he's long gone and dead as a herring." Despite two bullet wounds, Salazar wasn't dead, however, and later in the night dragged himself a half mile to another house, where he was cared for, and lived.

"The Big Killing" was the last straw. In September, President Rutherford B. Hayes removed Samuel B. Axtell as governor and replaced him with Lew Wallace, a former Union general who was busy writing a novel, *Ben-Hur: A Tale of the Christ*. Wallace arrived later that month, saying, "If peace and quiet are not restored in Lincoln County in the next 60 days, I will feel ashamed of myself."

He didn't quite understand how hard that task would be.

On November 13, 1878, he declared amnesty for all parties not already facing indictments for their actions during the Lincoln County War. Billy the Kid had been indicted for the murders of Buckshot Roberts and William Brady, so the amnesty did not apply to him. But on February 18, 1879, the first anniversary of Tunstall's death, a crusading Las Vegas, New Mexico, attorney named Huston Chapman was murdered by James Dolan in Lincoln. That murder was witnessed by Billy the Kid.

In March, Wallace was in Lincoln trying to get affidavits and arrest warrants. A few days later, he received a note from Billy the Kid, who said he had witnessed Chapman's murder and that he had "no wish to fight any more." Wallace met the Kid at Squire Wilson's home on March 17. Wallace offered the Kid a deal: "Testify before the grand jury and the trial court and convict the murderer of Chapman, and I will let you go scot-free with a pardon in your pocket for all your misdeeds."

The Kid lived up to his end of the bargain, but District Attorney William Rynerson, likely a puppet (if not directly part of) the Santa Fe Ring, reneged. "He is bent on going for the Kid ... he is bent on pushing him to the wall," lawyer and Wallace confidant Ira Leonard wrote the governor. "He is a Dolan man and is defending him by his conduct all he can."

In May, the Kid testified in a military court of inquiry that examined the actions of Fort Stanton commanding officer Nathan Dudley during the Five-Day Battle. Dudley would be exonerated, and the two people tried in civilian courts were both acquitted. The Kid saw what was happening. On the night of June 17, 1879, he rode out of Lincoln.

He gambled. He rustled livestock. By 1880, he was often riding with Tom O'Folliard/Folliard, Charlie Bowdre, a counterfeiter named Billy Wilson, a murderer named Dave Rudabaugh, and a forgotten cowboy named Tom Pickett. By October, John Chisum had persuaded Pat Garrett to run for Lincoln County sheriff, and the former buffalo hunter and bartender was elected in November. On December 19, the Kid and his pals rode into Fort Sumner, where Garrett and his posse were waiting.

O'Folliard/Folliard was killed, and the survivors fled, eventually finding shelter in

Lew Wallace, pictured as a Civil War general, before he became governor of New Mexico Territory (Library of Congress).

a stone house at Stinking Springs near present-day Taiban. Garrett's posse trapped the boys there on the morning of December 23. When Charlie Bowdre walked outside, he was mortally wounded. Eventually, Billy the Kid and the others were forced to surrender.

They were taken to Las Vegas, then to Santa Fe, where the Kid repeatedly wrote requests to see Lew Wallace, but Wallace was on his way out of New Mexico. Besides, with the publication of *Ben-Hur,* he was a literary star, too busy for trivial things like living up to his word. In March, Billy the Kid was shipped to Mesilla to be tried: Rynerson had arranged a change of venue away from Lincoln, where jury members might be sympathetic to the Kid, to Mesilla where the Kid wasn't as readily known.

On April 9, 1881, the Kid was found guilty of murdering Sheriff Brady, and a few days later, Judge Warren Bristol sentenced him to hang. He returned to Lincoln, and was confined in the Lincoln County Courthouse, a building that, ironically, had originally served as The House's store.

To guard the Kid, Garrett left two deputies, James Bell and a murderous cutthroat named Robert Olinger. On April 28, while Garrett was in nearby White Oaks either collecting taxes or buying lumber for the gallows, the Kid escaped.

A revolver was either planted in an outhouse for him, or he managed to take Bell's pistol. Bell was shot and killed. Shackled, the Kid then made it to the upstairs armory, grabbed Olinger's shotgun, and waited by a window. Olinger had been with the other prisoners eating supper at the Wortley Hotel. As he walked around the corner of the courthouse, the Kid called down at him and shot him to death with his own shotgun.

The Lincoln County Courthouse, formerly the Murphy-Dolan store, as it appears today. One staircase was added, but otherwise the building looks as it did in the late 1870s.

The Kid managed to free one leg from his shackles and rode out of town on a stolen, er, borrowed, horse.

On April 30, 1881, exactly one month before Lew Wallace was appointed minister to Turkey and left New Mexico, his last official act involving Billy the Kid was to offer a $500 reward for his capture.

Pat Garrett caught up with the Kid on July 14, ending Billy's life shortly before midnight.

Chapter Two

Billy the Kid in Pop Culture

Within a month of Billy the Kid's death, the Wide Awake Library had published a half-dime novel about his exploits, *The True Life of Billy the Kid*.[1] Also, almost immediately after the killing of the Kid, Pat Garrett found himself the subject of criticism and scorn. After all, he had killed the Kid in a darkened room, hadn't really given the boy a chance, and some people were saying the Kid was unarmed at the time. Approached to write a book about the life and death of Billy the Kid, Garrett jumped at the chance.

He wasn't a writer, so he got his good friend, an alcoholic ex–newspaper journalist named Ash Upson, to ghostwrite it for him. Upson moved in with Garrett's family in August 1881, and would support and defend Garrett until Upson died in 1894. Upson might have had a newspaper background, but he wrote like a dime novelist, and seldom let the facts get in the way of telling his hyperbolic, exaggerated story. Historians today point out, however, that the last third of the book, revealing Garrett's chase and killing of the Kid, might serve Garrett's interests, but remains fairly accurate.

That book, *The Authentic Life of Billy, the Kid, the Noted Desperado of the Southwest, Whose Deeds of Daring and Blood Have Made His Name a Terror in New Mexico, Arizona and Northern Mexico, by Pat. F. Garrett, Sheriff of Lincoln County, N. Mex., by Whom He Was Finally Hunted Down and Captured by Killing Him*, was published in 1882, and died a quick and merciful death.

Charlie Siringo, a Texas stock detective who had chased after the rustling Kid in 1880, fared better in 1885 with his book *A Texas Cowboy; or, Fifteen Years on the Hurricane Deck of a Spanish Pony*, as did Emerson Hough in *The Story of the Cowboy*, published in 1897. Both books were commercial successes, at least, but probably not historically accurate.

Pat Garrett was killed in 1908, shot in the back of the head while urinating on the road to Las Cruces. The man who claimed to have killed Garrett pleaded self-defense, and was acquitted.

On occasion Billy the Kid would pop up, but compared to the plethora of material being published about Jesse James and Buffalo Bill Cody, the Kid was rarely put in front of America.

In 1903, Walter Woods registered a play titled *Billy the Kid*, but it is doubtful that it was ever performed. A few years later, Woods and Joseph Santley apparently reworked his play and had it reregistered for copyright. That four-act melodrama opened on August 13, 1906, and become an enormous hit.[2]

"The popularity of melodrama is being demonstrated this week at the Lyric," the *Atlanta* (Georgia) *Constitution* reported, "where *Billy, the Kid* is drawing splendid audiences.

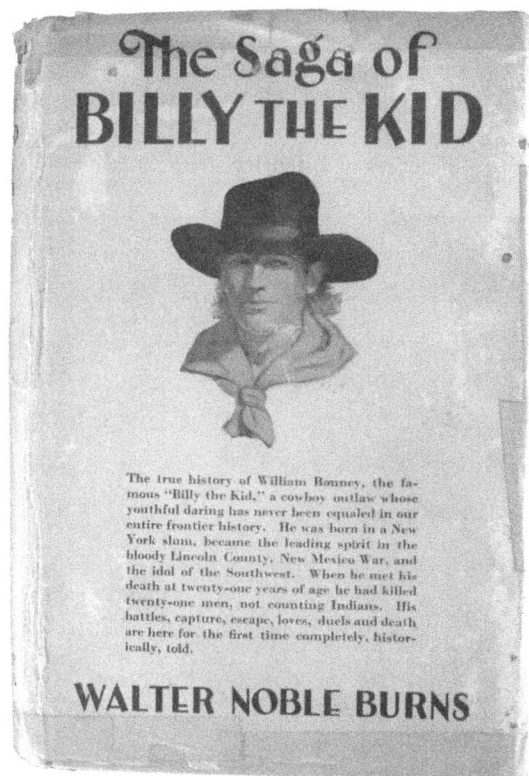 

Left: A later version of Walter Noble Burns's best-selling 1926 book that catapulted Billy the Kid back into the national spotlight. *Right*: A 1968 Charlton Billy the Kid comic book.

For thrills and melodramatic situations, this attraction holds the record...."[3] The *Syracuse (New York) Post-Standard* called it "a genuine thriller of the wild and woolly West, with some heart interest and considerable sentiment on the side."[4]

The play had absolutely nothing to do with the real Billy the Kid.

Thus, the Kid was likely on his way to second- or even third-tier Western celebrity. In 1925, Harvey Fergusson posed this question in an article for *The American Mercury*: "Who remembers Billy the Kid?"[5]

He went on: "He is no more than the echo of a name today, but in his time he stalked in glory across the front pages, and during the Lincoln County War in New Mexico he was almost a national hero."[6]

A year later, everything changed.

Walter Noble Burns's book *The Saga of Billy the Kid* was published in the spring of 1926. Book-of-the-Month Club made it a main selection, and it rose to best-seller status.[7] Its success might have prompted Houghton Mifflin to publish Siringo's *Riata and Spurs*, which included two chapters on Billy the Kid, in 1927. Almost immediately, Burns's book drew the attention of a Hollywood director named King Vidor.

Billy the Kid would soon be everywhere.

In 1938, a ballet titled *Billy the Kid*, scored by Aaron Copland and choreographed by Eugene Loring, debuted in Chicago. In Michael McClure's dramas, Billy would seduce Jean Harlow in *The Beard* (1959) and kill Tunstall and the McSweens in *The Blossom* (1965). He would show up in epic poems such as *The Collected Works of Billy the Kid* (1970) by Michael Ondaatje.[8]

Novels and nonfiction books about Billy became the norm. He appeared in comic books.

He would even outshine Jesse James (at least in terms of quantity if not quality) in Hollywood films.

CHAPTER THREE

The Silent Era, 1911–1916

Only two movies are known to have been made about Billy the Kid — loosely speaking — during the silent era, and both are presumed lost. Even the Dalton Gang was featured in more films during this period: *The Last Stand of the Dalton Boys* (1912), *The Dalton Boys* (1914), and *Beyond the Law* (1918), the latter a six-reeler starring Emmett Dalton, the only gang member to survive the catastrophic dual bank-robbery attempt in Coffeyville, Kansas, in 1892.[1]

At least a handful of silents were based on outlaw Jesse James's life and legend — the exact number might never be known — beginning with *The James Boys in Missouri* (1908), a one-reeler from Essanay released, and ending with Paramount's big-budget *Jesse James* (1927), a feature starring Western film hero (and former Boy Scout) Fred Thomson.[2]

Jesse James remained in the national consciousness through not only movies but dime novels, history books and plays. Jesse's brother, Frank, was off and on in the news until his death in 1915, as was former gang member Cole Younger, who died the following year. After his pardon in 1907, Emmett Dalton helped keep the Daltons' exploits remembered through a "Strictly Moral"[3] lecture circuit and his 1918 memoir *Beyond the Law*. (Another book by Dalton, 1931's *When the Daltons Rode,* would be adapted into a popular Randolph Scott Western in 1940.)

By the dawn of the 20th century, however, Billy the Kid had faded from the national spotlight, although Charlie Siringo, a former Texas cowboy, stock detective and Pinkerton agent, had given the outlaw his due in 1920 when he privately published a book, *History of "Billy the Kid,"* in Santa Fe.

After Walter Noble Burns's *The Saga of Billy the Kid* became a runaway bestseller, sending the Kid on his journey into immortality, King Vidor "tried for three or four years to get an approval for this story."[4] By the time Vidor got the go-ahead to film *Billy the Kid*, however, the silent movie era had ended.

Billy the Kid

(Vitagraph, August 1911, one reel) CREDITS: Director: Larry Trimble; Scenario: Edward J. Montagne. CAST: Edith Storey (Billy the Kid); Tefft Johnson; Ralph Ince; Julia Swayne Gordon (Billy's Mother); William R. Dunn.

Synopsis

It has been suggested that the first known movie about Billy the Kid was probably based on the play by Walter Woods,[5] and while that's a good guess, it's likely wrong.

According to a newspaper summary of the Vitagraph release, this is the movie's plot:

> A baby girl is born, just previous to the death of her mother, and is brought up by her grandfather, who thinks she is a boy. The girl leads the life of a cowboy until she is sixteen years of age, when her sex is discovered through an encounter with a band of outlaws, [and] the servant, who is the only one who knows the truth, and who was sworn to secrecy at the death of her mother, finds it necessary to disclose her identity. A rescue party is formed, and her pal, to whom she has always been "Billy, the Kid" marries her.[6]

Another newspaper summarized: "Billy the Kid is a boy until sixteen years of age then she becomes a girl and marries a cowboy."[7] It took sixteen years before anyone realized Billy was a girl? Little wonder a newspaper called the movie "decidedly different."[8]

So maybe it wasn't based on the hit play, but Vitagraph could definitely have been jumping on the Billy the Kid bandwagon after the success of Woods's hit play.

When Vitagraph released this one-reeler, the play *Billy the Kid* was still going strong on the boards. Woods had apparently revised his 1903 play into a four-act melodrama, which he co-wrote with Joseph Santley. Santley played Billy when the play opened on August 13, 1906, at New York's New Star Theatre, and it was received with enthusiasm. *The Dramatic News* critic called it "the best melodrama I expect to see this season." The new version of *Billy the Kid* would enjoy "twelve solid seasons."[9]

In 1910, a newspaper billed the play as "the Sensational Melodramatic Triumph" and "The Everlasting Success."[10] An advertisement in the *Evening Herald* in Dunkirk, New York, noted that this "True Story of Western Life" had been "witnessed by over Five Million people [in the] past six seasons," and praised its "Pathos Laughter Comedy Tears."[11]

So why wouldn't a film company like Vitagraph jump on the Billy the Kid bandwagon?

The History

The first documented movie about Billy the Kid really wasn't about Billy the Kid. Nor was it based on Woods's play. Its history came only from the imagination of the scenario creator, and of an actress — not actor Tefft Johnson, who has been mistakenly credited with playing cinema's first Billy the Kid — known for portraying male characters.

The Players

J. Stuart Blackton and Albert E. Smith founded American Vitagraph in Brooklyn, New York, in 1896 or 1897. A pioneer in the fledgling filmmaking business, Vitagraph quickly grew. In 1899, Blackton and Smith recreated the U.S. Navy's defeat of the Spanish fleet in Manila Bay "using a water tank, cardboard cut-out model ships, and plenty of smoke provided by Blackton's cigar." Around 1902, G.M. Anderson joined Vitagraph. Anderson would eventually form the Essanay Company and become America's first movie cowboy star, Broncho Billy Anderson. Vitagraph's studio at 14th Street and Locust Avenue in Flatbush opened in 1906 and became the country's first modern motion picture facility. Eventually, Vitagraph would also have a studio in California, but most of its productions were produced in Brooklyn.[12]

With film production moving to the Los Angeles area, Vitagraph remained in Brooklyn until 1925, when Warner Brothers bought the company's assets. After that, the studio was retrofitted to make Vitaphone shorts.

Its "golden era" fell between 1910 and 1915, and on July 1, 1911, *The Moving Picture World* reported that Vitagraph would release four movies a week, one of those being a Western.[13]

Enter Billy the Kid.

Billy the Kid featured the "leading Vitagraph players ... including Miss Julia Swayne, Miss Edith Storey, Mr. Harry Morey and Mr. Teft [*sic*] Johnson."[14] Many sources say Tefft Johnson played Billy in the Vitagraph production, but Storey had the title role.[15]

Born in New York City on March 18, 1892, Storey was performing as early as age nine, and even played in repertoire with legendary actress Sarah Bernhardt. Signing with Vitagraph in 1908, she was loaned to Melie for six months, and then to a Texas film company.[16]

Considered "America's first 'cowgirl' film star,"[17] Storey often played "an adventurous, tough tomboy affectionately known as Billy" in her short films.[18] In *As the Sun Went Down* (1919), she played "'Colonel Billy,' a female gunfighter whose past wild life has return to haunt her...."[19]

Actor Tefft Johnson appeared in *Billy the Kid* (1911), but not as Billy the Kid.

She didn't always play "male" Billys, but was "[e]qually adept as a Shakespearean tragedienne, a comedic cross-dresser, and a bonnie Irish lass." Perhaps her best-known movie, *A Florida Enchantment* (1914), had her taking a pill that transforms men into women and women into men.[20]

In 1911, she starred in a number of Westerns in which she "perfected her cowhand skills, leading a director to comment that she could 'ride anything with hair and four legs, throw a rope and shoot with the best of the cowpunchers.'"[21]

Westerns fit her. "Miss Storey is a great out-door girl. She is mistress of any horse she wishes to ride. She sails a boat with skill, is an excellent swimmer as well as a deep diver.... Her voice is a delight and she has beautiful hands — exquisite in their shape and coloring. On her slender figure rests a well poised head."[22]

In fact, Storey once said of playing cowboys in her films: "At that time my muscles were too hard to be easily bruised even from the severest bumps."[23]

Playing a girl mistaken for a man wasn't so hard for the actress either. "When it is necessary for me to play male characters, I am always careful to make them just as masculine as possible," she said in 1914. "Your audience, really looking through the keyhole, is so often offended by the obvious disguise of many girls who try to play male parts; and it therefore sees the artificiality that pervades the whole portrayal."[24]

She described her method: "It is here in my own studio that I study my script and work out new portrayals, the while practicing before my mirrors for the coming battle with the camera on the nine-foot line. When then I go before the director I am more capable of fitting into the picture as he has decided it shall be. Locked away in my own studio, I sometimes practice for an hour or more at a stretch the making of faces and perfecting of gestures before my mirrors."[25]

In 1917, she left Vitagraph and signed with the Metro Company before retiring from the screen in 1921. Storey, who never married, died in 1967 at age 75. Her star on Hollywood's Walk of Fame is at 1523 Vine.[26]

And what about the man several historians have mistakenly said was film's first Billy the Kid? Born in 1883 in Washington, D.C., Tefft Johnson was a leading man on stage before turning to film. In the early 1900s, he and his sister, actress Abby (or Abbe) Johnson, of Washington, D.C., "society," were also making their rounds promoting Peruna, a remedy for catarrh. "In all my experiments with medicines in the effort to improve a condition impaired by overwork, I have found nothing that has done so much good as Peruna," he was quoted as saying in advertisements featuring his and his sister's likenesses. "As a tonic it is grand. I take pleasure in recommending it to professional people and to the public generally."[27]

Johnson was a big man, and a reporter once described him as "he whose tremendous shoulders and biceps are rendered harmless by his kindly blue eyes."[28] Johnson had also directed child star Paul Kelly in "Buddy" comedies for Vitagraph.[29]

Actress Edith Storey, the screen's first "Billy the Kid."

Vitagraph had been "a happy family," but the film industry was growing. On August 11, 1916, *Variety* reported that Vitagraph was restructuring its "method of procedure." "The new order of things will mean that a 'jobbing system' is to be inaugurated, the company holding only the stars and engaging players for each production as it is put into work," *Variety* reported. Shortly thereafter, Tefft Johnson was gone. Edith Storey's contract was terminated the following year. "The Vitagraph family," historian Anthony Slide wrote, "was no more."[30]

After his film career, Johnson and his sister made news again when he tried to have set aside his mother's deed, which created a joint tenancy for mother and daughter at their D.C. home. The courts denied his plea.[31] Johnson died in 1956 at age seventy-three.[32]

Analysis

While the real Billy the Kid was not a girl, an early dime novel — *The Life of Billy the Kid, a Juvenile Outlaw* (John W. Morrison, 1881) — did have him escaping authorities by dressing as a girl.[33]

Historians have mistakenly credited the film as being based on Woods's hit play, but the published synopsis of the first movie does not match the play's plot. Likewise, historians have mistakenly credited Tefft Johnson as movies' first Billy the Kid. Actually, it was famed silent actress Edith Storey. Her role as "Billy" in *Billy the Kid* might have set a standard in filmmaking, too. Even after this 1911 one-reeler, few movies about Billy the Kid were really about Billy the Kid.

***

Logansport (Indiana) *Daily Reporter* (August 14, 1911): "a western caprice, with a strain of humor and a touch of pathos."

Billy the Bandit

(Victor, December 1916, 1 reel) CREDITS: Director-Scenario: John Steppling. CAST: Billy Mason, Peggy Custer,[34] "Mother" Sylvia Ashton, Fred Gamble, Countess Mary Du Cello

Synopsis

In this short comedy[35] distributed by Universal Film Manufacturing Company, "Billy first sells a sand lot to an unsuspecting woman purchaser, and then abducts his girl in cave man fashion."[36]

The History

The second known silent about Billy the Kid, like the first, really wasn't based on New Mexico's fabled outlaw, but the story of "Billy the Bandit" can be traced to the *National Police Gazette* when Billy the Kid was still alive.

The June 18, 1881, issue of the New York City–based *Gazette* ran the article "Billy LeRoy, the Bandit," about an alleged Colorado outlaw that historian J.C. Dykes suggests was likely the fictional creation of magazine publisher Richard K. Fox. Later that year, Fox published a book, *Billy LeRoy, the Colorado Bandit; or, the King of American Highwaymen*, by Thomas F. Daggett. Another dime novel by Daggett followed that year, also published by Fox: *The Life and Deeds of Billy LeRoy, alias The Kid, King of American Highwaymen*. The *Gazette* had published an account of the real Billy the Kid's escape from jail in May when Billy the Kid became national news, but whether the magazine was trying to mislead the public into thinking Billy the Kid and the alleged Billy the Bandit were one in the same is unknown, although a later 1881 Fox release by Daggett, *The Life and Deeds of Billy LeRoy, alias The Kid, King of American Highwaymen*, obviously did try to capitalize on Billy the Kid's newsworthy name. That version, reportedly a revised edition of Daggett's first book, was advertised in the *Gazette*: "[T]his history of Billy the Kid is the most sensational and authentic narrative of outlaw life ever published." An August 1881 version of the book, published after the real Kid's death, contained two chapters "remotely related to the Kid. The rest of the book is about a Colorado bandit."[37]

The Players

Director-writer Steppling was better known as an actor. His career began in the early 1900s and continued through almost 250 movies in the silent era. His last known role, albeit uncredited, came as a townsman in *Broken Lullaby*, which was released in 1932 a few months before his death.[38]

In 1916, Steppling returned to Universal City to direct "Smiling Billy" Mason "in slap-bang comedies." The director and comedic actor had worked together at Essanay in Chicago. Also joining the cast were Peggy Custer, Countess Du Cello, a "Mrs. Ashton" and Fred Gamble. The first film was reportedly to be titled *Betty's Bandit*, but no other information can be found to verify that film was produced by Victor, or at least that the film was released under that name.[39] It is possible that *Betty's Bandit* became *Billy the Bandit*, which was produced by Victor and distributed by Universal.

Billy the Bandit, Steppling's only confirmed writing credit, came while he was directing a handful of comic shorts. Between 1915 and 1917, he directed himself often for American Film Manufacturing Company, then directed Billy Mason in one-reel comedies for Victor, including *A Charming Villain*, *The Beauty Doctor* and *A Box of Tricks*, along with *Billy the Bandit*.[40]

Born in South Dakota in 1888, blond-haired, blue-eyed "Smiling Billy" Mason, who likely played the title role in *Billy the Bandit*, had a career in vaudeville and the circus— "I'd rather be in the circus than Ambassador to Mexico," he told *Motion Picture Story Magazine* in 1913 when he was with Essanay— before landing in motion pictures.[41]

In fact, Mason ran away from home to join a circus, and when he returned, he was sent back to his parents' native Denmark, where he attended the University of Copenhagen. He finished his studies in Chicago and returned to show business as a chorus boy, eventually appearing on New York stages in the production *The Shepherd King* and *Girl of My Dreams*.[42]

"Smiling Billy" Mason likely had the title role in *Billy the Bandit* (1916).

According to Mason's obituary, Thomas A. Edison selected Mason to play in the first double-exposure movie that Edison filmed. Other sources say he made his screen debut in 1912 for Pathé Freres before returning to Chicago to work for Essanay.[43]

He worked for Solax, Imp, Victor, Vitagraph, and several other film companies on the East and West coasts, but is best remembered as an Essanay player in one- and two-reelers. His earliest known credit, *Billy and the Butler*, was released in March 1912, and he went on to appear with Essanay stars Beverly Bayne, Dolores Cassinelli and Gloria Swanson. His first known feature film, *A Prince of India*, was an adventure-comedy produced in 1914 by Ted Wharton, an old friend.[44]

"I'd need an adding machine to count the characters I've done," said the prolific, "fair-cheeked" actor, but he preferred comedies over melodramas. "[C]ut out the cheap melodramas full of naughtiness and rot and give us good two-reel comedies," he said. "I hand over my nickel every time I can find one of them, but the 'Deadwood Dick' stuff doesn't make a hit with Smiling Billy."

In 1915, Mason left Essanay for the Independent Motion Picture Company (IMP), which eventually became Universal, then moved to Keystone—appearing with Wallace Beery and Gloria Swanson in *A Dash of Courage* (1916)—and finally landed at Universal, but his career was on the downturn. By 1920, Mason was out of pictures, although he reportedly attempted a comeback in 1922 with more comedies. He wound up in Orange, New Jersey, where he died in 1941 at age 53 after a long illness.[45]

"Ingénue"[46] Peggy Custer, "one of the pretty young things of Universal City,"[47] married cameraman Jack McKenzie (or MacKenzie) in San Diego while at Universal. Billed as one of "the famous Universal Juvenile players,"[48] Custer starred in comedies and dramas including *The Valley of Beautiful Things* (Victor, 1917), *The Lair of the Wolf* (Universal, 1917) and *Putting One Over on Ignatz* (Universal, 1917). Silent film-era records are sparse, and Custer seems to have faded from pictures and history after her marriage.

Analysis

Another silent short that is presumed lost, *Billy the Bandit* did not please critics. "The action is so jerky that it interferes with the plot development at times," *Moving Picture World* noted.[49]

Other than the name, it had nothing to do with the real outlaw, but that would soon change, thanks to a best-selling book by Walter Noble Burns that once again put Billy the Kid in the national spotlight.

***

Moving Picture World (January 6, 1917): "The number is one of only fair strength."

CHAPTER FOUR

Early Billy, 1930–1938

Jesse James would become a major movie character thanks to the success of 20th Century–Fox's *Jesse James* (1939), a huge hit that prompted an immediate sequel, *The Return of Frank James* (1940). Billy the Kid, however, had no such luck. The first sound movie about the outlaw, *Billy the Kid* (1930), bombed at the box office, and the Kid would rarely ride the cinematic screen again until Producers Releasing Corporation began a series of Billy the Kid programmers in 1940.

In 1932, Tom Mix came out of movie retirement and signed with Universal Studios to make a series of Westerns and be paid $30,000 a picture. He went on to make nine talkies with Universal, routine B's for the most part, before an on-set accident forced his retirement again.[1]

Modern sources list Billy the Kid as a character in two of those Universals — *The Texas Bad Man* and *The Fourth Horseman*, both from 1932 — yet no character is ever identified as "Billy the Kid" in either film.

Lynton Wright Brent, who received no on-screen credit, played Billy in *The Texas Bad Man*, but nobody is ever called that name in the final film version or in the movie tie-in book by A.J. Sharick published in 1934. Brent had a long career as a minor player, usually without on-screen credit, in feature films and Three Stooges shorts. He wrote a humorous, short memoir, *Gittin' in the Movies*, published in 1936, and went on to write a number of Western novels such as *The Bird Cage* (1945) and received an original story credit for *The Texas Kid* (1943), a Johnny Mack Brown Western in which Brent played one of the henchmen. If he's remembered at all, however, it's for a string of sexploitation novels from the 1960s, including *Lesbian Gang*, *Flaming Lust*, and *The Sex Demon of Jangal*. Brent died in 1981 at age 83.[2]

Likewise, Paul Shawhan is listed in modern sources as playing "Billy the Kid" in *The Fourth Horseman*, yet again there's no character going by that name in the film. Publicity articles published in newspapers at the time of the movie's release did mention Shawhan as one of the members of the cast.[3] *The Fourth Horseman* is the only movie Shawhan is known to have appeared in. After that, he faded out of film history.[4]

Billy the Kid

(MGM, October 1930, 95 minutes) CREDITS: Director: King Vidor. Screenplay: Wanda Tuchock (Continuity), Laurence Stallings (Dialogue), Charles MacArthur (Additional Dialogue). CAST: John Mack Brown

(Billy the Kid); Wallace Beery (Pat Garrett); Kay Johnson (Claire); Wyndham Standing (Tunston); Karl Dane (Swenson); Russell Simpson (McSween); Blanche Frederici (Mrs. McSween); Roscoe Ates (Old Stuff); Warner P. Richmond (Ballinger); James Marcus (Donovan); Nelson McDowell (Hatfield); Jack Carlyle (Brewer); John Beck (Butterworth); Christopher Martin (Santiago); Marguerita Padula (Nicky Whoosiz); Aggie Herring (Mrs. Hatfield).

Synopsis

In the first known movie about Billy the Kid that was actually based on Billy the Kid, cattlemen Tunston and McSween arrive in the Pecos region, where William P. Donovan — sheriff, notary public, justice of the peace, postmaster, saloon boss and storekeeper — claims all of the country. "I am the law," Donovan tells the newcomers, and encourages them to move on.

"Well, I guess we'll have a fight wherever we settle," Tunston tells his partner, and they decide to remain in the area despite Donovan's threats. "Right or wrong," a title card proclaims, "Donovan was the Law of the Southwest."

Movie tie-in novel (1934) for the Tom Mix Western *The Texas Bad Man* (1932).

Donovan and his hired gun, Ballinger, run off (even kill) homesteaders, burn homes and steal livestock, which prompts Tunston to call a meeting of the good guys to put a stop to this reign of terror.

The sheriff and his men decide to break up the meeting, and when Tunston accuses one of them of stealing his cattle, it's up to Billy the Kid — "the most dangerous man in all of Lincoln County" — to save Tunston's life. "Killin' rats comes natural to me," Billy tells Tunston.

With Billy's arrival, peace comes to the region, and Tunston sends for his fiancée, Claire. Things won't stay peaceable, of course.

Ballinger tries to prompt a drunken gunman named Grant to kill Tunston, but Deputy Sheriff Pat Garrett prevents any gunplay between Grant and Tunston's protector, Billy. Billy tries to talk Garrett into working for Tunston, but Garrett declines: "Someone's got to maintain law and order." When Billy suggests that Garrett's taking orders from Donovan, Garrett says angrily: "I'm not working for Donovan. I'm just doing what I think's right."

Having Claire in Lincoln and a wedding the next day calls for a party, but when Billy hears that Grant's threatening to kill Tunston, he slips out in the night and (off-screen) kills the gunman.

Donovan orders Tunston's arrest, and sends Ballinger out the next morning to bring in the Englishman. Posse members murder Tunston, who dies in Billy's arms. "Before I die," Billy says, "I'm gonna shoot down like a dog ever man that had anything to do with this."

The war's on. Billy kills two of Tunston's assassins in Donovan's saloon, and Donovan orders McSween's arrest. A violent, fiery showdown at McSween's place leaves McSween, Donovan, and many others dead. Ballinger and his henchmen disarm Garrett, who's still trying to do things peacefully, and burn out Billy and the boys holed up in McSween's store.

The king of cool, Billy lights a cigarette from a fallen, burning rafter before coming outside with guns blazing and making his escape.

Law and order arrives in Lincoln County in the form of the Army. General Lew Wallace, military commander of New Mexico Territory, agrees to grant amnesty to the two men still fighting the war: Billy and Ballinger. Ballinger's game, but Billy's stubborn. Wallace hopes Claire will persuade Billy to take the offer, but she tells the Kid: "I want you to do whatever your heart tells you to do." That's enough for Billy, who tells Garrett to inform General Wallace "that there's gonna be peace in this country, and justice, the very next time I see Bob Ballinger."

Garrett tells Billy that he'll be coming after him. "Then come shootin', Pat," Billy says.

After Garrett and his posse trap Billy in a cave, the lawman manages to persuade Billy to surrender by frying a skillet-full of bacon, the Kid's favorite food, just outside the entrance.

Back in Lincoln, with Billy facing a hangman's noose, he is tormented by Ballinger. Billy tricks Garrett into playing some poker, and disarms the lawman. Then he kills Ballinger with his own shotgun. He tells Garrett that now he's ready to take the governor's amnesty offer, but Garrett says the only thing he'll get now is a rope.

Garrett tricks Claire into going to Billy, and follows her. Kindhearted as he is, however, he allows Billy to escape and lets Claire follow him into Mexico to live happily ever after.

The History

In 1930, William E. Johnson took his mother to see *Billy the Kid*. His mother, Camelia Olinger, had known all the principals in the Lincoln County War. Eighteen years later, Johnson told Eve Ball that, after the movie, his mother had told him that "the only thing in the picture true to the facts was the Scotch brogue of McSween."[5]

Maybe. But compared to the movies followed, *Billy the Kid* sometimes resembles a documentary. For one thing, King Vidor brought his crew to film in New Mexico. Gallup, on the western edge of the state, isn't exactly Lincoln, in southeastern New Mexico, but Vidor and MGM took great pains to make the sets look right. The "Lincoln" filmed often has an uncanny resemblance to the actual town, especially the courthouse. Vidor also shot footage at Arizona's Grand Canyon, which doesn't look anything like Lincoln County.

The story, on the other hand, is part history, part fantasy.

When he was only twelve years old, Billy tells Tunston, someone killed his mother in cold blood while another shot his father in the back. "My father was a kind-lookin' gent," Billy says, "just like you." We'll likely never know if Billy's dad was kind-looking or not, or if he was shot in the back, but the Kid's mother was not the victim of a cold-blooded murder. Catherine McCarty Antrim died of tuberculosis on September 16, 1874, in Silver City, New Mexico. If we go by the reported birth date of Billy as being November 23, 1859 — "in spite of marginal provenance," Bob Boze Bell points out — that would have made Billy almost fifteen years old, not twelve.[6]

Among the hands working for Tunston are Charles Bowder, Tom O'Folliard and Dick Brewer. The name of Billy's employer, of course, was John Henry Tunstall, not Tunston, but Charles Bowdre (not Bowder), Tom Folliard/O'Folliard, and Dick Brewer were supporters of Tunstall. Brewer managed his own ranch and served as Tunstall's foreman. Bowdre had bought a ranch or farm with Doc Scurlock in Lincoln County in 1875. Folliard/O'Folliard did not arrive until later, coming up from Texas in May or June — months after Tunstall's death — and asking Frank Coe for work. He became one of Billy's closest pals.[7]

Tunstall wasn't on a buckboard when he was killed, he was on horseback, and his killers shot his horse, too — but although the only witnesses to Tunstall's death were his murderers, several Tunstall riders, including Billy the Kid, were nearby. And Billy did vow revenge while staring down at Tunstall's body, not where he was killed, but when the body was laid out at the McSween home.[8]

That revenge wasn't wreaked in a Lincoln saloon. William "Buck" Morton and Frank Baker, who were part of the posse that killed Tunstall, were captured and killed on the trail to Lincoln by a posse that included Billy. Sheriff William Brady was ambushed on Lincoln's main street.[9]

This publicity still from King Vidor's *Billy the Kid* (1930) has actor Johnny Mack Brown silhouetted in a cave scene.

"I hear tell the Mexicans have been hiding him," Pat Garrett says of Billy. "He's pretty friendly with them, you know." That relationship helped the real Kid in New Mexico. Although he was "pure gringo," he learned to speak Spanish fluently. "Unlike other Anglos who referred to all Hispanics as greasers, a derogatory label that had originated in Texas, Henry was drawn to the Hispanic culture and people," Michael Wallis writes. "He fancied their spicy food, their style of dress, and especially their music."[10]

Brown's wardrobe is that of a dime-novel gunfighter. He is dressed in black with a bib-front shirt and hat, and sports two holstered six-shooters. In reality, the Kid donned "simple, serviceable clothing," more fitting for a working cowhand. "His only conspicuous garb was an unadorned Mexican sombrero," Robert M. Utley writes, but even that was serviceable with its wide brim protecting him from the blistering sun and numbing rain.[11]

Tunstall had no fiancée, and Pat Garrett was not a deputy sheriff during the early stages of the Lincoln County War. He wouldn't be elected sheriff until 1880.[12]

Joe Grant wasn't threatening to kill Tunstall — the Englishman was long dead when Grant rode into Fort Sumner — but was threatening to kill the Kid at Bob Hargrove's saloon when Billy shot him dead in 1880.[13]

The burning of the McSween home, while not historically accurate, does recreate the spirit of the scene Walter Noble Burns depicted in *The Saga of Billy the Kid*. "He had prayed for peace," Burns wrote of McSween. "Bullets were his answer." The film recreates the murder of McSween, the burning of the home, and has Billy light a cigarette from a burning rafter. In Burns's book, the burning roof just misses the kid, and a bullet knocks the cigarette out of his mouth. "Now that's too bad," the Kid says. "I'll have to roll another."[14]

"The Kid was the last to leave," Burns wrote, and that's the way Vidor depicts it, with Billy mounting his horse, sitting backward in the saddle, firing revolvers in both hands as he gallops to freedom. Burns had "the Kid's trigger fingers" working "with machine-gun rapidity," taking out Bob Beckwith, who had killed McSween, and wounding two others.[15]

What actually happened was that the Kid and others decided to race out of the kitchen, the only relatively safe part of the house by that night, and sprint for the Tunstall store, drawing fire from the Murphy men, thus allowing McSween and the others to make a dash for the back gate and possibly reach the river. It was a desperate plan, and the burning home turned the darkness into daylight. The Kid and three others made it, but a bullet killed Harvey Morris. Instead of running then, McSween and the others waited too long, and were trapped by gunfire. McSween was then killed.[16]

On the other side, Bob Beckwith, a deputy from Seven Rivers, was killed, too, but not by Billy the Kid. The Kid did, however, manage to rip off John Kinney's mustache with a pistol shot.[17]

Lew Wallace had been a general during the Civil War, but he wasn't military commander of New Mexico. He was appointed territorial governor by President Rutherford B. Hayes to replace the ineffective Samuel Axtell, arriving on September 29, 1878, and being sworn in the following day. On November 13, Wallace issued his "amnesty" declaration, a "general pardon" for misdemeanors and offenses in Lincoln County between February 1 and November 13, 1878. It would not apply to Army officers stationed in Lincoln County (at Fort Stanton). Nor would the amnesty apply to civilians currently under indictment, disqualifying Billy the Kid, already indicted for the murders of Sheriff William Brady and Buckshot Roberts.[18]

When Pat Garrett and his posse captured Billy the Kid in December 1880, the outlaw wasn't hiding in a cave, but at a rock house at Stinking Springs near present-day Taiban, New Mexico. Garrett did, however, did lure Billy and his friends out by cooking. After inviting the Kid and his cohorts out for coffee, the Kid, not feeling humorous, snapped, "Go to hell, Pat." Morning faded, and by late afternoon, another meal was being made. The aroma proved too much for the outlaws, who, upon Garrett's guarantee of protection, came out and shook hands with Garrett before being shackled.[19]

By most accounts, Robert Olinger (called Ballinger here) was a bully. Even Pat Garrett said his deputy was "born a murderer at heart." Commissioned a deputy U.S. marshal in October 1880, he had been appointed a deputy sheriff of Doña Ana County to deliver Billy the Kid to Lincoln County after the Kid's conviction for the murder of Sheriff William Brady. He also tormented his prisoner with his Whitney ten-gauge double-barrel shotgun, loading it with two shells containing eighteen buckshot each, and staring at the Kid while saying, "The man that gets one of those loads will feel it."[20]

Walter Noble Burns has the Kid playing monte with Deputy James Bell, disarming him, then shooting the deputy dead as he ran down the stairs. The movie replaced Bell with Pat Garrett, but allowed Garrett to live. Garrett wasn't in Lincoln when Billy made his escape. He had gone to nearby White Oaks to collect taxes and/or to buy lumber for the Kid's gallows.[21]

Around 6 P.M. on April 28, Olinger led three or more prisoners from the upper-story jail across the street to the Wortley Hotel for supper. James Bell remained behind to guard Billy the Kid. The Kid asked to be taken to the privy. A pistol was either planted in the outhouse, or the Kid disarmed Bell once back in the courthouse. Either way, Bell ran down the stairs, and the Kid shot him. Bell staggered outside, dying in the arms of Godfrey Gauss. "I did not want to kill Bell," the Kid later said, "but I had to do so in order to save my own life. It was a case of have to, not wanting to."[22]

Shackled, the Kid managed to get Olinger's shotgun and waited for him by an upstairs window. Olinger hurried out of the Wortley toward the courthouse. One version has Gauss calling out a warning to Olinger, "Bob, the Kid has killed Bell," at which point Olinger saw the Kid and the shotgun, and said, "Yes, and he's killed me too." Another version doesn't give Olinger the chance to say anything. Billy called down, "Look up, old boy, and see what you get"; or, "Hello, old boy"; or merely, "Hello, Bob." He pulled both triggers, sending thirty-six buckshot (instead of the eighteen Billy announces in this film) toward the deputy. Bob Olinger was soon dead.[23]

Once Billy was freed from his shackles, he busted Olinger's shotgun over the porch railing, and threw the broken shotgun at the dead man. "Here is your gun, God damn you," he shouted before he rode out of town. "You won't follow me with it any longer."[24]

Naturally, history tells us that Billy the Kid wasn't allowed to ride off into the sunset with Claire and live happily ever after, but this was Johnny Mack Brown, former superstar for the University of Alabama, and audiences, at least in America, would not allow him to be cut down by Pat Garrett.

"The old-timers may not agree with this brand-new personality of a New Mexican bandit in all details," the *Los Angeles Times* reported, "but a lot of them will probably approve it just the same. You see, the reason is that Billy the Kid, even despite his badness, was something of a popular idol. His daring and the legends of the Southwest have given him an aura which is decidedly not 'all wrong.'"[25]

The Players

In the spring of 1926, Chicago newspaper journalist Walter Noble Burns's book *The Saga of Billy the Kid* was published. The Book-of-the-Month Club picked it up as a main selection, and it became a bestseller. Several months earlier, Harvey Fergusson had asked in *The American Mercury*, "Who remembers Billy the Kid?" By the end of 1926, practically everyone knew about the New Mexico outlaw.[26]

Less than two years later, New York publisher Macmillan released a reprint of Pat F. Garrett's *The Authentic Life of Billy the Kid,* revised by Lincoln County War scholar Maurice G. Fulton and wrapped in "a facsimile of the board covers of the original edition of 1882."[27]

Burns's book drew the attention of movie director King Vidor, who wanted to film a Western. Born in Galveston, Texas, in 1894, Vidor — King was his real name — had become interested in films while working as a ticket-taker and projectionist at a Galveston theater. Before long, he was making amateur newsreels and a two-reel comedy titled *In Tow*. In 1915, he struck out for Hollywood. His career went up and down until he directed MGM's

The Big Parade (1925), a surprise hit that made Vidor "a valued artist able to choose his subjects and stars, courted by actors anxious to share his highbrow status."²⁸

Having read Burns's book, Vidor tried to get a movie deal. "I have always felt that there was a great dramatic opportunity in this production," Vidor told the *Los Angeles Times*. "The hero is one who is widely known in the West, and he had qualities which seemed to draw many people toward him. He undoubtedly possessed some very likable characteristics, or this could not have been so."²⁹

By 1929, sound was taking over for silent movies, and rapid improvement in sound recording and a new wide-screen medium made an outdoor epic Western attractive to the studios. Fox, which had released the first Western talkie *In Old Arizona* (1929) and gotten Warner Baxter a best actor Oscar, was banking on *The Big Trail*, directed by Raoul Walsh and starring a former bit player now being called John Wayne; it was to be filmed in widescreen 70mm. Paramount had put Gary Cooper in *The Virginian* (1929) and had cast him in *Fighting Caravans* (1931), based on Zane Grey's novel. MGM wasn't interested in *Billy the Kid* until one or two other people approached studio executive Irving Thalberg, who remembered Vidor's interest in the project. Although actor John Gilbert was reportedly attached to the film at one time, Vidor recalled Thalberg telling him that he could make the movie if he cast Johnny Mack Brown as Billy the Kid.³⁰

"I didn't think that Brown was ideal for the part," Vidor recalled, "but I wanted to do it, and I was afraid that if I didn't do it, somebody else would. I didn't think that Brown had the violent look of a killer."³¹

Born in 1904 in Dolthan, Alabama, Johnny Mack Brown had been a standout high school football player when he enrolled at the University of Alabama in 1923 and successfully tried out for the team. He quickly became a star, working part-time in a local shoe store and participating in dramatics. Selected captain of the team in 1925, Brown earned national attention when he led Alabama to a come-from-behind Rose Bowl victory against the University of Washington. George Fawcett, a character actor who was in Alabama filming *Men of Steel*, attended an Alabama-Vanderbilt game and suggested that Brown try his luck in Hollywood. "Why, thanks," Brown said, "that's awfully nice of you, but I'm not an actor. Gee, I'd be scared to death out there. You don't need me. All I can do is run around with a pigskin." Later, however, Brown decided to head to Hollywood. He took a screen test, and MGM signed him to a $75-a-week contract.³²

Grossett & Dunlap reissued a version of Walter Noble Burns's *The Saga of Billy the Kid* in conjunction with the 1930 release of MGM's movie *Billy the Kid*, starring Johnny Mack Brown.

Four — Early Billy, 1930–1938

With the advent of talkies, MGM feared that Brown's Southern accent would work against him, but cast him as a cowboy who falls for Manhattan girl Joan Crawford in the Western-comedy *Montana Moon* (1930). Brown's accent fit, even if the movie was a box office flop.[33]

Vidor had considered casting an up-and-coming actor named James Cagney or an unestablished actor (such as Raoul Walsh was doing with John Wayne in *The Big Trail*). "That was the ideal casting I was thinking about," he said, "but I had to abandon all of those thoughts when they told me I was to use Johnny Mack Brown."[34]

Brown, on the other hand, was ecstatic. "Every boy who ever lived has played a bandit at some time in his life, and every boy who ever lived read all the adventure stories he could find. It's just human nature, I reckon, for us to like to hear about folks who do things we wouldn't dare to do or wouldn't want to do. That's why I was so tickled when they gave me the part of Billy."[35]

Vidor didn't want Wallace Beery to play Pat Garrett, but "I supposed Irving Thalberg and the executives at MGM were looking for box office appeal. It was always a battle between names and personalities to get the film sold."[36]

Vidor wanted Helen Hayes as the love interest. Thalberg, according to Vidor, *didn't* want her, so, Vidor said, "We made a bad choice because we were halfway through the picture with another girl, and discovered that she just couldn't act at all."[37]

The daughter of an architect, Kay Johnson had made her Broadway debut in 1923 and moved to motion pictures, as a lot of Broadway talent was doing, by 1929. Her starring roles weren't very strong, but "she came into her own as a screen actress after being demoted to supporting roles later on" in *Of Human Bondage* (1934) and *The Real Glory* (1939). Married to actor-director-producer John Cromwell, she moved from theater to film, then focused on her family and was out of acting altogether by the late 1940s. She died in 1975.[38]

MGM decided to experiment with a 70mm wide-screen film called Realife. Cinematographer Gordon Avil shot footage in both 70mm and standard 35mm. "The difference was tremendous," Vidor said. "There was just no comparison. The 70mm film seemed to see around each object. This sold me forever on wide-screen films."[39]

There was a problem, however. Only twelve theaters across the country could show the 70mm film.[40]

Vidor took his film crew to Arizona's Grand Canyon and Utah's Zion National Park, and they even got close to Utah's Monument Valley. Vidor wanted "large, sweeping shots" for the wide screen, something straight out of *The Covered Wagon* (1923).[41]

At Zion, he ran into something of a communication problem while shooting down from the mountains to a wagon train. Boy Scouts were stationed along the way so he could communicate, through semaphore signaling, with the crew down below. When that didn't work, Vidor sent someone in search of a heliograph. The assistant found a park ranger at a station and asked if the ranger had something they could use. The ranger replied: "No, I haven't, but if you'd like to use it there's a telephone up there."

"Telephone?" the assistant cried out. "Where's the telephone?"

"It's on a tree up there at the top."[42]

Which certainly proved easier than flags or heliographs.

In the San Fernando Valley of Southern California, the town of Lincoln was recreated from photographs. "We might have used our imagination for the [Tunstall] house, and the bar," Vidor said, "but everything else is very realistic."[43]

Shooting in Gallup provided the filmmakers with "wonderful" skies and "beautiful thunderhead clouds," and the crew took advantage of a nearby cave, dubbed Kit Carson's Cave, to shoot the scene in which Garrett has trapped a starving Billy.[44]

Sophie Poe, widow of Pat Garrett's deputy John Poe, visited the set at Kit Carson's Cave, and complained to Vidor about how Billy the Kid was being portrayed. "Sir," she said, "I knew that little buck-toothed killer, and he wasn't the way you are making him at all." Vidor replied, "Mrs. Poe, I understand your feelings, but this is what the people want."[45]

Yet shooting at the cave left Vidor with one terrible memory about the production.

> When we were shooting there, I told the crew that we needed a dead horse out near the mouth of the cave, and the property man and the assistant director had forgotten to bring the dead horse we had arranged for. I was up in the top part of the cave yelling, "Where's the dead horse?" Unbelievably, they brought out some old Indian horse and hit it over the head to kill it. I could hear the blows way up inside the cave. They were killing it right there for the shot. I'll never forget the sound echoing through the cave. I look at the film and see the dead horse lying there, and it makes me sick. Even at that time I got sick, and I was very angry with my assistant director for doing it.[46]

When filming moved back to California, a rider on horseback kept appearing on a hill in the distance, causing Vidor to change camera angles to keep him out of the scene. Eventually, the rider drew nearer and the crew learned that it was retired actor William S. Hart, star of silent Westerns such as *Hell's Hinges* (1916) and *Tumbleweeds* (1925). "All he wanted to do was come out and look me over, because his favorite character was Billy the Kid," Brown said. (This could have been a publicity stunt set up by MGM.[47])

Hart brought out a revolver that he said had belonged to Billy the Kid, and reportedly showed Brown how to turn his body, and protect his heart, while shooting in gunfights. It impressed Brown, who would later visit the actor at his ranch near Newhall. It didn't impress Vidor. "I don't think he knew any more about Billy the Kid than we did," Vidor said. "By then I'd done a lot of research."[48]

When filming came to an end, Vidor and Thalberg wondered if the film would be too violent for American tastes, but that wasn't the problem. Vidor's movie was supposed to have "a tragic ending, as it was in real life." Vidor filmed the scene in which Garrett shoots down Billy, who dies in his arms as Claire wails. That's the version that was shown to preview audiences. That's the version that American audiences would not accept. New footage was filmed in which Garrett allowed Billy to escape. Only in the European release, titled *The Highwayman Rides*, did Billy die. Paul Andrew Hutton wrote, "The Europeans, more accustomed to tragedy, could evidently cope with this sad conclusion to the saga."[49]

Billy the Kid opened in October 1930, one month before Fox's *The Big Trail* premiered. Brown "is Billy the Kid with a southern accent," the *Los Angeles Times* said, and his first starring turn in a big-budget film "didn't take," MGM historian John Douglas Eames noted. Both *Billy the Kid* and *The Big Trail* had huge production costs and, with theaters already paying to put in sound equipment and unable to afford to show a 70mm movie, both films failed. *Big Trail* star John Wayne would immediately be demoted to small roles and programmers. Brown would last a little, but not much, longer as an A-list star. His next role was in a frontier historical epic, *The Great Meadow* (1931), about pioneers heading from Virginia to Kentucky. It wasn't a box office hit, either. Brown had been cast with Joan Crawford to appear in *Laughing Sinners*, but Crawford complained to Thalberg that there was no chemistry between the two. She asked Thalberg to re-shoot the film with Clark Gable instead of Brown, and Thalberg agreed. MGM decided to back Gable as its rising star, and when Brown's contract ran out, the studio did not renew it.[50]

Brown made films for Paramount, Warner Bros., and Universal, then found a niche in B-Westerns at Mascot and other Poverty Row operations. Wayne eventually rose to A-list material and superstar status after John Ford directed him in *Stagecoach* (1939), but Brown would remain, albeit as a star, in B Westerns. He made 111 B Westerns and five Western serials during his career. When his B run ended, he moved to guest roles in second-tier productions, even playing a "lecherous sheriff" in A.C. Lyles's Paramount cheapie *Apache Uprising* (1966).[51] On November 14, 1974, Brown died of kidney failure in Woodland Hills, California, at age seventy.[52]

Vidor's failure didn't turn him off Westerns. He went on to make *The Texas Rangers* (1936), *Northwest Passage* (1940), *Duel in the Sun* (1946), and *Man Without a Star* (1955), none a classic, and, arguably, none very good.

"[T]he Western was a chance to take people in cities, the ones who were sitting in the theatres, and allow them to experience all these great open spaces and vistas," Vidor said. "The Western permitted this. Those were my main interests with the Westerns." Vidor died in 1982 of a heart ailment at age eighty-eight. A year before his death, he played a grandfather in *Love & Money* and *New York Times* critic Vincent Canby called his performance the best in the film.[53]

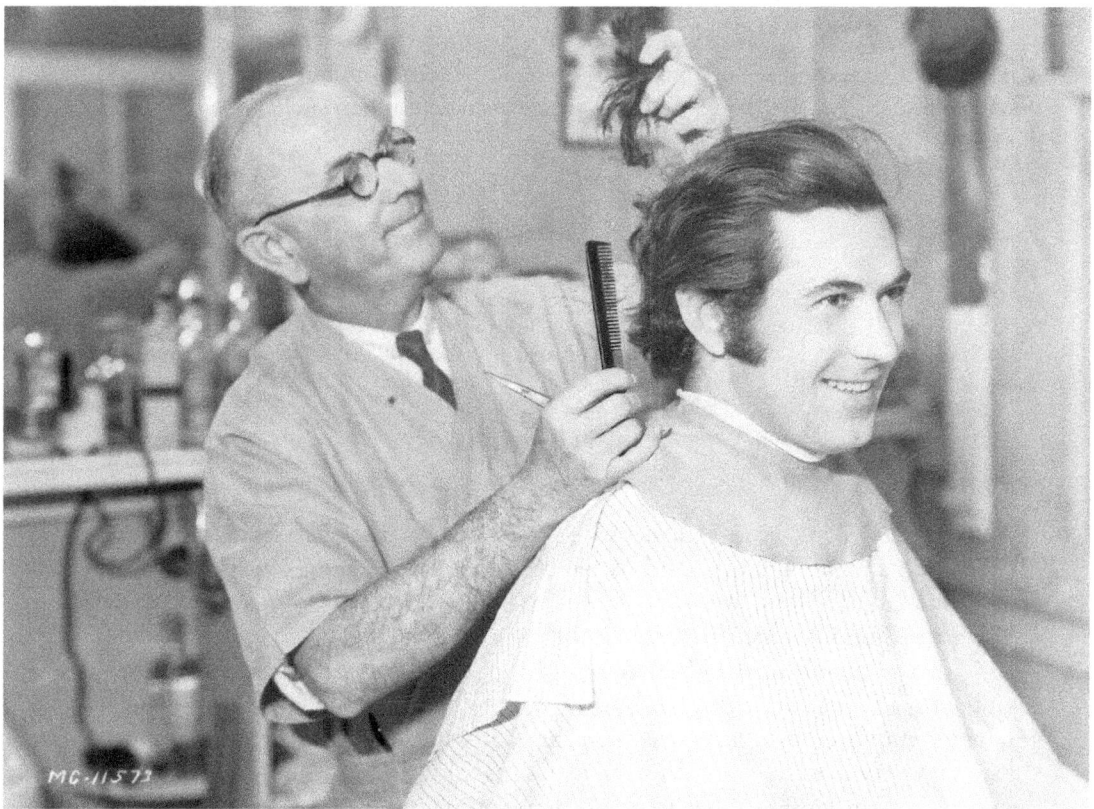

Johnny Mack Brown gets a haircut after letting his locks grow for two feature films, *Billy the Kid* (1930) and *The Great Meadow* (1931).

Analysis

"I was more interested in photography than anything else," King Vidor said. "At least this was one of my biggest interests, and I thought that we could always get great scenic stuff in these pictures."[54]

Therein lies the problem with *Billy the Kid*. The scenery is often great, but the story isn't. Johnny Mack Brown was certainly athletic. Even Vidor gave him that much credit, saying, "He did all of the stunts himself, even jumping on the horse and riding backwards, which is terribly difficult."[55] But Brown couldn't act. Wallace Beery, usually the gruff, likable good bad man, wasn't effective as Pat Garrett.

Today, *Billy the Kid* is an interesting movie to watch, but it's not a good movie. Like many early Westerns (or many early sound movies, for that matter), it's often creaky, plodding and filled with former silent actors still displaying their dated, animated histrionics. The Western really wouldn't find its footing until after World War II.

Walter Noble Burns had made Billy the Kid a name known, if not across the world, then certainly across America, but *Billy the Kid* the movie would not be like *Jesse James*. When 20th Century–Fox released *Jesse James* in 1939, it became such a huge hit, practically every studio would come out with a Jesse movie in a few short years.

MGM's *Billy the Kid* was a box office failure in 1930, which relegated Billy to mostly programmers until the 1950s.

***

Los Angeles Times (November 3, 1930): "Essentially this is a mannish feature, marked with a melodramatic intensity, and only here and there hinting at the gentler and more romantic purposes.... [It] seems to glory in scenes where its male characters fight it out to the finish."

Billy the Kid Returns

(Republic, September 1938, 53 minutes) CREDITS: Director: Joe Kane. Associate Producer: Charles E. Ford. Screenplay: Jack Natteford. CAST: Roy Rogers (Billy the Kid/Roy Rogers); Mary Hart [Lynne Roberts] (Ellen Moore); Smiley Burnette (Frog Millhouse); Morgan Wallace (J.B. Morganson); Fred Kohler (Matson); Wade Boteler (Pat Garrett); Edwin Stanley (Nathaniel Moore); Horace Murphy (Miller); Joseph Crehan (U.S. Marshal Dave Conway); Robert Emmett Keane (Page).

Synopsis

A scroll tells us as the camera focuses on a reward poster, "In the history of New Mexico appears the name of 'Billy the Kid,' a bandit, who at the age of twenty had a record of twenty-one killings."

Let the shooting start.

With a store burning and bullets flying, a man (let's assume it's Alexander McSween) comes out of the inferno, pleading, "Wait," only to be shot down by Matson, one of many gun hands employed by a hard-case merchant and rancher named Morganson. Others are killed as they try to escape, but Billy the Kid waits until the last minute. Naturally, he gives the bad guys fair warning: "Get set, boys, I'm coming out."

Firing two Colt revolvers, Billy makes it to a horse, murders its owner, and escapes. Matson and cronies pursue, and terrorize a sodbuster's wife who they think knows where

Lobby card for the Roy Rogers programmer *Billy the Kid Returns* (1938) showing Smiley Burnette, Edwin Stanley and Mary Hart.

Billy's hiding. Billy's not hiding. He comes to the rescue, shooting Matson in the hand and running off the bad guys. Matson then meets Sheriff Pat Garrett, who's on Billy's trail. Garrett finds Billy sleeping on the floor in a shack, and gets the drop on the outlaw, but Billy refuses to go "peaceably," forcing Garrett to shoot him dead.

Ah, but who should arrive in Lincoln County the next day but a singing Roy Rogers, who stops Morganson's raiders from running off a nester's horses. A dead ringer for the Kid, he scares off some of the gunmen, leaving Roy unimpressed with New Mexico badmen. "They wouldn't make common chicken thieves back in Texas," he tells his horse, Trigger.

Roy runs into an old friend, Frog Millhouse, a peddler for Dixie Brand Musical Instruments. Turns out, Roy is a former deputy sheriff whose boss thought he was too young for the job, so Roy has come west looking for work. Convincing Lincoln County residents that Roy isn't Billy proves harder, except to two newcomers from Connecticut, Nathaniel Moore and his daughter Ellen. Naturally, Roy is smitten by Ellen.

In town, Roy, still mistaken for Billy, is caught and taken to the marshal's office. Garrett arrives and tells the marshal that Roy isn't Billy, "because I killed Billy last night." Roy's resemblance, however, gives the sheriff an idea: Have Roy pose as Billy and keep protecting the nesters. Billy's game, but Garrett doesn't think that Roy would risk his hide just to save some nesters. "Every time I look at you I see another boy," Garrett tells Roy, "who talked the same line you do. A boy I finally had to kill."

The plan, however, works. "Life and property safe again," Marshal Adams tells Garrett, "all because an outlaw's on the job."

Trouble might be resurrected, however, when Moore opens a bargain store that threatens Morganson's monopoly. Morganson tries to make Moore sell out, but Roy comes in and forces Morganson and his men to buy Frog's musical instruments at inflated prices.

More gunplay, more horse chases, more mayhem. When Garrett tells Roy that "cattlemen don't fear a thing but federal court," Roy comes up with a new plan.

Frog tells Morganson and Matson that Billy has stolen his (Frog's) horses and plenty more, for the nesters. The badmen force Frog to lead them to those horses, which they promptly steal. When they run into an Army patrol, Morganson and Matson realized they have been duped. The horses they have are Army mounts, and they are arrested to face a U.S. court and serve out their time in a federal pen.

"He's made the country safe for settlers," Garrett tells the villains after revealing Roy's true identity, "and he's going to be my chief deputy."

The History

Before 1942, when Republic president Herbert J. Yates decided that Roy Rogers's movies needed to be more like the Broadway musical *Oklahoma!*,[56] some Rogers's programmers had some elements of history. *Billy the Kid Returns* was the first, followed by *Days of Jesse James* (1939), *The Arizona Kid* (1939), *Young Buffalo Bill* (1940), *Young Bill Hickok* (1940) and *Jesse James at Bay* (1941). The latter film again cast Rogers in a dual role: as a good Jesse James and an evil lookalike. "[W]e tried to give each picture a historical flavor," Rogers said.[57]

Which isn't to say that *Billy the Kid Returns* is a documentary.

Take the opening reward poster, for example. It puts a price of $5,000 on Billy's head. The amount Governor Lew Wallace set was $500. Yet the burning of the store and the killing of McSween have shreds of truth, although in the movie Pat Garrett tracks down Billy the Kid and kills him that same night. In reality, McSween was killed in 1878, and Billy didn't die until three years later.

"My father was a nester," Billy tells a woman homesteader. "Besides, you folks come in mighty handy for a meal or a bed when a fellow's on the dodge."

Historians have never been able to track down Billy's birthfather, so he could have been a farmer. He might have been killed during the Civil War. His stepfather, William Antrim, was a Civil War veteran who held jobs as a driver and a clerk in Indianapolis and as the family moved west, worked as a real estate investor, bartender, carpenter, miner, butcher, and gambler.[58] The Kid, however, certainly had many friends in New Mexico who were willing to help him out.

There's another element of truth when a photo displayed at a saddle shop advertises that it's the only picture of Billy the Kid. Although many photos have been proclaimed as showing Billy, only one has been documented. That tintype was likely taken in late 1879 or early 1880 by an itinerant photographer in Fort Sumner and probably cost Billy twenty-five cents. In 2011, when the last remaining original tintype was auctioned off at Brian Lebel's 22nd Annual Old West Show & Auction in Denver, Colorado, it took a bid of $2.3 million to win it for Palm Beach, Florida, businessman William Koch.[59] The original image has Billy holding a rifle, and the photo in the movie, although not quite the same, likewise has Roy holding a rifle.

"I knew Billy well," Garrett says in the movie, "rode the range with him and was his friend until he went wrong."

That has become the legend, and it makes for a good story, but Mark Lee Gardner points to an "obscure" account by White Oaks, New Mexico, newspaper editor James E. Sligh: "Sligh said Garrett told him that while he knew the Kid well, they were neither friends nor enemies: 'He minds his business and I attend to mine.' That struck me as very believable."[60]

However, when a sodbuster laughs that "Billy the Kid never spent a day in school his whole life" and the marshal declares that Billy the Kid can't sing, history says something different. Actually, the Kid was pretty well-educated for the time, attending the first public school in Silver City, New Mexico, in 1874 and continuing school for a year after his mother's death, earning room and board by working in a hotel.[61]

From his mother, he inherited a love of music. As historian Michael Wallis writes: "It was well known that [Billy the Kid] enjoyed singing."[62] The real Billy might not have been able to play a guitar as well as Roy Rogers, but at age fourteen, he helped raise money for the Silver City school by performing as "the head man" in "minstrel shows." Wallis writes: "Perhaps one of his favorite songs, 'Silver Threads Among the Gold,' was included in the boy minstrel's repertoire."[63]

The Players

The year 1938 found Republic Studios' singing cowboy star Gene Autry holding out for more money, forcing studio head Herbert J. Yates to find a replacement. That led him to Cincinnati-born Leonard Slye, who had appeared in a few movies already, often credited as Dick Weston. Slye became Roy Rogers. ("I like it," Yates said of the new name. "It's alliterative.") He was cast in *Under Western Stars*, which became a 1938 hit for the studio.[64]

"This lad isn't the pretty boy type," the *Dallas Morning News* wrote of Rogers, "but a clean cut youngster who looks as if he had grown up on the prairies, not backstage with a mail order cowboy suit. An engaging smile, a good voice and an easy manner ought to put him out in front before very long."[65]

Next up was *Billy the Kid Returns*.

Republic re-teamed Rogers with director Joseph Kane and co-star Smiley Burnette, both of whom had been working in Autry movies since 1935. Kane, a one-time cellist, had moved from editing films for Paramount in 1926 to directing at Republic in 1935. Over a fifty-year career, he directed roughly 115 movies. More than 100 of those were Westerns, and some forty starring Rogers. "I love making westerns," Kane said. "I like the scenery and the outdoors. The sense of excitement. The horses and the cowboys." By 1939, Kane was also earning credit as an associate producer credit. He worked with Rogers through *The Yellow Rose of Texas* (1944) before Republic promoted him to direct some of the studio's higher budgeted movies, including the John Wayne vehicles *Flame of the Barbary Coast* (1944) and *Dakota* (1945). By the late 1950s, he was working mostly in television, including the hit Western series *Bonanza*, *Cheyenne*, and *Rawhide*. Kane died in 1975.[66]

Burnette, born Lester Alvin Burnette in Summum, Illinois, in 1911, had appeared with Autry on the *National Barn Dance* radio program and on stage for several years. When the two landed at Republic in 1935, Burnette assumed the part of Autry's comic sidekick, Frog Millhouse. With Autry holding out, Republic saw no reason that Frog Millhouse couldn't be Roy Rogers's comic relief. Burnette was an accomplished songwriter (more than 300 songs); for *Billy the Kid Returns*, he co-wrote with Eddie Cherkose "The Dixie Instrument Song," "The Man in the Moon Is a Cowboy," "Parade Song" and "Sing a Little Song About Anything." By the fall of 1938, Autry and Yates had agreed to terms, so Burnette once again became Autry's sidekick, and Roy got Raymond Hatton and, eventually, George "Gabby" Hayes.[67]

Burnette, however, played one major part, off-screen, in Roy Rogers's film career.

A few days before shooting began on *Under Western Stars,* Rogers was searching for a horse. He knew he had found the perfect mount when he swung into the saddle on a palomino stallion from Hudkins Stables. The horse, who had carried Olivia de Havilland in *The Adventures of Robin Hood* (1938), was named Golden Cloud. "His name got changed when Smiley Burnette and I were hanging around the set one day and I was practicing my quick-draw," Rogers recalled. "Smiley said, 'Roy, as quick as that horse of yours is, you ought to call him 'Trigger.'"[68]

As Pat Garrett, native Californian Wade Boteler once again found himself playing a peace officer. Boteler "is remembered for outstanding roles in several Universal cliff-hangers," William C. Cline writes, including Inspector Scott in *Red Barry* and as the hero's father in *Buck Rogers*. Between 1919 and his death of a heart attack in 1943, Boteler appeared in more than 400 motion pictures. Yet at almost fifty years old when *Billy the Kid Returns* was filmed, he was too old, really, for the role. Pat Garrett was thirty-one when he killed Billy the Kid.[69]

El Paso, Texas-born Lynne Roberts would co-star with Rogers in eight Westerns, billed as Mary Hart in the first seven of those. "You see, when she started making Westerns," Rogers said, "Mr. Yates made her change her name to Mary Hart just so he could bill us as 'Republic's own Rogers and Hart,' like the successful Broadway musical writing team."[70]

Actually, in 1937 Roberts had already been billed as Mary Hart in Warner Bros.' *Love Is on the Air* and as Lynne Roberts in Warner Bros.' *Dangerous Holiday*. And *Billy the Kid Returns* billed Roy Rogers and Smiley Burnette above the title.

Hart was cast to give the plots some romance, Rogers said. "We never kissed or anything; but she balanced all the action with a nice, soft touch and gave the movie someone I could sing to. Studio publicists labeled us 'Sweethearts of the West.'" (Rogers tries to kiss Hart at the end of *Billy the Kid Returns*, but Smiley Burnette won't let them.)

"Like other female stars of B Westerns, her main function was visual — to be the central shot while Rogers was singing," film historian Paul Varner writes. "Only in one film, *Billy the Kid Returns* (1938), did her character actually have a job — as a clerk in her father's store."[71]

Hart quit the series — "[S]he had had her fill of sagebrush romance," Rogers writes[72] — after *In Old Caliente* (1939), and in 1943 became Lynne Roberts. She returned to the Roy Rogers series once more, as Lynne Roberts, in director William Witney's *Eyes of Texas* (1948). "[D]espite the new name and a good measure of talent and charm she never hurdled the barrier to big-time stardom," Ephraim Katz noted. She retired from film in 1953 and died in 1978.[73]

Rogers was still learning the ropes in 1938. "I eventually learned acting pretty much the way I learned music — by ear," he said. "I would read a script and I'd hear it a certain way in my head, and that's the way I did it. If I was a bad guy, I didn't smile; if I was a good guy, I had plenty of pleasant personality and a lot of smiles. That was about it...."[74]

He was sued by a vaudevillian named Roy Rogers, but Republic settled out of court.

"I'm not sure exactly what they paid the other Roy Rogers," Rogers said, "but he walked away a happy man; and I walked away with a whole new identity."[75]

Rogers, of course, went on to become the King of the Cowboys, supplementing his $150-a-week Republic salary with evening performances at theaters for $150 a night. His celebrity status grew so much that he was one of many actors invited to the White House for the March of Dimes Ball on President Franklin D. Roosevelt's sixty-first birthday in 1943. In 1944, after a string of leading ladies that included Sally Payne, Gale Storm, Peggy Moran, Ruth Terry and Linda Hayes, Rogers was cast with Dale Evans in *The Cowboy and the Señorita*. They married in 1947, and their fame continued to grow through movies, television, and personal appearances. Rogers amassed a wealth estimated at almost $100 million before his death in 1998. "Today there will be a lot of sad and grateful Americans, especially of my generation, because of his career," President Bill Clinton said when Rogers died. Dale Evans died in 2001.[76]

Analysis

There isn't much history, but you don't expect that from a Roy Rogers programmer. What you expect is what you get: kiddie action, Roy Rogers's charm, Smiley Burnette's vaudevillian humor, and some pretty good songs, including "Born to the Saddle" and "When Sun Is Setting on the Prairie."

***

Zanesville (Ohio) *Times Recorder* (March 8, 1939): "Following right on the heels of *Under Western Stars*, which sky-rocketed young Roy Rogers to stardom, *Billy the Kid Returns* will establish this likable cowboy as one of the really great western stars of all time."

CHAPTER FIVE

The PRC Programmers, 1940–1943

Republic Studios had introduced Billy the Kid to the kiddie crowd with *Billy the Kid Returns* (1938), but it would take cheap Producers Releasing Corporation to turn the outlaw into a cowboy hero. In 1940, PRC launched a new Saturday matinee series about Billy the Kid. Bob Steele played the hero in the first six programmers, then was replaced by Buster Crabbe, who continued until the series ended in 1943 and afterward, when the character's name was changed to Billy Carson, until 1946, the year before PRC became Eagle Lion.[1]

The films, usually with a budget around $23,500, presented Billy as a Robin Hood who pals around the West, saving the day, usually with his two pals Fuzzy and Jeff. Later, as the budgets grew even cheaper, Billy was reduced to riding around the West with only one pal, Fuzzy.[2]

"Although far removed from any historical reality," Paul Andrew Hutton writes, "the films created a Billy the Kid brand name that elevated the outlaw into a position alongside fictional westerners such as Red Ryder, Hopalong Cassidy, and the Lone Ranger."[3]

Surprisingly, some of the early movies were quite dark in tone. As the series continued, the plots grew more similar and the production values lessened steadily until they were borderline ridiculous, even for Poverty Row. In fact, some critics have suggested that PRC should have stood for "Pretty Rotten Crap."[4]

Billy the Kid Outlawed

(PRC, July 1940, 52 minutes) CREDITS: Director: Sam Newfield (billed as Peter Stewart). Producer: Sigmund Neufeld. Screenplay: Oliver Drake. CAST: Bob Steele (Billy the Kid); Al St. John (Fuzzy Jones); Louise Currie (Molly Fitzgerald); Carleton Young (Jeff Travis); John Merton (Lije Ellis); Joe McGuinn (Pete Morgan); Ted Adams (Sam Daly); Walter McGrail (John Fitzgerald); Kenne Duncan (David Hendricks); Reed Howes (Whitey); George Chesebro (Tex); Budd Buster (Clem); Steve Clark (Shorty); Karl Hackett (Sheriff Long); Sherry Tansey (Outlaw).

Synopsis

"In the year 1872," the scroll reveals, "Lincoln County, New Mexico, was ruled by a reign of terror. Range wars swept the country and only one law prevailed — GUN LAW!"

Sam Daly (the credits spell it Daly but one poster spells the name Daley, only later it's spelled Daly) is running for sheriff, but he's a Morgan man, and Pete Morgan has plans to own all of the richest section of New Mexico. Two law-abiding ranchers, the Bennett broth-

Bob Steele (right) first played Billy the Kid in *Billy the Kid Outlawed* (1940). He is shown here with Kenne Duncan and Louise Currie.

ers, oppose Daly and are asking the Department of Justice to investigate, so Morgan has them killed.

Billy the Kid, ramrodding a cattle drive, plans to drop in to see Bob and Hal Bennett, who grew up with Billy in Arizona, but by the time he gets to Lincoln County, "the best friends I got" are dead. Unfortunately for Morgan and Daly, a hired hand named Shorty was left only wounded, and as Billy digs a bullet out of Shorty's shoulder, the hired hand tells Billy and his pals Fuzzy and Jeff what has been going on.

In town, Sheriff Long is powerless to do anything to end the murders and raids, but Billy and his pals find some of the Bennett murderers in a saloon. That's a good place for a brawl when the bad guys try to escape. One of them makes it outside, taking cover behind a stagecoach that has just pulled into town. He's killed, but the stagecoach's team panics and takes off, pulling the stage and two passengers away. Billy leaps on his horse and saves Molly Fitzgerald and her father, Judge Fitzgerald, who has been sent by the Justice Department to investigate the shady dealings in Lincoln County.

Morgan and Daly try to have Billy arrested for murder, but Judge Fitzgerald won't hear of it. Billy, Fuzzy, and Jeff are going to work at the judge's ranch, and Billy issues a warning to the villains: "Before I'm through, you're going to wish you never heard the name of Billy the Kid."

After two weeks of relative peace, Morgan, Daly, and the gang come hunting the judge.

Despite Billy's warning that to talk to those boys is suicide, Judge Fitzgerald meets them on the trail. Fitzgerald is so naive, he raises his hand and calls out, "I understand you men are looking for me." They gun him down.

Bill tells Sheriff Long: "If you'll deputize me and my boys, we'll wipe out the Morgan and Daly gang out legally. If you don't, we're gonna wipe them out anyway." Long swears them in.

They capture a number of the killers, but by then Daly has been elected sheriff and declares Billy, Fuzzy, and Jeff outlaws. Once Billy sees a wanted poster offering a $500 reward for him, Fuzzy, or Jeff, he sees red. "That settles it," he says, ripping up the poster. "As long as we're outlawed, we'll give 'em a reason."

"It's a bad move, Billy," Jeff warns him. "Once we get started, there's no turning back."

"They shot the Bennetts," Billy says. "They shot Judge Fitzgerald, and they're out to get us. Why? Just because we tried to enforce justice. If that's what the law can do, I don't want any part of it."

So they start robbing the "cutthroats." Billy plans to strip Morgan and Daly of everything they own, then go after them. The reward goes up — $1,000 ... $1,500 ... $2,500 ... and Daly and Morgan come up with a plan: Get the governor to offer Billy a pardon, persuade Molly to ask Billy to give himself up, and kill him when he rides in. Expecting a double cross, Billy bags Morgan and Daly and forces them to ride to Molly's ranch.

Good move. Because the bad boys have captured Molly and Dave Hendricks, the late judge's partner, and are ready to ambush the Kid. Instead, the bad guys kill their bosses, and the killers are either captured or killed.

The pardon offer is real, but Billy doesn't trust the law. Molly wants Billy to stay, but Billy knows "the cards are stacked against me." He, Jeff, and Fuzzy ride off.

The History

This Lincoln County War begins in 1872 — before Billy the Kid had even arrived in New Mexico and six years before the Lincoln County War began.[5] Billy says he grew up with the Bennetts in Arizona, but the Kid didn't reach Arizona until the fall of 1875.[6]

One scene, however, is somewhat close to history since Judge Fitzgerald is loosely based on John Tunstall. When the posse members approached Tunstall late in the afternoon of February 18, 1878, John Middleton pleaded with Tunstall, "For God's sake, follow me." Middleton dashed for cover, but the confused Tunstall froze when he recognized the posse. Tom Hill told Tunstall he would not be harmed if he gave himself up, so Tunstall rode toward them. Instead, William "Buck" Morton shot Tunstall out of his saddle, and Hill ran up to Tunstall and put a bullet in his head. Tunstall's horse was also killed.[7]

After that, *Billy the Kid Outlawed* is completely fiction.

Billy the Kid in Texas

(PRC, September 1940, 63 minutes) CREDITS: Director: Sam Newfield (billed as Peter Stewart). Producer: Sigmund Neufeld. Screenplay: Joseph O'Donnell. CAST: Bob Steele (Billy the Kid); Terry Walker (Mary Morgan); Al St. John (Fuzzy Jones); Carleton Young (Gil Cooper); Charlie King (Dave); John Merton (Flash); Frank La Rue (Jim Morgan); Charles "Slim" Whittaker (Windy).

Synopsis

When three armed men try to rob a wagon carrying $30,000, the guard gallops after them. Problem is, guard Gil Cooper is in on the holdup. "Billy the Kid couldn't have engineered that any better himself, Gil," one of the baddies says. Because while Gil's pretending to be chasing off the gunmen, two other bandits rob the driver.

Ah, but Billy the Kid is happening by, and he holds up the two bad guys with the loot.

Gil isn't that bad. He has turned to crime but just wants to ride to New Mexico to help his brother, who has been framed. His brother? Billy the Kid.

Meanwhile, in Corral City, Texas, folks are getting ready for the Lazy A boys to come shoot up the town, it being the first of the month. Billy and Fuzzy have come there to get away from the New Mexico law, but as Fuzzy says, "She's not as peaceful as she looks."

The Lazy A boys are part of the outlaw gang, but Billy makes them back down only to get shot in the back after he walks out of the saloon. Fuzzy and Jim Morgan, one of the town's leading citizens, take Billy to Mary's place, and he's fixed up in no time. Since Billy plans on going up against the Lazy A, Morgan offers him the job of sheriff. Billy's not interested, but Fuzzy says he "always wanted to wear a badge," so Billy takes the job. Fuzzy, of course, sees the badge as a way to make a buck, but Billy plans on doing things "on the level."

Which sure doesn't set well with the Lazy A. After some roughhousing, Gil Cooper decides to shoot it out with Billy, but then Gil recognizes his brother. Billy lets Gil get away.

The brothers meet up, and Gil explains how he joined the outlaw gang. He had tried to raise money to help Billy, but got turned down because his brother was Billy the Kid. Billy doesn't want his brother "to be in the same fix I'm in, dodging people the rest of your life." They decide to get the money from the first two holdups. Instead of Billy going, Gil says he'll walk in and get the money without any problem. But the bad guys have figured out that Gil and Billy are brothers, and they devise a plan to trap Billy and Gil. The plan doesn't work, of course, and Billy and his pals rob Windy of the payroll to keep the money from the Lazy A.

Mary Barton has discovered a wanted post for Billy and shows it to Jim Barton. He and the posse catch the Kid with his saddlebags full of the express money. Billy lands in jail, but Gil and Fuzzy break him out. The Lazy A gang arrives, ready to steal the money, but the good guys are ready.

The bad guys are routed, and as his last act as deputy sheriff, Fuzzy makes Gil Cooper sheriff. Billy and Fuzzy "have a hankering to travel on" and ride off.

The History

The only time Billy the Kid was a lawman was in New Mexico when he served as one of the Regulators, sworn in by Squire Wilson after Tunstall's death. Billy did wind up in Texas, usually selling stolen livestock in the raw Panhandle town of Tascosa. His brother Joseph wound up gambling in Arizona and Colorado. The closest Joseph ever came to being a lawman was twice in New Mexico in 1883, when he reportedly helped prevent the lynching of W.H. "Doc" Kane (or Cain) in Silver City. A few months in Las Vegas later, he persuaded gambler Joe Silks to put away his gun, thus preventing a shooting.[8]

Billy the Kid's Gun Justice

(PRC, December 1940, 63 minutes) CREDITS: Director: Sam Newfield (billed as Peter Stewart). Producer: Sigmund Neufeld. Screenplay: Tom Gibson. CAST: Bob Steele (Billy the Kid); Al St. John (Fuzzy Jones); Louise Currie (Ann Roberts); Carleton Young (Jeff Blanchard); Charlie King (Ed Baker); Rex Lease (Buck Mason); Kenne Duncan (Bragg); Forrest Taylor (Roberts); Ted Adams (Sheriff); Al Ferguson (Cobb Allen); Karl Hackett (Lawyer Martin); Edward Piel Sr. (Barlow); Julian Rivero (Carlos); Blanca Vischer (Juanita).

Synopsis

Billy and his pals Fuzzy and Jeff are trapped in a cabin by bounty hunters who are after the $5,000 price on the Kid's head. "You seem to forget, Billy, that you've been accused of everything but Lincoln's assassination," Jeff says. Billy quips: "Yeah, and if I were a little older they'd probably hang that on me."

Naturally, our three heroes outwit the posse, and Jeff suggests that they hide out at his uncle's ranch in Little Bend Valley. On the way there, they stop Buck Mason and Ed Baker from terrorizing homesteader Ann Roberts. Cattlemen don't like nesters in these here parts. The threesome escort Ann home, which turns out to be Jeff's uncle's old place. Ann's father tells them that Jim Blanchard disappeared and that they bought the place from Cobb Allen. Now, Allen has diverted the stream that once ran through the ranch and is selling water to homesteaders. Billy smells a bad fish. An attorney tells him that he thinks Allen killed Blanchard. Billy tries to get Allen to return the money, but that doesn't work.

Poster for *Billy the Kid's Gun Justice* (1940).

Now it's Fuzzy's turn. He shows a map to Allen and says $50,000 is buried there. Allen decides to buy the land, but Baker and Mason overhear that plan and want the loot for themselves. Jeff finds out that Allen killed Blanchard and buried the body under the floorboards of the cabin.

Billy, Allen, and Baker-Mason bid on the ranch, and the price keeps going up. Finally, Baker and Mason join forces and buy the property for $25,000, which Billy plans to distribute to the homesteaders.

Jeff tells the sheriff what has happened, and Jim Blanchard isn't the only body buried below that cabin. Jeff tells the law that he'll likely find all the evidence he needs to hang Allen, and asks what will happen to Billy and him. The sheriff plans to "be deaf, dumb, and blind for the next twenty-four hours." Jeff asks for one favor: let Billy, Fuzzy and Jeff to help round up the killers.

When the bad guys search for the expected treasure, they find they've been cheated. Billy has left behind a note: "How does it feel to be sold a gold brick? Billy the Kid." With Billy's help, the sheriff captures the killers. Billy, Jeff and Fuzzy ride off.

The History

For the rest of this series of programmers, it's pretty safe to surmise that there is no history. Nothing even close.

Billy the Kid's Range War

(PRC, January 1941, 60 minutes) CREDITS: Director: Sam Newfield (billed as Peter Stewart). Producer: Sigmund Neufeld. Screenplay: William Lively. CAST: Bob Steele (Billy the Kid); Al St. John (Fuzzy Q. Jones); Joan Barclay (Ellen Gorham); Carleton Young (Jeff); Rex Lease (Buck); Milton Kibbee (Leonard); Karl Hackett (Williams); Ted Adams (Sheriff Black); Julian Rivero (Romero); Alden Chase (Dave Hendrix); Howard Masters (Ab Jenkins); Buddy Roosevelt (Spike); Ralph Peters (Jailer); John Ince (Hastings).

Synopsis

An outlaw named Buck, posing as Billy the Kid, is responsible for a string of robberies and the murder of a freight company operator. The real Billy finds himself pursued by his old friend Jeff, now a U.S. marshal, and Sheriff Black, who's one crooked cop. Sheriffs are notified across the Southwest to shoot Billy the Kid on sight.

Ellen Gorham, who thinks Billy killed her father, is determined to get a road built from West City to Pebble Creek. If that happens, her father was promised a mail contract, and Ellen plans to see things through. Trouble is, accidents keep happening on that construction. There's another guy in town, Williams, who wants that contract. Williams has killed Gorham's foreman and asked outlaw Ab Jenkins to take over and to keep up the troublemaking.

When Billy learns this, he kidnaps Jenkins and poses as him. Things are going good until Jeff shows up and arrests his old pal. Fuzzy breaks Billy out. He also lets Jenkins escape, and the outlaw tells the villains they've been duped.

Williams decides he might as well kill Ellen. First, however, he has his hired killer Buck get rid of her guardian Leonard, whom Williams had been blackmailing. Ellen thinks Buck is Billy, the killer of her father.

Poor kid. Her pa's dead. Now her guardian. Despondent, she decides to sell to Williams, but Billy interrupts that deal. And when Buck rides up on that paint horse, Ellen figures out that Billy isn't her enemy, but Buck. Williams kills Buck and has plans to dynamite the road, but Fuzzy gets the drop on the bad guy, and Billy stops the explosion.

With that government contract secured, Ellen asks Billy, Fuzzy and Jeff to stay on and help. A chance to go straight. You bet.

Oops. Here comes another posse, so the boys hit the saddles.

Bob Steele (center) in *Billy the Kid's Range War* (1941). Steele played Billy the Kid in PRC's first six programmers that portrayed Billy as a "B" hero.

Billy the Kid's Fighting Pals

(PRC, April 1941, 62 minutes) CREDITS: Director: Sam Newfield (billed as Sherman Scott. Producer: Sigmund Neufeld. Screenplay: George Plympton. CAST: Bob Steele (Billy the Kid); Al "Fuzzy" St. John (Fuzzy Jones); Phyllis Adair (Ann); Carleton Young (Jeff); Charles King (Badger); Curley Dresden (Burke); Edward Peil Sr. (Hardy); Hal Price (Burrows); George Chesebro (Sheriff); Forrest Taylor (Hanson); Budd Buster (Mason); Julian Rivero (Lopez).

Synopsis

Our three pals decide to get out of the country and head down to the border town of Paradise, five miles away. Paradise sure isn't peaceful.

Fuzzy poses as the new marshal. Two bad hombres, Badger and Burke, are forcing newspaper editor Mason out of town, and auctioning off the paper, but Billy not only wins the bid to take over the paper, he beats up Badger. The Mexican bartender, Lopez, writes up the contract. The celebration is short-lived. As the town banker, Hardy, and his ward, Ann, are congratulating Billy, word comes that Mason has been murdered.

Opposite: Poster for *Billy the Kid's Fighting Pals* (1941).

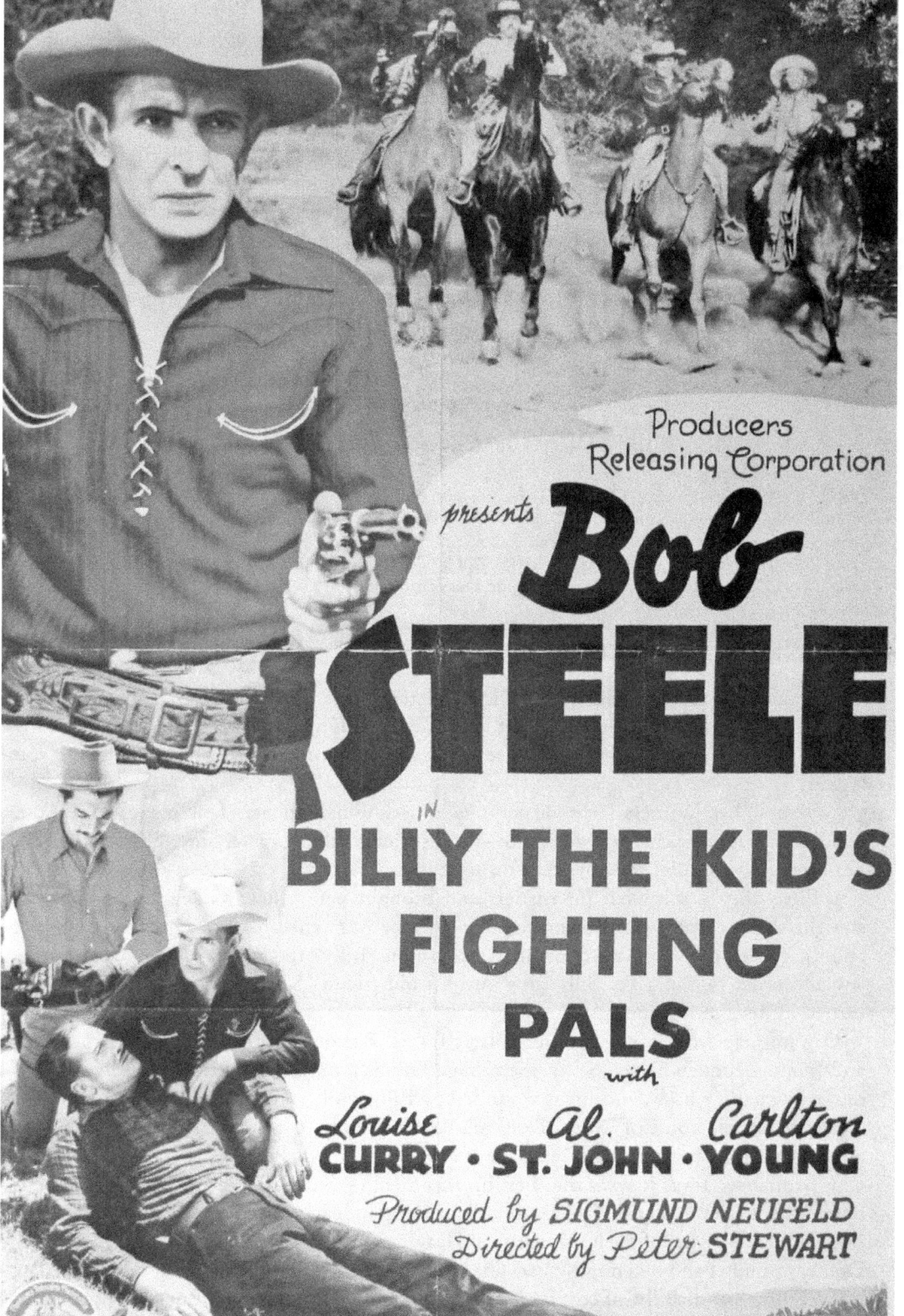

Ann's a great gal, but Hardy's not all that he seems. Fact is, he's the brains behind all the evil doings in Paradise. He and Badger hope to take over the town and use it as the base of a smuggling operation by digging a tunnel connecting the United States with Mexico.

Hardy keeps trying to get rid of Billy and Fuzzy, to no avail. Complicating matters is the fact that Ann happens to be in love with that no-account Badger. That is, until Billy takes Ann and Badger to meet Lopez, who isn't just a bartender. He's a Mexican secret service agent, and he has enough evidence to put Badger and Hardy in jail. Which is what happens when the sheriff rides into town.

Seems like a good time for Billy and the boys to get out of town, which they do, but not before shooting up the Paradise sign until it says Pards.

"That's us."

Billy the Kid in Santa Fe

(PRC, July 1941, 66 minutes) CREDITS: Director: Sam Newfield (billed as Sherman Scott). Producer: Sigmund Neufeld. Screenplay: Joseph O'Donnell. CAST: Bob Steele (Billy the Kid); Al "Fuzzy" St. John (Fuzzy Jones); Rex Lease (Jeff); Marin Sais (Pat Walker); Dennis Moore ("Silent" Don Vincent); Karl Hackett (Bert Davis); Steve Clark (Allen); Hal Price (Sheriff); Charlie King (Steve Barton); Frank Ellis (Hank Baxter); Dave O'Brien (Texas Joe Vincent); Kenne Duncan (Scotty).

Synopsis

Framed for murder, Billy the Kid is convicted in the town of Red Gap and sentenced to hang. "I'll be looking you up one of these days," Billy warns.

"I'll be the one looking up. Because I'll be standing under those gallows watching you kick."

Want to bet? Witness Texas Joe perjured himself under rancher Hank Baxter's direction, and Baxter sends the crooked witness to visit his friend, saloon owner Steve Barton, in Santa Fe. After Billy escapes, the boys take off for Santa Fe.

First, they're mistaken for rustlers and brought before Pat Walker, "a rip-snortin', straight-shootin' gal" who has known Billy since he was "knee-high to a grasshopper." Pat and the cattlemen's association members believe that Billy's the one person who can restore law and order to Santa Fe. Billy runs into his old friend "Silent Don" Vincent, who has turned in his gun for books.

With help from bad-guy rancher Bert Davis, Barton murders rancher Charlie Bates and frames drunken Texas Joe for the crime. Things look bad for Joe when Billy and Jeff discover Charlie's body, and Joe is wounded by Billy while trying to escape. The outlaw is discovered at the home of "Silent Don" and arrested, only to be freed from jail by Barton's boys. Davis forms a posse and Texas Joe is captured and lynched.

Bad move. Texas Joe was the "best brother a fellow ever had," and his brother happens to be "Silent Don" Vincent. Old Don starts dressing in black and takes off on his vengeance ride, killing members of the lynch party and leaving a playing card on each body. Eventually Don is wounded and taken in by Pat. She tells him that he should go about taking the law into his own hand. Billy, of course, is forced to go after his old pard. But Fuzzy organizes an ad-hoc court which acquits Don of murder. It was justifiable homicide.

Heroes Rex Lease, Fuzzy St. John and Bob Steele take on bad guys in *Billy the Kid in Santa Fe* (1941), Steele's last film as the young outlaw.

Not knowing of Fuzzy's dealings, Billy and "Silent Don" face each other down, but neither can shoot the other. That's all right, of course, since they soon learn that "Silent Don" is a free man. Our three heroes ride off in search of another adventure.

Billy the Kid Wanted

(PRC, October 1941, 64 minutes) CREDITS: Director: Sam Newfield (billed as Sherman Scott). Producer: Sigmund Neufeld. Screenplay: Fred Myton. CAST: Buster Crabbe (Billy the Kid); Al "Fuzzy" St. John (Fuzzy Jones); Dave O'Brien (Jeff); Glenn Strange (Matt Brawley); Charles King (Jack Saunders); Slim Whitaker (Sheriff); Howard Masters (Stan Harper); Choti Sherwood (Jane Harper); Joel Newfield (Joey Harper); Budd Buster (Storekeeper); Frank Ellis (Bart).

Synopsis

"Billy ain't breakin' no laws," Fuzzy complains to Jeff, "yet every sheriff in the state's looking for him." (Actually, New Mexico wasn't a state until 1912.) Here comes Billy, with a posse right on his tail. The three pals narrowly escape. Later, at a campsite Fuzzy finds a flyer that promotes a new land development called Paradise Valley. Fuzzy's sold. Tired of being on the run, he says goodbye to Jeff and Billy and sets out for a new life.

Buster Crabbe (right) took over for Bob Steele beginning with *Billy the Kid Wanted* (1941). He and Dave O'Brien (left) round up the baddies.

Turns out that Paradise Valley is far from Heaven. Matt Brawley, president of the land company, is swindling the new homesteaders, charging them "robber prices" at the company store and making them pay for water. He even owns the sheriff.

Fuzzy fights Brawley and winds up in jail, so he sends a note to Billy and Jeff. They quickly ride to the rescue and bust Fuzzy out, fleeing to the homestead of Stan Harper and his family.

Brawley asks his gunman, Saunders, to shoot down Billy, but he knows Saunders won't win, so he tells the sheriff to be there and take care of Billy after Saunders is dead. Sounds good, but then Jeff pretends to be sick of Billy. He says one thing; Billy says another, so suddenly it looks like Jeff's with Saunders and Billy's with Brawley.

Not really, of course. It's a trick, and the rival gangs are suddenly fighting each other. Billy gets the homesteaders to unite against the bad guys. In the end, Billy shoots Saunders, the homesteaders arrive to catch Brawley and his bunch, and peace comes to Paradise Valley. Homesteader Stan Harper is made sheriff, and Billy tells him, "Don't you ride too hard when you're on my trail."

Billy the Kid's Round Up

(PRC, December 1941, 58 minutes) CREDITS: Director: Sam Newfield (billed as Sherman Scott). Producer: Sigmund Neufeld. Screenplay: Fred Myton. CAST: Buster Crabbe (Billy the Kid); Al "Fuzzy" St. John

(Fuzzy Jones); Carleton Young (Jeff); Joan Barclay (Betty); Glenn Strange (Vic Landreau); Charles King (Ed Slade); Slim Whitaker (Sheriff Jim Hanley); John Webster (Dan).

Synopsis

In Gila Valley, Square Deal Saloon owner Vic Landreau tries to get Sheriff Jim Hanley off his back, but Hanley is an honorable man. "What this town needs is a good housecleanin', and I'm sending for a friend of mine," Hanley says, decking Landreau and walking out.

That friend, of course, is Billy the Kid.

But then Hanley is killed, shot in the back, before he can tell newspaper editor Dan Webster and his daughter Betty who he suspects are terrorizing the country.

At a nearby camp, a gunman tries to kill Billy, but the hired killer is caught by Billy, Fuzzy, and Jeff. He tells them Landreau hired him to stop Billy from coming. The boys bring Butch to Gila Valley, but Landreau denies the accusations. Butch escapes.

Landreau sends some hoods to tear up the newspaper office. Naturally, Billy and the boys stop that ruction. Fuzzy decides to run for sheriff. When Betty rides out to deliver newspapers, Landreau mentions to the boys, "I wouldn't mind if she didn't get back till after

Heroes Carleton Young (second from left), Fuzzy St. John (fourth from left) and Buster Crabbe (right) with guns drawn in *Billy the Kid's Round Up* (1942).

the election." Jeff finds Betty's abandoned wagon. He, Billy, and Fuzzy rescue her. They also capture crooked deputy sheriff Ed Slade and make him confess, which will be printed in the paper.

The newspaper office is wrecked again, but they print the papers by hand and Billy makes sure Vic Landreau gets a copy personally. Naturally, there's a fight. Naturally, Billy wins.

Fuzzy's elected sheriff, so Billy and Jeff ride out.

Billy the Kid Trapped

(PRC, February 1942, 52 minutes) CREDITS: Director: Sam Newfield (billed as Sherman Scott). Producer: Sigmund Neufeld. Screenplay: Joseph O'Donnell. CAST: Buster Crabbe (Billy the Kid); Al "Fuzzy" St. John (Fuzzy Jones); Bud McTaggart (Jeff Walker); Anne Jeffreys (Sally); Glenn Strange (Stanton); Walter McGrail (Judge McConnell); Ted Adams (Sheriff Masters); Jack Ingram (Red Barton); Milton Kibbee (Judge Clark); Eddie Phillips (Dave); Budd Buster (Montana).

Synopsis

Billy, Fuzzy, and Jeff are in jail, waiting to be hanged for a murder they didn't commit. You know how things are. "They'll be accusin' us of startin' the Civil War next."

Masked bad guys pretend to be Billy, Fuzz and Jeff in *Billy the Kid Trapped* (1942).

Outlaws help them escape. Turns out these outlaws have been impersonating the threesome, and framing them. It's better if they're out and about, so the bad guys can *keep* framing the boys. After witnessing the lookalikes wound Sheriff Masters, the heroes rescue the lawman and convince him of their innocence. Masters lets Billy and his pals know the gang is working out of Mesa City, so that's where the boys are headed.

A crook named Stanton is running the gang, with help from gang leader Red Burton. A stagecoach is robbed; the driver, Dave Evans, believes Billy the Kid was the leader and that the Kid also murdered his brother, once sheriff in these parts. Dave's sister Sally says Billy couldn't have robbed the stagecoach. Billy and Sheriff Masters, who has arrived in Mesa City, come up with a plan.

A judge is coming to town by stagecoach to end the lawlessness. Stanton and his blackhearts attack the stage, and are surprised to find the passengers include Billy, Jeff and Fuzzy. The bad guy named Montana confesses and gets gunned down by Stanton, who in turn is captured by Billy.

Billy the Kid's Smoking Guns

(PRC, May 1942, 63 minutes) CREDITS: Director: Sam Newfield (billed as Sherman Scott). Producer: Sigmund Neufeld. Screenplay: George Milton. CAST: Buster Crabbe (Billy the Kid); Al "Fuzzy" St. John (Fuzzy Jones); Dave O'Brien (Jeff); John Merton (Morgan); Milton Kibbee (Dr. Elmo Hagen); Ted Adams (Sheriff Carson); Karl Hackett (Hart); Frank Ellis (Carter); Slim Whitaker (Roberts); Budd Buster (Rancher); Joel Newfield (Dickie Howard); Joan Barclay (Mrs. Howard).

Synopsis

Having been chased into a new county, Billy, Fuzzy, and Jeff immediately hear gunshots and ride to an overturned wagon defended by little Dickie Howard, whose father has been gravely wounded.

The sheriff arrives, arrests Billy and his friends, and takes Dickie's pa to Stone City's Doc Elmo Hagen. Oh, no! Hagen, a doctor of death, discretely kills Howard, chastising the sheriff for not doing it himself.

Billy and the boys escape and take little Dickie home only to find Dickie's mother being terrorized by bad men. They beat up the ruffians, then hide when the sheriff drops in and tells Mrs. Howard that her husband was murdered by Billy the Kid.

There's a scam going on in Stone County. A ranchers' coop association has been crediting ranchers for their supplies and having them sign liens against their ranches. See, the leader of the association, Morgan, knows the government wants to buy all the land for a cavalry post, so Morgan's after the land so he can clean up. Of course, the real villain is Doc Hagen.

Billy, Jeff, and Fuzzy decide to open a rival store. Supplies are coming in by wagon, but the driver is shot. Billy takes the wounded man to Doc Hagen, and the Kid becomes suspicious. Seems like none of the doc's patients live. Billy finds the proof he needs, but is arrested by the sheriff. Then Fuzzy and Jeff help free Billy. A posse is formed among Billy and the ranchers. Bullets fly. Jeff is shot, and Fuzzy, who hasn't been informed of Doc Hagen's evil intentions, takes Jeff to the doc. When Billy finds out, he rides to the rescue, stopping Hagen from giving Jeff a lethal injection.

Buster Crabbe (right) as Billy the Kid in *Billy the Kid's Smoking Guns* (1942).

Morgan and the bad guys are all in jail, the liens are burned, and Billy rides out with Fuzzy and Jeff.

Law and Order

(PRC, August 1942, 57 minutes) CREDITS: Director: Sam Newfield (billed as Sherman Scott). Producer: Sigmund Neufeld. Screenplay: Sam Robins. CAST: Buster Crabbe (Billy the Kid/Ted Morrison); Al "Fuzzy" St. John (Fuzzy Jones); Tex O'Brien (Jeff); Sarah Padden (Aunt Mary); Wanda McKay (Linda); Charles King (Mil Crawford); Hal Price (Simms); John Merton (Turtle); Kenne Duncan (Durgan); Ted Adams (Sheriff).

Synopsis

Arrested by the Army and wrongly accused of various crimes, Billy, Fuzzy and Jeff are brought to a fort. Things look bad. Then things look double. Turns out, Lieutenant Ted Morrison is an exact lookalike for Billy the Kid. Billy turns the tables on Morrison, steals his uniform, and leads Fuzzy and Jeff to safety.

Outside, folks shoot at Billy. The Kid knows, of course, that they must have been shooting at Morrison, and inside a coat pocket, Billy finds an invitation to the wedding of Mary Todd, Ted's wealthy, blind aunt. They decide to see what's up.

Mary's beau, George Fremont, has arrived, only it's not George Fremont, but an impostor set up by Mil Crawford, the justice of the peace who plans to steal Mary's fortune. Crawford sends hired killer Turtle to murder the real Fremont and the real Ted Morrison. Billy arrives too late to save them. He then arrives at Mary's house, but Crawford attempts to get Billy lynched.

Fuzzy, donning an Army uniform, saves the day, saying that Billy is really Ted Morrison. Then Linda, Fremont's niece, arrives and agrees to help Billy. She interrupts Mary's wedding, points out the impostor, and the bad guys are caught. Linda agrees to stay and help Mary, and our heroes ride off.

Sheriff of Sage Valley

(PRC, October 1942, 57 minutes) CREDITS: Director: Sam Newfield (billed as Sherman Scott). Producer: Sigmund Neufeld. Screenplay: George W. Sayre, Milton Raison. CAST: Buster Crabbe (Billy the Kid/Kansas Ed); Al "Fuzzy" St. John (Fuzzy Jones); Tex O'Brien (Jeff); Maxine Leslie (Janet); Charles King (Sloane); John Merton (Nick); Kermit Maynard (Slim); Hal Price (Harrison).

Synopsis

Billy, Jeff, and Fuzzy plan to rob the stagecoach of wanted posters, but another gang beats them to it. Only they don't steal posters but a payroll, and the sheriff of Sage Valley, riding inside the coach, is killed.

Strange. The sheriff was shot in the back. Billy's suspicious.

Turns out two of the passengers, Janet and Sloane, work for Kansas Ed, an outlaw trying to take control of the town. When Mayor Harrison won't renew the lease on Ed's saloon, Ed tries to have the mayor killed. Billy saves the mayor and is offered the job of sheriff. That job, Billy says, is "way out of my line." But he'll help.

After another killing in Kansas Ed's place, Harrison threatens the gambler again, and Kansas Ed tries to have the mayor murdered. Again, Billy saves Harrison's life, and this time he takes the job of sheriff.

After some brawls and such, Fuzzy, Billy, and Jeff notice that Kansas Ed looks a whole lot like Billy, causing Billy to think that maybe Ed is the brother he long thought dead.

Janet lures Billy into a trap, the Kid is captured, and Kansas Ed changes clothes with Billy. It's part of a plot to make the ranchers think that Billy's a crook. Jeff and Fuzzy free Billy, but then they're all captured and jailed until Harrison, who has recovered, frees them.

The boys get caught again. Ed beats up Jeff, then fights Billy. Before Ed can kill Billy, Jeff shoots him. A dying Ed admits that he's Billy's brother.

The ranchers aren't satisfied, and demand that Billy, Jeff and Fuzzy be arrested. Harrison does, but then lets them go, and the pals leave Sage Valley.

The Mysterious Rider

(PRC, November 1942, 54 minutes) CREDITS: Director: Sam Newfield (billed as Sherman Scott). Producer: Sigmund Neufeld. Screenplay: Steve Braxton. CAST: Buster Crabbe (Billy the Kid); Al "Fuzzy" St. John (Fuzzy Jones); Caroline Burke (Martha Kincaid); John Merton (Dalton Sykes); Edwin Brien (Johnny Kincaid); Jack Ingram (Trigger Larson); Slim Whitaker (Rufe); Kermit Maynard (Joe); Ted Adams (Marshal).

Synopsis

Billy and Fuzzy elude another posse by heading to Laramy, now a ghost town after most citizens fled from Billy the Kid. 'Course, some citizens are still around, including Dalton Sykes, who's looking for a gold vein. A rancher named Frank Kincaid found that gold, but Sykes murdered him and has been scaring off new settlers.

When Martha and Johnny, the children of the murdered Kincaid, arrive at the ranch, Billy and Fuzzy rescue them. They didn't even know their father was dead.

Fuzzy plays Kincaid's old violin, scaring off some of Sykes's bad guys who think it's Kincaid's ghost. The fiddle's soon broken in a gunfight, and Billy discovers a gold map hidden inside it.

Billy sends Johnny to get help from the neighboring town, but Sykes tricks Martha into trusting him and she tells him about the map. When Sykes demands that map from Billy, the Kid gives him a fake one. Finally realizing that he has been tricked, Sykes returns to get the real map and make ghosts out of Billy and Fuzzy.

Johnny and the marshal arrive. Sykes tries to escape, but is captured by Billy. The map is given to Johnny and Martha, and citizens begin returning to Laramy. Billy and Fuzzy ride away.

By 1942, PRC had dropped Billy the Kid from its titles, as in *The Mysterious Rider*.

The Kid Rides Again

(PRC, January 1943, 60 minutes) CREDITS: Director: Sam Newfield (billed as Sherman Scott). Producer: Sigmund Neufeld. Screenplay: Fred Myton. CAST: Buster Crabbe (Billy the Kid); Al "Fuzzy" St. John (Fuzzy Jones); Iris Meredith (Joan Ainsley); Glenn Strange (Tom Slade); Charles King (Vic); I. Stanford Jolley (Mort Slade); Ed Peil Sr. (Ainsley); Ted Adams (Sheriff); Slim Whitaker (Texas sheriff).

Synopsis

Billy escapes jail and heads to Sundown, where Fuzzy's running a saddle shop. Billy's not just here for a reunion, or to get away from the law. He thinks the Slade brothers, Mort and Tom, have framed him and are behind a string of crimes. He's right.

Mort and Tom and their gang have been forcing ranchers to sell their mortgages to Mort. When the banker, Ainsley, says he won't sell any more mortgages, Mort figures he'll just get rid of the banker. Billy warns Ainsley and his daughter Joan, but they believe Billy's the bad guy.

Billy kills Mort's hired gun Vic and gets arrested. Then Mort robs the bank, and Billy, having been freed from jail by Fuzzy, is seen nearby and suspected of that crime, too.

Mort spreads rumors that the bank's broke, but Billy and Fuzzy ride to the hideout, fool the gang members, get the stolen money, capture a gang member, and head back to

Frequent villain Charles King (left), Buster Crabb (throwing punch) and Fuzzy St. John (right) in a brawl in *The Kid Rides Again* (1943).

town. The money is returned to Ainsley, stopping a bank run. Billy hands the bad guy over to the law, then goes after Mort. He finds him in the saloon. "How do you want it?" Billy asks him. "By rope or gunsmoke?" Gunsmoke. Billy kills the villain.

Fugitive of the Plains

(PRC, April 1943, 56 minutes) CREDITS: Director: Sam Newfield. Producer: Sigmund Neufeld. Screenplay: George W. Sayre. CAST: Buster Crabbe (Billy the Kid); Al "Fuzzy" St. John (Fuzzy Jones); Maxine Leslie (Kate); Jack Ingram (Dillon); Kermit Maynard (Spence); Karl Hackett (Sheriff Packard); Hal Price (Sheriff Conley); George Chesebro (Baxter); Frank Ellis (Dirk); John Merton (Deputy).

Synopsis

Bandits are running roughshod over border towns, and Billy the Kid's getting the blame. Willow Springs Sheriff Conley knows Billy's innocent, but warns his friend that the Red Rock sheriff is after him. Billy and Fuzzy decide to do some investigating.

Almost immediately in Red Rock County, they find the murdered body of a deputy with a note pinned to it: "It ain't healthy sending deputies out alone. Billy the Kid." They follow the trail to a cabin, where Billy discovers that the leader of the gang is a black-clad woman named Kate.

She takes Billy in, although bad guy Dillon is against it. Billy's plan is to capture Kate's gang members — "She can't operate alone"— but Fuzzy is captured by the sheriff. Billy breaks him out and captures two gang members. Back at the outlaw camp, Billy tells Kate that they got caught trying to rob a stagecoach.

Growing sick of Billy's preaching, Kate decides it's time to rob that bank. And blame Billy, of course. "This is gonna be one of your biggest jobs and I'm gonna see you get all the credit." Billy's captured, and the gang rides off.

Problem is, Billy has warned the sheriff about the planned robbery. The gang is driven off, and Kate is badly wounded.

Having escaped, Billy rescues Kate, but Dillon comes by to kill Billy. Billy drops his gun by Kate, who picks it up and kills Dillon, saving Billy's life before she dies. The sheriff realizes Billy's innocent, and tears up the wanted poster.

Western Cyclone

(PRC, May 1943, 62 minutes) CREDITS: Director: Sam Newfield. Producer: Sigmund Neufeld. Screenplay: Patricia Harper. CAST: Buster Crabbe (Billy the Kid); Al "Fuzzy" St. John (Fuzzy Jones); Marjorie Manners (Mary Arnold); Karl Hackett (Governor Jim Arnold); Milton Kibbee (Senator Peabody); Glenn Strange (Dirk Randall); Charlie King (Ace Harmon); Hal Price (Sheriff); Kermit Maynard (Hank).

Synopsis

Fuzzy Jones is driving a stagecoach that is held up by a masked bandit. The passengers are Senator Peabody, Governor Arnold, Dry Springs banker Dirk Randall, and the governor's niece, Mary. The horses spook and take off with the stage, with only Mary inside, and the bandit rescues her.

He's not really a bandit. He's Billy the Kid, and the robbery was a stunt to show Senator Peabody how tough it is to keep law and order in the state.

Jim Arnold and Billy the Kid are on friendly terms. The word is, someone is trying to get Arnold out of office. That someone is Dirk Randall, who hires Ace Harmon to frame Billy for the murder of a loose-lipped outlaw named Rufe Meeker. They trick Rufe into picking a fight with Billy. When Meeker and Billy draw, Randall shoots Meeker in the back, and Billy's arrested for murder.

Ever the detective, Fuzzy finds a shell casing near the murder site and discovers that the gun that fired it had a defective hammer. Problem is, he can't find the murder weapon.

Billy's tried, convicted and sentenced to hang, and Fuzzy is jailed for stealing guns. They escape. Randall orders Mary kidnapped, then demands that Billy turn himself in. He won't let Mary go until after the Kid is executed.

The sheriff and governor give Billy twelve hours to prove his innocence. Fuzzy and Billy find the hideout, free Mary and head back to town.

Randall and Harmon rob the bank and shoot Billy. Thinking Billy's dead, Randall murders Harmon. Randall comes back to town and says Billy was caught robbing the bank and killed Harmon, only to be shot by Randall. Oops. Here's Billy, who lets everyone know that Randall's the bad guy. Randall's hauled off to jail, and Billy and Fuzzy escort the stage carrying the governor, Senator and Mary out of Dry Springs.

Cattle Stampede

(PRC, August 1943, 58 minutes) CREDITS: Director: Sam Newfield. Producer: Sigmund Neufeld. Screenplay: Joe O'Donnell. CAST: Buster Crabbe (Billy the Kid); Al "Fuzzy" St. John (Fuzzy Jones); Frances Gladwin (Mary Dawson); Charles King (Brandon); Ed Cassidy (Sam Dawson); Hansel Werner (Ed Dawson); Ray Bennett (Stone); Frank Ellis (Elkins); Steve Clark (Turner); Roy Brent (Slater); John Elliott (Doctor); Budd Buster (Jensen).

Synopsis

Outlaws plan on capturing Billy and Fuzzy, but they are forewarned by a stranger named Ed Dawson. Ed is wounded escaping the bad men, and asks Billy and Fuzzy to help his father and sister. A land grabber named Coulter has been sending raiding parties against their cattle drives. The Dawson foreman, Brandon, is actually working for Coulter. Brandon leaves the Dawson spread, and Billy is made boss.

Coulter's boys run off 1,500 cattle from the Dawsons. Coulter promises to help round them up and pay half the market value, but Billy won't take that deal. He's suspicious of Coulter.

A lot of other ranchers have had problems with Coulter, so Billy organizes the ranchers to protect the cattle trails. That stops some of the attacks. Billy robs Coulter's money from a stagecoach and puts it in a bank. Mary Dawson recognizes Billy and thinks he's a bad man, until Coulter kidnaps her.

Coulter's plan is to force Mr. Dawson into signing over his ranch. Billy and Fuzzy ride to the rescue, Mary's saved, the bad guys are caught, and things are peaceful once more.

The Renegade

(PRC, August 1943, 58 minutes) CREDITS: Director: Sam Newfield. Producer: Sigmund Neufeld. Screenplay: Joe O'Donnell. CAST: Buster Crabbe (Billy the Kid); Al "Fuzzy" St. John (Fuzzy Jones); Lois Ranson (Julie Martin); Karl Hackett (John Martin); Ray Bennett (Mayor Hill); Frank Hagney (Saunders); Jack Rockwell (Sheriff); Tom London (Pete); George Chesebro (Bart).

Synopsis

After a robbery, Pine Bluffs bank president John Martin rides to a neighboring town to borrow cash for his customers. The town mayor wants to make sure Martin doesn't get back home with that money; he wants to get his hands on 10,000 acres of the best oil land in the country. Hill orders his hired man Pete to handle the dirty work.

Martin and his friend Fuzzy Jones take shelter at Fuzzy's ranch, and Fuzzy tries to lure the bad guys away, but the gang catch Martin and take the $50,000.

Bad move. That means Fuzzy will send for his pal, Billy the Kid, who arrives just in time to save John Martin from being lynched. Turns out Pete has been spreading nasty rumors that Martin's an embezzler.

Hmmmm. Looks like someone is forcing ranchers into foreclosure and taking away their pasture lands.

Hill hires an outlaw named Bart to kill Billy and Fuzzy, but it's Bart who winds up dead. Billy's arrested, but a neighboring sheriff sends word that Billy's a good guy, so the sheriff lets him go. John lands in the calaboose. Eventually, Billy and Fuzzy are ambushed, and Fuzzy falls into a pool of oil. That's the clue Billy needed. He figures the bad guys want the oil. Pete and his gang are captured, and the good guys figure out that Hill's the mastermind. Hill is arrested.

Looks like everybody else is going to wind up really wealthy.

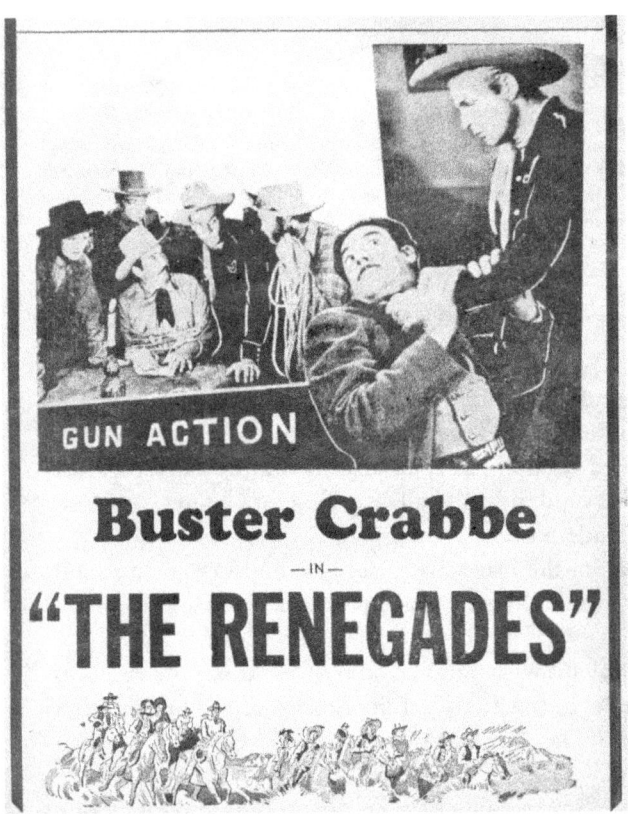
Cornelius card for *The Renegades* (1943), or *The Renegade.*

Blazing Frontier

(PRC, September 1943, 59 minutes) CREDITS: Director: Sam Newfield. Producer: Sigmund Neufeld. Screenplay: Patricia Harper. CAST: Buster Crabbe (Billy the Kid); Al "Fuzzy" St. John (Fuzzy Jones); Marjorie Manners (Helen Barstow); Milton Kibbee (Clem Barstow); I. Stanford Jolley (Luther Sharp); Frank Hagney

(Sheriff Ward Tragg); Kermit Maynard (Deputy Pete); George Chesebro (Deputy Slade); Frank Ellis (Deputy Biff).

Synopsis

Railroad agent Luther Sharp and detective Ward Tragg are cheating Red Rock County ranchers out of their leases. When a judge upholds the contracts as legal, lawyer Lem Barstow sends word to Billy the Kid.

Once Billy shows up, Tragg tries to hire him to run off the settlers. Billy says no, but recommends his friend, a ruthless killer named Fuzzy Jones.

Sharp and Tragg tell Fuzzy to rob the stagecoach that's carrying Sharp's payments. Fuzzy does, only he gives the money back to the settlers. Then the bad guys learn that Barstow is asking for a railroad vice-president to investigate what's been going on. Tragg decides the Barstow house must be destroyed, but Fuzzy gets word to Billy and Barstow, who manage to escape.

Tragg tries to incite a mob to lynch Barstow, but Billy and Barstow escape and save the railroad VP. Several bad guys are killed, Tragg and Sharp are caught, and the settlers head back to their ranches, which the railroad has agreed to sell at fair prices.

Blazing Frontier (1943) was PRC's last Billy the Kid programmer. Buster Crabbe (left) continued playing Billy, but his name was changed to Billy Carson.

The Players

Founded in the spring of 1939 by distributor-turned-producer Ben Judell, Producers Distributing Corporation (PDC) quickly announced plans to produce eight George Houston–starring "Billy the Kid" quickies for the 1939–40 season. PDC planned on releasing low-budget films, most of which would be Westerns, to small independent theaters. Veteran producer Sigmund Neufeld was named executive producer.[9]

The Houston series never made it, and PDC only produced seven films before the company was facing bankruptcy. In April 1940, Neufeld formed Producers Releasing Corporation, with Harry Rathner as president. By December, Pathé Corporation had absorbed PRC, but kept the PRC title. O. Henry Briggs became president, with Leon Fromkess general sales manager overseeing production and George Batcheller acting as production supervisor. Fromkess had previously worked as treasurer for Monogram Pictures, and Batcheller had been boss at Chesterfield Pictures.[10]

Sigmund Neufeld Productions included his wife, Ruth, as vice-president and brother Samuel as secretary, with Bert Sternbach production manager-casting director. Samuel Neufeld was better known as Sam Newfield, who had directed numerous comedy shorts before moving to feature films in the early 1930s. Between 1933 and 1958, he directed between 150 and 200 films, moving fast with low budgets and tight schedules for cheap studios like Tower, Ambassador, Puritan, and PRC. He would direct all of PRC's Billy the Kid programmers, starting off using the pseudonyms Sherman Scott and Peter Stewart before finally taking credit, beginning with *Fugitive of the Plains* (1943).[11]

Bob Steele had made his screen debut in 1920–21 with his twin brother Bill in a series of one-reel shorts titled *The Adventures of Bill and Bob*. Bill went on to become a doctor; Bob became a Hollywood star. He was born Robert N. Bradbury, Jr., in Pendleton, Oregon, in 1907. The family moved to Glendale, California, so that Bob's father could direct movies. With his dad directing Westerns for Sunset Productions, Bob appeared in a number of films, including *With Davy Crockett at the Fall of the Alamo* (1926), then got a starring role in Film Booking Offices' *The Mohave Kid* (1927) with a new name, Bob Steele. "Steele was not a big man, but he had a cheerful boyish expression, he was a good rider and an even better fighter," George N. Fenin and William K. Everson wrote. Once *The Mohave Kid* made him a Western star, he moved to a number of studios, with Republic signing him in 1936.[12]

Steele played Billy in PRC's first six programmers, but caught a break, since he was under contract with Republic, when he joined that studio's *Three Mesquiteers* series starring Robert Livingston. (John Wayne had also played the lead hero in eight programmers before *Stagecoach* changed his career.) Steele played Tucson Smith, with Livingston as Stony Brooke and Rufe Davis as Lullaby Joslin, beginning with *Under Texas Skies* (1940). Steele was bumped up to the lead hero after Livingston's Republic contract ran out and Tom Tyler became Stony. Livingston went over to PRC to become the lead in the *Lone Rider* series.[13]

To replace Steele, PRC signed Buster Crabbe, the 1932 Olympic swimming gold medalist, born Clarence Linden Crabbe in 1907. Crabbe had played in ten of Paramount's Zane Grey Westerns but was likely best known for playing Flash Gordon in three Universal serials between 1936 and 1940.[14]

"Crabbe fits nicely into the title role, although not looking particularly like a cowpuncher," *Variety* noted of Crabbe's Billy debut.[15] Jon Tuska counters, "The series did not improve when Buster Crabbe replaced Steele."[16]

Crabbe remained busy. "All during this heavy shooting," Don Miller writes, "Crabbe would still find time to do another jungle number for PRC, or sneak over to Pine-Thomas for some villainy to plague Richard Arlen."[17]

The one consistent actor throughout the series was Al "Fuzzy" St. John. The nephew of Roscoe "Fatty" Arbuckle, St. John began working for Mack Sennett in 1913 and starred in short comedies such as *Out West* (1918) with Arbuckle and Buster Keaton. He worked for Paramount, Fox and Educational in the 1920s, and moved to the sound era easily, usually as a Western comic sidekick. St. John appeared in 116 Westerns.[18]

Character actor Carleton Young, who had started in films in 1936, played the third pal in the first five Billy the Kids, then Rex Lease, a bad guy in *Billy the Kid's Gun Justice* and *Billy the Kid's Range War*, took over as Jeff. Lease had appeared in Westerns for Tiffany, World Wide, Syndicate, and Superior, then moved into more supporting roles in Westerns in the 1950s. Dave O'Brien, later billed as "Tex" O'Brien, also played Jeff, until PRC decided two pals were enough. Beginning with *The Mysterious Rider*, Billy and Fuzzy were the stars.[19]

Sam Newfield's young son, Joel (or Joe, or Joey) had roles in *Billy the Kid Wanted*—*Variety* called his appearance "a worthwhile bit"—and *Billy the Kid's Smoking Guns*.[20]

Anne Jeffreys, who played Sally in *Billy the Kid Trapped*, would rise above movies like this at RKO, where she came back to play in another Billy the Kid movie, *Return of the Bad Men* (1948). Kermit Maynard, Western star Ken Maynard's younger brother, had been a stuntman and double, then starred in his own Westerns in the 1930s, but by the time the Billy the Kid series came around, he was reduced to character bits, usually as a villain.[21] Crabbe's horse was a palomino named Falcon, who had also been ridden by Lee Powell and Tim McCoy.[22]

The one consistent factor was that the Billy series was incredibly cheap. *Outlaws of the Plains* was completed in four days. PRC made Republic look like MGM.[23] Kalton C. Lahue points out:

> [F]ancy trimmings like rehearsals, retakes, a variety of camera angles and script motivation were looked upon as luxuries not to be indulged in. If the scene didn't go quite right, you could always chalk it up to realism; after all, what real western hero could leap on his horse's back without missing once or twice during his career? Doubles were all over the place, and in many cases there was little or no attempt to hide the fact....[24]

Technically, the Billy the Kid series ended in 1943, when the character's name was changed to Billy Carson, partly because censorship groups were still protesting the glamorizing of outlaws but more on account that in 1943, Howard Hughes released his controversial film about Billy the Kid, *The Outlaw*.[25] Billy Carson wasn't based on Billy the Kid, however. "He *was* Billy the Kid," Crabbe said.[26]

The Billy Carson series ran for 23 programmers between 1943 and 1946, and production values got cheaper and sloppier with few retakes. Don Miller points out one scene in *Frontier Outlaws* (1944) in which Crabbe backs out a window, cracking his head against the sill so hard that theater audiences "would wince spontaneously at the accident." By *Gentlemen with Guns* (1946), riders could be seen falling onto a mattress in plain view. You could even hear one rider calling out the cue, "One ... two ... three ... *hup!*" before Crabbe's double leaped from his horse to knock the bad guy out of his saddle.[27]

In 1946, while filming *Outlaws of the Plains*, Crabbe had had enough. He quit the series, and Billy the Kid's ride at PRC came to an end.[28]

PRC wouldn't last much longer, either. The company was already suffering from internal disagreements. O. Henry Briggs resigned as president in 1944, reportedly over disagreements with the Young family, who controlled Pathe. Fromkess replaced Briggs, but he was out by September 1945, also citing disagreements with the Youngs. Board chairman Kenneth Young became president. Meanwhile, British filmmaker J. Arthur Rank wanted to form an international distribution company so his company, Eagle Lion Corporation, absorbed PRC in 1947.[29]

Steele and Crabbe moved on. Neither was finished with Billy the Kid.

Analysis

It's hard to find much good to say about the PRC series, although they started out with surprisingly dark elements. Billy the Kid, for one, holds the law in contempt. He's a good guy, sure, but says in *Billy the Kid Outlawed*: "As long as we're outlawed, we'll give 'em a reason." In *Billy the Kid in Santa Fe*, after his brother is lynched, one character goes off on a vengeance raid, murdering the members of the lynch mob. And gets away with those crimes! Justifiable homicide, the jury decides.

The series was so cheap, lobby cards were later issued allowing the individual theaters to insert the name of the programmer being shown, no matter the movie. This is a Mascot reissue of *Terrors on Horseback* (1946) picturing (left to right) Buster Crabbe, an unidentified actor and Fuzzy St. John.

Wow. And the Hays Office let that through?

What the series *isn't*, is entertaining. Al St. John's comedy grates on one's nerves, the acting is typically bad, and the production values horribly cheap. Everything got worse as the series continued.

Republic's programmers, be it *The Three Mesquiteers*, or Roy Rogers's "historical" tries like *Billy the Kid Returns, Days of Jesse James* and *Jesse James at Bay*, at least moved and, if viewers were in the right mood, entertained. Besides, Roy Rogers could sing.

PRC's tries left you bored and annoyed.

***

Michael R. Pitts, *Hollywood and American History* (1984): "These films had no relationship at all to history outside of using the outlaw's name."[30]

Chapter Six

The 1940s: Bs, As and *The Outlaw*

Producers Releasing Corporation wasn't the only company dedicated to Billy the Kid in the 1940s. The success of 20th Century–Fox's massive hit *Jesse James* (1939) had other studios looking at other outlaws for profit.

Billy the Kid joined those ranks, and while he was mostly relegated to B programmers, every now and then he would rise up to A-list star, including MGM's Robert Taylor film *Billy the Kid* and the controversial Howard Hughes Western *The Outlaw*.

Billy the Kid

(MGM, May 1941, 94 minutes) CREDITS: Director: David Miller. Producer: Irving Asher. Screenplay: Gene Fowler. CAST: Robert Taylor (Billy Bonney); Brian Donlevy (Jim Sherwood); Ian Hunter (Eric Keating); Mary Howard (Edith Keating); Gene Lockhart (Dan Hickey); Lon Chaney, Jr. ("Spike" Hudson); Henry O'Neill (Tim Ward); Guinn Williams (Ed Bronson); Cy Kendall (Sheriff Cass McAndrews); Ted Adams ("Buz" Cobb); Frank Conlan (Judge Blake); Frank Puglia (Pedro Gonzales); Mitchell Lewis (Bart Hodges); Dick Curtis (Kirby Carton); Grant Withers (Ed Shanahan); Joe Yule (Milton); Earl Gunn (Jesse Martin); Eddie Dunn (Pat Shanahan); Carl Pitti ("Bat" Smithers); Kermit Maynard (Thad Decker); Ethel Griffies (Mrs. Hanky); Chill Wills (Tom Patterson); Olive Blakeney (Mrs. Patterson).

Synopsis

Billy the Kid arrives in Lincoln, New Mexico, to free his friend, a guitar-strumming Mexican named Pedro, from jail. They go to a nearby saloon, where thieving cattleman Dan Hickey recognizes Billy by his left-handed draw. Billy, lured by the chance of some "hot" action, agrees to ride with Hickey's gunmen and stampede the cattle herd of Hickey's rival, an English rancher named Eric Keating.

They stampede the herd, all right, but when the foreman puts a bullet hole in Billy's hat, Billy heads in for the kill. Instead of killing the foreman, Billy recognizes him as a childhood friend from Silver City, Jim Sherwood. The next morning, Sherwood goes back to the Keating ranch, and Billy returns to Hickey.

Keating's a peaceable man who doesn't even pack a gun, but in reality he's just building up more evidence to convince the authorities to bring law and order to the territory. He rides to town to warn Hickey to cease and desist.

Hickey sics Billy on the Englishman, but Billy's impressed with the man. He just can't figure him out, and follows him back to the ranch. Along the way, they discover a dying

Six — The 1940: Bs, As and The Outlaws 65

Backed by town citizens, Brian Donlevy disarms Robert Taylor in this lobby card scene for *Billy the Kid* (1941).

cowboy, mortally injured during the previous night's stampede. (No one missed him before then?) That shames Billy, and when he meets Keating's beautiful sister Edith, he decides to quit Hickey and join Keating.

Happy times ensue. Billy starts becoming more human, and even puts away his six-shooter. He and Pedro decide to gentle a colt for Edith, but Pedro is murdered by some of Hickey's boys.

Keating again talks Billy out of taking the law into his own hands. In fact, Keating has been appointed U.S. marshal and has managed to get Billy paroled into his custody. Keating hopes that, within a year, parole will become a full pardon. Sherwood is appointed Keating's chief deputy.

Keating is murdered, shot in the back, and Sherwood insists on doing this "the way Eric would want it done." Says Billy: "I'll play along with this marshal stuff, Jim, as long as it works out the way I want."

Naturally, it doesn't.

Sherwood has Billy locked up — "to keep you from getting into more trouble," Edith tries to explain to him — but when Hickey tries to have the Kid shot while trying to escape, Billy kills the sheriff and begins his vengeance raid. He kills four of Keating's suspected murderers, then shoots a fleeing Donovan in the back, forcing a showdown between Sherwood and Billy.

"I'm coming in to get you," Sherwood says.

"I'm coming out," Billy says.

But wait! Billy has shifted his gun belt so that he's now drawing right-handed. He's too slow that way, allowing Sherwood to shoot him down.

"I never knew you to draw with your right hand, Hothead," Sherwood says.

"I won't do it again, Holy," Billy says, before dying in Jim's arms.

"Thus," viewers are informed, "as the ways of law came to the last frontier, the last of the men of violence found his peace."

The History

This strange Billy film, billing itself as "the first true story" about the outlaw, is pure fiction. No Tunstall, no Murphy, no Lew Wallace, not even Pat Garrett. The only historical figure in this one is Billy the Kid.

"Metro," the *New York Times* noted, "decided not to hamper itself with known facts about the Kid and as a consequence the screenplay is based largely on legend to which the scenarists have added liberally."[1]

Sherwood (a Pat Garrett character) explains to Keating (a John Tunstall character) that when Billy was twelve years old, his father was killed with a bullet in his back. After the murderer was acquitted, Billy "went and got a gun and shot it out, killed his man." He turned outlaw. Even Ash Upson never got that far-fetched. In *The Authentic Life of Billy the Kid*, Billy's father died in Coffeyville, Kansas, when Billy was maybe three or four years old—a little young to go gunning for a killer.[2]

John Tunstall was never appointed U.S. marshal; Pat Garrett didn't know Billy the Kid in Silver City; Tunstall's sister was in England, not New Mexico; and Billy the Kid wasn't left-handed.

Instead of being nicknamed "Little Casino" and "Big Casino," as Miguel Otero said the Kid and Garrett were called, here they are called "Hothead" and "Holy." Hothead might fit the Kid, but Garrett was agnostic, going so far as requesting no religious rites be conducted at his funeral.[3]

Billy's death comes nowhere close to the facts, but as the *Los Angeles Times* pointed out in its review, his death was "an unpleasant but unavoidable bit of business decreed by Hollywood's censoring body."[4]

Of course, Gene Fowler's screenplay, from a story by Howard Emmett Rogers and Bradbury Foote, was only "suggested" by Walter Noble Burns's book *The Saga of Billy the Kid*.

The Players

MGM's pretty boy Robert Taylor had wanted to do a Western since he had started acting, but the closest he had gotten was in *Stand Up and Fight* (1939), which while set in pre–Civil War western Maryland contained plenty of Western elements, including brawls, gunfights, and a stagecoach line. With the death of Irving Thalberg, Louis B. Mayer was running MGM, and the studio took notice of the success Warner Bros. was having by casting leading actors Errol Flynn (1939's *Dodge City*) and James Cagney (1939's *The Oklahoma Kid*) in Westerns. 20th Century–Fox had scored a mammoth hit with Tyrone Power in *Jesse James*.[5]

"I was just a guy gifted with looks I had done nothing to earn, who fell into a career that I was never overly ambitious about," Taylor said. He was born in 1911 in Filley, Nebraska, played the cello, wanted to become a doctor like his father, but wound up in a drama club at Pomona College in Claremont, California. After he screen tested at Samuel Goldwyn studio, MGM signed him to a seven-year contract in 1934. In 1939, he married actress Barbara Stanwyck and, after a string of box office duds, starred in *Flight Command* and *Waterloo Bridge* in 1940, giving his stalling career a bit of a boost.[6]

"Mayer liked beautiful pictures," Jon Tuska writes in *The Filming of the West*, "pictures that stressed the importance of motherhood (and mothers were always good cooks), that showed the stability of the family, that glamorously and sentimentally depicted the essential good nature of nearly all men. *Billy the Kid* ... was made to fit this formula."[7]

Ostensibly it would be a remake of MGM's *Billy the Kid*, although King Vidor's 1930 film came closer to history, or at least Walter Noble Burns's idea of history, than this one.

The movie was filmed in Technicolor — a first for a Taylor film — and shot predominantly on location in Arizona around Flagstaff, Sedona, and Tucson, and in Utah, around Kanab and in what would become known as John Ford country, Monument Valley. Ford's *Stagecoach* (1939) had highlighted the Navajo country's picturesque desert, but *Billy the Kid* would reveal its grandeur in color. For MGM newcomer producer Irving Asher, this was

Robert Taylor's first true Western was *Billy the Kid* (1941) in which he played the title role.

his first feature for the studio. Frank Borzage, who had won Oscars for *7th Heaven* (1927) and *Bad Girl* (1931), was assigned to direct, with his brother Lew to be assistant director. Filming began in December 1940 in Monument Valley, where "weather trouble" plagued the production. Then, Borzage was reassigned to a Joan Crawford movie, *Bombay Nights*— a movie that was never filmed — or, suffering from mental exhaustion or too much alcohol stemming from his divorce, he was simply relieved. In any event, Borzage was replaced by David Miller.[8]

Miller, who had started out as an assistant editor at Columbia, had joined MGM in the mid–1930s, directing two-reelers, mostly sports shorts. *Billy the Kid* was his first chance at directing a feature, but since it *was* his first outing, MGM sent Norman Taurog, the Oscar-winning director of *Skippy* (1931) who had been nominated for MGM's hit *Boys Town* (1938), as a "supervisor" to help him. Although *Billy the Kid* would be "distinguished more by the outstanding Technicolor work of Leonard Smith and William V. Skall than by any directorial qualities," Miller would eventually prove his workmanship with *Sudden Fear* (1952) and *Lonely Are the Brave* (1962). He died in 1992 at age ninety-two.[9]

There was another change, too. Maureen O'Sullivan, Taylor's co-star in 1938's *A Yank at Oxford* and *The Crowd Roars*, began production as Edith Keating, but left for Canada to join her husband, director John Farrow, who was serving in the Royal Canadian Air Force, according to press reports. Or she left because after a script rewrite her role was reduced. She was replaced by Mary Howard, a former Broadway actress who had played Ann Rutledge in *Abe Lincoln in Illinois* (1940). Howard's Hollywood career was cut short by World War II, during which she toured service camps and helped start the USO in Los Angeles. In 1945, she returned to New York, married Broadway producer-director Alfred de Liagre, Jr., and died in 2009.[10]

Ian Hunter, a South Africa–born actor who had appeared in a number of British and American films since 1934, played Keating. A year after *Billy the Kid*, he returned to England to serve in the war. He would appear in almost 100 films before his death in 1975.[11]

Brian Donlevy, who had made his mark playing the sadist soldier in 1939's *Beau Geste* (getting an Oscar nomination) and had played a bad guy in *Jesse James*, got to play a nice guy this time. He even got nice reviews, with the *Los Angeles Times* noting that he "brings a solid, common-sense assurance to his role," and *Variety* calling his performance "excellent." Donlevy had started out in New York in the early 1920s and would continue playing mostly "tough guy roles" for the rest of his career, although he showed his deftness at comedy in the title roles of *The Great McGinty* (1940) and *The Remarkable Andrew* (1942). He died of cancer in 1972.[12]

Taylor was warned not to repeat Johnny Mack Brown's errors in MGM's original *Billy the Kid* (1930). According to veteran MGM crew members, "Brown always telegraphed his lethal intentions by screwing up his face before he went for his weapons. And every time he pulled a trigger he'd flinch." MGM's research department provided Taylor with a copy of the famous tintype of Billy the Kid, so the right-handed Taylor spent months practicing his left-handed draw. As previously noted, tintypes were reversed; the real Billy the Kid was right-handed. When Taylor visited retired actor William S. Hart, one of Taylor's "earliest film idols," who had reportedly coached Taylor on the art of fast draws, the former silent screen star and a Colonel Archer Adams informed Taylor that Billy was right-handed. By then it was too late to change, so Billy remained a southpaw.[13]

When it came to film his death scene, Taylor said he wanted a "hard glint" in his eyes, but because he didn't think he could do that in Technicolor, he got eye drops from a doctor to make his pupils contract. "He fixed me up all right," Taylor said. "Then as the lights trained on me for my death scene I went blind and production had to be called off. Next time I did it straight — with my own blue eyes."[14]

By the time the moviemakers returned to Hollywood, MGM had recreated the town of Lincoln, New Mexico, on its back lot.[15]

With the exception of Republic's *Billy the Kid Returns* (1938) and PRC's new series of programmers starring Bob Steele, New Mexico's legendary outlaw hadn't been the subject of a movie since MGM's 1930 flop. But the success of 20th Century–Fox's *Jesse James* had studios turning to stories for A-list productions about dead outlaws. In 1940, Fox had released a sequel, *The Return of Frank James*, and Universal had scored a hit with *When the Daltons Rode*. Fox's *Belle Starr* would go into production in the spring of 1941, although it bore more resemblance to *Gone with the Wind* (except in quality) than to any Western.

Billy the Kid was the cover story for *Movie Story* magazine picturing Robert Taylor, Mary Howard and Brian Donlevy.

Suddenly, MGM found itself in a race to get out a Billy the Kid movie first. Howard Hughes was filming his own story about Billy the Kid in Arizona with the working title *Billy the Kid*. That left MGM executives apprehensive. "For past experience has proved that when subjects conflict, the first to the box office is the one that does the business," the *New York Times* noted. Hughes wound up taking over the direction from Howard Hawks, moving at Hughes's "own bizarre pace." MGM's production was taking its time, too. It was the longest production on the MGM lot since *Gone with the Wind*, which was only partially shot on the studio. Filming halted on March 26, 1941, but then retakes began in mid–April. Still, MGM finished first — and Hughes still had to get his "sexy love story" past censors — so MGM "stole" the title *Billy the Kid*. Hughes protested to Mayer, but MGM wasn't about to change, forcing Hughes to title his film *The Outlaw*.[16]

The movie opened in May, a quick turnaround, but the rush wasn't necessary. Hughes's *The Outlaw* would be delayed for years.

Taylor had told friends that he sort of wished he had lived in the 19th Century West, although he admitted, "I'd have probably gotten myself shot to death very young."[17]

Film critics were about to gun the actor down.

"Robert Taylor proves a much less fantastic choice for the role of William Bonney, the Kid, than you might suppose," Philip K. Scheuer wrote for the *Los Angeles Times*. "He acts real tough and he means business. But because he is Robert Taylor, because he is the 'hero' of the tale, the studio is at great pains to show you that no matter what he does or how many lives he snuffs out, the moral justification was sufficiently strong to prod him into it."[18]

That was one of the kinder assessments. The *New York Times* said that Taylor "gives the impression of a kid in a new cowboy suit."[19] *Life* magazine said "Taylor, even in Technicolor, creates a poor copy of the fleet, slim killer of the border country."[20]

It wasn't all bad. *Variety* said, "Robert Taylor will surprise, and make plenty of progress toward strongest marquee voltage, as a rough and tough man's man type of western outlaw. Characterization puts a mat of hair on Taylor's chest in a big way and opens new angles for future rugged assignments."[21]

The *Chicago Tribune* called it "an engrossing, colorful film," and said, "They couldn't make a toreador out of Tyrone Power but, O boy, what a 'Billy the Kid' Robert Taylor turned out to be!"[22]

There were other good reviews, too. While Taylor's performance garnered mixed reactions, everyone raved about the cinematography. Directors of photography Leonard Smith and William V. Skall would be nominated for an Academy Award, losing to Ernest Palmer and Ray Rennahan for *Blood and Sand*. "But somehow," Bosley Crowther wrote for the *New York Times,* "a lot of Mr. Taylor is scarcely able to compare with even a moderate amount of stunning outdoor scenery — with the coral and copper-colored monoliths of Monument Valley, their tops wreathed in billowing mists; with deserts stretching off into pink distance and red cattle grazing on the rolling plains. And the scenery is by far the most spectacular part of this bulging film."[23]

It made money. Lots of it, becoming one of Taylor's biggest hits. And *Variety* was right, as Taylor moved from MGM pretty boy to "rugged assignments," playing the crooked hood who falls for Lana Turner in *Johnny Eager* (1942) and the heroic G.I. in *Bataan* (1943). Taylor wouldn't make another Western until *Ambush* (1950), but after that, he made quite a few in the genre, including the excellent *Devil's Doorway* (1950) and *Westward the Women* (1951) and giving arguably his best performance as the racist buffalo hunter in *The Last Hunt* (1956). Between 1949 and 1967, he made eleven feature Westerns.[24]

Taylor spent twenty-five years at MGM, before leaving the studio in 1958, and the quality of his films declined. So did his looks, from the effects of smoking. He was diagnosed with cancer, had part of a lung removed, and died on June 8, 1969.[25]

Analysis

"They've got a good script, practically all of it true; at least there'll be no such outrageous history-twisting and moral whitewashing as 20th-Fox gave to Jesse James," Hollywood correspondent Paul Harrison wrote.[26]

The script wasn't that good, practically none of it was true, and it was full of history-twisting and moral whitewashing. *Billy the Kid* also wasn't anywhere near as entertaining as *Jesse James*.

Taylor was only twenty-nine when filming began, but he played the role like, and certainly looked like, a much older gunman.

The cinematography was first-rate, capturing Monument Valley's beauty, but the movie never struck solid footing in entertainment or, especially, in history.

"Once again the studio sought to whitewash William Bonney, making him the Robin Hood–like figure invented by Walter Noble Burns," Jim Hitt writes in *The American West from Fiction (1823–1976) into Film (1909–1986)*, "and once again both reality and history are left behind in this inferior remake."[27]

***

New York Times (June 20, 1941): "[I]n spite of its elaborate coloring and its highly reputed star, *Billy the Kid* is just another routine horse opera — another glorified fable about one of the West's more notorious outlaws — and not a very good one at that."

West of Tombstone

(Columbia, January 1942, 59 minutes) CREDITS: Director: Howard Bretherton. Producer: William Berke. Screenplay: Maurice Geraghty. CAST: Charles Starrett (Steve Langdon); Russell Hayden ("Lucky" Barnet); Cliff Edwards (Harmony Haines); Marcella Martin (Carol Barnet); Gordon DeMain (Wilfred Barnet/Billy the Kid); Clancy Cooper (Dave Shurlock); Jack Kirk (Sheriff); Budd Buster (Wheeler); Tom London (Morris).

Synopsis

After a stagecoach is robbed, a wounded passenger informs the stage driver, "Lucky" Barnet, that one of the bandits was none other than Billy the Kid. As Billy has been dead for twenty years, Lucky thinks the old man is just addled, but the man insists, pointing to the fact that one of the masked riders used "Mexican lingo," which Billy was prone to do; and besides, that old man had tangled with some of those boys in the Lincoln County War.

As rumors increase, the U.S. marshal sends Deputy Steve Langdon to Fort Sumner to investigate. Harmony Haines is a flimflam artist leading tourists on a Billy the Kid tour and selling them buttons for $5 a pop that he swears he took off the clothes on Billy's body; Steve forces him to help dig up Billy's grave. "Seems a shame to disturb him after all these years," Harmony laments.

When the coffin is opened, Steve and Harmony find only a saddle, holster, rifle, and gun belt. Someone takes a shot at them. The gunman gets away, but Steve spots the Swinging J brand on the rider's palomino horse.

That clue takes the two to the Crescent City stagecoach line. It's a family operation, owned by Wilfred Barnet, whose son is Lucky, while his daughter Carol runs and rides around in a fringed skirt and six-shooter looking pretty and acting feisty. Lucky has recovered from the injury sustained in the holdup, and rides off to look for clues at the site. Sister tags along. Harmony spots the Swinging J brand on Lucky's palomino. Naturally, Harmony informs Steve, and they follow.

After a chase, Steve tries to arrest Lucky. Carol intervenes, insisting that her brother was just able to ride this very day. Her father owns the stagecoach line, so what reason would they have to rob it? That makes sense to Steve — or does it?

He breaks into the Barnet home and discovers a letter, and Carol discovers him sneaking around. But when Steve shows her a letter written to her father by none other than Pat Garrett, the slayer of Billy the Kid, even Carol has suspicions. She confronts her father, who tells her that he was a hired gun in the range war years, and the only way he could escape all those trigger-happy kids looking to build a reputation by killing a fast gun was to become someone else. Yep, he is Billy the Kid.

Uh-oh. The company's clerk, Wheeler, overhears that confession, and Wheeler is in

cahoots with the outlaw gang that has been robbing those stages. He takes off, Lucky follows him, and gets the drop on the bad guys. But the leader of the gang says if they are turned in, it'll be curtains for Lucky's old man. He's Billy the Kid.

"And I'm Jesse James," Lucky says.

Still, Lucky gives the leader a chance to prove his story by going to town with him. Sure enough, Wilfred Barnet pays off the bad man and warns him to get out of town. But the outlaws have other plans. He tells Barnet, er, Billy that they'll rob one more stage and that he'd better keep his son from driving. Of course, Lucky has informed Steve and the sheriff that he suspects that the stage will be held up and dispatches them to trap the bad guys. When Barnet/Billy sends the stage off without Lucky driving, Barnet/Billy knocks out his son.

The outlaws rob the stage. Steve, believing that he has been double-crossed by Lucky, goes back to the house and arrests him. Meanwhile, Barnet/Billy uses one of the dead outlaw's horses to take him to the hideout. He's followed by Steve and Harmony.

Barnet/Billy catches up with the outlaws, and the shooting starts. Steve sends Harmony to town to bring back a posse, then he rides to help Barnet/Billy stop the bad guys.

Steve's wounded, but he and Billy manage to hold off the robbers until help arrives. Unfortunately, it's too late for Barnet/Billy, who was mortally wounded during the fracas. Steve lets Billy die as Barnet.

"I guess [Billy the Kid] never did figure into this after all," Steve says.

The History

The opening scroll says, "William H. Bonney, alias Billy the Kid, was killed at Fort Sumner, New Mexico, on July 14, 1881. So the official records state. But was he? The supposed killing was done by his lifelong friend, Sheriff Pat Garrett, and has long been disputed, even by members of Billy's outlaw band."

Writes Billy biographer Robert M. Utley:

> The "Billy Rides Again" syndrome appealed to people's gullible fondness for conspiracy and cover-up as historical determinants. Garrett shot the wrong man, or faked a killing in a pact with the Kid, or conspired in some other secret maneuver that set the young man free to disappear into another life.[28]

The most famous of the alleged Billy the Kids was Ollie L. "Brushy Bill" Roberts, who petitioned New Mexico Governor Thomas J. Mabry for a pardon in 1950. On November 29 of that year, Roberts and his attorney, William Morrison, met Mabry in the governor's mansion. Afterward, the three men convened with reporters, historians and people like Oscar and Jarvis Garrett (Pat Garrett's sons), Cliff McKinney (son of Kip McKinney, one of Garrett's deputies when he killed the Kid) and Arcadio Brady (William Brady's son). Roberts performed so poorly, the governor declared: "I am taking no action, now or ever, on the application for a pardon for Billy the Kid because I do not believe this man is Billy the Kid." Roberts returned to Texas and died the following month in Hico, where many residents still believe he was, indeed, Billy the Kid. Predating Brushy Bill's claim was that of John Miller, whom many said looked like the Kid and was rather secretive. Miller died at the Prescott, Arizona, Pioneer's Home, on March 12, 1937, without ever getting his chance to "set the record straight."[29]

Opposite: Poster for *West of Tombstone* (1942).

Then, of course, there's this matter of Billy the Kid robbing stagecoaches. On the other hand, the stagecoach company owner (who turns out to be Billy) says that's the "first time I ever heard of him holding up a stagecoach. That wasn't in his line." Since he was Billy, he should know — and did. Billy the Kid is not known to have ever robbed any stagecoach or bank.

During the shootout with the robbers, Steve hands Barnet/Billy a Colt, saying that Billy the Kid never was much of a shot with a Winchester. When Barnet/Billy begins shooting with his right hand, Steve tells him: "Use your left hand, where it belongs." As pointed out already, Billy the Kid was right-handed.

The Players

Promotional releases noted that *West of Tombstone* had "Not one, but two stars, Charles Starrett and Russell Hayden" to bring "western thrills never experienced before."[30]

Charles Starrett is best remembered for playing the Durango Kid, playing "the Robin Hood–like masked avenger" in *The Durango Kid* (1940) and then, beginning with *The Return of the Durango Kid* (1945), in sixty-four features that ran until 1952. He was, however, anything but a Westerner. Heir to a tool and die company, he was born in Athol, Massachusetts, attended Worcester Academy, a prestigious prep school, and played football at Dartmouth. While at Dartmouth in 1926, he landed a job as an extra in *The Quarterback*, starring Richard Dix, which was partially filmed on the college campus. He won a scholarship to the American Academy of Dramatic Arts and worked in regional theater in the Midwest before moving to New York, where he performed on Broadway. In 1930, he began his film career at Paramount, playing youthful romantic roles. When he moved to Columbia in 1935, he became a cowboy star (replacing Tim McCoy), beginning with *The Gallant Defender*.[31]

"Charles was a handsome cowboy, so good-looking," recalled Louise Currie, who worked with Starrett on *The Pinto Kid* (1941). "But he looked like an Eastern dude, not the cowboy type. He seemed to be having a hard time riding his horse, just like I was. I got to know him very well, but I felt he should have played the visiting Easterner, rather than being a cowboy."[32]

After joining Columbia, Starrett ranked in *Motion Picture Herald*'s annual list of top ten moneymaking Western stars, but studio executives decided in the mid–1940s that his series needed something. Producer Colbert Clark decided to bring back The Durango Kid, and Starrett returned to the list of top ten Western moneymakers. He went on to make more than 130 Westerns for Columbia.[33]

"The Durango Kid stories were the Western stereotype stripped down to the mare's back," Buck Rainey wrote in *Heroes of the Range*. "The theory that the grinding out of the same plot, with only minor variations, will still result in a successful film, particularly if it happens to be a Western, is nowhere more strongly (and somewhat mistakenly) illustrated in the Durango Kid series. The same old stagecoach holdup, the same old suave villain masquerading as a benefactor, the same old cattle stampede and a few other standard props were constantly assembled ... and while the result probably produced no audible complaints from oater fans, the whole series seemed rather tired."[34]

West of Tombstone wasn't much better.

No matter. Starrett probably laughed all the way to the bank. Not that he needed it, having "received a sizable income from a block of stock" he inherited from his grandfather (owner of the tool and die company). Starrett retired from acting in 1952, and died in 1986 of cancer at age eighty-two.[35]

Second-billed Russell Hayden started in movies as a grip, and moved to sound recorder, film cutter, and assistant cameraman before becoming an actor in the mid–1930s. He played Lucky Jenkins in William Boyd's Hopalong Cassidy series, but had left that hit series to freelance. *West of Tombstone* publicity releases practically gave Hayden equal billing with Starrett, noting "not one, but two stars." Hayden almost always played "Lucky" in the movies. In the early 1950s, Hayden moved behind the camera as a producer and director of TV Western series such as *Cowboy G-Men* (1952–1953), *Judge Roy Bean* (1956), and *26 Men* (1957–1959). He died in 1981.[36]

Iowa-born Gordon DeMain (born Floyd Wood), whose career began in the silents, was equally unsuited for Westerns, though he would appear in several under a variety of pseudonyms (Gordon De Maine, Gordon Demaine, Gordon Wood, G.D. Wood, G.A. Wood, G.D. Woods, J.D. Wood, Bud Wood, etc.). He was in his mid-fifties when *West of Tombstone* was filmed; his "heavy French accent makes his portrayal of a middle-aged Billy the Kid slightly exotic by any standard." DeMain died in 1954.[37]

Analysis

Another routine programmer that is easily forgotten. Well, maybe screenwriters Ron Ormond and Ira Webb and the rest of the gang at Western Adventures Productions didn't forget it. They'd revise many of the elements in another programmer, seemingly close to the point of plagiarism, this one starring Lash LaRue: *Son of Billy the Kid* (1949).

***

Joplin (Missouri) *Globe* (March 11, 1942): "Sixty minutes of riding and shooting."

The Outlaw

(Hughes Productions/United Artists/RKO, February 1943, 121 minutes) CREDITS: Director-Producer: Howard Hughes. Screenplay: Jules Furthman. CAST: Jack Buetel (Billy the Kid); Thomas Mitchell (Pat Garrett); Jane Russell (Rio McDonald); Walter Huston (Doc Holliday); Mimi Aguglia (Guadalupe); Joe Sawyer (Charley Woodruff); Gene Rizzi (Stranger); Emory Parnell (Dolan); Martin Garralaga (Waiter); Julian Rivero (Pablo); Bobby Callahan (Boy); Arthur Loft (Swanson); Ethan Laidlaw (Deputy).

Synopsis

Lincoln County Sheriff Pat Garrett is pleased to hear that his old friend Doc Holliday is in town. When Doc goes after a horse thief, Garrett promises to help. Turns out the horse thief is Billy the Kid. He and Doc size each other up, and when Garrett shows up to arrest the horse thief, Doc introduces him to Billy.

Garrett tries to pull one of his old ruses. He walks forward to shake Billy's hand, with the intention of knocking him out, but it's Billy who decks the lawman. "It's the first time a sheriff ever wanted to shake hands with me," the Kid explains.

Doc helps set Billy up to be arrested by Garrett—after all, Doc does want his horse back—but the thought of having to get a sheriff to help him out sticks in Doc's craw, and he walks out with Billy. That annoys Garrett, who tells the two gunmen: "I want the two of you out of town by sundown."

Doc takes most of Billy's money in a poker game, but Billy still has his horse. He decides to sleep in the livery to make sure Doc doesn't steal the strawberry roan away from him. During the night, someone tries to kill Billy. When Billy disarms the assailant, he discovers it's a beautiful young woman, Rio McDonald; Billy was forced to kill her brother in Socorro. They roll around in the hay.

The next day, Billy and Doc are back in the saloon, where Billy kills a stranger who was trying to con Garrett into making him a deputy. Garrett brings in some deputies to arrest the Kid for murder, but Doc backs Billy's play. When Garrett shoots Billy with a Winchester, Doc steps in, shooting the rifle out of Garrett's hands and killing two of his deputies.

That's about all Garrett can take. "Doc, this finishes you and me for good and all."

"I'm sorry," Doc says, and takes Billy to the home of his girlfriend and her aunt. Yep, Doc's gal is Rio. "Now, do your best for this boy," Doc tells his lover before riding off to lead the posse away.

Rio will certainly do that. It's not like her aunt, Guadalupe, will "lift a finger" to help Billy.

The stars of *The Outlaw* (1943): (left to right) Thomas Mitchell, Walter Houston, Jane Russell and Jack Buetel.

It's touch and go for the wounded gunman for a while, and when Billy is chilled, Rio decides to crawl into bed with him. "I'll get you warm," she tells him, and lets her Aunt Guadalupe know that she can fetch a preacher to marry them if it'll make her feel better.

Apparently, that's what happens.

Wouldn't you know it, a night in bed with Rio brings Billy around just like that, and before you shout a warning to censor Joseph Breen, Rio's in love with the Kid. Heck, Billy has even managed to charm Guadalupe. "He can charm a bird right out of a bush," she says.

That's when Doc Holliday returns. He's a bit perturbed at how things have turned out, but Billy blames him for what has happened between him and Rio. "Who brought me here?" he asks.

The two men decide to pick, Rio over the horse Red. That's not the way to a woman's heart, but Doc picks Red, and Billy rides off with his friend, leaving Rio more than just miffed. Pat Garrett is on their trail.

It's a long way to Fort Sumner, and Billy's infuriated when he discovers that Rio has filled their canteens with sand. What was he to expect? He takes off during the night to exact revenge, leaving Doc alone to be caught by Garrett.

On the way back to Lincoln, Garrett and Doc discover Rio. Billy has left her tied with wet rawhide between two rocks. Doc's convinced that Billy's in love with Rio, which makes Garrett think that he'll likely come back for her. So he sets an ambush.

Sure enough, it works. Now Garrett has captured Billy and Doc, but Mescaleros are on the warpath, blocking the way to Lincoln. They decide to go to Fort Sumner instead.

The Indians close in, and Garrett lets Billy and Doc have their guns after they promise to give them back if they get out of this mess alive. Billy takes the lead, and he, Garrett and Doc rope down cacti and drag them behind their horses as they flee the Mescaleros. The thick dust caused by the cacti and horses stops the Indians, and the foursome arrive at a home about forty miles from Fort Sumner. Garrett sends the owner to Fort Sumner to bring back the marshal.

Doc's ready to leave — breaking his word to Garrett — on Red, but Billy keeps saying that horse is his. They push and prod until it becomes evident that there must be a showdown, and Garrett's not going to intervene. "You and me never had any trouble till he came along," he tells his ex-pal Doc.

They agree to draw when a cuckoo clock chimes its last note at eight o'clock. But while waiting for that signal, Billy has a change of heart. He doesn't draw, and Doc doesn't shoot. Not even when Doc fires a bullet scratching his hand, and nicks Billy's two ears. He just won't fight Doc. "You're the only pardner I ever had," he says.

The two men make up. They decide to leave, but that pushes Garrett past the breaking point.

"I might have know you'd do something like this to me!" Garrett explodes in an unnerving homosexual, homicidal rant. "Ever since you met him, you've treated me like a dog. The very first day you sided with him against me and made me the laughingstock of the town."

"Be careful," Doc warns. "You know you haven't got a chance against me."

They draw. Doc has him beat, but can't pull the trigger on his old friend. Garrett fires, and Doc is mortally wounded, but tells Billy to leave Garrett alone. Doc is buried the next morning.

Garrett offers Billy Doc's guns, and suggests that Billy leave his own guns with Garrett. That way, Garrett can pass Doc's grave off as Billy's, leaving Billy free to get out of the country and live a life in peace. Billy buys into the plan, but Garrett has taken the firing pins out of Doc's guns. Now he's ready to bring Billy in.

Only, Billy accidentally switched one of Doc's revolvers for his, so the gun Garrett's holding has no firing pin. Poor Pat Garrett's foiled again.

Garrett's left chained to an adobe column at the house. Billy tells him that he's leaving his guns, suggesting that Garrett would feel a lot better claiming that it was Doc Holliday — and not Billy the Kid — who left him chained.

Rio brings Billy canteens — full of water this time, not sand — and he starts to ride away, but stops and turns back to Rio. She smiles widely, understanding, and climbs onto the saddle behind him. They ride into the desert together.

The History

"It sure is funny," Thomas Mitchell's Pat Garrett laments toward the end of this movie, "how two or three trails can cross and get all tangled up."

The Outlaw certainly crossed a few trails and got history all tangled up.

Pat Garrett (Thomas Mitchell) is helpless to prevent his deputies from getting killed in *The Outlaw* (1943).

For instance, Garrett says of Doc Holliday: "He's my best friend." And Doc tells Billy: "I know [Garrett] better than you do." Likewise, Billy says that he has admired Doc Holliday since he was "in short pants." If Pat Garrett ever met Doc Holliday, history hasn't recorded it. The same can be said of any Billy the Kid–Doc Holliday meeting. Holliday's best friend wasn't Pat Garrett, but lawman Wyatt Earp. "I am a friend of Doc Holliday because when I was city marshal of Dodge City, Kansas, he came to my rescue and saved my life when I was surrounded by desperadoes," Earp testified. It was Earp who had a reputation for pistol-whipping lawbreakers into submission; Pat Garrett's reputation was pretty much shooting down an outlaw in a darkened bedroom.[38]

When Billy says of women, "I don't trust 'em," history tells us otherwise. Frank Coe called Billy "a ladies' man. He talked the Mexican language and was also liked by the women." George W. Coe said Billy "was so popular there wasn't enough of him to go around. He had a beautiful voice and sang like a bird."[39]

"That's the one thing I've always been afraid of," Doc tells Rio. "Dying in bed." Ironically, for an alcoholic gunman and gambler with a death wish and violent temper, that's how the real Doc Holliday died. Suffering from tuberculosis, Holliday's health finally broke, and in October 1887, he checked into a hotel in Glenwood Springs, Colorado. Practically bedridden, he ordered room-service breakfast — a bottle of whiskey — every day before drifting into a coma and dying, at age thirty-six, on November 8.[40]

The marker over Doc's grave proclaims: "Here Lies Billy the Kid Killed by Pat Garrett July 13, 1881." According to the historical record, Garrett shot Billy dead on the night of July 14 — not the 13th — but that's just one problem with the history of *The Outlaw*. If Doc Holliday was killed on July 13, how did he take part in the Gunfight at the O.K. Corral in Tombstone, Arizona Territory, some three months later?[41]

The Players

Houston, Texas–born Howard Hughes was a designer, builder, daredevil, aviation enthusiast and millionaire with an interest in films. Since 1927, he had owned a production company in Hollywood, underwriting *Hell's Angels* (1930) and *Scarface* (1932). Even in pre–Code Hollywood, his 1932 film *Cock of the Air* was deemed by the Producers Review Board of the Studio Relations Committee "obscene and immoral in title, theme, and portrayal." Undeterred, Hughes appealed to the Motion Picture Producers and Distributors of America Board in New York — a first for a producer — but the board sided with Hollywood, forcing Hughes to cut scenes, although he kept the title "and the titillation."[42]

The Hays Code, named after the MPPDA's powerful president Will Hays, had been adopted by the MPPDA in 1930, but enforcement did not begin until 1934. Hughes had been out of movies for eight years when he decided to make *The Outlaw*, and he was about to run into a concrete wall known as the Hays Code.[43]

At a post–*Gone with the Wind* party in 1939, Hughes approached publicist Russell Birdwell and told him he wanted to get back into the motion picture business but needed a publicist, and Birdwell readily accepted. The subject of Hughes's planned movie surprised Birdwell: Billy the Kid.[44]

Billy the Kid had interested Hughes for years. He once invited Johnny Mack Brown, who had starred as Billy in King Vidor's MGM spectacular flop *Billy the Kid,* to supper, then screened the 1930 film. "He was utterly fascinated by the character of Billy the Kid,"

Brown said of Hughes years later. "I had no idea that Howard was picking my brain and was planning even back then to make his own film called *Billy the Kid*."[45]

Hughes explained that he wanted not only a complete unknown to play Billy (which had been Vidor's idea in 1930), but also an unknown to play the Kid's love interest. After all, Hughes had "discovered" Jean Harlow in *Hell's Angels*.[46]

Hired as director was Howard Hawks, the veteran who had worked with Hughes on *Scarface*. Writing the script was Ben Hecht, who had won Academy Awards for *Underworld* (1927) and *The Scoundrel* (1935); his other credits included *Scarface*, *Viva Villa!* (1934), *Barbary Coast* (1935), and *Wuthering Heights* (1939). Hecht never produced an outline that Hughes liked so, at Hawks's suggestion, Hughes hired Jules Furthman, who had been writing since the silents and whose credits included *Mutiny on the Bounty* (1935) and *Come and Get It* (1936), earning an Oscar nomination for the former. Hughes had no intention of making "an ordinary western."[47] 20th Century–Fox, which had scored a mammoth hit with *Jesse James* in 1939, was to distribute Hughes's independent production.[48]

The film would also be sexy. Very, very sexy.

"Hughes ... was determined not only to test the limits of censorship but to best censorship itself. His would be not so much a motion picture as a media event designed to challenge the system of controls devised by the majors."[49]

The first publicity stunt was the search for the two youngsters. Hughes's office was flooded with photographs, but Billy was found when agent Gummo Marx (the one Marx brother who never acted in a movie) introduced him to a 23-year-old actor from Dallas named Jack Buetel. Hughes signed the novice actor for $75 a week.[50]

Finding someone to play the love interest, Rio, wasn't as easy. Then Hughes saw a photograph of a 19-year-old named Ernestine Jane Geraldine Russell. "Give this Jane Russell a test," he said. Russell hadn't sent the photo. A Minnesota native who had arrived in Hollywood in 1932, she was working as a receptionist at $10 a week, supplementing her salary by modeling dresses and coats for photographer Tom Kelley. Agent Levis Green had seen the photo at Kelley's studio, "swiped" it, and began showing it to various casting directors around Hollywood.[51]

The screen test arranged for Russell would be the barn scene. "They gave me this peasant blouse to wear," Russell recalled, "and it was 'Janie, bend down and pick up those pails.' I did it, and the next thing I know, they're aiming the camera down to my navel."

Russell turned for help to Hawks, who said, "You're a big girl. If you don't want to do something, say 'No' loud and clear. Nobody's going to look after you but you."

When she saw the photos, she complained to Hughes, who said, "That's the way to sell a picture."[52] He signed Russell to a contract.[53]

Hughes hired Thomas Mitchell to play Pat Garrett and Walter Huston to play Doc Holliday. Character actor Mitchell was coming off his Academy Award–winning turn as the drunken doctor in John Ford's *Stagecoach* (1939), made the year in which he had also appeared in *Only Angels Have Wings*, *Gone with the Wind*, and *Mr. Smith Goes to Washington*. A former newspaper reporter and playwright, Mitchell would continue acting pretty much until his death in 1962. Like many other Broadway actors, Huston had been lured to Hollywood by the money. Although he was already in his forties by the time he began his career as a film actor, he landed lead (sometimes romantic) roles and character parts, earning acclaim for his performances in *Abraham Lincoln* (1930), *The Beast of the City* (1932), *Dodsworth* (1936), and many others. Directed by his son, John Huston, he would win an

Jane Russell made her film debut in *The Outlaw* (1943).

Oscar for Best Supporting Actor in *The Treasure of the Sierra Madre* (1948) before his death in 1950.[54]

With actors in place, the production began in November 1940 near Tuba City, Arizona, with Hawks directing, Lucien Ballard as director of photography, and Birdwell arranging sexy photographs of Russell and concocting provocative slogans for the revealing photos like "Mean, moody, and magnificent." Second-unit shooting was done near Socorro, New Mexico.[55]

The movies of 1939 had revitalized the Western genre. 20th Century–Fox's *Jesse James*, Warner Bros.' *Dodge City*, Universal's *Destry Rides Again,* and United Artists' *Stagecoach* had proved commercial and critical hits. Hughes had planned on titling his film *Billy the Kid*, but once he began shooting, he learned that MGM had a Western in production starring Robert Taylor in the title role, *Billy the Kid*. Hughes complained to MGM boss Louis B. Mayer. Mayer said he had every right to remake MGM's 1930 film and suggested that Hughes film another movie or change the title. Hughes had no choice but to change *Billy the Kid* to *The Outlaw*.[56]

The title was the least of the production's problems.

Hawks reportedly told Hughes, "Jane and Jack are nice kids, but neither one of them can act." To which Hughes replied: "The horses will do the acting."[57]

Hughes had dailies flown in to Los Angeles daily, and began telephoning Hawks, regardless of the hour, with complaints. He told Hawks not to worry about money, that he was rushing things, and that he wanted more clouds in the background. (Hughes had a thing about clouds; when filming the John Wayne movie *Jet Pilot* [1957], he ordered cinematographer William Clothier not to shoot anything unless the clouds were beautiful.) Hawks countered that his salary, on top of the $3,500 a week, included a percentage of profits so it made sense to keep costs down. Eventually, Hawks grew fed up. "We just can't agree on how the picture should be done," Hawks told Russell. "I told Howard he'd better do it himself, because no one tells me how to shoot a picture." Hawks left the production, later saying that he had an offer from Warner Bros. to film *Sergeant York*. Hughes took over as director, and cinematographer Gregg Toland, coming off *Citizen Kane*, replaced Ballard, who left with Hawks. Production was shut down, then moved to the Samuel Goldwyn lot.[58]

Legend has it that when filming the scene in which Russell was tied between two trees with leather thongs and trying to free herself, Hughes came up with the idea for a new brassiere. "Relying on his knowledge of aerodynamics and stress ... Hughes sketched a bra for Russell that would, at the pull of a string, accentuate her already impressive endowments."[59]

Another story has Hughes filming two versions of *The Outlaw*, the commercial release and another for his personal viewing, showing Russell naked from the waist up.[60] Which makes sense when you consider yet another story, this one having Hughes tell Toland: "We're not getting enough production out of Jane's breasts. I want her knockers to be the real star of the picture."[61]

Russell and Buetel were novices. "Howard was always very kind and soft-spoken," Russell recalled, "but he always wanted one more take. 'Jack, you lifted your left eyebrow,' he'd say. 'I'd like to try it without that. It may give Billy a smart aleck attitude.' Over and over we did it until, instead of just concentrating on lines and intent in a scene, we were both thinking of eyebrows. Don't move your left thumb, don't lean too far to the right, and on and on. We were like wooden dummies. But we didn't know there was another way."[62]

In the scene in which Billy talks beside Doc's grave, Hughes demanded 103 takes.[63] Mitchell and Huston often threatened to quit, with Mitchell calling *The Outlaw* "a bastard of a film."[64]

Hughes reportedly started filming each day at 11 A.M., the time he typically liked to begin work. He had all of the Hawks-Ballard footage re-shot but, as the *New York Times* noted, "He has the money to do it and the consensus is that he will spend as much as may be necessary to make *The Outlaw* a good picture...."[65] Initial filming was completed on February 7, 1941. Retakes were then scheduled, costing Hughes another $127,000.[66]

When the finished film was sent to the Hays Office, Joseph I. Breen, head of the Production Code Administration, objected. "In my more than ten years of critical examination of motion pictures I have never seen anything quite so unacceptable as the shots of the breasts of the character Rio. Throughout almost half the picture the girl's breasts, which are large and prominent, are shockingly uncovered."[67] Breen demanded 108 cuts.[68]

Hughes appealed. Arguments went back and forth, and after Hughes agreed to a number of minor cuts and changes, *The Outlaw* was given a Seal of Approval on March 23, 1941. In mid–August, however, the PCA learned that Hughes, trying to do an end-around on the PCA, had sent unedited copies of the film to various state censors only to discover that some state censors were even more rigid than Breen. That was enough for 20th Century–

Fox, which could have been slapped with a $25,000 fine for releasing an un-approved movie. The studio backed out of its distribution deal. Hughes continued his fight, but when the United States entered World War II, he shelved the picture, put movies aside, and focused on his airplane enterprise.[69]

Toward the end of 1942, Hughes was ready to resurrect his movie. It opened at San Francisco's Geary Theatre on February 5, 1943, but not before Birdwell had supervised advertising billboards across the city featuring Russell's "charms" and the slogan, "How'd you like to tussle with Russell?" When Russell's aunt complained that billboards made Russell look like "some cheap stripper," Hughes responded: "I can't very well sell her like Shirley Temple." Hollywood's press was flown in for the premiere. *Newsweek* opined, "*The Outlaw* turns out to be a bust in more ways than one." The Catholic Legion of Decency banned it. So did New York's State Board of Regents. After the movie ran ten weeks in a limited release, Hughes shelved it again, only to revive it three years later when it was distributed by United Artists.[70]

This time, Hughes's advertising reached, *Newsweek* said, "literally a new high in vulgarity" after a skywriter spelled out "The Outlaw" followed by two circles with dots in the centers. The League of Decency said the movie glamorized crime and immorality. Boston banned it, not because of the sex, allegedly, but because it "Glorifies Crime." Censors responded by yanking the seal of approval. Hughes not only sued the Motion Picture Association of America, he made the film available to theaters willing to run it without a seal. Hughes eventually backed down, agreeing to some cuts. *The Outlaw* played in four Music Halls in Los Angeles—a blimp promoted the movie the night before it opened—with crowds lining up early for its opening. Los Angeles filmgoers bought one hundred thousand tickets in the opening week. In Atlanta, Georgia, *The Outlaw* earned $22,413 in ticket sales during its first week—$3,091 more than *Gone with the Wind* had racked up in its first week. By the end of the decade, the film had made up its $2.5 million cost by more than ten times.[71]

The Outlaw made Jane Russell a star forever linked to the movie, but it didn't do much for Jack Buetel's career. Howard Hawks reportedly considered Buetel (even though he had told Hughes that Buetel couldn't act) for the role of Matthew Garth in *Red River* (1948), but by then Buetel and Hughes were feuding, Hawks went with Montgomery Clift, and Buetel would not appear in another movie until RKO's *Best of the Badmen* (1951). Buetel made a few more movies and appeared on some TV shows but was out of the limelight by the early 1960s. He died in 1989. Russell would make roughly two dozen features, most of them between 1948 and 1957, including *The Paleface* (1948) and *Gentlemen Prefer Blondes* (1953). She began singing and appearing in Las Vegas in 1957 and even performed on Broadway in 1971. Yet until her death in 2011, and even afterward, she would always be linked to *The Outlaw* as a sex symbol.[72]

In 1948, Hughes become production head at RKO and sold *The Outlaw* to his new studio. By late 1949, he had decided to release the movie again. That October, the National Legion of Decency removed *The Outlaw* from its Class C (condemned) category and made it a mere Class B ("morally objectionable in part for all"). RKO rereleased the movie again in 1950. By April 1952, *The Outlaw* had grossed $2.6 million for RKO alone.[73] In 1968, *The Hollywood Reporter* said the movie had grossed more than $20 million.[74]

The Outlaw proved to be, as the *Chicago Daily Tribune* reported in 1946, "a horse opus to end all equine opera."[75]

Analysis

By today's standards, *The Outlaw* is tame, not titillating, but by any standards, it's bad moviemaking. Buetel is terrible, and even old pros Mitchell and Huston aren't very good. Russell isn't good, either, but she does possess a screen presence (and not what you're thinking). Hughes's direction is weak and unfocused, and the story drags. The history, of course, in nonexistent.

"Howard did all right when he hired a strong director and let the man make his picture without interference," longtime aide Noah Dietrich said in 1972. "But when Howard tried to take over and make the picture himself, as in the case with *Hell's Angels* and *The Outlaw*, the result was pretty godawful."[76]

Would the film found better footing had Hawks remained director? Hawks knew how to move a film along, even a bad one, and he would prove to be pretty good in the Western genre with *Red River* (1948) and *Rio Bravo* (1959). Even a pro like Hawks, however, could not likely have overcome this weak cast and weaker script.

Yet give *The Outlaw*, and Hughes, credit for challenging film censorship. *The Outlaw* also added an adult sexuality into the Western genre.

When you rank it as a Billy the Kid movie, you'd be hard-pressed to find another as controversial as this one. Nor are you likely to find a bigger box office success.

***

Variety (December 31, 1942): "Beyond sex attraction of Jane Russell's frankly displayed charms, picture, according to accepted screen entertainment standards, falls short. Plot is based on legend Billy the Kid wasn't killed by the law but continued to live on after his supposed death."

Alias Billy the Kid

(Republic, April 1946, 57 minutes) CREDITS: Director: Thomas Carr. Associate Producer: Bennett Cohen. Screenplay: Earle Snell, Betty Burbridge. CAST: Sunset Carson (Sunset Carson/The Kid); Peggy Stewart (Ann Marshall); Tom London (Dakota); Roy Barcroft (Matt Conroy); Russ Whiteman (Peewee); Tom Chatterton (Ed Pearson); Tex Terry (Buckskin); Pierce Lyden (Sam); James R. Linn (Jack); Stanley Price (Frank Pearson); Edward Cassidy (Sheriff).

Synopsis

Don't expect to find Billy the Kid in this one, except in the title. Sunset Carson is an undercover Texas Ranger posing as a horse thief, and when he's asked his name, he says, "Alias the Kid." Not Billy the Kid. Just the Kid.

Sunset shows up before Peewee, part of a gang of suspected cattle rustlers and killers, is to be hanged. Peewee has been convicted of back-shooting a Ranger who was bringing him in. He swears he's innocent, but isn't about to turn on his friends, so Sunset decides to pose as a horse thief and is locked in the same cell.

Before Peewee can say anything, however, he is shot in the back. His dad and sister have just arrived, hoping to take the boy's body back home after the hanging. Turns out, they'll get him sooner.

The body is loaded into the back of a wagon, but Sunset and the sheriff follow. That's because Sunset knows Peewee isn't dead as he was "breathing very heavy for a dead person."

Half-sheet poster for *Alias Billy the Kid* (1946) starring Sunset Carson and Peggy Stewart.

That's not Peewee's sister and dad, but Ann Marshall, leader of the outlaw gang since her father's death, and Dakota, one of her hired men. They spot the tail and get away, but Sunset decides to go after them, even if it means crossing what a title card tells us is "the turbulent Pecos River, west of which there existed no law or god or man."

"The governor gave orders to push law west of the Pecos," he says, "and here's where I start pushing."

He shows up in Denton City, where Matt Conroy has forced bankers Ed and Frank Pearson to help him rip off the ranchers by buying their cattle at "starvation prices" and stealing the stock, selling it at a handsome profit, and blaming all the crimes on Ann Marshall and her gang.

In fact, shortly after Sunset's arrival, Ann and her boys pay a visit to Conroy, robbing him and the bankers of the money belt. A tough customer, she tells the trio: "I know how much you like money. And I'm gonna strip you of everything you own before I call a showdown."

Ann's wounded in the getaway, but Sunset comes to her rescue and gets her safely back to camp. Ann tells him she's not stealing the money for herself, but plans to give it back to the ranchers Conroy has been cheating.

Sunset already suspects Conroy, but he needs proof. Besides, there's another problem. During the getaway from Denton City, weak-livered banker Frank Pearson was shot in the back by Conroy, and the crime has been pinned on the Marshall gang. That, Sunset agrees, will be tougher to pin on Conroy. Sunset finds two shells, one fired, one unfired, on the spot where the Ranger was murdered. When he comes back to Denton City, he finds Conroy with a bolt-action rifle which its proud owner says is likely "one-of-a-kind west of the Pecos." Yep, that's enough for Sunset.

Sunset makes a deal to bring in Ann and returns to the hideout, revealing his true identity and persuading Ann to give herself up. Not so fast, Dakota says. He followed Sunset into town and believes that he's working for Conroy. Fistfights and other shenanigans follow, and Sunset handcuffs Ann and takes her back to Conroy.

Conroy is growing tired of Ed Pearson, who wonders how his brother wound up shot in the back by the Marshall gang, and orders one of his gunmen to kill him. Sunset saves his life, and sends the banker out, on Sunset's horse, to bring back the Marshall gang and help him take care of Conroy.

Bullets and fists fly again, but as Sunset and Ann run out of bullets, the gang arrives. The bad guys are dispatched, and Sunset arrests Conroy, bringing law and order to the Pecos country as last.

The History

Considering that the closest Billy the Kid actually comes to being in this movie is in the title, there's no history, really, to contradict. Regarding Billy the Kid, anyway.

The Players

"Vivacious" Peggy Stewart appeared in seven Westerns at Republic with Sunset Carson, whom she "adored." She would marry another Republic B-Western star, Don Barry in 1940, divorcing him four years later. One of Republic's cowgirl queens, she had first appeared in Paramount's *Wells Fargo* (1937) and signed with Republic in 1944, staying there for three years, then moving on to play in mostly Westerns for other studios. As late as 2012, she was still an active actress, although well before then she had finally broken out of being typecast in Westerns.[77]

Sunset Carson's run as a cowboy hero, on the other hand, was short-lived. Born Michael Harrison in Plainview, Texas (or maybe Winifred Maurice Harrison in Gracemont, Oklahoma), he reportedly had been a rodeo star as a teenager, and got bit parts in a few movies before landing a role in *Stage Door Canteen* (1943). In 1944, he signed a three-year term contract with Republic Studios that paid him $150 a week in 1944, $200 a week in 1945, and $250 a week in 1946. His name was changed to match the cowboy hero he would portray on film. For Republic, he made fifteen programmers, with average budgets of $88,333, before "carousing himself out of a job." Studio president Herbert J. Yates fired Carson when he showed up at a Republic party — not only drunk, but with an underage girl.[78]

"Sunset Carson was a big athlete, with a broad Southern drawl. His films were jammed with action, and were very fast-moving, but Carson himself was a poor actor, and his period of popularity was brief," historians George N. Fenin and William K. Everson wrote.[79]

After Republic, Carson appeared in a few more programmers for fly-by-night production companies like Astor Pictures. His days as a cowboy hero were over after 1950, although he did tour with Wild West–circus shows and appeared in a science fiction flick, *Western Alien Outlaw* (1985). He also found religion, and led campaigns against drugs, violence, sex and foul language in film and television. He even helped launch a public television series, *Six Gun Heroes*, that featured sixty-eight films starring him as well as Ken Maynard and Roy Rogers, but filed suit in 1987 against South Carolina Educational Television Producers and Ken Heard Releasing Inc., saying he was never paid for videocassette sales and promotional materials sold on the show since 1982. The suit was settle out of court for an undisclosed amount. Carson died, apparently of a heart attack, in 1990 in Reno, Nevada, at age sixty-three.[80]

Analysis

Thomas Carr, film historian Jon Tuska writes, "directed Republic's best action Westerns."[81] This wasn't one of them.

It's a typical programmer, but the production is cheap, the acting atrocious, and the plot ridiculous. By this time, Carson was on his way out as a Republic cowboy hero. And considering the only thing about Billy the Kid in this movie is the title, it's not even worth watching if you're a Billy buff.

***

Mason City (Iowa) *Globe-Gazette* (September 27, 1946): "Republic's most thrilling western to date...."

Return of the Bad Men

(RKO, June 1948, 90 minutes) CREDITS: Director: Ray Enright. Producer: Nat Holt. Screenplay: Charles O'Neal, Jack Natteford, Luci Ward. CAST: Randolph Scott (Vance Cordell); Robert Ryan (Sundance Kid); Anne Jeffreys (Jeanie McBride "Cheyenne"); George "Gabby" Hayes (John Pettit); Jacqueline White (Madge Allen); Steve Brodie (Cole Younger); Richard Powers (Jim Younger); Robert Bray (John Younger); Lex Barker (Emmett Dalton); Walter Reed (Bob Dalton); Michael Harvey (Grat Dalton); Dean White (Billy the Kid); Robert Armstrong (Wild Bill Doolin); Tom Tyler (Wild Bill Yeager); Lew Harvey (Arkansas Kid); Gary Gray (Johnny Allen); Walter Baldwin (Muley Wilson); Minna Gombell (Emily); Warren Jackson (George Mason); Robert Clarke (Dave); Jason Robards (Judge Harper).

Synopsis

It's 1889, and the land rush is about to open Oklahoma Territory to settlers, which means bandits will soon have a new place to plunder. That's why Wild Bill Doolin has recruited some of the West's top names, including Billy the Kid, the Sundance Kid and the Younger brothers (Cole, Jim, and Bob).

Doolin's pistol-packing, hard-riding niece, Jeanie McBride, who goes by the nickname "Cheyenne," informs the new gang — since Wild Bill isn't around — about the plan to rob a bank in Braxton. Sundance isn't happy with letting her tag along. "Bustin' banks is men's work," he tells her.

"Belle Starr did all right," she fires back.

"You ain't Belle Starr," he says.

Billy the Kid is okay with letting Cheyenne ride with them. "If it's all right with Bill Doolin, it's all right with us. This is his show, Sundance."

Meanwhile, ex–Texas Ranger Vance Cordell is auctioning off his ranch as he prepares to give up law enforcement and the new territory for a peaceful life in California with his bride-to-be, the widow Madge Allen, and her son Johnny. Madge works at the bank owned by her father, John J. Pettit. Just so happens, that's the bank Doolin's gang plans on robbing.

The gang makes off with a lot of bank notes, but one bandit is killed, and Cheyenne catches a bullet in her arm. Barely clinging to the saddle, she rides past Cordell, who catches up with her and takes her to his almost-abandoned ranch. Cordell sends his Indian friend Gray Eagle to fetch a doctor, and as Cheyenne recovers, he preaches at her. After all, outlawing is no life for a lady. "Pretty soon, if you play your cards right," he tells her, "you'll be one of the richest outlaws buried on Boot Hill."

When the posse swings by the ranch, Cordell doesn't turn in Cheyenne. He figures the judge will go easier on her when she gives herself up, and before you know it, they are riding to Braxton.

Shortly after they leave, Sundance, Billy the Kid, and Cole Younger arrive at the ranch, searching for their wounded partner in crime. They find Gray Eagle, and when he refuses to talk, Sundance guns him down in cold blood. Then the outlaws head Cordell and Cheyenne off at the pass. Billy ropes Cordell and pulls him off the saddle. Cordell's knocked out, and Cheyenne takes off with the trio of outlaws. But by then, Billy has had enough. "I think I'll check out about here," he says.

"What's eatin' you?" Sundance asks.

"You," Billy snaps. "I don't like the way you operate."

"You're getting particular."

"I always was. That's why I'm pulling out now."

As he rides off, Sundance starts to draw his pistol to put a bullet in the Kid's back, but Cheyenne warns him not to try it: "He's got eyes in the back of his head."

So, thirty minutes into the feature, Billy the Kid rides away, never to be seen or heard from again.

Cordell's words haunt Cheyenne, and she quits Cole and Sundance, taking the money they stole back to Braxton, where she surrenders to the law. She even gives Cordell Sundance's pistol, prompting Cordell to say: "Someday, I'll be giving this back to the Sundance Kid."

The land rush begins, Braxton is abandoned, and Pettit and Cordell settle in Guthrie, which soon balloons to a city of more than fifteen thousand. After a while, the U.S. Army, which had been responsible for law and order, announces that it's leaving, and the colonel appoints Cordell U.S. marshal.

Cordell's about to decline the offer, citing his upcoming nuptials, until he learns that a stagecoach has been held up and that the Sundance Kid is likely behind it. That's enough for Cordell, who wants to avenge Gray Eagle's murder. Of course, that makes things hard on Madge. After all, her first husband was a peace officer killed in the line of duty. The couple agree to postpone the wedding until they're off to California.

The stagecoach idea was Sundance's plan, but Doolin urges the bandits to follow him and start something big. Things are always tense between Doolin and Sundance, but Doolin won't get rid of Sundance. "He's a good man," he says. "So long as you keep him in front of you."

In Guthrie, Cheyenne is paroled to Cordell and gets a job as a telegrapher. On the owlhoot trail, the Daltons brothers join Doolin's gang and the crime wave begins. Banks, stagecoaches, and trains are robbed, but Cordell finds the outlaws hard to track down. Then he learns that a dance hall girl is leaving Guthrie after depositing $800 in Pettit's bank and that a drunk claimed to have seen a ghost sweeping out a saloon in the ghost town of Braxton. Suspicious, Cordell decides that Doolin's men are holing up in Braxton, so he forms a posse and heads there.

He's right. Doolin and the outlaws are having a dance in the saloon, but Doolin's touchy. "I've just got a feelin' something's wrong," he says. Sundance snips and gripes, and is about to face down Doolin, when Cordell announces that the place is surrounded and that the bad men better give up. They don't, and lead starts flying. Most of the outlaws get away, but Doolin is captured.

Sundance promises to get Doolin out of jail, but most of the outlaws have had enough. The Daltons head back to Kansas. The Youngers abandon Sundance, too, leaving him with two outlaws, the Arkansas Kid and Wild Bill Yeager.

They go to Guthrie, hoping to persuade Cheyenne to tip them off when the law moves Doolin. When Cheyenne refuses to help, Sundance strangles her. Which really ticks off Cordell. He rides out alone to get the murdering scum.

When Arkansas's horse goes lame, Sundance kills the outlaw. Before long, Wild Bill Yeager decides to quit Sundance and ambush Cordell. That foolhardy plan leaves Yeager dead and Sundance alone. He holes up in Braxton, where he and Cordell fight. It's a rough-and-tumble free-for-all, but in the end, right prevails as Cordell, as he had promised, returns Sundance's revolver. Well, he gives him a bullet, anyway.

With Sundance dead, law and order has been restored. Cordell is free to move to California with his future bride Madge, but they have decided to stay in Guthrie.

The History

"Obviously," Robert Nott writes in *The Films of Randolph Scott*, "historical accuracy was not important to the scenarists of this film."[82]

During the heyday of Billy the Kid (1878–1881), Cole, Bob, and Jim Younger were serving a life sentence at the Minnesota prison in Stillwater for the murder of Joseph Heywood during the 1876 bank robbery in Northfield. State law did not allow the death penalty for anyone who pleaded guilty to murder. A tubercular Bob Younger died in prison thirteen years later. Cole and Jim were paroled in 1901, and Jim killed himself in 1902. Cole eventually returned to Missouri, wrote an autobiography, toured with fellow Confederate guerrilla and outlaw Frank James in a Wild West show and died in 1916.[83]

The Daltons (Bob, Emmett, and Gratton), on the other hand, would not start their outlaw gang until almost a decade after Billy the Kid's death. Their claim to fame happened in their hometown of Coffeyville, Kansas, on October 5, 1892, when they tried robbing two banks simultaneously. End result: Four dead townsmen, two dead Daltons, two other dead Dalton gang members. Emmett survived and went to prison for almost fifteen years. Pardoned in 1907, he went on to write two fanciful memoirs, *Beyond the Law* (1918) and *When the Daltons Rode* (1931), before he suffered a stroke and died on July 4, 1937.[84]

Bill Doolin lucked out in that he didn't take part in the Coffeyville raid with the Daltons, but he and his gang pulled off a number of jobs between 1892 and 1894 in Arkansas, Kansas, Missouri, and Oklahoma Territory. In fact, Doolin became such a priority, U.S. Marshal Ed Nix sent a who's-who trio of lawmen—Chris Madsen, Bill Tilghman, and Heck Thomas, nicknamed the "Three Guardsmen"—after Doolin. Doolin was captured—not in a saloon in some fictitious ghost town, but at a health spa in Eureka Springs, Arkansas, in 1895 by Tilghman. He was jailed at Guthrie and even signed autographs. He escaped six months later, but freedom didn't last long. Acting on a tip from an informer, Thomas tracked Doolin down to his farmhouse in Lawson, Oklahoma Territory, and shot him dead in August 1896.[85]

The Sundance Kid also came along after Billy the Kid. Born in 1867, Harry Longabaugh was jailed for horse theft in Sundance, Wyoming, from 1887 to 1889, and thus became "the Sundance Kid." As a member of Butch Cassidy's Hole-in-the-Wall Gang or Wild Bunch, he robbed banks, trains, and mines in the 1890s. Many believe that he and Cassidy were killed by Bolivian police in 1908 after a payroll robbery — not by an ex–Texas Ranger in Oklahoma in the 1890s.[86]

There was no Arkansas Kid riding with Doolin, but there was Arkansas Tom, an alias of Roy Daugherty. He was captured in a shootout with lawmen in Ingalls, Oklahoma Territory, in 1893, went to prison, was released, and died in a gunfight with lawmen in Joplin, Missouri, in 1924.[87]

Belle Starr did exist in history, but George Mason, Wild Bill Yeager and "Cheyenne" McBride were dreamed up by the screenwriters.

One A-list outlaw was linked to Billy the Kid. In his memoir *A Frontier Doctor*, Henry F. Hoyt recalled an 1879 meeting at Hot Springs, a resort six miles from Las Vegas, New Mexico, in which Billy was introduced to a "Mr. Howard from Tennessee." After dinner, the Kid told Hoyt, after swearing him to secrecy, that Mr. Howard was in reality Jesse James. Hoyt was skeptical (as are some historians today), but the Kid convinced him. The *Las Vegas Daily Optic* did note in December 1879, "Jesse James was a guest at the Las Vegas Hot Springs, July 26th to 29th. Of course it was not generally known."[88]

No matter. Jesse and Frank turned up in *Badman's Territory*, but not in *Return of the Bad Men*, and Billy wasn't in the former.

Government surveyors laid out the town site of Guthrie — and Kingfisher, Oklahoma City and Norman, as well — before the Unassigned Lands were open to white settlers, and Guthrie became a boomtown. But the land run didn't begin until April 22, 1889, when Billy the Kid was dead and the Youngers were in prison. Congress passed the Oklahoma Organic Act on May 2, 1890, making Guthrie the territorial capital. Congress also made No-Man's Land part of the new territory. Before that, it had been a haven for outlaws because what is now the Oklahoma panhandle did not fall under the jurisdiction of any state or territory. In addition to No-Man's Land, the strip was also called Public Land Strip, Cimarron Territory, and Robbers Roost. Cattlemen and homesteaders had settled in No-Man's Land during the 1880s, even forming vigilante committees to remedy the outlaw problem.[89]

There is, however, one moment of truth regarding Billy the Kid in this movie, and that's after he ropes Vance Cordell and says, "I'm getting to be a pretty good hand." Well, Billy did work (and rustle) cattle, so he probably knew how to use a lariat.

The Players

In 1946, RKO released a Randolph Scott Western, *Badman's Territory*. In that one, Scott played Texas lawman Mark Rowley, who finds himself in the lawless Indian Territory (present-day Oklahoma) town of Quinto. Scott's character met up with Sam Bass, Belle Starr, the Dalton brothers, and Frank and Jesse James. "A bona fide Western film fan might wonder how all those famous outlaws could have still been around," film historian Robert Nott writes, "since Scott had worked to bring about their downfall in previous films" like *When the Daltons Rode* (1940) and *Belle Starr* (1941). With a budget of $831,211.29, *Badman's Territory* came close to A-movie standards ($1 million), and, despite reaping mostly negative reviews, made a $500,000 profit. When Scott's next RKO Western, *Trail Street*, proved a box office success, the studio followed with a not-quite-sequel to *Badman's Territory*.[90]

It wasn't quite a sequel since Scott was playing a different lawman, and the Daltons had been gunned down near the end of *Badman's Territory*. Gabby Hayes also appeared in both movies, but his character was killed in the first one. Both movies borrowed from Universal's all-star horror movies of the 1940s: *House of Frankenstein* and *House of Dracula*. The more monsters, or, in this case, outlaws, the better.[91]

Production began in May 1947, primarily at RKO's Encino ranch (a fire reportedly broke out during filming and damaged the Western set). Other scenes were shot near Bakersfield, Saugus, and Fillmore. There were some minor setbacks—airplanes flying nearby cost one or two days of production, and a reflector fell on Anne Jeffreys's horse, requiring stitches in its mouth.[92]

RKO signed Broadway actor Dean White to play Billy the Kid, after White assured executives that he was an expert horseman. Which he was. English, however, not Western. His time on camera was delayed for a week while "some of Hollywood's old cow hands taught him how to ride a stock saddle." White was a Navy combat flyer who played Novak, the farmer who gets an unsecured loan from banker Fredric March, in *The Best Years of Our Lives* (1946). He made only a handful of films—his last known role was in *The Stratton Story* (1949)—before disappearing from movies.[93]

Screenwriters Charles O'Neal, Jack Natteford and Luci Ward (Mrs. Natteford) also kept the actors guessing. "A lot of the dialogue was written day by day," actress Jacqueline White said. "The general plot stayed the same, but you'd come in ready to work and they'd have something new for you that day."[94]

Directing was Ray Enright, who worked with Scott seven times between 1942 and 1948. Enright started out with Warner Bros. directing *Rin Tin Tin*s, comedies, musicals and war films; he didn't really do a Western until he began directing Scott at RKO, Paramount and Columbia. "He was a very jolly, outgoing kind of guy," Jacqueline White recalled. "But he wasn't the sort that sat and talked about the character with you." Instead, as David Quinlan pointed out: "The films he made with Scott are vigorous and action-filled, and have memorable fistfights that climb all over the screen." *Return of the Bad Men* was the last Enright-Scott pairing. Enright died in 1965.[95]

Greensboro, North Carolina, native Anne Jeffreys (1923–) and had been an opera singer, often appearing on Broadway, and model before RKO signed her. Robert Nott called her "one of the unsung heroines of 1940s cinema," though she never got many decent roles. *Return of the Bad Men* ended her run at RKO, and afterward she appeared mostly on TV, including a co-starring turn with husband Robert Sterling on *Topper* (1953–1955).[96]

Child actor Gary Gray took the role of Johnny. He would also appear in the Western *Rachel and the Stranger* (1948) and was signed by MGM after playing the son of Nancy Davis and James Whitmore in *The Next Voice You Hear...* (1950). His claim to fame might be in that he appeared in MGM's final Lassie movie, *The Painted Hills* (1951). Gray died of cancer in 2006 at age sixty-nine.[97]

Scott had been involved in Westerns since reportedly helping Gary Cooper as dialogue coach and appearing as an extra in *The Virginian* (1929), but his best films would come after *Return of the Bad Men*. In the late 1950s, he teamed with director Budd Boetticher in a series of solid, memorable Westerns such as *Seven Men from Now* (1956), *The Tall T* (1957) and *Comanche Station* (1960). "Randy was a lovely man to work with — a gentleman," White recalled. "When you worked one on one with him, he was a very good actor." Scott retired from acting after appearing in Sam Peckinpah's *Ride the High Country*, and died in 1987 at age eighty-nine.[98]

If *Return of the Bad Men* did anything to advance anyone's career, it was Robert Ryan's. The Chicago-born, Dartmouth-educated actor had tried several jobs — seaman, sandhog, sewer builder, bodyguard, paving supervisor — before turning to acting at age twenty-eight. He made a few movies before World War II, but after the war came into his own as an actor. He was coming off a mesmerizing performance as the anti–Semite killer in *Crossfire* (1947) for which he was nominated for an Academy Award as Best Supporting Actor. He had a turn as a good guy with Scott in *Trail Street* (1947), but *Return of the Bad Men* gave Ryan another chance to do what he did so well: playing the pure embodiment of evil.[99]

Critics singled out his performance. "Robert Ryan has managed to come through unscathed with a cool, expert performance as a prairie sadist," the *New York Times* noted. The *New York Herald-Tribune* said: "Robert Ryan, as the murderous Sundance Kid, comes off best in the film, duplicating the viciousness of his portrayal in Crossfire."[100] *Time* magazine remarked: "The only heavy who throws his weight around to any effect is the Sundance Kid (Robert Ryan, a thoroughly hissable villain)."[101]

Ryan certainly made an impression on Jeffreys. "He was a very intense actor and murdered my character in both *Trail Street* and *Return of the Bad Men*. He choked me to death in one and shot me in the back in the other," recalled Jeffreys, whose memory was slightly off seeing that Steve Brodie killed her in *Trail Street*. "He seemed to enjoy it, so I was a little leery of him [*laughs*]. However, he was really a very nice, warm person and a terrific actor."[102]

While RKO promoted *Return of the Bad Men* as a "big-budget epic," it didn't live up to the hype. It did, however, help secure Ryan a place in Westerns. He would make nineteen over his career, ranging from bad-guy roles in this and *The Naked Spur* (1953) to good-guy turns in *Day of the Outlaw* (1959) and *The Professionals* (1966), to an honorable good-bad guy in *The Wild Bunch* (1969). He died at age sixty-three in 1973.[103]

Analysis

Billy the Kid makes what amounts to pretty much a cameo in *Return of the Bad Men*, so it's just a minor film for Billy aficionados. As a Western, it is better than *Badman's Territory*, but it's certainly not great. It's worth watching only to see Ryan's mesmerizing performance.

***

Christian Science Monitor (August 20, 1948): "[It's] is a typical western. Everything runs according to formula right up to the final man-to-man duel between the marshal and the chief desperado."

Son of Billy the Kid

(Screen Guild, April 1949, 65 minutes) CREDITS: Director: Ray Taylor. Producer: Ron Ormond. Screenplay: Ron Ormond, Ira Webb. Additional Dialogue: Guy Tedesco. CAST: Lash LaRue (Jack Garrett); Fuzzy St.

John (Fuzzy); June Carr (Betty Raines); Johnny James (Colt Thorn); Marion Colby (Norma Berry); Terry Frost (Cy Shaeffer); George Baxter (Jim Thorn/Billy the Kid); Clark Stevens (Yantis Henchman); Stan Jolley (Matt Fergus); Eileen Dixon (Dance Hall girl); Bob Duncan (Clem Yantis); Cliff Taylor (Jake); William Perrot (Billy the Kid); Rosa Turich (Rosa Gonzales); Jerry Riggio (Sanchos); Felipe Turich (Jose Gonzales); Bud Osborne (Guard).

Synopsis

Around midnight on July 14, 1881, Billy the Kid visits the home of his friends Jose and Rosa Gonzales and their son Sanchos. Rosa promises to cook him a meal, and Billy volunteers to cut the ham himself. Of course, walking out with his gun belt might arouse suspicion, so Billy unbuckles his rig—which Sanchos puts on—and goes to cut some ham. While Billy is performing this task, he hears something. "*¿Quién es?*" he asks, and is gunned down by several shots.

Fast-forward to 1896 in a town called Baldwin City. Bandits try to hold up a stagecoach carrying banker Jim Thorn, but Jack Garrett hears the commotion and rides to the rescue. After the guard is shot off the stage, Garrett leaps on board, tells the driver to keep driving, and shoots down two of the badmen. The others have had enough, and let the stage head into Baldwin City. Garrett—no relation to Pat Garrett, slayer of Billy the Kid—tells Thorn that he's a marshal whose job is to protect the railroad's interests as it expands into Baldwin City.

The man behind the outlaw gang, land speculator Cy Shaeffer, has sent for Clem Yantis, who once was part of Billy the Kid's gang. Word of Yantis's arrival has already reached Fuzzy, the stagecoach driver, justice of the peace, sheriff and holder of just about every other city job. Shaeffer's men try to rob the bank, but "someone with a stick of dynamite" beats them to it.

Garrett is always playing hunches. He lets word slip out that the railroad plans to bring in its next payroll by prairie schooner, follows a suspicious hombre to a cabin, unearths a clue, and outwits the bad guys.

Suddenly, the plot starts getting similar to Columbia's Charles Starrett programmer *West of Tombstone* (1942). Yantis recognizes bank prez Thorn as none other than Billy the Kid. He tells Thorn that his (Thorn's) son Cole is part of the gang and "sort of followin' in his father's footsteps." Which makes it easier for Yantis to blackmail the bank president into bringing him the railroad money.

Garrett and Fuzzy join the prairie schooner, and when Thorn's niece, Norma, pulls a gun on Thorn, admitting that she's part of the outlaw gang, Cole arrives and gets the drop on her. Thorn takes off to help Garrett and Fuzzy.

The outlaws rob the prairie schooner, but that's a setup. The wagon is filled with posse members who start shooting at the bad men upon Garrett's command: "All right, boys, let 'em have it." Outlaws take to the rocks. Thorn rides up—"Never seen a bank president ride like that," Fuzzy comments—and joins the fracas on the side of the good guys. He shoots with a rifle, until Garrett offers him a six-shooter. When Thorn fires right-handed, Garrett suggests, "Why don't you try your left hand?"

That works. Thorn dispatches a bad guy.

"You know," Garrett says, "there's only one man I've ever heard tell who could shoot like that with his left hand. His name was Billy. Billy the Kid. 'Course, he's been dead for almost twenty years."

About then, Cole kills Yantis, and Garrett goes after Shaeffer. They fight, and Shaeffer falls to his death.

Back in Baldwin City, all those loose ends are tied up. Cole was just pretending to be part of the outlaw gang (uh ... so why didn't he let the authorities know Shaeffer was behind it all before now?) and even robbed the bank first to keep the outlaws from getting away with the dough.

And, yes, Thorn indeed is Billy the Kid. Seems like a sheriff from Santa Fe was tipped off about the Kid's visit to the Gonzales family and set a trap. Pat Garrett, Billy's old friend, learned of it and offered his help. "After Garrett fired three times," Billy/Thorn says, "I fell to the floor as if I had been killed." He laid there until it was safe, but the plan didn't work out the way everyone had expected.

When Garrett fired three times, one of the bullets went through the wall and killed Sanchos. (Apparently Garrett never thought about firing blanks.) Billy changed clothes with Sanchos, and the next morning Garrett identified Sanchos's body as Billy's.

That's why Thorn has been sending the Gonzales family money all those years. "It was the least I could do," Thorn admits, and says that he's ready to give himself up.

Garrett tells Thorn he doesn't think the governor will be too hard on Billy the Kid after his record as an honest banker.

The History

The plot of *Son of Billy the Kid,* the *Denton* (Texas) *Record-Chronicle* noted, "is predicated on the theory that the notorious Billy the Kid was not killed in 1881, as generally believed, but lived on under the name of Jim Thorn to become a banker...."[104]

Let's see:

Many thought John Miller was really Billy the Kid, but Miller, who died in 1937, lived in Prescott, Arizona. In 1950, Ollie L. "Brushy Bill" Roberts claimed to have been Billy the Kid, but he lived in Hico, Texas.[105]

There was no Gonzales family, but Billy visited friends on the night he was killed. "He may have ended up with Bob Campbell, or Celsa Gutiérrez, or Deluvina Maxwell, or Jesús Silva and Francisco Lobato, among others," biographer Robert M. Utley says. Later historians have said he left the home of Celsa and Saval Gutiérrez to go cut meat, not from a ham but a butchered yearling hanging from a rafter on Pete Maxwell's front porch. The Gutiérrezes — in-laws of Pat Garrett — did have a son, not Sanchos, but seventeen-year-old Candido.[106]

Billy did ask, "¿Quién es?"— several times, in fact — before Pat Garrett shot him dead in Pete Maxwell's bedroom. Garrett fired only twice. One bullet struck the Kid; the other ricocheted and lodged in the headboard of Pete's bed. The only persons in danger of being killed by the ricocheting second bullet were Maxwell and Garrett. Billy the Kid was already dead.[107]

Of course, there was no Clem Yantis in Billy the Kid's "gang," and when one character comments that a planned bank job "might not be as big" as some bank robberies pulled off with Billy the Kid ... well ... Billy the Kid never robbed any bank.

Opposite: Pressbook for the Lash LaRue programmer *Son of Billy the Kid* (1949).

The Players

Winning a jitterbug contest inspired Venice, California, high school student Marion Colby to seek out Hollywood, although she got her start in New York on Broadway and radio before returning west to be with her family. *Son of Billy the Kid* was her first credited film role. June Carr, who would be better known as a Hollywood producer, was a Broadway stage comedienne who also got her first feature role in this programmer. The other big star was a prop: A covered wagon used in the film had also been a prop in *The Big Trail* (1930) "and every Western epic since," including *Cimarron* (1931). That is if you believe the movie's pressbook.[108]

But this wasn't about actresses or covered wagons. It was a Lash LaRue film!

As a hero of Western programmers, Lash LaRue looked and sounded more like Humphrey Bogart than Gene Autry or Roy Rogers. Most sources cite his birthplace anywhere from Michigan to Chicago to Gretna, Louisiana, where he grew up. And his age? "Age is a psychological trap," he said in 1987. "If I started thinking about how old I was, I wouldn't be able to get up in the morning." He was born in 1921, or maybe 1917, and his real name was Alfred Larue. In any case, by high school, he was in Los Angeles, graduating from St. John's Military Academy and attending the College of the Pacific, where he took some drama courses. He worked in a variety of jobs before George Brent arranged a screen test at Warner Bros. Although Warner Bros. didn't hire him, Universal did, casting him in small roles in films such as *Christmas Holiday* (1944) and *Lady on a Train* (1945) and the serial *The Master Key* (1945).[109]

His career took a major turn in 1945 when LaRue, who had grown up idolizing Western stars William S. Hart, Tom Mix, Hoot Gibson, and Ken Maynard, played the Cheyenne Kid in *Song of Old Wyoming*, an Eddie Dean programmer for Producers Releasing Corporation. LaRue got the part by saying he could use a bullwhip, then went home and "beat myself to death trying to get that sucker out in front of me. I had welts on my back that never did go away!" LaRue's was killed off in the film, but audiences loved the cowboy dressed in black who used a whip.[110] "[S]omehow the notion of a tough Lower East Side Kid punk with a Bronx accent as a semi-villianous hero caught on with postwar youth," Jon Tuska writes.[111]

Knowing a good thing when they saw it, PRC officials brought LaRue back in *The Caravan Trail* (1946) and *Wild West* (1946). Eddie Dean was the star of both programmers, but Buster Crabbe's Billy the Kid series was coming to an end, so PRC decided to create a new character. Thus, Lash LaRue was born, beginning with *Law of the Lash* (1947).[112]

PRC, however, was at the end of its run, which began in 1939. Eagle Lion Corporation, owned by British filmmaker J. Arthur Rank, absorbed PRC in 1947 because he sought to form an international distribution company. United Artists would later absorb Eagle Lion.[113]

But Lash LaRue wasn't done. In 1948, Ron Ormond started Western Adventure Productions to film more LaRue Westerns, which would be released by Screen Guild. "This first series for Western Adventure Productions was on a par with the PRC series — no better, no worse," Chuck Thorton and David Rothel write in *Lash LaRue: King of the Bullwhip*. "It was very apparent to the discerning eye that no money was being wasted on the series. The sets were skimpy, as were the number of people in the casts."[114]

Shooting for Western Adventure Productions generally took five days. "We didn't waste any time or money!" LaRue recalled.[115] LaRue liked director Ray Taylor and his longtime comic sidekick, Fuzzy St. John. Taylor "never got mad. He was *so* calm. I remember in one picture I had a scene with four names and two different towns. I kept messing it up; I must have done it thirteen different times! We couldn't afford to do that. I got mad at him for not getting mad at me!"[116]

On Fuzzy: "He was a beautiful person and a lot of fun to work with. His important dialogue was generally shot in the morning because during lunch somebody would slip him a drink and he'd mumble."[117]

The last LaRue programmer, *The Frontier Phantom*, was released in 1952. Television was killing off programmers, and the incredibly cheap productions of these films certainly didn't help. LaRue continued to act occasionally — including a recurring role as Sheriff Johnny Behan on TV's *The Life and Legend of Wyatt Earp* (1959–1960) — and eventually wrote scripts for pornography films before he "got religion." His fame got a bit of a revival when he wound up in Tucson and met Johnny Cash and Waylon Jennings, who gave him a role in their 1986 TV movie *Stagecoach* and mentioned him in the liner notes of their 1986 duet album *Heroes*. LaRue died in 1996 in Burbank, California.[118]

Analysis

Lash LaRue had a face and voice that brings to mind Humphrey Bogart — and Bogie never was much in period Westerns. The plot borrows heavily, and sometimes verbatim, from *West of Tombstone* (1942), the budget's cheap, the action lethargic and the story pretty much ridiculous.

Even by programmer standards, there isn't much to like about this one.

***

Variety (December 31, 1948): "Except for the variation on the Billy the Kid theme, pic is typical...."

Chapter Seven

The 1950s: The Kid Moves Forward

Billy found new life, and new direction, as Westerns began to dominate movie theaters during the 1950s. As the programmers slowly faded, the Kid moved into higher budgeted B Westerns and even the occasional A.

The 1950s would also see the widest range of actors playing Billy, from cut-rate actors like Don Barry and Allan "Rocky" Lane, to mid-listers such as Scott Brady, to World War II hero Audie Murphy (in his first Western role) and rising superstar Paul Newman.

The Kid from Texas

(Universal, February 1950, 78 minutes) CREDITS: Director: Kurt Newmann. Producer: Paul Short. Screenplay: Robert Hardy Andrews, Karl Kamb. CAST: Audie Murphy (Billy the Kid); Gale Storm (Irene Kain); Albert Dekker (Alexander Kain); Shepperd Strudwick (Jameson); Will Geer (O'Fallon); William Talman (Minninger); Martin Garralaga (Morales); Robert H. Barrat (General Lew Wallace); Walter Sande (Crowe); Frank Wilcox (Pat Garrett); Dennis Hoey (Major Harper); Ray Teal (Sheriff Rand); Don Haggerty (Morgan); Paul Ford (Sheriff Copeland); John Phillips (Sid Curtis); Harold Goodwin (Matt Curtis); Zon Murray (Lucas); Tom Trout (Denby); Rosa Turich (Maria); Dorita Pallais (Lupita); Pilar Del Rey (Marguarita).

Synopsis

On July 11, 1879, a deputized gunman named Minninger and two other deputies enter the office of lawyer-merchant Alexander Kain and his ranching partner, an Englishman named Jameson, attempting to arrest the two for murder. Kain argues that the men were caught stealing cattle, and that he won't be arrested by gunmen working for his competitors, Major Harper and his flunky, Sheriff Rand. Besides, Kain and Jameson have their own sheriff, and the killers of those rustlers were acting under the cover of law.

Minninger notices a young kid standing in the office, a boy named William H. Bonney. When Minninger tries to take away the Kid's guns, Billy opens fire, shooting the guns out of the hands of two of the deputies and killing a third.

Jameson offers the Kid a job at his ranch, and Billy tells him a little about his past. He has been on the run for seven or eight years, since killing a man who insulted his mother in Silver City, Colorado. Jameson doesn't care about the boy's past, but wants him to focus on his future — a future without guns. He asks the Kid to put away his two Colts in a cabinet. "Any time you think you need them," Jameson tells the Kid, "they'll be right there."

(From left) Audie Murphy, Gale Storm, Shepperd Strudwick and Albert Dekker in *The Kid from Texas* (1950), Murphy's first Western.

Kain brings his young wife Irene to visit the ranch, with news that he is to meet — with Major Harper — the new territorial governor, General Lew Wallace, who is focusing on bringing law and order to Lincoln County. When Irene plays the piano, Billy is captivated by her beauty and charm. Her much-older, jealous husband is miffed.

While Kain and Harper are getting lectured by General Wallace about keeping the peace, a mob of drunken posse men ride to Jameson's ranch to exact revenge on the English lord and Billy the Kid. Billy starts to buckle on his guns, but Jameson talks him out of it, and walks outside to greet the posse, who shoot him down.

At Jameson's funeral, Billy stands over the grave and tells Kain: "He was the only man who ever treated me like I was good enough to shake hands with.... I'll get every man that had a hand in this killing, if it's the last thing I do."

Kain takes over Jameson's ranch, and has his sheriff deputize Jameson's foreman Morgan, Billy and most of Jameson's riders. Kain sends them after the killers of Jameson but warns them: "This is not a raiding party."

The posse captures some of the killers at a line shack. Morgan, O'Fallon, and Billy take three of the killers, including Minninger, to Lincoln. Along the way, Minninger grabs Morgan's pistol and kills him, and the three gunmen make a break for freedom. Billy kills two with rifle shots, but Minninger gets away.

Since Billy was acting as a deputized lawman, Sheriff Rand can't arrest him, and Kain reluctantly agrees to take Billy into his custody. Everything's okay until rustlers steal some of Kain's cattle. He sends Billy out on another posse, saying, "Major Harper wants war, he'll get war."

All of this really puts a strain on the Kains' marriage, and when more men are killed by Billy, General Wallace takes action. He removes sheriffs Rand and Copeland and appoints Pat Garrett sheriff of Lincoln County. Kain washes his hands of Billy the Kid, even agrees to put up a reward, although Wallace is reluctant to make the boy a fugitive (what about that murder warrant for killing the fella who insulted his ma?).

In the spring of 1880, General Wallace meets with Billy the Kid. Wallace has granted amnesty to the other participants in the Lincoln County War, and offers Billy a pardon. But the Kid won't bite. He's still carrying on his personal war, so Wallace is forced to put a price on Billy's head: $10,000. Dead or alive.

Minninger's posse captures Billy in a line shack, and the Kid is tried, convicted, and sentenced to hang. While awaiting execution, Billy sees Minninger wearing his guns. A friendly deputy, Barnes, agrees to play poker with the Kid, but the Kid grabs Barnes's gun and forces the deputy to remove the chains on his hands and feet. When Barnes tries to fight, Billy kills him, then waits for Minninger to come back. He blows Minninger away with a shotgun blast to the face (rather bloody by 1950 standards. After getting his guns back, Billy rides off.

His friends O'Fallon and Morales join him, and before long, Billy is leading a gang of outlaws. Eventually, he returns to Kain's store, but the posse arrives. Billy forces Kain into his house.

The house is surrounded. Billy agrees to send Mrs. Kain and her "help" out, but she refuses. "My place is here with my husband," she says.

"Suit yourself."

That riles Mrs. Kain. "You're nothing but a savage. Everything Mr. Kain said you were."

Pat Garrett tries to parley with the Kid, and get the women out of the building, but now it's Mr. Kain who won't agree to those terms, saying, "Mrs. Kain doesn't leave unless I do."

The Kid snaps back: "You had me do your killing. When I got through with it, you put a price on my head."

Kain admits that he contributed to the reward, which disgusts Irene Kain. She leaves with her Mexican helpers, and the posse set fire to the house. Billy hands Kain his rifle, saying Kain will lead them out of the inferno. Kain tries to kill Billy, only to be shot dead by the mortally wounded O'Fallon. Billy and Morales make a break for it, but only Billy gets away.

It's July 14, 1881, and Mrs. Kain is leaving. Pat Garrett is wondering why the Kid hasn't fled, why that boy's still running around the territory, and then he plays a hunch: Billy's in love with Mrs. Kain, so Garrett follows her to Pete Maxwell's place.

Sure enough. Billy shows up, listening outside the window as Mrs. Kain plays the piano — the same song Billy had heard her play back at the ranch. Garrett calls out for the Kid to surrender, but Billy draws and is shot dead.

The History

As the movie begins, the narrator tells us, "Many stories have been told of him that are more fiction that fact. In some instances, we've changed names and slightly altered chronology. But the facts were as you see them."

Well, here's a fact. Audie Murphy was a kid from Texas, but Billy the Kid wasn't.

The filmmakers certainly altered the chronology, and not just slightly. The movie opens on July 11, 1879. By that time, John Tunstall, Alexander McSween, and Sheriff William Brady were long dead, and Lew Wallace had already been appointed territorial governor.

For some reason, many names were changed. Lawrence G. Murphy (or maybe it was James Dolan) became Major Harper. Brady was turned into Sheriff Rand. Tunstall was named Jameson, and McSween became Kain. Charles Bowdre/Tom Folliard was a composite called O'Fallon, and deputy Olinger was turned into Minninger. About the only characters whose names weren't changed were Billy the Kid and Lew Wallace.

In an early scene, Billy carves his name on a building's column in Lincoln. "Go to the town of Lincoln today," the narrator tells us, "and you can still see where Billy the Kid carved his name nearly three-quarters of a century ago."

Guess again.

Billy tells Jameson that his mother is alive in Santa Fe. That his father died in Kansas. That his mother remarried a drunk. That he killed a man in Silver City, Colorado.

Catherine Antrim, Billy's mom, died on September 16, 1874, at age forty-five. We don't know anything about Billy's father, but it's doubtful he died in Kansas, unless his mother was a bigamist. Billy's stepfather, William Antrim, met Catherine in 1865 in Indianapolis and came with her and her two sons to Wichita in 1870. They were married in Santa Fe on March 1, 1873. William Antrim said his wife's former husband had died in New York, which follows the legend that Billy the Kid was born in New York. Ash Upson/Pat Garrett noted in *The Authentic Life of Billy the Kid* that Billy's dad had died when Billy was young, and that the family moved to Coffeyville, Kansas, in 1862. The problem there, of course, is that Coffeyville wasn't founded until 1869, and not incorporated until three or four years later.[1]

Was Antrim a drunk? He had worked as a part-time bartender in Wichita, worked as a carpenter, did odd jobs around Silver City, gambled, and pretty much abandoned his stepsons. Drunk? Perhaps. Bad father? Definitely. Silver City's Henry Whitehill once said that had Antrim "taken [Billy] in then [before the Kid fled to Arizona] Billy would have been all right. But he didn't and the kid turned bad."[2]

And that story about Billy's killing a man in Silver City, Colorado, for insulting his mother? It's a story often told since *The Authentic Life of Billy the Kid*, but it never happened in Silver City, *Colorado*. For one reason, Billy the Kid lived in Silver City, *New Mexico*, but never killed anyone there. Nor is there any documentation that he killed four Chiricahua Apaches.

In this version, Jameson/Tunstall is killed at his ranch. In reality, Tunstall was killed on the trail away from his ranch — and while that was happening, Murphy/Dolan and Brady were not meeting with Lew Wallace. Wallace wasn't governor at the time of Tunstall's murder, and when he became governor, Sheriff Brady was already dead.

On the positive side, while Billy didn't attend Tunstall's funeral, the scene where he tells McSween/Kain "I'll get every man that had a hand in this killing, if it's the last thing I do," has some history behind it. Before the Kid was arrested, historian Mark Lee Gardner writes, Tunstall's body was laid out on a table in Alexander McSween's home. "I'll get some of them before I die," Billy reportedly said.[3]

After Tunstall's death, foreman Dick Brewer (called Morgan, another one of those name changes) was appointed special constable and led the posse of Regulators after Tunstall's killers. The posse captured William "Buck" Morton and Frank Baker, both of whom were conveniently shot while attempting escape, but Bob Olinger (here Minninger) wasn't there. And Dick Brewer wasn't killed by Olinger, but by Buckshot Roberts at Blazer's Mill.[4]

The meeting between Billy the Kid and General Wallace "in the spring of 1880," the narrator says, was "one of the strangest events in history." Wallace, we are told, rode sixty miles to keep a rendezvous with Billy the Kid. Actually, Lincoln is more like two hundred miles from Santa Fe, and Wallace's reward for the capture of the Kid was $500, not $10,000.[5]

The script gets the dates of Billy the Kid's murder trial and conviction slightly off. Convicted for the murder of William Brady, he was sentenced to hang on May 13, 1881. He escaped, gunning down deputies Bell (Barnes) and Olinger (Minninger), maybe not quite the way it's depicted this time, although Olinger was killed with a shotgun blast.

After that, we get some more of those changes in chronology. Billy arrives in Lincoln, asking for .45 and .30–30 rounds (the .30–30 wouldn't come into use until 1894)[6], seeking help from McSween/Kain. This is 1881. McSween died in 1878.

McSween's wife was Susan. Billy was rumored to have many girls, but not Susan McSween. Colonel Nathan Dudley produced affidavits challenging Susan McSween's character, calling her a "lewd woman" who had had numerous affairs. There was no love lost between Dudley and McSween, who despised one another, and Dudley was seeking to save his reputation and career during a Board of Inquiry. One person McSween was rumored to have been involved with was cattle baron John Chisum.[7]

The Kid was killed at Pete Maxwell's house, but not while listening to Sue McSween (or anyone else) play the piano, and he didn't kill twenty-one men, that we know of.

Well, as our narrator puts it: "Many stories have been told of him that are more fiction that fact." He could have added:

"This is one of them."

The Players

Born in Kingston, Texas, in 1924, Audie Leon Murphy grew up poor. While his mother worked in a cotton patch, he hunted game for the supper table. His father abandoned the family when Audie was twelve. When Audie was sixteen, his mother died. His three younger siblings were placed in an orphanage. Then the Japanese bombed Pearl Harbor, and the United States went to war.[8]

At first, Murphy could not enlist because he was underage. As soon as he turned eighteen, he tried again. "I was looking for trouble," he wrote. Turned down for service by the Navy, Marines and Army paratroopers because of his height (about 5'7") Murphy hit up the Army infantry, which had no such reservations. He saw action during World War II in Italy, France, and Austria, rising in rank from private to first lieutenant, and becoming the most decorated American soldier in history. In one engagement, while manning a machine gun on a burning tank destroyer, he shot down a hundred German soldiers. All told, he killed roughly 240 German soldiers in combat. Discharged in 1945, he came home, hoping "to look at life through uncynical eyes, to have faith, to know love." He was a *Life* magazine cover story on July 16 and drew the attention of actor James Cagney, who had formed his own independent film company in 1943.[9]

Cagney and Murphy's longtime friend David "Spec" McClure managed to get the kid from Texas in a few bit roles, and in 1948, producer Paul Short gave Murphy the starring role as Billy the Kid. J. Edgar Hoover wanted to narrate the film, but Parley Baer would get that assignment. Short also sought to cast Lloyd Nolan, Herbert Marshall, Charles Bickford, and Mona Freeman as co-stars. Shelly Winters was also considered for a role.[10]

Not under contract, Murphy was hired as "outside talent" and paid $10,000. Gale Storm also earned $10,000.[11]

Murphy's first featured role, however, would be an Allied Artists cheapie, *Bad Boy* (1949), which cast the war hero as a juvenile delinquent.

That movie became a surprise hit, and with his autobiography, *To Hell and Back* going through five printings and reaching best-seller status in 1949, Murphy was suddenly a hot name.[12]

The Kid from Texas was shot at the Jack Garner Ranch near Idyllwild, California, as well as at Pine Meadows, Hurkee Creek, the Morris Ranch, and on the Universal back lot. It was filmed quickly between late May and late June 1949.[13]

Murphy (or at least his press agents) recalled that he had long been interested in Billy the Kid; he wrote in a *Saturday Evening Post* article:

> As a youngster, I read everything about Billy I could get my hands on. I always figured him as a boy who might have gone straight under different circumstances. So I was glad when producer Paul Short agreed I could play him as a quiet guy, a real human being who made mistakes at times, instead of as a swaggering superman.[14]

On the first day of shooting, Murphy's stunt double reportedly broke his collarbone, so Murphy filled in. It became standard for Murphy, who would use only two stand-ins for the rest of his career. There were other accidents and injuries, and on June 21 a brush fire burned four buildings on Universal's back lot and threatened nearby residences. Helping studio firefighters battle the flames were cast members, including Murphy and Albert Dekker.[15]

Gale Storm remembered Murphy as "a very professional person and always knew his lines.... He was very serious and didn't really let his hair down."[16]

"What's odd about *The Kid from Texas* is how it mirrors Murphy's life," Robert Nott writes. "He plays an orphaned kid with a chip on his shoulder who turns out to have an amazing capacity for violence and a great talent for shooting people."[17]

Shot in color at a budget of under $700,000, the movie became a hit. It opened at the Majestic Theatre in Dallas, Texas (where *Bad Boy* had premiered on February 16, 1949, setting an attendance record). *The Kid from Texas* broke those records.[18]

Murphy began making personal appearances in Texas. At one, he warned would-be hecklers: "If you try to louse me up I'll come down and punch you right in the nose." Which got this response from Universal-International's contract player Scott Brady: "I'd hate to say that in Brooklyn."[19]

The Kid from Texas went on to break box office records for the studio. While *Variety*'s reviewer relegated the film to the "minor league," it did praise Murphy for handling "the Kid assignment in commendable fashion." The *Hartford Courant* said, "In the title role and doing a highly realistic job of it is Audie Murphy...."[20]

Hollywood columnist Erskine Johnson predicted that "Audie Murphy is a good bet to become UI's western star...."[21]

Universal needed no such encouragement, signing Murphy to a seven-year contract at $2,500 per week, or $12,000 per picture. His next movie was a Western with his wife Wanda

Hendrix, *Sierra* (1950), in which the studio sought to capitalize on the couple's marriage. That didn't quite work out. The couple announced their separation during filming and divorced in 1951.[22]

Afterward, Murphy played another outlaw, a young Jesse James, in the Civil War Western *Kansas Raiders* (1950). Yet another bad guy? "It wouldn't be at all surprising to see Audie Murphy as Joaquin Murietta one of these days since Hollywood apparently has a predilection for casting the young actor in desperado roles," the *Christian Science Monitor* reported.[23] At least in *Kansas Raiders*, Murphy finally got to kiss the girl: "With a luscious smooch upon the lips of lovely Marguerite Chapman, one that lasted 34 seconds and skirted every rule of the Johnston office, Audie Murphy won the final round in his long battle for the western kiss."[24]

Murphy had been battling Universal to put a little sex in his Westerns. He wasn't alone. Shelley Winters complained that she never got to kiss Joel McCrea in *Frenchie* (1950) or James Stewart in *Winchester '73* (1950). Said Murphy: "I figured that a horse opera hero who doesn't kiss the gal is just plain sucker. And they were sure making a sucker out of me. So I did something about it."[25]

Murphy became a bona fide Western star, although Universal often kept him playing outlaws and gunmen: Bill Doolin in *The Cimarron Kid* (1951), the black-clad young gunman in *The Duel at Silver Creek* (1952), the hired killer in the excellent paranoia-filled *No Name on the Bullet* (1959). He would slip out of character on occasion, in John Huston's *The Red Badge of Courage* (1951) and Joseph L. Mankiewicz's *The Quiet American* (1958), and would turn in a memorable performance in Huston's underrated A-list Western *The Unforgiven* (1960). For the most part, however, Murphy stuck to second-tier Westerns for the rest of his career. Later in the 1950s, he usually wasn't playing the baby-faced bad guy—*Night Passage* (1957) being one exception—but the baby-faced good guy. His last starring role came in *40 Guns to Apache Pass* (1967).

In 1970, Don Siegel, who had directed Murphy in *The Duel at Silver Creek,* gave Murphy the screenplay of a crime drama he was set to shoot, *Dirty Harry*. Siegel wanted Murphy to play the psychotic sniper. Murphy read the script, but said he couldn't do that. What would it do to his good-guy image?

On May 28, 1971—his mother's birthday—Murphy was on a business trip when his airplane crashed during a rainstorm in the Virginia mountains.[26] Audie Leon Murphy, Medal of Honor winner and cinematic cowboy hero, was dead, just one month shy of his forty-seventh birthday.

Analysis

At this stage in his career, Audie Murphy wasn't comfortable in front of the camera, but his wooden acting sometimes works as Billy the Kid. It's not a great performance by any means, and it wouldn't be until the late 1950s that Murphy found something of a stride as an actor. That stride—which wasn't long—would be a limp by the early 1960s.

Still, considering Murphy's background, he seems a closer fit to the historical Billy the Kid than other actors who had played and would play him. Murphy was about twenty-five years old during shooting—Robert Taylor was a much older-looking twenty-nine when he filmed *Billy the Kid* (1941)—and Murphy certainly had experience killing. He just wasn't much of an actor.

The Kid from Texas is a strange — not good — movie, with historical characters names often changed, and Alexander McSween turned from religious pacifist good guy, as he was typically portrayed, into a vindictive, double-dealing bad guy (named Kain).

How does it compare to history? Perhaps the *Christian Science Monitor* put it best at the time of this movie's release: "The saga of Billy the Kid turns up every few years in a new film version, each of which takes blithe liberties with the facts to produce fresh fictions."[27]

The Kid from Texas would fade from memory, only to find a literary rescue. Future Pulitzer Prize and Academy Award winner Larry McMurtry would make Murphy's first Western the last movie shown in the old theater in his 1966 semi-autobiographical novel *The Last Picture Show*.

"The boys planned to" like the movie, McMurtry writes, "but somehow the occasion just didn't work out. Audie Murphy was a scrapper as usual, but it didn't help. It would have taken *Winchester '73* or *Red River* or some big movie like that to have crowded out the memories the boys kept having."[28]

When Peter Bogdanovich turned the novel into a 1971 movie, however, he changed the last picture show to Howard Hawks's 1948 classic *Red River*.

***

New York Times (June 2, 1950): "[D]espite an occasional bit of gunplay and the facts as supplied by the commentary, *The Kid from Texas* doesn't give special stature to a noted saga."

I Shot Billy the Kid

(Lippert, August 1950, 57 minutes) CREDITS: Director-Producer: William Berke. Screenplay: Orville Hampton. CAST: Don Barry (Billy the Kid); Robert Lowery (Pat Garrett); Wally Vernon (Vicenti); Tom Neal (Charlie Bowdre); Wendy Lee (Francesca): Claude Stroud (General Lew Wallace); John Merton (Ollinger); Henry Marco (Juan); Bill Kennedy (Poe); Archie Twitchell (Grant); Jack Perrin (Mann); Richard Farmer (McSween); Felice Richmond (Mrs. McSween); Jack Geddes (Sheriff); Tom Monroe (Maxwell).

Synopsis

Old Pat Garrett walks to Billy the Kid's grave in Fort Sumner, where he tells the viewers that he was supposed to have been the Kid's twenty-second victim. And in a flashback, we learn what happened.

In the last major fight of the Lincoln County War, Billy and several men are holed up in the house of attorney Alexander McSween and his wife, fighting it out with the Murphy gang. Mrs. McSween asks her husband if he'll trade the Bible for a gun, but he refuses. "I may perish by the sword, but I'll never live by it." A moment later, he's killed.

Billy and friend Charlie Bowdre sneak out of the house and escape. It's a good thing Billy's lover, Francesca, has been waiting with two horses.

He and Bowdre steal horses and cattle, and murder and raid.

Time for another scroll: "You wouldn't think that the toughest buscaderos in the Southwest would join up with a cocky kid, not old enough to vote! But they did! And took his orders, too! Then Hell really broke loose in New Mexico."

After more rustling and violence, Billy and his gang save buffalo hunter Pat Garrett

Don Barry (left) and Robert Lowery (center) as Billy the Kid and Pat Garrett in the Lippert cheapie *I Shot Billy the Kid* (1950).

from an Indian attack. The Indians are run off, but Garrett's horse has been killed. Billy gives him his. "I'll get another one," Billy says. "Same way I got that one."

Back at Francesca's place, Billy learns that her father is in jail. Ever the nice guy, Billy breaks Vicenti out. Later, Billy's in Fort Sumner about to head into a bar, when he runs into Pat Garrett. Garrett warns him that there's a drunk in the saloon threatening to kill Billy the Kid.

Billy thanks his friend, meets the would-be gunman and, in a bit of trickery, takes the bullets out of the drunk's Colt. When the drunk tries to shoot the Kid in the back, Billy calmly punches him. "I should have killed him," he tells Bowdre. "He'll shoot someone in the back one day." Outside, Billy runs into the sheriff and his deputy, and guns both of the men down.

More rustling. More riding. Meanwhile, Garrett is elected sheriff, and Governor Lew Wallace ends the Lincoln County War by declaring amnesty.

Wallace asks to meet with the Kid, and Garrett gets word through Francesca about the arrangement. Billy's suspicious at first, but he trusts Garrett, and meets with the governor. The governor's terms of amnesty aren't acceptable to the Kid: He must give up his guns. "I couldn't do that, general," he says. "I wouldn't last an hour."

Garrett encourages him to take the offer, and Billy agrees to think it over. Yeah, right. He holds up stagecoaches. He frees prisoners from a city jail. His reign of terror increases until Garrett and his posse catch up with the Kid and his gang. Charlie Bowdre is killed, and the gang is forced to surrender. Billy's the last to surrender, and he does it, smiling.

Tried for murder in Mesilla, the Kid is convicted and sentenced to hang. Now he must wait to see if Wallace will pardon him, as he had promised.

While waiting in jail, Billy escapes, disarming one guard, then killing Ollinger on the stairs. Vicenti is waiting outside with a horse, and they ride away. When Garrett learns what happened, he heads back to his office. He pulls Billy's pardon out from his pocket and rips it into shreds. "Billy," he says, "had double-crossed himself."

Thinking that the gang will show up again at Caliente Springs, Garrett and his posse set up an ambush. Tom O'Folliard is shot from the saddle and killed, but the Kid escapes.

Garrett sends a deputy to Francesca's place to see if the Kid will return there. Sure enough, the Kid arrives, promising to take Francesca and the family to Mexico, and heads to Pete Maxwell's room to tell him they're leaving.

Garrett and his posse reach Maxwell's. Garrett sneaks into Pete's bedroom, and Billy enters the room. Garrett tells Billy to give up, but Billy goes for his gun. Both men fire, with Garrett wounded and Billy killed. "He died as he lived," Garrett says, "with a gun in his hand."

The flashback ends, and the old Garrett says, "So that was Billy the Kid, and that's his story." Walking away from the grave, Garrett says, "*Hasta luego*, Billy."

The History

The opening scroll informs us: "This picture is based directly upon the true facts in the life of William H. Bonney — 'Billy the Kid' — outlaw and killer. Except for a few names and places, all characters and incidents are shown as they actually were."

Uh. Not really. Not even close.

Take the Five Day Battle, for instance. There is no fire this time, but there was in 1878. That's what sent everyone fleeing the McSweens' house, and Alexander McSween — again depicted as the pious, Quaker-like Christian — wasn't killed inside the house.

McSween was one of the last to leave the burning building, and found himself trapped with others, some hiding against adobe walls, others behind a chicken coop. Eventually, he said he would surrender, then changed his mind, yelling, "I shall never surrender." Five bullets dropped McSween. Bob Beckwith, Vicente Romero, and Francisco Zamora also fell dead. Yginio Salazar was wounded, believed to be dead, but crawled away later. A few others, some wounded, managed to escape. Andy Boyle, who had helped start the fire, called it "the big killing."[29]

Susan McSween, however, was not in the house. She left at about 5 P.M., joining other refuges in the Tunstall store next door.[30]

By the time McSween was being riddled with bullets, Charlie Bowdre was long gone. Bowdre, Doc Scurlock, and John Middleton had abandoned the Ellis store with roughly forty other McSween supporters. "A handful made a half-hearted attempt to relieve McSween in the afternoon," Robert M. Utley writes, "but allowed themselves to be driven off by a few shots from George Peppin's Winchester and, possibly, the threat of [Colonel Nathan] Dudley's artillery."[31]

Pat Garrett hunted buffalo but Billy the Kid never, as far as history records, saved him from death by an Indian. The two likely first met at Beaver Smith's bar in Fort Sumner.

Also, in this version, Billy the Kid doesn't kill Joe Grant after removing bullets from the drunken gunman's revolver. Instead of punching Grant, the Kid killed him.[32] Grant died in 1880. Sheriff William Brady and Deputy Hindman were killed in 1878. Brady might have been, as Billy tells Governor Wallace, "a Murphy man, using that badge to get me cold," but he and Hindman were shot dead, by ambush, on the streets of Lincoln, not Fort Sumner.[33]

The newspaper headline says Garrett wins election as Lincoln County sheriff "in overwhelming vote for local man." Garrett wasn't local. He was born in Alabama, grew up in Louisiana, and spent a lot of time in Texas before drifting to New Mexico. Garrett did, however, win the 1880 election easily, getting 328 votes to incumbent Sheriff George Kimbrell's 179.[34]

In the fall of 1878, Governor Samuel B. Axtell was ousted as New Mexico's governor and replaced by Lew Wallace. In November, Wallace did issue an amnesty. Unfortunately for Billy the Kid, the amnesty didn't apply. Wallace's decree freed from prosecution all parties involved in the Lincoln County War *except* those already under indictment, and Billy was facing charges for the murders of Sheriff Brady and Buckshot Roberts. He would meet with Wallace, at Squire Wilson's place in Lincoln and would testify before a grand jury and at a military board of inquiry examining Dudley's conduct, for which Wallace promised the Kid "a pardon in your pockets for all your misdeeds." Wallace would break that promise. The Kid was never pardoned.[35]

Bowdre was killed at Stinking Springs (not Caliente Springs), and Billy was tried and convicted of murdering Brady. No pardon came from Wallace. "I can't see how a fellow like him should expect any clemency from me," he told a reporter.[36] When Billy escaped from the Lincoln County jail, he didn't disarm Deputy Bell and kill Olinger on the staircase. He shot Bell dead on the stairs, then, from an upstairs window, shot Olinger on the street with the deputy's own shotgun.[37]

Tom O'Folliard/Folliard wasn't killed after Billy's legendary escape. He had been shot dead in December 1880 at Fort Sumner.[38]

Of course, Billy might have been visiting his favorite girl in Fort Sumner on the night he was killed. Not Francesca, but Paulita Maxwell. Whether the Kid was armed when he stepped inside Pete Maxwell's bedroom can be debated, but Billy never got off a shot. Garrett fired twice, and the Kid was dead. Garrett was not injured.[39]

Yet the opening and closing scenes have some history behind them. In October 1905, Garrett and writer Emerson Hough, working on his book *The Story of the Outlaw*, visited Fort Sumner. Garrett told the author about the killing of the Kid, and then they drove to the cemetery. Upon finding the grave, Garrett stared at it in silence for a while, then walked back to the buckboard. He found a canteen, opened it, and made a little toast. He didn't say, "Hasta luego, Billy," but "Well, here's to the boys, anyway. If there is any other life, I hope they'll make better use of it than they did of the one I put them out of."[40]

The Players

After appearing in supporting and minor roles, Donald "Red" Barry's career took off when he starred in the Republic serial *Adventures of Red Ryder* (1940). Studio president Herbert J. Yates saw Barry as Republic's answer to James Cagney. Short (reports of Barry's height ranged from 5' 4½" to 5' 9"). Feisty. Rough-and-tumble. He also had a tremendous ego, often earning him the animosity of co-stars, directors, and others.[41]

Virginia Carroll, who starred with Barry in *The Phantom Cowboy* (1941), said he "was very difficult. A little man; a short man, with a very big disposition!"[42] Vivian Austin, Barry's *Adventures of Red Ryder* co-star, said "he wasn't a very nice fellow."[43] Film historian Jon Tuska called him "a second-rate talent."[44]

"Not exactly handsome," wrote Kalton C. Lahue, "but good-looking in a sense of the word, Don had the appearance of an outlaw written all over his face."[45] He played Jesse James twice, in Republic's Roy Rogers programmer *Days of Jesse James* (1939) and in the abysmal *Jesse James' Women* (1954). He played plenty of bad guys, including Lee Marvin's crony in Budd Boetticher's *Seven Men from Now* (1956). Boetticher said, "[H]e was lucky to get the part."[46]

In 1949, Robert L. Lippert reorganized his Screen Guild Pictures as Lippert Pictures Inc. An adopted orphan, Lippert had started in the film business at 14 as an organ player for silent movies in Alameda, California. In the 1940s, he started a chain of theaters, and by 1945 his Screen Guild Productions was releasing low-budget films produced by his Action Films, Inc. One of his first successes was *I Shot Jesse James* (1949), Sam Fuller's first directing job.[47]

Lippert was known as the Quickie King, and the string of movies he made with Donald Barry Productions in 1949 (*The Dalton Gang*, *Square Dance Jubilee*, *Tough Assignment*) and 1950 (*I Shot Billy the Kid*, *Gunfire*, *Train to Tombstone*) were no exception. Much of the footage in *I Shot Billy the Kid* shows Barry and Co. riding around California's Vasquez Rocks, much as much of the footage in *Gunfire* shows Barry and Co. riding around California's Vasquez Rocks. (Actress Julie Adams worked on six James Ellison-Russell Hayden Lippert films that were shot simultaneously over a six-week period.[48])

Consider this 1950 lineup: Lippert's *Gunfire* was released in July, *Train to Tombstone* and *I Shot Billy the Kid* in August, and *Border Rangers* (starring Barry, Lowery and Vernon but produced by Lippert Productions) in October.

"The Lippert westerns were poorly scripted and badly produced," Lahue writes. "[T]he youthful Barry of a few years before had been bushwhacked and the fans had not remained around to rescue him."[49]

Barry's career continued to slide, although he kept appearing in films and on television into the 1980s. On July 17, 1980, Barry quarreled with his wife at his North Hollywood home. Police were summoned, and as officers escorted his wife and their ten-year-old daughter away, Barry re-entered his home, stepped outside with a revolver, and shot himself to death.[50]

Analysis

A routine and cheap Western, *I Shot Billy the Kid* never comes close to reaching the level of Lippert's, *I Shot Jesse James*. Frequent Barry co-star Wally Vernon (the two made twelve movies together) and his vaudeville schtick grow tiresome quickly, but this time he's playing a Mexican, making everything even worse.

Robert Lowery never had great range, but he wasn't a horrible actor. He just stayed in B productions forever and never got a real chance.

Screenwriter Orville Hampton knew enough of the Billy the Kid story to follow, sometimes, an accurate trail. Of course, he also took plenty of liberties with the truth. Hampton, whose credits would range from *Outlaw Women* (1952) and *Young Jesse James* (1960) to *Rock-*

etship X-M (1950) and *One Potato, Two Potato* (1964) would get other cracks at Billy the Kid, but his interest seemed to hone in on Pat Garrett. Hampton also wrote *Last of the Desperados* (1955) and *Badman's Country* (1958).

I Shot Billy the Kid is a mix of programmer and historical Western. The mix doesn't work, but it's watchable. Forgettable, often bad, but watchable — especially if you like watching riders galloping past California's Vasquez Rocks.

* * *

Variety (August 2, 1950): "Adequate western-type story about tracking down of Billy the Kid."

Captive of Billy the Kid

(Republic, January 1952, 57 minutes) CREDITS: Director: Fred C. Bannon. Associate Producer: Harry Keller. Screenplay: M. Coates Webster, Richard Wormser. CAST: Allan "Rocky" Lane (Allan "Rocky" Lane); Penny Edwards (Nancy McCreary); Grant Withers (Van Stanley); Clem Bevans (Skeeter Davis); Roy Barcroft (Piute); Clayton Moore (Paul Howarth); Mauritz Hugo (Randy Brown); Garry Goodwin (Pete); Frank McCarroll (Deputy Marshal); Richard Emory (Sam); Steve Clark (Telegraph Operator); Tex Terry (Stagecoach Driver); Art Dillard (Wagon Driver).

Synopsis

Allan "Rocky" Lane is sitting by his campfire about to enjoy some coffee when two riders begin firing on a buckboard carrying a man and woman. Rocky puts out the fire — because we can't risk a prairie fire, can we? — and rides to the rescue.

The wagon driver is killed, but Rocky shoots down one of the outlaws, scares off the other — a tough hombre named Piute — and saves the woman, a handsome gal named Nancy McCreary who's heading to the town of Junction.

In town, Rocky sends a couple of telegraphs and introduces himself as a range detective. A local rancher, Van Stanley, finds it odd that a range detective is here since this isn't cattle country. Hmmmm. Not cattle country, yet Stanley and just about everyone else in these parts lives on a ranch? Maybe they're raising horses, or goats.

Rocky heads to the ranch of Skeeter Davis. Actually, Rocky's a deputy marshal who has come here at the request of Davis, an old ex-carnival barker who knows a dark secret.

The late Billy the Kid drew a map that led to his buried treasure, then tore the map into five pieces. Skeeter took one part. So did Van Stanley, Nancy's father and two other men, Gorman and Brown. When Nancy's father was killed — giving her possession of his piece of the map — Skeeter grew suspicious.

It has been decided that Billy the Kid's fortune should go back to its rightful owners, but maybe somebody wants all that loot for himself. About the only person Skeeter thinks he can trust is Van Stanley, "a nice feller, ain't worried about him."

That's a mistake, because Stanley's actually behind the gunplay and killings. He sends Piute out to kill Brown and get that part of the map because Brown's coming in on a stagecoach. Rocky rides to intercept the stage and find Brown.

He's too late. A fellow named Brown is killed when Piute and another man attack the stage. Rocky runs off the bad guys before they can do any more damage and take Brown's map.

Another Billy programmer, this one with Allan "Rocky" Lane (right): *Captive of Billy the Kid* (1952).

Only Brown doesn't have a map. There's another guy on the stage, a handsome mustached man. Rocky thinks he might be Gorman, but, nope, the man says he's Paul Howarth.

Back in Junction, Rocky tangles with Piute, but the villain gets away. Then Paul asks for directions to Skeeter's ranch. It turns out that Paul won the part of a map in a card game.

Randy Brown shows up at Skeeter's; he, too, thought someone might be up to no good, so he sent a fellow on the stagecoach to pretend to be Brown. Too bad for that fellow. After Van Stanley arrives, they agree to set out for the buried treasure of Billy the Kid.

With all of the parts of the map in Skeeter's home, Piute attacks, announcing that they have the place surrounded and want that map. Well, they don't have all of the house surrounded. In fact, all three outlaws are hiding behind a well. Rocky easily slips out the back door, kills a couple of the henchmen and captures Piute. Van Stanley frees Piute by clobbering Skeeter on the head, and the next morning, they take off for the treasure.

Stanley kills Brown with a nice knife throw, and takes his part of the map. "We can count Brown out" as a suspect, Rocky tells Nancy. Before he can search the remaining suspects for that map, Piute opens fire. Again, Rocky runs him off.

The treasure is near Remargo, so when they arrive there, Rocky comes up with a plan. He poses as a bad guy and takes all the pieces of the map. But Piute and Van Stanley are on to him: They know he's a lawman and is expecting two deputies to come help him. Instead, two of Stanley's men pose as those deputies in an attempt to fool Rocky.

Rocky is no dummy. He kills one of the bad guys, knocks out another, and finally puts a bullet into Piute. Van Stanley takes the parts of the map from Skeeter and tries to make a getaway. He doesn't make it. Rocky catches up with him and, after a brutal fistfight, Van Stanley falls to his death.

A headline screams: "BILLY THE KID'S LOOT FOUND." The outlaw gang has been broken up, and Nancy is free to court the handsome Paul. Skeeter says he might start a new carnival, and Rocky rides off for further adventures on his trusty horse, Blackjack.

The History

Billy the Kid isn't in this movie (lucky him) since he has been dead for a while, but his buried treasure is around. On the other hand, seeing that Billy the Kid never robbed banks or trains or stagecoaches, merely rustled and killed, it's doubtful that the real Billy the Kid buried any treasure.

The Players

Allan "Rocky" Lane was born Harold Albershart in 1904 in Mishawaka, Indiana. He played football at Notre Dame, was a commercial photographer and appeared on Broadway before moving to motion pictures in 1929. He didn't become a Western hero until World War II. He started at Republic in serials: *King of the Royal Mounted* (1940), *King of the Mounties* (1942), *Daredevils of the West* (1943), and *The Tiger Woman* (1944).[51]

In 1944, Republic signed Lane to a term contract and he made six programmers for the studio's "Action Western" series over two years at $250 a week, then replaced Bill Elliott as Red Ryder, getting a pay raise to $350 a week. Stephen Slesinger had created Red Ryder as a comic book hero, drawn by Fred Harman, in 1933, and the series claimed a readership of 14 million in the 1940s. Comic books, novels, and a radio show followed — not to mention cowboy hats, toy guns and BB guns — and in 1940, Republic filmed a twelve-chapter serial, *Adventures of Red Ryder,* starring Don Barry. Programmers followed, and the series continued with Republic and Equity until 1949. Playing the popular Red Ryder likely helped Lane's exposure and salary, because in 1947, when he returned to play Allan "Rocky" Lane, he was making $450 a week, a salary that would increase to $700 a week by the time the series ended in 1953. Between 1947 and 1953, Lane appeared in thirty-eight programmers.[52]

What Lane wasn't was a good horseman, although he thought he was, according to some of his peers. Stunt men performed most of his hard riding and trick shots. Many co-stars found him to be a jerk. Lane, however, found longer-living fame after hanging up his spurs as a cowboy hero. From 1961 to 1966, he was the voice of television's iconic talking horse, Mr. Ed. "Rocky" Lane might not have known how to ride a horse well, but he could talk like one. He died of cancer at age sixty-four in 1973.[53]

Missing from this film was Eddie Waller, who played an "old coot" named Nugget Clark in thirty-two Lane programmers, but *Captive of Billy the Kid* still boasted a pretty good cast. Sporting a mustache instead of a mask was Clayton Moore. Moore had appeared in several Republic serials and films before turning to television in 1949 and starring in *The Lone Ranger,* the first Western series specifically produced for television. In 1952, producer George Trendle fired Moore "without warning or explanation," Moore recalled. "One day

I was doing a job I loved, idolized by children all across the country. The next, I was out of a job. And I didn't know why."[54]

John Hart replaced Moore as ABC-TV's masked man, and Moore went back to finding other jobs in things like the Republic serial *Radar Men from the Moon* and a United Artist Western, *Buffalo Bill in Tomahawk Territory*, whose budget "made Republic's budgets seem astronomical" ... and *Captive of Billy the Kid*, which Moore didn't mention in his autobiography. In 1953, Hart was out as the Lone Ranger and Moore was back. He would ride Silver until 1957, and keep wearing that mask — except between 1979 and 1984 when Wrather Corporation, which bought the *Lone Ranger* rights in 1957 for $3 million, got a court order that forced Moore to don sunglasses instead of the fabled mask. "It's my symbol, it's the Lone Ranger, and if I may say, it's Americana," Moore said of that black mask. "I guess when I go up to the big ranch in the sky, I'll still have it on." Moore died at age eighty-five in 1999.[55]

Blue-eyed Penny Edwards was considered one of the most popular heroines in B Westerns, appearing in six Roy Rogers films. She was born in 1929 in New York; her christened name was Millicent, but because it ended in "cent," she soon was being called Penny. By the time she was twelve, she was with the Ziegfeld Follies and later appeared on Broadway, doing dance specialties. She made her film debut in *My Wild Irish Rose* (1947) and got her first leading role the following year, opposite Dennis Morgan and Jack Carson in the musical *Two Guys from Texas*. When Dale Evans retired, Republic signed Edwards to appear in a Roy Rogers vehicle, *Sunset in the West* (1950). The movie proved to be one of Rogers's biggest draws, so the studio signed Edwards to a contract. After *Captive of Billy the Kid*, Edwards moved briefly to 20th Century–Fox, appearing with Tyrone Power in *Pony Soldier* (1952) and Rory Calhoun in *Powder River* (1953). One of her best roles came as a woman driven to outlawry in director Reginald LeBorg's *The Dalton Girls* (1957). Eventually, she moved into television. She died in Texas in 1998 three days short of her sixty-ninth birthday.[56]

After working as a salesman and newspaper reporter, Grant Withers wound up in Hollywood in the late 1920s. Although he had been a star in A features as well as Bs and serials, he had moved into supporting roles by the 1940s, including the 1941 *Billy the Kid* with Robert Taylor. He appeared in two of the movies in director John Ford's famed Cavalry Trilogy, *Fort Apache* (1948) and *Rio Grande* (1950), but his biggest claim to fame might have been in 1930. That year, he eloped with Loretta Young, then only seventeen years old, to Yuma, Arizona. The marriage was annulled in 1931. He later married actress Estelita Rodriguez, best known for appearing in several Roy Rogers programmers. Withers committed suicide in 1959.[57]

Born in 1880, character actor Clem Bevans got his start in stock, vaudeville, and burlesque before heading to Hollywood in 1935. Almost always, he played some country old-timer, in A pictures like *Come and Get It* (1936), *Abe Lincoln in Illinois* (1940), *Sergeant York* (1941), *The Yearling* (1946), *The Paleface* (1948) and *Harvey* (1950) plus plenty of Bs. Bevans died in 1963.[58]

Roy Barcroft, Republic's (if not *Hollywood's*) most active bad guy, was one of the few actors who actually got along with Lane. Usually. "You just couldn't take what he said seriously," Barcroft said. "We got along fine away from the studio, but once he stepped in front of the cameras, he became a different person." They certainly made enough movies together with Barcroft appearing in thirty-eight of Lane's fifty-one films.[59]

Barcroft recalled one amusing — to Barcroft, not Lane — incident during filming: "Rocky insisted his fight scenes look realistic. One day, he kept on about my performance. I got mad, and popped him right on the chin, and asked him if that was realistic enough."[60]

Analysis

The plot might be a little more inventive than plenty of kiddie Westerns, but Lane's a poor actor, and even Republic's programmers had turned rather dull by the 1950s. Besides, this is yet another Billy the Kid movie *sans* Billy the Kid.

***

Phil Hardy, *The Western: The Complete Film Sourcebook* (1984): "This is one of Lane's best series Westerns."

The Law vs. Billy the Kid

(Columbia, August 1954, 72 minutes) CREDITS: Director: William Castle. Producer: Sam Katzman. Screenplay: Bernard Gordon (billed as John T. Williams). CAST: Scott Brady (Bill Bonney); Betta St. John (Nita Maxwell); James Griffith (Pat Garrett); Alan Hale, Jr. (Bob Ollinger); Paul Cavanagh (John H. Tunstall); William "Bill" Phillips (Charlie Bowdre); Benny Rubin (Arnold Dodge); Steve Darrell (Tom Watkins); George Berkeley (Tom O'Folliard); William Tannen (Dave Rudabaugh); Richard Cutting (Pete Maxwell); John Cliff (Carl Trumble); Otis Garth (Governor Lew Wallace); Martin Garralaga (Miguel Bolanos); Frank Sully (Jack Poe); William Fawcett (Parsons); Robert Griffin (L.G. Murphy).

Synopsis

Billy the Kid is digging fence holes for a New Mexico rancher named Parsons. One of the ranch hands, Carl Trumble, tries to provoke the Kid into a fight, and Billy almost guns him down. Another hand, Pat Garrett, stops him. "Never go for one of those, Billy," Garrett tells him, "unless you're willing to use it."

When Parsons tries to cheat Billy out of his pay, he takes the money, slaps around Parsons, and leaves. Parsons tries to get Garrett to help him get the Kid; Garrett won't, so Parsons fires him. Trumble's ready to help, though, and they go after Billy.

Billy shoots Trumble out of the saddle, and Parsons lets the Kid go. Soon, Garrett catches up with the Kid, and they ride to Lincoln County together. Billy's hungry, so he kills a steer. While he's butchering the beef, up ride shotgun-wielding Bob Ollinger and rancher John Tunstall. Ollinger thinks the two strangers are working for Murphy and Watkins, their enemies, but Tunstall doesn't believe that, and offers them a job. His English accent amuses the Kid. "Where did you learn to speak English, mister?" the Kid asks.

"In England, my home. Why do you ask?"

"You talk real funny."

Back at the ranch, Tunstall introduces his niece, Nita Maxwell, and Billy is smitten. That makes Ollinger jealous, and he beats the tar out of the Kid, forcing Tunstall to fire Ollinger.

"I hope I'm wrong, Ollinger," Garrett says, "but you'd have been better off if you'd killed him. Now, he'll kill you."

Ollinger joins the Murphy-Watkins faction. When they learn that Billy's working for

The Law vs. Billy the Kid (1954) starred Scott Brady and Betta St. John.

Tunstall, it gives Murphy a plan of action. A reward poster is found for Bonney, so Watkins is ordered to arrest Tunstall for harboring a fugitive.

At the Tunstall ranch, the posse shows the reward poster for the Kid. Tunstall reaches inside his coat for his eyeglasses. Thinking he's going for a gun, one of the deputies kills him.

Billy vows revenge. Some of Tunstall's employees, Charlie Bowdre, Tom O'Folliard and Dave Rudabaugh, join him. Violence in Lincoln County escalates.

Garrett, who has been running Tunstall's ranch, meets Governor Lew Wallace. Wallace has fired Watkins as sheriff and makes Garrett pin on the badge. If Garrett refuses, Wallace says, "I'll declare martial law, and order my troops to shoot Bonney on sight."

When Billy meets the governor and hears the terms, he's unmoved. The murderers of Tunstall will also go free under this amnesty deal, and Billy won't have that. "You stick to legal, governor," he says. "I'll stick to right and wrong."

In a saloon, he's forced to kill ex-sheriff Watkins, and beats Ollinger to a pulp. Garrett's forced to go after his old friend. He tracks him down at Farrow Springs, but is forced to deputize Ollinger as well.

At a Farrow Springs shack, Ollinger blows away Bowdre with his shotgun. Rudabaugh and O'Folliard are also killed, and Billy's captured. It's Christmas Day. Billy knows a hangman's noose awaits him, but he tells Nita: "The noose isn't there yet, and it won't be, Nita."

While waiting in jail, the Kid disarms Jack, his jailer, and tracks down Ollinger at the Lincoln Hotel. He shoots Ollinger with his own shotgun. The reward for the Kid, once $100, rises to $500, and eventually $1,000.

Tipped off that Billy's at Pete Maxwell's ranch, Garrett takes his posse there. Billy arrives to see Nita, asking her to cross the border into Mexico with him. She agrees, and Billy walks into Pete's room to tell him they're leaving. A gunshot sounds, and Billy staggers out into the courtyard and falls dead. The deputies are excited that Garrett had killed the Kid, but Garrett isn't happy.

"Yeah, I got him," he says, and throws his gun to the ground in disgust. He walks away, leaving Nita cradling Billy in her arms.

Where's Garrett going?

"Away," he says. "Just away."

The History

John Tunstall is again played as the older father-figure to the Kid, but he was not uncle to Billy's alleged lover Paulita (here called Nita) Maxwell. Paulita always denied that she was one of Billy's *queridas*, but she did admit that the Kid "fascinated many women."[61] Robert Olinger never worked for Tunstall — he was always on the other side — and the Lincoln County sheriff killed by the Kid was Brady, not Watkins.

General Lew Wallace, was appointed governor by President Hayes — replacing Samuel Axtell — and promised to come to Lincoln to investigate the lawlessness. He met the Kid on March 17, 1879, at the home of Squire Wilson.[62]

Billy the Kid's background is clouded by obscurity. Here, we're told, "New York killed my father. Lungs." Which could be true, since the Kid is said to have been born in New York City and on an 1868 census in Indiana, his mother was reportedly listed as the widow of one Michael McCarty.[63]

"After that," the Kid says, "Ma was on the run." Certainly, Catherine McCarty moved around a bit, from Indiana to Wichita, Kansas, and possibly Denver, before settling in New Mexico.[64]

He calls her marriage in Kansas "a mistake." Actually, Catherine McCarty married Henry Antrim at the First Presbyterian Church in Santa Fe, New Mexico Territory, on March 1, 1873.[65]

Screenwriter Bernard Gordon also falls back on the legend that Billy the Kid was "drifting since I was twelve." If we go with the unsubstantiated birth date of November 23, 1859, the Kid would have been twelve years old in 1871, when he was living with his mother and brother in Kansas and possibly Colorado in 1872. He didn't run away until 1875.[66]

After Tunstall is murdered, the Kid and others take out after his killers, and Billy manages to shoot one dead. In reality, the Tunstall hands who witnessed his murder were not so eager to pursue (and possibly get shot). It was not until Dick Brewer, the Kid and others were sworn in as "Regulators" that they went after Tunstall's killers, capturing posse members Morton and Baker. On or about March 9, 1878, Morton and Baker — and William McCloskey — were killed. It takes no stretch of the imagination to argue that Billy the Kid at least had a hand in their deaths.[67] As pointed out previously, the amnesty offered by Lew Wallace could not apply to Billy the Kid since he was already facing felony indictments.[68]

Here, the capture of the Kid occurs at Farrow Springs (instead of Stinking Springs) and Bowdre, O'Folliard and Rudabaugh are killed. Charlie Bowdre was killed that cold December morning (not quite Christmas, but screenwriters do get poetic license), but O'Folliard/Folliard was mortally wounded on the night of December 19, 1880, when the outlaws rode into an ambush at Fort Sumner.[69]

The passionate kiss of Nita (Paulita) has some basis in history. Jim East, a member of Garrett's posse that had captured the Kid, said that before the prisoners were transported to Las Vegas, New Mexico, Paulita Maxwell and Billy embraced, and Paulita "gave Billy one of those soul kisses the novelist tell us about, till it being time to hit the road for Vegas, we had to pull them apart, much against our wishes, for you know, all the world loves a lover."[70]

Sheriff Brady wasn't killed in a saloon, but on the streets. And Bob Olinger wasn't killed in a saloon, either. He was killed by the Kid with his own shotgun, but that happened on April 28, 1881, not New Year's Day. Brady had been killed on April 1, 1878.[71]

Why Billy was at Fort Sumner on the night of July 14, 1881, can be — and certainly has been — debated. He was probably visiting Paulita Maxwell, who could have been pregnant at that time. He certainly felt comfortable there.[72]

The Players

Cast as Billy — "much too old for the part and wearing a typical 1950s-style haircut" — was Scott Brady (1924–1985) in yet another B Western role. The younger brother of actor Lawrence Tierney, Brady was born Gerald Kenneth Tierney in Brooklyn. His brother Lawrence had played the title role in *Dillinger* (1945), so after World War II, Brady (a former Navy light-heavyweight boxer) came to Hollywood with $700 on what was planned as a six-month vacation. A scout for producer Hal Wallis saw him and arranged a screen test, and Brady soon enrolled at the Bliss-Hayden School in Beverly Hills to study acting. He landed some leading roles for Eagle-Lion in *Canon City* and *In This Corner* (both 1948). By 1950, after Brady had signed with Universal, he and Eagle-Lion would sue one another in contract disputes. He moved from studio to studio (Allied Artists, MGM, 20th Century–Fox, etc.). Brady seemed well-suited for urban roles in films like *He Walked by Night* (1948), *Port of New York* (1949), *Undertow* (1949) and *I Was a Shoplifter* (1950), but he wound up in Westerns: *Kansas Raiders* (1950) and *Bronco Buster* (1952). Just before going to work on *The Law vs. Billy the Kid,* he had completed Republic's quirky cult Western *Johnny Guitar* (1954), playing the Dancing Kid. He never quite made it out of the Bs, eventually moved to television and supporting roles, and died of respiratory failure in Los Angeles at 65 years old.[73]

Ever-reliable character actor James Griffith took the role of Pat Garrett. "James Griffith should have had the career Zachary Scott had, because he would have made much more of it," film historian Robert Nott says. "His presence, whether he was in a bit part or a second lead, elevated many a B Western in the 1950s, mostly because he seemed incapable of striking wrong notes."[74]

Griffith struck the right note at Pat Garrett, as James Fidler pointed out in his Hollywood column: "James Griffith as sheriff Pat Garrett is the best portrayal of Garrett that I can remember."[75] Griffith died of cancer in 1993 at age seventy-seven.[76]

Born in New Britain, Connecticut, in 1918, Bernard Gordon grew up in New York City and moved to Hollywood about 1940. Declared physically unfit for the military, he worked in the film industry during World War II. He also joined the Communist Party, although he eventually quit it because of Stalin's crimes. When the House Un-American Activities Committee began its witch hunt, Gordon was blacklisted.[77] "Where was J. Edgar Hoover when they wrote the First Amendment?" Gordon wrote in his autobiography.[78]

Before getting snared by the blacklist and fired, Gordon had been hired by Universal Studios' William Alland and went to work as a screenwriter, working on a B boxing movie, *Flesh and Fury* (1952), starring up-and-coming Tony Curtis, and *The Lawless Breed* (1953), a romanticized, Raoul Walsh–directed Western about Texas gunman John Wesley Hardin. It starred another rising star at Universal, Rock Hudson.[79]

Officially, Gordon was out of work in Hollywood, but he was not without friends. Charles H. Schneer had seen *The Lawless Breed*. An assistant producer for Columbia's B unit, Schneer called Gordon and said he was looking for another Western. Gordon went to work, borrowing the synopsis of a play about Billy the Kid written by Janet and Philip Stevenson, who were also blacklisted. While working at his day job of selling plastics, Gordon collaborated with another blacklisted writer, Bob Williams, on the script.[80] "The success of this work started me," Gordon recalled, "with many fits and starts, into a busy career as a blacklisted screenwriter."[81]

Gordon followed with a flurry of scripts, including *Earth vs. the Flying Saucers* (1956), *Zombies of Mora Tau* (1957), *The Man Who Turned to Stone* (1957), *Escape from San Quentin* (1957), *Hellcats of the Navy* (1957), and *The Case Against Brooklyn* (1958), all as Raymond T. Marcus. Marcus was the name of Gordon's friend who had hired him to sell plastics. Schneer produced *Hellcats* and *Brooklyn*. The others were produced by Sam Katzman.[82]

"You did what you could," Gordon said after the Writers Guild of America began restoring proper film credits in the 1980s. "I knew so many people who were blacklisted. They scattered all over. They went to Mexico or London or Paris to find work. Some succeeded, some didn't. Some wrote under pseudonyms or had fronts; some started to sell insurance or became salesmen. It was not a good time."[83]

No fan of the House Un-American Activities Committee, producer Sam Katzman gave plenty of blacklisted writers the opportunity to work, albeit under pseudonyms. As Wheeler Winston Dixon points out, Katzman "got their services at bargain-basement prices."[84] Wheeler writes:

> In all his work, Katzman created a sealed, hermetic universe, within which he could operate with generic impunity. There were no rules to break because Katzman had created the rules and, with them, the concept of the genre "hot-wire" (in which several genres are combined to create a new twist on an existing format, such as the comedy/western, the horror/musical, and the like). Using this concept to bring new life to existing and often overused genres, Katzman created a cinematic vision that was his alone.[85]

Katzman had been producing movies since the 1930s. He went on to produce *Rock Around the Clock* (1956), *Twist Around the Clock* (1961), a couple of 1960s Elvis Presley offerings — *Kissin' Cousins* (1964) and *Harum Scarum* (1965) — and *The Fastest Guitar Alive* (1967), starring Roy Orbison. His last movie, an action film starring Brady and Gloria Grahame, was *Loners* (1972). Katzman died on August 4, 1973.[86]

Kirk Douglas and Otto Preminger effectively ended the blacklist in 1960 when they demanded that Dalton Trumbo get credit for writing *Spartacus* and *Exodus*, respectively but Gordon, and other writers, still often had to use fronts and pseudonyms for a few more years (although Gordon got credit for *55 Days at Peking* and *The Thin Red Line*). When Elia Kazan was selected to receive an honorary Oscar in 1999, Gordon led a protest. Kazan had named names during the blacklist. Gordon, who later moved to Spain, where he wrote and produced movies, died in 2007 at age eighty-eight. His last movie was *Surfacing* (1981).[87]

Analysis

As a Billy the Kid movie, *The Law vs. Billy the Kid* is routine, historically flawed and dull to boot, although James Griffith is excellent (as he always seemed to be) as a pleasant Pat Garrett.

What makes the movie important isn't its rather even-tempered portrayal of Billy the Kid as neither good guy or villain (one might wonder how much better the movie could have been with a younger and better actor as Billy). The movie is important merely because it was written by a blacklisted screenwriter.

***

Nevada State Journal (August 11, 1954): "I've never been too strong for pictures that have a tendency to glorify an outlaw, but this one gets over that bridge by neither glorifying nor condemning the man."

The Boy from Oklahoma

(Warner Bros., February 1954, 87 minutes) CREDITS: Director: Michael Curtiz. Producer: David Weisbart. Screenplay: Frank Davis, Winston Miller. CAST: Will Rogers, Jr. (Tom Brewster); Nancy Olson (Katie Brannigan); Lon Chaney, Jr. (Crazy Charlie); Anthony Caruso (Barney Turlock); Wallace Ford (Wally Higgins); Clem Bevans (Pop Pruty); Merv Griffin (Steve); Louis Jean Heydt (Paul Evans); Sheb Wooley (Pete Martin); Slim Pickens (Shorty); Tyler MacDuff (Billy the Kid); James Griffith (Joe Downey).

Synopsis

Folksy Oklahoma cowboy Tom Brewster rides into Blue Rock, New Mexico Territory, hoping to mail his examination papers to a Kansas City law school. The post office is closed because it's election day. Tom finds postmaster Wally Higgins in Mayor Barney Turlock's saloon and persuades him to open the post office so he can get his papers out on the stagecoach. Justice of the Peace Pop Pruty takes advantage and drops off a letter himself. It's addressed to the U.S. marshal in Lincoln, and Higgins recognizes the handwriting.

To celebrate election day, there's going to be a horse race. When Brewster learns that the winner will get $100, he enters. The race ends in a dead heat between the trick-roping Brewster and Katie Brannigan, who dresses in men's garb and packs a gun. To break the tie, she suggests a shooting contest, which she easily wins. Brewster's mighty handy with a lariat, but he's no good with a six-shooter.

Brewster's on his way to Lincoln to study law with an uncle, but Turlock offers him the sheriff's job, which will pay $100 a month. "You look honest," Turlock tells him. "You don't drink, and you're no gunslinger." Brewster's not interested in the job—though he is interested in Katie Brannigan—until the stagecoach is robbed and the mail is taken. He decides to pin on a badge until he can get replacement papers from Kansas City, but he won't wear a gun. "People ought to respect the badge," he says, "not the gun behind it."

Barney Turlock isn't liked by everyone in town, but Katie respects him. "Barney Turlock gave my father the best funeral this town has ever seen," she tells Brewster. Turns out,

Nancy Olson assists Will Rogers, Jr., in bringing bad guy Anthony Caruso to justice in *The Boy from Oklahoma* (1954), which inspired the *Sugarfoot* TV series.

Katie's dad had been the town's quick-drawing sheriff until he was murdered and his body found out on the prairie on a rainy night. Rustlers were suspected, but Brewster — and Pop Pruty — think otherwise. So Brewster starts investigating. "If you do find the men who did it, let me know," Katie tells him. "I'll do the shooting."

Brewster's investigation leads him to one of Turlock's riders, Pete Martin, so Turlock sends for his cousin, Billy the Kid. Brewster is summoned to Turlock's saloon, and everybody in town knows it's a setup to have Brewster killed. They try to talk him out of going to face down Billy the Kid.

Brewster admits that he's scared, but says there are "lots worse things than bein' scared."

"Yeah," Pop Pruty tells him, "bein' dead's one of 'em."

In Turlock's saloon, the two-gun Billy tries to provoke Brewster into a fight, calls him yellow, rips off his badge, shoots at his feet. Brewster won't bite, but he's counting Billy's bullets.

The problem is he miscounts. Thinking Billy is holding an empty gun, he approaches him, warning him that his actions — he's not wanted for anything now — will land him in jail or a grave. In a fit of rage, Billy fires his last shot above the bar, and warns Brewster, "I'll be back here again someday. You better not be around." Then he storms out of the saloon.

Everybody's happy, but not Turlock, especially when Brewster threatens to arrest him for selling liquor to a minor, which carries a penalty of $1,000, loss of license, and six months in jail.

Turlock leads Brewster to his office, where he pulls out IOUs for gambling debts from Katie's father, and a confession. He had been helping the rustlers. So Brewster is in a quandary: keep after the truth, and reveal Katie's dad as a crook, or let things slide.

He decides to leave. But Katie talks him out of it — after learning the truth from Pop Pruty — and they set up a plan to snag the crooks. She perfectly matches her father's handwriting on an envelope addressed to the U.S. attorney in Lincoln, and Pruty drops it off for the afternoon stage. Wally Higgins informs Turlock, and riders go after the stage. As soon as they take the letter, Brewster leads a posse and rounds up the bad guys. Robbing the U.S. mail — even if all they took is a envelope full of blank paper — is a federal offense.

Some members of the posse are ready to lynch Pete Martin for killing Katie's dad, but he confesses that all he did was drop the body in the gulch. Sheriff Brannigan, he says, was murdered by Barney Turlock.

Back in town, Turlock tries to murder Pruty, but Katie stops him. Knowing neither will shoot him in the back, Turlock walks away and, seeing the posse bringing back his men, tries to ride away. He's no match for Brewster's rope, and is hauled off to jail.

Brewster heads to Lincoln to start his apprenticeship, but lets Katie know that he'll be back in Blue Rock some day to set up his law office. Katie says she'll be waiting.

The History

Again, Billy only shows up for a cameo in this film. Brewster warns Billy the Kid that he isn't wanted for anything — yet — but, of course, by the time Billy the Kid was known around New Mexico Territory, authorities in New Mexico and Arizona would have liked to have him in custody. In 1877, he shot and killed bullying blacksmith Francis P. "Windy" Cahill in Camp Grant, Arizona Territory. A coroner's jury declared it murder, although in all likelihood, had he stuck around for a trial, a jury would have acquitted him on grounds of self-defense. On April 1, 1878, he participated in the ambush that killed Lincoln County Sheriff William Brady and was indicted for murder. In 1881, a jury found him guilty of first-degree murder.[88]

And while we don't know much about Billy's background, we do know he had a brother, Joseph Antrim. Long after Billy's death in 1881, a few people popped up claiming to be Billy the Kid. No cousins, however, have ever surfaced.[89]

The Players

Hungarian-born Michael Curtiz became one of the golden directors of Hollywood's golden era — *The Adventures of Robin Hood* (1938, which he finished after William Keighley left), *The Sea Wolf* (1941), *Casablanca* (1942, his lone Oscar win), *Yankee Doodle Dandy* (1942), *Mildred Pierce* (1945). He started in the silents and kept at it until 1961 with *The Comancheros*, before he died in 1962.[90]

He also directed a number of Westerns, including some starring Errol Flynn: *Dodge City* (1939), *Virginia City* (1940), *Santa Fe Trail* (1940). Since he directed *The Story of Will Rogers* (1952), which starred Will Rogers, Jr., Curtiz must have seen the obvious choice to direct *The Boy from Oklahoma*.

The screenplay was based on Michael Fessier's short story "The Sheriff Was Scared," which appeared in the May 3, 1952, *Saturday Evening Post*. Fessier was adept at humor. Another tongue-in-cheek Fessier—*Saturday Evening Post* story became an oddball Republic picture, *Woman They Almost Lynched* (1953). His novels included *Fully Dressed and in His Right Mind* (1935) and *Clovis* (1948), about a "highly educated, highly opinionated" parrot.[91]

Curtiz liked the Frank Davis-Winston Miller script so much, he asked for five weeks to shoot rather than the four Warner Bros. had set. Jack Warner countered that Curtiz should reduce his percentage of profits (twenty-five percent). Curtiz, never one to hold back, said the percentage clause in his contract was a joke and that he was willing to end his career with Warners at any time. Needless to say, Jack Warner kept the shooting schedule at four weeks, with filming at the Warner Ranch in Calabasas, California. *The Boy from Oklahoma* also proved to be Curtiz's last film for Warners as a contract director. He completed the film on March 21, 1953. Warners released him from his studio contract on April 18.[92]

"*The Boy from Oklahoma*," Curtiz biographer James C. Robertson writes, "was Curtiz's way of showing that gory, gratuitous violence and new dramatic situations were not necessary to make entertaining Westerns."[93]

Warners didn't back the movie, however, abstaining from a New York City opening and generating little publicity. "No studio likes to trumpet the wares of its rivals," historian John Howard Reid wrote, noting the fact that Curtiz was gone by the time the movie was released. "And two, it was undoubtedly felt that the movie lacked star power and had nothing to offer the 1954 teenage market." The movie made a profit of only $454,000.[94]

Although Ronald Reagan was considered for the lead, the studio returned to Will Rogers, Jr. He had played his famous father, the folksy humorist and actor from Oklahoma, in an uncredited cameo in *Look for the Silver Lining* (1949) and got the starring role in *The Story of Will Rogers*. He also had a supporting role in *The Eddie Cantor Story* (1953).[95]

"The younger Rogers hadn't quite followed in his father's boot steps, but he certainly had been successful before he became," as *Life* magazine put it, "an imitator of his famous father." Born October 20, 1911, in New York City while his dad was working in Ziegfeld Follies, Jr. graduated from Stanford University in 1935. He worked as a journalist (publisher of the *Beverly Hills Citizen* and, in 1938, Spanish Civil War correspondent for McNaught Syndicate) and served as a Democratic congressman from California from 1942 to 1944.[96]

In Congress, he not only called for the abolishment of the House Committee on Un-American Activities, he promoted assistance for European Jews, helping push President Franklin D. Roosevelt to establish the War Refugee Board. "I just did what anybody would have done," he said. He resigned from Congress in 1944, and joined the Army. As a tank commander during the Battle of the Bulge, he was promoted to first lieutenant and awarded the Bronze Star. On April 9, 1945, he was hit by shrapnel in the knee during the Battle of the Ruhr. A run for the U.S. Senate in 1946 failed.[97] Even though he remained active in politics, he eventually tried Hollywood.

"[Rogers] does his manhuntin' by some neat rope work in a good Western," *Boys' Life* magazine noted in its *Boy from Oklahoma* review. But actually, Rogers had to re-learn the rope tricks his father had taught him while preparing for his role in *The Story of Will Rogers*, based on Betty Blake Rogers's book. Warners had wanted to make that movie since 1941, and after a long search, decided to cast the humorist's son in the lead. Even then, Rogers wasn't available to start production for three years. *The Story of Will Rogers* was a hit, and got mostly favorable reviews.[98]

"You know," he told columnist Louella O. Parsons, "I never spoke any lines, not even 'shut the door, open the window,' until I played my father [in *The Story of Will Rogers*]. I hadn't even been in plays in college." He had won a playwright competition for his play *Judge Lynch* when he was twelve years old in 1924.[99]

As far as acting goes, Rogers said, "I'm not an actor. I can't do anything outside of my own character, so I just try to be natural and not act."[100]

After *The Boy from Oklahoma*, Rogers appeared mostly, and not often, on television, although he also had top billing (but a supporting role) in another Western, Universal's *Wild Heritage* (1958), and radio. He played the publisher of a small-town newspaper in Eugene O'Neill's play *Ah, Wilderness!* at the Pasadena Playhouse in 1954. He hosted the syndicated TV series *The Pioneers* in the late 1950s. He served as assistant to the U.S. commissioner of Indian Affairs from 1967 to 1969. In 1993, at age eighty-one, troubled by failing health, he shot himself to death in Tubac, Arizona.[101]

Warner Bros. might not have done much to promote *The Boy from Oklahoma*, but the studio wasn't done with the character Rogers created, Tom Brewster. Will Hutchins resurrected the role of the tenderfoot lawyer on TV's *Sugarfoot*. Although Warners had also released a Randolph Scott Western titled *Sugarfoot* in 1951, based on a novel by Clarence Budington Kelland, the only thing that movie had in common with the TV series was Max Steiner's original score. Ray John Heindorf adapted that score, with Paul Francis Webster adding lyrics. *Sugarfoot* was never a weekly show, however. From 1957 to 1959, it ran on an alternate-week basis with Clint Walker's hit series *Cheyenne*. When Walker walked off from *Cheyenne* during a contract dispute for the 1959–60 series, *Sugarfoot* alternated its time slot with *Bronco*, starring Ty Hardin. For the final season, *Cheyenne*, *Bronco* and *Sugarfoot* rotated under the all-encompassing title *The Cheyenne Show*.[102]

Analysis

It's not really a Billy the Kid movie seeing that the Kid shows up for one barroom cameo, and *The Boy from Oklahoma* doesn't have much of a reputation. That's too bad.

"Superbly photographed both indoors — [cinematographer Robert] Burks can be justly proud of such suspenseful low-key lighting as the sequences in the barn — and out (Curtiz gets the most in dramatic value out of some only moderately attractive locations by using tightly composed shots with lots of pans and running inserts, all sharply cut together), and lensed on a sizable budget with lots of extras milling about its large sets, *The Boy from Oklahoma* is a western with pace, charm, style and artistry," John Howard Reid writes in *Movie Westerns: Hollywood Films the Wild, Wild West*.[103] It's a sweet movie, suitable for adults and children.

Will Rogers, Jr., might have a 41-year-old "boy" (?) when filming started, but his down-home style fits the character perfectly. Gentle — maybe the most of any Billy the Kid film — *The Boy from Oklahoma* is an enjoyable minor Western that deserves a wider audience.

***

Los Angeles Times (February 25, 1954): "Will Rogers, Jr., follows in the footsteps of his father as adept with the lariat in *The Boy From Oklahoma*, because he is a sheriff who uses a rope rather than a gun. And this serves okay in the production...."

Strange Lady in Town

(Warner Bros., April 1955, 112 minutes) CREDITS: Director-Producer: Mervyn LeRoy. Screenplay: Frank Butler. CAST: Greer Garson (Julia Garth); Dana Andrews (Rork O'Brien); Cameron Mitchell (David Garth); Lois Smith (Spurs O'Brien); Walter Hampden (Father Gabriel Mendoza); Pedro Gonzalez (Trooper Martinez-Martinez); Joan Camden (Norah Muldoon); Anthony Numkena (Tomasito Diaz); Jose Torvay (Bartoloa Diaz); Adele Jergens (Bella Brown); Robert J. Wilke (Karg); Frank DeKova (Anse Hatlo); Russell Johnson (Shadduck); Gregory Walcott (Scanlon); Douglas Kennedy (Slade Wickstrom); Harry Hines (Chicken Feathers); Jack Williams (Ribstock); Joe Costarello (Alfredo); Nick Adams (Billy the Kid); Bob Foulk (Joe); Julian Rivero (Manuel); Ralph Moody (General Lew Wallace); Louise Lorimer (Mrs. Wallace); Paul Birch (Sheriff); John Stephenson (Captain Taggart); William Boyett (Lieutenant Keith).

Synopsis

In 1880, New England–born Julia Garth comes west—"My farewell to Boston was without a tear," she says—to join her Army officer brother in Santa Fe and hang her shingle as a doctor.

A woman doctor? In Santa Fe? "We've never seen a woman doctor out here," she's told at a cow camp. Besides, Santa Fe already has a doctor, widower Rork O'Brien, who is trying to raise his tomboy daughter Spurs. O'Brien is also a sexist hard rock who thinks a woman's place is in the home. On the other hand, O'Brien spends more time raising thoroughbred trotters than peddling pills. Spurs, however, is captivated by this beautiful, red-haired lady. In fact, Spurs bring in the new doctor's first patients.

Billy the Kid's pard, Joe, has a toothache, and when it comes time for Julia to pull the tooth, Billy whips out a six-shooter and buffaloes his pard. "All right, ma'am," Billy then says. "He's all yours."

Julia refuses payment—it's not right to charge her first patient—and Billy and Joe ride out of the movie.

"What a nice boy," Julia says to Spurs.

"They call him Billy the Kid," Spurs tells him.

That shocks Julia. "Billy the Kid. But he's so young!" (Hey, Doc, maybe that's why they call him "The Kid.")

"Nineteen years old," Spurs concedes, "and he's killed nineteen men. The trouble with Billy is he's too sensitive. You'd never know how many people don't understand him."

"Well," Julia says, "offhand I can think of at least nineteen."

That's it for Billy. He's never mentioned and never appears again in the movie. Julia, however, does run into some of Apache leader Geronimo's "boys" while on a horseback ride with O'Brien, who has taught the strange lady how to ride Western-style, not sidesaddle. And Governor Lew Wallace shows up at the Governor's Ball, where Julia upsets O'Brien yet again by contradicting O'Brien's evaluation of the governor's health. It's not his heart, Julia says, but a tight collar that is cutting off blood circulation to his head.

The rest of the movie finds Julia and O'Brien sparring, falling in love, sparring, sparring, falling in love ... you get the idea. Julia also learns that her brother, Lieutenant David Garth, is not quite an officer and a gentleman. "You ought to know by this time that I'm not always a proper person," he tells her.

O'Brien thinks Garth will be "laughed out of town in three months," but she begins helping out in Father Gabriel Mendoza's makeshift hospital, much to O'Brien's displeasure. More sparring.

Greer Garson can't save Cameron Mitchell in *Strange Lady in Town* (1955). Lois Smith stands on the porch.

Julia tells him that she left Boston "because of the intolerance of men like you.... I didn't expect to find the same intolerance, the same bigotry out here."

More sparring. More making up. Eventually, O'Brien proposes, but Julia can't accept. "You're the symbol of everything I ran away from," she tells him.

Yet everything Julia does in the hospital turns out perfectly. She's part psychiatrist, part surgeon. Everything her brother does, however, backfires. After he is accused of cheating at cards, he strikes a superior officer, which lands him in the guardhouse. He breaks jail, and then plots to rob the Santa Fe bank during Fiesta.

The robbery goes badly. Poor Father Mendoza is trampled to death while the bad guys try to get away. One outlaw is killed, another is captured and hanged, and David is trapped, holed up in a cabin outside of town. Julia tries to talk David into surrendering. David starts out but, seeing the mood of the crowd, panics and tries to flee, only to be gunned down.

That's too much for Santa Fe. They've had enough of the Garths. So Julia decides to leave "because they hold me responsible for David."

Before she can ride out, however, O'Brien arrives. He slashes out at the crowd, and informs those bigots and back-stabbers that Julia Garth is staying in Santa Fe. Together they will work to make the Santa Fe hospital the finest in the territory. "She's going to stay," O'Brien says, "because she's the best doctor Santa Fe ever hand."

She's also going to marry O'Brien.

The History

Here's another movie in which Billy the Kid makes only a cameo appearance. Since the legend has it that he killed twenty-one men, he's only up to nineteen when he shows up at the doctor's office in Santa Fe. That would leave him deputies Bell and Olinger to kill during his jailbreak in the spring of 1881, I guess. Not counting his mother's wedding in 1873, Billy the Kid wasn't known to hang out in Santa Fe — except for that time he spent in jail after Pat Garrett's posse captured him at Stinking Springs in December 1880.

"He is shut up in a stone cell to which even the light of day is denied admittance, and only when some of the jailers or officers enter can he be seen at all," the *Santa Fe New Mexican* reported. During his stay, he wrote letters to Governor Lew Wallace that went unanswered, and then he was sent to Mesilla to be tried for murder.[104]

Wallace was finishing his novel *Ben-Hur: A Tale of the Christ* while serving as territorial governor, so he possibly could have been "working on a great chariot race." According to Wallace's autobiography, "It was written in purple ink with fastidious care, every sentence wrought to the most perfect finish of which the author was capable."[105]

Wallace had started writing the novel in 1875, originally thinking of it as a magazine serial. *Ben-Hur* was published by Harper Brothers on November 12, 1880, selling out its initial print run before Christmas. In thirteen years, the novel had sold six hundred thousand copies. By 1911, it had reached the one million mark. Small towns were named Ben Hur. The novel inspired a popular Broadway production that opened in 1899 and toured the country for twenty-one years, not to mention motion pictures, including the 1959 version that won eleven Academy Awards.[106]

When Geronimo's "boys" interrupt Julia and O'Brien's riding, O'Brien warns Julia that they want to see her red hair: "If you want to keep it, you'd better humor him." Historically, Apache Indians did not practice scalping all of their enemies.[107] On the other hand, by 1880, Geronimo would have been confined to Arizona, Mexico, and southern New Mexico.

The "Fiesta" celebration in which "sorrows go up in flame and smoke" still goes on today with the annual burning of Zozobra each September. The United States' oldest continuously observed festival, it was first held in Santa Fe in 1712 in commemoration of Don Diego de Vargas's re-entry into the city after the Pueblo Revolt of 1680. But the burning of Zozobra, a forty-foot-tall papier mache puppet known as "Old Man Gloom," did not take place until 1926. Burning away one's troubles in the form of Zozobra was the idea of Will Shuster, a Los Cinco Pintore who helped start the Santa Fe art colony.[108]

Julia arrives in Santa Fe to be near her brother, who is stationed at a military post. Fort Marcy was established in Santa Fe when General Stephen W. Kearny arrived in 1846 during the Mexican War. The original post was abandoned in 1867, and a new fort was built north of the Palace of the Governors. In 1894, the War Department abandoned the fort, sending men and equipment to Fort Sill in present-day Oklahoma.[109]

Julia says the "fairly new" stethoscope is "not in general use yet." The stethoscope has its origins in early 1800s Paris, and was first used in 1817. Its inventor, Dr. René Laennec, contracted tuberculosis and soon died. Pierre Adolphe Piorry improved Laennec's design in 1828 and it was used until the 1850s and the debut of a new version of the device, this one a "binaural" instrument that used both ears. In 1851, a Cincinnati doctor used a commercially marketed stethoscope, and a new version, with ivory earpieces on metal tubes held together

Strange Lady in Town (1955) was Greer Garson's first film away from MGM.

by a hinge joint, was invented in New York in 1855. An 1870 American encyclopedia noted that the stethoscope was "now in general use," a decade before Dr. Julia Garth arrived in Santa Fe.[110]

Despite her vast education and healing powers, Dr. Garth sure didn't do so well at the history of medicine.

The Players

Redheaded Greer Garson had rocketed to fame with her Oscar-winning performance in *Mrs. Miniver* (1942), which drew praise from *The New York Times* and England Prime Minister Winston Churchill. At New York's Radio City Music Hall, it ran a record ten weeks (the previous mark was six weeks for 1940's *The Philadelphia Story* and *Rebecca*), bringing in just under 1.5 million viewers. Its box office total reached $8,878,000.[111]

Garson was born in London (though she often claimed Ireland) in 1904 (though she often claimed 1908). A successful stage actress in Great Britain, she got her Hollywood break when Sam Wood directed her in *Goodbye, Mr. Chips* (1939), which was filmed in Britain. Garson earned an Oscar nomination. Other hits followed, and then came *Mrs. Miniver*, a role she got when Norma Shearer turned it down because she didn't want to play the mother of an adult son. Garson also received Oscar nominations for *Blossoms in the Dust* (1941), *Madame Curie* (1943), *Mrs. Parkington* (1944), and *The Valley of Decision* (1945).[112]

By the 1950s, Garson's storybook seventeen-year career at MGM had turned bitter. On March 1, 1954, she decided to freelance. Nine days later, she signed a $10,000 deal to star in *Strange Lady in Town*, a Western being produced for Warner Bros. by Mervyn LeRoy, Garson's good friend who had directed her in *Blossoms in the Dust, Random Harvest* (1942), and *Madame Curie*.[113]

LeRoy said his main education from age fourteen was vaudeville. Over forty years, he made seventy-five movies and bragged, "I never repeated myself." His movies ranged from musicals to epics to comedies to Westerns, and he also was a producer, including *The Wizard of Oz* (1939). After starting out as wardrobe assistant, laboratory assistant, assistant cameraman and extra, he moved to writing and then directing, first at Warner Bros., where he produced hits like *Little Caesar* (1930) and *Three on a Match* (1932), then heading to MGM in 1938, where he directed *Waterloo Bridge* (1940) and *Thirty Seconds Over Tokyo* (1944). In 1955, he was back at Warner Bros. LeRoy died in 1987. He was eighty-six.[114]

Nebraska-born Buddy Fogelson had moved from wildcatter to oil man, rancher, lawyer, and philanthropist when he met Garson. Fogelson invited Garson and her mother to relax at his Forked Lightning Ranch in Pecos (northeast of Santa Fe), which he had bought in 1941. Garson fell in love with the ranch, New Mexico, and Fogelson. On July 15, 1949, she married Fogelson in a small ceremony at the Santa Fe home of Dr. Fletcher A. Catron, one of Fogelson's friends.[115]

Years later, at a dinner party in Hollywood, Garson happened to be seated next to screenwriter Frank Butler, whose credits included the Oscar-nominated *Road to Morocco* and *Wake Island* (both 1942) and the Oscar-winning *Going My Way* (1944). She told him, "I read at least a dozen books about the early days of Santa Fe and love to question very old residents who remember what it was like in the last century." Not long afterward, Butler told Garson he was working on a screenplay set in Santa Fe around 1880. "I didn't know he was also writing in a role for me," Garson recalled, "and a red-headed woman at that."[116]

Butler completed the script on April 22, 1954, but Warner boss Jack L. Warner was nervous because of a studio system that was falling apart, rising costs of production, falling revenues and the competition with television. "With the exception of a handful of pictures," Warner warned LeRoy, "in this past year there have not been many profitable ones."[117]

Warner ordered that the movie be filmed in CinemaScope and WarnerColor to lure people away from their TV sets. Garson even offered the studio the chance to shoot on location at the Forked Lightning Ranch in Pecos, but the studio decided to film at the "Old Tucson" set in Arizona.[118]

Dana Andrews got the role of Rork O'Brien. Although this native Texan had appeared in Westerns — *The Westerner* (1940), *Kit Carson* (1940), *Belle Starr* (1941) and *The Ox-Bow Incident* (1943) — he was more of an urban actor, often wooden but sometimes shining in war movies like *The Purple Heart* (1944) and *A Walk in the Sun* (1945) and noirs like *Laura* (1944) and *Where the Sidewalk Ends* (1950), and as the returning GI in William Wyler's classic *The Best Years of Our Lives* (1946). "But with some significant exceptions, Dana's pictures after 1954 lack not just good scripts but basic veracity and credible co-stars," author Carl Rollyson writes in *Hollywood Enigma: Dana Andrews*.[119]

He was also drinking heavily. In 1957, Andrews pleaded guilty to drunken driving. The next year, he was sued by producer Benedict Bogeaus and Waverly Productions, who claimed that during filming of *Enchanted Island* in Mexico, Andrews's stay was "interrupted only by infrequent and occasional periods of sobriety." By 1963, however, Andrews was president of the Screen Actors Guild, and later did a public service announcement about alcoholism. Hospitalized in Orange County for pneumonia, 83-year-old Andrews died on December 17, 1992, of congestive heart failure and pneumonia.[120]

Cameron Mitchell landed the part of David Garth after Richard Eagan, Tab Hunter and Robert Stack had been considered. A bombardier in World War II, Mitchell had made an impression on Broadway as one of Willy Loman's sons in *Death of a Salesman* in 1949. Mitchell moved to Los Angeles and signed with MGM. He worked steadily in Hollywood, later in European productions in the 1960s, and on television, where he played Buck Cannon on NBC's *The High Chaparral* (1967–1971). He died of lung cancer at age seventy-five in 1994. LeRoy liked Mitchell, and had built up his role in MGM's Clark Gable-Lana Turner vehicle *Homecoming* (1948).[121]

For the small role of Billy the Kid, LeRoy picked Nick Adams. The young actor tried to keep the mood light on the set. When filming on a Warner Bros. sound stage, Adams would answer the telephone doing impersonations of Marlon Brando, James Cagney or Cary Grant. "He was a fine boy...." LeRoy wrote of Adams. "Every nickel he made he sent to his brother, who was studying to be a doctor. As a result, Nick lived a Spartan life in Hollywood, where Spartan lives are exceedingly rare. So, whenever I could, I hired him." Adams became a star when he played Johnny Yuma in the TV Western *The Rebel* (1959–1961) and would be nominated for a supporting actor Oscar for *Twilight of Honor* (1963). In February 1968, Adams was found dead in a bedroom of his Coldwater Canyon home. He was thirty-six, and officials said he either committed suicide or died from an accidental overdose. He was being treated for nervous disorders and alcoholism. "[H]is death was a terrible shock to me," LeRoy wrote. A crowd of two thousand attended Adams's funeral as he was buried on a hillside in Briar Creek Township.[122]

The role of Spurs went to Lois Smith, a twenty-one-year-old actress who had just finished filming *East of Eden* (1955) with James Dean. Natalie Wood had tested for that part, even dying her hair brunette, but when Victor Saville saw her, he "thought she was a young Virginia Mayo," and Wood instead got the part as Mayo's character as a young girl in *The Silver Chalice* (1954).[123]

Garson arrived at Warner Bros. on August 3, 1954, for wardrobe and makeup tests. On the night of August 14, cast and crew left for Tucson for a five-week shoot.[124] It would be a grueling shoot—LeRoy called it "a mess"[125]—and almost left Garson dead.

The heat was brutal—"130 degrees in the shade," LeRoy said. Between waiting in the scorching heat and undergoing a hot-oil treatment "to keep her hair WarnerColor red" in the evenings, Garson lost seven pounds. Andrews's alcoholism made LeRoy's job harder. Then Garson became sick.[126]

"She isn't the complaining sort, so when se said she felt poorly, I knew she must have felt rotten," LeRoy recalled. Doctors were summoned, and all agreed that she needed an immediate appendectomy. Garson refused, saying, "There is an entire company depending on me."[127]

Ice bags were piled on Garson's abdomen each night. During shooting, she took pills from her Beverly Hills doctor and a Tucson clinic, and had a nurse checking her temperature after every scene. She jokingly told the media, "My body will be a battleground of opposing bacteriological forces for the next few weeks."[128]

When filming fell behind schedule, Jack Warner sent a memo to LeRoy, complaining: "Stop being a perfectionist. If you hit it right on the first take, go to the next scene.... I don't know how we are ever going to make a buck unless we make pictures at a price within reason."[129]

Garson's husband was more concerned with his wife's health than Warner's budget. He came to Tucson to return to California with her for the final weeks of shooting. But this was October, and the wardrobe remained the same—airy and comfortable in the desert, but chilly in Southern California. On October 11, Garson was rushed to a hospital after a severe attack in her home. An emergency appendectomy saved her life, but the production was shut down for twenty-seven days as the actress recovered. That took longer when she came down with the flu.[130] "For the sake of a movie," LeRoy wrote, "she literally risked her life."[131]

Meanwhile, LeRoy was feeling the pressure to finish *Strange Lady* so that he could take over directing *Mister Roberts* from John Ford. Some *Strange Lady* scenes were scrapped. Warner backed off temporarily, telling Garson not to worry, to get well: "If you do not have good health, you do not have anything."[132]

To help promote the film, Frankie Laine recorded the theme song, written by Ned Washington and Dimitri Tiomkin, and the song was playing on radio and jukeboxes when the film was previewed in February 1955 at Huntington Park. Music and dubbing snafus, which would be fixed, made Warner even more nervous. He asked Garson to go on an extensive promotional trip for its April 12, 1955, premiere in Austin, Texas, and other stops in major Texas cities. All of which worked. By the time Garson was back in Los Angeles, *Strange Lady in Town*, which had cost $3 million to film, was a commercial hit.[133]

But critically?

The *Los Angeles Times* called it a "strange picture in town," while the *New York Times* remarked, "We've got to hand it to Miss Garson that she does all these brave and noble things without showing the least discomposure, except when a little trace of personal feeling is apt. Then she delivers it dryeyed, with her jaw firm and her head thrown back. Her dresses are always crisp and stylish. Her hair is always beautifully done. She is probably the most fine and gallant woman ever to turn up in a Western film."[134]

Jack Warner called Garson's performance "magnificent," and the film got some good reviews.[135]

Garson did have one complaint about the movie: "I've always wanted to point a six-gun at someone on the screen," she said with a laugh. "And I know how! I used to shoot lots of times when I was on the stage. However, I've never aimed a revolver in a film. I guess that makes me an exception in Hollywood."[136]

After *Strange Lady in Town*, and almost dying in the process, Garson took only occasional roles. She kept her sense of humor, too. When offered a guest role on NBC's Western series *The Men from Shiloh* (previously called *The Virginian*), she is said to have asked a Universal executive: "Do I dispense booze or justice?" Told "justice," she said in disappointment, "I was already thinking of myself in spangles and tights."[137]

Asked if she missed Hollywood, Garson answered, "No. I have at long last learned to be interested in where I am."[138]

Her husband died in 1987. On April 6, 1996, Garson, who had a long history of heart ailments, died in Dallas. She was ninety-two.[139]

Analysis

"I'm still mighty noble in [*Strange Lady in Town*]—but I'm also a woman with a woman's weaknesses," Garson told reporters. "I'm not infallible—as a matter of fact I make mistakes with men and on occasions I'm downright mean."[140]

Not mean enough. Not infallible enough. And the movie sure isn't interesting enough.

Carl Rollyson is harsh on Garson's performance, calling her "the worst example of inauthenticity, doing her star turn in a Technicolor dud.... Garson does nothing to modify her movie star voice and mannerisms to suit her character. Even while working long hours as a doctor in primitive conditions, she remains fresh and always smiling."[141]

Basically, the film just sits there. Andrews is too wooden. Garson is too pure and pretty (still an MGM star, I guess, lacking that Warner Bros. grit). The plot rambles, and the script is weak.

For Billy fans, he's in early and out quickly. Lucky him.

***

Christian Science Monitor (April 18, 1955): "There is nothing strange about Greer Garson's performance in the title role of *Strange Lady in Town*.... In fact it is all too familiar. Perhaps for that reason it seems as artificial as the script's contrived succession of sentimental, humorous, and melodramatic incidents."

Last of the Desperados

(Associated Film Releasing Corp., December 1955, 71 minutes) CREDITS: Director: Sam Newfield. Producer: Sigmund Neufeld. Screenplay: Orville Hampton. CAST: James Craig (Pat Garrett); Jim Davis (John W. Poe); Barton MacLane (Mosby); Margia Dean (Sarita McGuire); Donna Martell (Paulita); Bob Steele (Charlie Bowdre); Myrna Dell (Clara); Dick Elliott (Walter "Wally" Stone); Stanley Clements (Bert McGuire); Holly Bane (Dave Rudabaugh); Ralph Brooks (Doctor); Thomas Browne Henry (Pete Maxwell); Brad Johnson (Tip McKinney); Hank Patterson (Wagon Driver); Frank Sully (Tim); Herb Vigran (Coroner).

Synopsis

One evening in Fort Sumner, Sheriff Pat Garrett arrives at Pete Maxwell's house with deputies Tip McKinney and John Poe. Acting on a tip that Billy the Kid is in the area, Garrett leaves McKinney and Poe outside ("Just in case I miss") and sneaks through the window of Maxwell's bedroom, wakes Maxwell, and begins questioning him. Maxwell is scared to cooperate. If he talks, the Kid's sure to kill him.

Down the hallway, Billy leaves the bedroom of his girlfriend, Paulita, hears voices, grabs his revolver, and enters Maxwell's bedroom. Garrett fires, and the Kid falls dead over Maxwell's body. Maxwell runs out of the house, covered with Billy's blood, and is stopped by McKinney and Poe. Upset over the death of her lover, Paulita calls Garrett a murderer. "You shot him down in the dark." She flees to the barn, where she gallops away (apparently, she can saddle a horse in record time) to the hideout of the Kid's gang.

Those bad hombres return from a train robbery and hear of the Kid's death. "Ever since the Lincoln County War we've had our own way in the territory, because of Billy," Mosby says. Half the people in the county liked him, and the others were too scared to try to stop him, and that's how Mosby, who is taking over the gang, plans to keep things. Gang member Charlie Bowdre, enraged, wants to kill Garrett himself, but Mosby says, "We get Garrett or he's gonna get us."

Margia Dean and James Craig pose in this lobby card for *Last of the Desperados* (1955).

The gang realizes that Garrett could be considered a hero for killing Billy, and that might change how easy the gang has had things. But Mosby has plans to nip that in the bud.

A coroner's inquest rules that Garrett had just cause to kill the Kid, and the judge even says, "The whole territory owes you a vote of thanks," to which Garrett replies, "I wouldn't advise you to take that vote here in Fort Sumner." Sure enough, when he's outside, a punk tries to draw on him, but John Poe steps in and disarms the would-be killer.

"You would have stood right here and let the kid gun you down, wouldn't you?"

"I don't know, John."

Back in Lincoln, the lawmen find the town engulfed by fear of the Kid's gang. Garrett tries to form a special posse to run Billy the Kid's gang out of the territory, but no one will join him except one man named Tim. Just then, the Kid's gang rides through town, firing — and killing Tim — and dumping the body of Pete Maxwell in the street.

The townspeople, especially Tim's widow, blame Garrett for this violence. In a saloon, Wallace, one of the Kid's gang members, kills George Graham (the drunk who tipped off Poe that Billy was at Pete Maxwell's). When Garrett tries to arrest Wallace, he draws, but is shot in the arm by the lawman. McKinney takes the prisoner to jail, but Bowdre and others free him. Bowdre then shoots McKinney dead, saying, "Too bad you're not Garrett."

That's about all Garrett can take. Over Poe's protests, Garrett resigns. He even tells his fiancée Clara that they must postpone the wedding. More bullets fly, which makes everything even clearer to Garrett: "If I can find someplace where we can live a decent, peaceful life, I'll send for you."

Off he goes, shaving his mustache, and wandering to Stone Center, which is "so far out of the way, even the Apaches don't bother us." No train. No bank. Not even a post office. Just a store, which Garrett buys. He goes to work under the name Jim Patrick.

With Garrett in hiding, Mosby has his men spy on Garrett's fiancée, figuring at some point he'll contact her. Sure enough, after months of peace, Garrett writes her a letter and has a wagon driver carry it to the nearest post office. The letter arrives, but Mosby's men are waiting. Bowdre has no intention of telling his boss. He wants to kill Garrett himself, so he takes off to Stone Center with Wallace.

They question two Stone Center residents, threatening to kill one if Garrett isn't brought out. Garrett sees what's happening and knows his identify has been discovered. He calls out the bad guys. Wallace is killed; Bowdre, wounded, escapes on his horse. Garrett is hit in the leg, but his dander's up, and wounded leg or not, he's going after Bowdre.

He loses Bowdre's trail, and winds up in the border town of Tascosa, walking into a saloon and fainting. He's nursed back to health by the saloon owner, Sarita McGuire. She wears an interesting bracelet, which she tells Garrett that her husband gave her instead of a wedding ring. Her husband's dead. He was killed. His name was Billy the Kid.

Oh, my. Garrett's in a jam, but he owes Sarita, so he takes a job at the saloon as bartender and gunman — at least until Sarita's brother returns — but he's wondering, "Billy, am I ever gonna get you off my back?"

Eventually, Bert McGuire returns to Tascosa. He's a punk kid, looking for a reputation, and wants to kill Pat Garrett. "With Billy dead, I'm gonna take his place."

While serving bar, Garrett sees John Poe and they share a drink and information. Lincoln wants Garrett back. The county's ready to run that gang out for once and all, but Garrett's not certain. Poe sticks the badge in Garrett's shirt pocket, telling him, "You just can't keep on running. Eventually, you'll find yourself in a corner."

"I may be in one now," Garrett says.

Bert reads a newspaper article about the Kid's death and notices the photo of Pat Garrett. He recognizes Jim Patrick as the lawman and killer of his friend, and goes gunning for him.

After being outed as Garrett, the lawman tries to talk Bert out of making a fool's play, saying that the Kid was once his friend. "Then he wasn't anybody's friend, especially his own." Bert draws, but Garrett wings him, then takes him to Sarita's where Bert tells her the truth about himself. Sarita slaps the killer of her husband, but Garrett's angry. Billy was a "mad-dog, degenerate killer," he says, and goes on to say that he must have "married a half-dozen girls in the territory, for the same reason." Garrett can't run forever, Sarita says, but by now, Garrett's finished running. He'll be waiting for Mosby and his boys right here. She rides off to Mosby's hideout. (Seems everybody knows where Mosby and the gang are hiding out but the law.)

Mosby, Bowdre, Tom (O'Folliard?) and Dave Rudabaugh take off for Tascosa, leaving Sarita alone with Paulita. Interesting, Paulita has a bracelet just like the one Billy gave Sarita. Turns out, Billy gave that to Paulita. Knowing the truth about Billy, Sarita realizes her mistake and gallops back to Tascosa.

Garrett's ready. The gang splits up, and the gunmen start hunting for the lawman. If this seems a lot like *High Noon*, just wait.

Garrett catches Tom and Bowdre in the open. Guns fire. Tom and Bowdre are killed, and then Rudabaugh and Mosby come running up. They're also caught in the open. Rudabaugh's hit, and Mosby takes cover behind the omnipresent water trough. Garrett's hiding behind a hitched wagon. They exchange shots, then Mosby fires at a lantern and startles the team, which takes off, leaving Garrett exposed. Mosby shoots Garrett in the chest, and the lawman falls. But Garrett's only playing dead. He guns down Mosby, and tries to sit up, stunned by the shot to his chest.

Barely alive, Dave Rudabaugh tries to finish off Garrett but is dispatched by Sarita, who has arrived in the nick of time to shoot Rudabaugh in the back (just like Grace Kelly kills Robert J. Wilke in *High Noon*).

Garrett rises and pulls the badge out of his shirt pocket. It stopped the bullet that would have killed him.

After all that, Garrett's ready to ride to Lincoln and resume his work as sheriff. "Billy," he says as he leaves the saloon with Poe, "I've finally got you off my back."

The History

For a B movie, *Last of the Desperados* has some accuracy in its depiction of Pat Garrett's killing of Billy the Kid. That night, Garrett arrived at Pete Maxwell's home in Fort Sumner with two deputies, John W. Poe, who had been a lawman in Texas, and Thomas McKinney. McKinney was nicknamed "Kip" instead of this movie's "Tip," but that's closer than most movies depict the killing. Leaving the two deputies outside, Garrett slipped into Maxwell's bedroom to question him.[142]

The Kid was rumored to have been visiting his sweetheart Paulita Maxwell, who might have been pregnant with the outlaw's child. "[T]his was the reason the Kid had gone to Sumner," historian Frederick Nolan says, "this was the reason he was still there." The movie's pressbook, on the other hand, says, "Although Billy the Kid is said to have had nine wives ... *Last of the Desperados* ... deals with only two of these unhappy lasses."[143]

When the Kid entered Maxwell's room, Garrett shot him dead. The gunfire sent Maxwell screaming out of the house, and Garrett had to hurry outside to stop his two deputies from accidentally shooting Maxwell. When Garrett told Poe that he thought he had killed the Kid, Poe was skeptical. "Pat, the Kid would not have come here," he said. "You've shot the wrong man."

Garrett, however, was positive. "I'm sure it was him," he said. "I know his voice too well to be mistaken."

One woman berated Garrett upon seeing Billy's body, but it wasn't Paulita. Deluvina Maxwell, a Navajo woman serving as the Maxwell servant, shot out at the killer: "You pisspot! You sonofabitch." Other young women consoled Paulita, who did not gallop off to warn Billy's gang.[144]

By that time, Charlie Bowdre had been dead for more than six months. Dave Rudabaugh was in jail in San Miguel County awaiting execution for murder, and the Kid is not known to have ridden with anyone named Mosby. In December, Rudabaugh would tunnel out of jail and escape the hangman. His fate remains a bit of a mystery. The most common version is that he wound up in Mexico, where on February 18, 1886, an angry mob in Parral chopped his head off and paraded it across the plaza. Another version, certainly not as dramatic, has him ranching in Montana before dying in Oregon in 1928.[145]

The morning after the Kid's death, Justice of the Peace Alejandro Segura asked Milnor Rudolph to convene a coroner's jury. The inquest was held in Maxwell's bedroom, where the jury ruled that not only was Garrett's act justifiable, but that "he deserves to be rewarded."[146]

All in all, that's not a bad mix of history and poetic license. Of course, *Last of the Desperados* got one major fact wrong. Billy the Kid was killed on July 14, 1881, not July 13.[147]

After that opening, of course, the movie takes a wide arc around history. There was no violent uprising against Garrett, and he didn't go into hiding. There were rumors, however, of retaliation. Garrett even met up with the Kid's brother, Joe Antrim, in Trinidad, Colorado. Antrim told the lawman that he didn't begrudge Garrett, and the two men parted. The biggest problem Garrett faced was trying to collect the reward for the Kid.[148]

Garrett certainly didn't postpone his marriage after the Kid's death. He had married Apolinaria — not Clara — Gutiérrez on January 14, 1880.[149]

On the other hand, Garrett knew how to run a store, and he had experience in saloons. He never wound up in Stone Center, New Mexico — no such town exists — but he certainly was no stranger to Tascosa, Texas. Billy the Kid frequented the town, too. Tascosa is depicted as a border town. Actually, it was located in the Texas Panhandle, near present-day Amarillo, and after its founding in 1877 rose to legend "for rustling, vice, and violent death."[150]

The Players

Prolific Sam Newfield, who had completed *eighteen* features in 1943 alone under his own name and various aliases, was still at it. Having directed PRC's Billy the Kid programmers, he was no stranger to the story, but this time Billy would be dead in minutes and the story would focus on Pat Garrett.[151] "Newfield's best films are filled with an air of unrelenting mortality and incessant menace and bear witness to the paranoia and hysteria of the McCarthy era," historian Wheeler Winston Dixon writes.[152]

His movies were still cheap. *Last of the Desperados* was shot on 16mm film (used in low-budget features to be blown up to the standard 35mm).[153]

Jim Davis was then starring in the Emmy-winning syndicated Western TV series *Stories of the Century* (1954–55). Born in Missouri in 1909, the gravelly-voiced son of an undertaker had various jobs before landing at MGM. World War II cut his acting career short, and he joined the Coast Guard. After the war, he resumed acting, and costarred with Bette Davis, at her insistence, in *Winter Meeting* (1948); Warner Bros. dropped him after that movie bombed. Soon, however, he found steady work, usually as heavies in Westerns. *Stories of the Century*, in which he played a railroad detective, upgraded Davis into some lead or second lead roles in Bs, such as *Last of the Desperados*. By the 1960s, he was again landing mostly supporting or bit roles in movies and on TV. That changed in 1978 when he played the patriarch of the Ewing family on CBS's hit series *Dallas*. While the series was at its peak in 1981, however, Davis died at age sixty-five, having recently undergone surgery on a perforated ulcer and being treated for a brain tumor.[154]

A Clark Gable lookalike, James Craig (born James Henry Meador in 1912) had been discovered by talent scout Oliver Hinsdell. Craig moved from Paramount to Columbia to Universal, getting an occasional lead in a B movie. He appeared on Broadway in 1938 in *Missouri Legend* (Elizabeth Beall Ginty's comic play about Jesse James), but it closed after forty-eight performances. (Craig would resume the role, albeit playing the El Paso Kid and not Jesse James, ten years later in the movie *The Man from Texas*.) After RKO cast him with Ginger Rogers in her Oscar-winning *Kitty Foyle* (1940), MGM signed him. He was briefly romantically linked to Joan Crawford, but was out at MGM by 1951. Although he made a number of Westerns, he's likely best remembered for his work in the film noirs *Side Street* (1949), *The Strip* (1951) and *While the City Sleeps* (1956). "He's just too killing for words," the *Los Angeles Times* said of Craig's performance in *Side Street*. Unfortunately, Craig also carried that tough-guy, bad-boy image into his personal life. Reports of spousal abuse and excessive drinking first came in the early 1950s. Over the next decade, he would marry, divorce and remarry. More claims of spousal abuse followed. In the early 1960s, wife Jane Craig said, "He's a wonderful man when he's not drinking. He needs help and he knows it." They divorced in 1964. Three years later, Jane Craig shot her eleven-year-old son to death and then committed suicide. Craig never commented publicly on the incident. By 1971, Craig's Hollywood career had slid so much he obtained a real estate license. He died of lung cancer on June 28, 1985.[155]

Craig might have garnered a bad reputation, but Donna Martell recalled that "everyone was compatible" during shooting of *Last of the Desperados*. "We had a good time."

Martell was pregnant with her first child during shooting, and her mother would drive her to the shooting location north of Hollywood from their home in East Los Angeles. One time, her mother ("a fabulous cook") made pizza and brought it for the entire cast and crew. "Everything stopped while we all had the pizza," she says.[156]

The big mystery then is:

Who played Billy the Kid?

He had no lines, and was not credited in the film or in the movie's pressbook. Nor has his name been revealed on movie databases online such as www.imdb.com or www.afi.com. Even Martell couldn't recall.

"He must have not made an impression on me," she says.[157]

Analysis

It's obvious that screenwriter Orville Hampton knew a good bit about Pat Garrett and Billy the Kid (after all, he had written 1950's *I Shot Billy the Kid*). He also knew what he was writing, not history but a screenplay for a standard, cheap Western movie. What he, or the producers, didn't know was how to spell *desperadoes*.

Last of the Desperados isn't great, but it moves at a rapid pace. The acting is inconsistent. While James Craig had a troubled off-screen life, his on-screen persona makes him easy to watch.

That's a good word to describe this one. Watchable.

Another good word? Forgettable. It won't stick with you for long, but you won't be bored watching it.

***

Variety (January 19, 1956): "Overall, release shapes as a good programmer, with story line sustaining interest and James Craig coming through with a good performance in the lead role."

The Parson and the Outlaw

(Columbia, September 1957, 74 minutes) CREDITS: Director: Oliver Drake. Executive Producer: Robert Gilbert. Producer: Charles "Buddy" Rogers. Screenplay: Oliver Drake, John Mantley. CAST: Anthony Dexter (Billy the Kid); Sonny Tufts (Jack Slade); Marie Windsor (Tonya); Charles "Buddy" Rogers (The Rev. Jericho Jones); Jean Parker (Mrs. Sarah Jones); Robert Lowery (Colonel Jefferson Morgan); Madalyn Trahey (Elly McCloud); Bob Steele (Ace Jardine); Joe Sodia (Ben); Bob Duncan (Pat Garrett); Bob Gilbert (Piute); Paul Spahn (Lieutenant Paul Nash).

Synopsis

Pat Garrett knocks on the door to the room where Billy the Kid's lying on a cot. "*Quién es?*" the Kid asks, and Garrett announces his name.

"Come on in, Pat," Billy says, and Garrett comes in, firing three times, and dropping the young outlaw to the floor.

On a rainy day, the Rev. Jericho Jones, who baptized the Kid, preaches at the Kid's funeral, and he's not kind to Garrett. "May the Lord have mercy on you, Pat Garrett," Jones says.

As soon as the crowd's gone, Billy comes out from hiding. It's not every day that a man gets to attend his own funeral. Turns out, Garrett and the Kid have concocted a plan. By faking the Kid's death, Billy is free to ride out — as long as he doesn't wear his guns. Garrett even gives the Kid a deed to his homestead way off in the territory. The Kid leaves for a new life, draping his guns over his own cross.

On the way to that spread, he happens upon a group of four hostile Indians who are about to ambush a stranger. Billy knifes two of them, and the stranger kills the other with his six-shooter. Apparently, the last Indian sneaked away while the continuity editor was asleep on the job.

Billy introduces himself as Bill Antrim. The stranger is Jack Slade, who has made a name for himself by gunning down men like Cherokee Bill and Wes Hardin. Now he's after Billy the Kid. In fact, he's been chasing Billy for two long years. He's upset to learn from

Marie Windsor and Anthony Dexter starred in *The Parson and the Outlaw* (1957).

Antrim that Pat Garrett has robbed him of that opportunity. "Now I'll never be able to prove I could beat him to the draw."

Well, Slade knows he owes Bill Antrim his life, so they decide to ride the trail together for the Four Corners area. They arrive in town just as Colonel Jefferson Morgan, the unscrupulous, corrupt land baron who founded the town and area, kills the newspaper editor in a duel. Apparently, the editor has been exposing Morgan and saying that the territory would be better off if it were annexed by Texas. The editor's daughter, Elly McCloud, vows to continue her father's fight. When Billy decides to help take care of the dead editor, Morgan's top gun, Ace Jardine, warns him off, and Slade steps in. He finds it interesting that a man not packing firearms would take a stand so early, but Billy lets him know he's not taking any sides: "I just happen to believe kinfolk have a right to their dead."

Turns out, Jack Slade and Ace Jardine have some bad history. Jardine's still carrying a slug Slade gave him, but that was because they were on opposite sides. Now both men are working for Morgan, so they ride off.

Billy learns that Morgan's men are squatting on his place — well, the spread hadn't been worked on for years — but rides out there anyway, passing the Reverend Jones and his wife. They recognize him, and Jones is torn. He should turn in Billy, but his wife says maybe God's telling him something. After all, Billy isn't wearing guns. Well, Jones decides not to squeal, and he starts preaching his gospel sermons on Sundays in a tent in town. It'll be the first time a preacher has preached in Four Corners in fifteen years.

Seven — The 1950s: The Kid Moves Forward

At Billy's new home, Jardine, Slade and other gunmen play poker while Jardine abuses his girl, Tonya. Then Billy shows up and announces that he owns this place, even has a bill of sale. He breaks a chair over Jardine's head, and Slade announces they should leave. After all, it's Billy's place, fair and legal. The gunmen walk out, but Jardine's fed up with Slade butting into his affairs. He tries to gun him down, but Slade's quicker. Ace Jardine falls dead.

"This about squares us, Bill," Slade says, and rides off with Morgan's gunmen. Tonya, naturally, decides to stick around with this Antrim fella.

The Army's coming in to protect the polls for the annexation vote, and Morgan wants this Antrim guy run out of the territory. He hands that job off to Slade. Meanwhile, Elly prints that Morgan is a murderer and pushes for annexation in *The Weekly Bugle*. Newspaper delivery man Ben is pummeled by Morgan's men.

Jericho tells Elly that this Bill Antrim is the one person who can help their cause. She rides out to see Billy, finds Tonya there, and pleads with Billy, who still won't help. She thinks it's because he doesn't want to go up against his friend Jack Slade, but Billy says, "A Man like Slade is no friend." Elly, upset, rides back to town. And Billy's not too happy with how Tonya has treated Elly, so he carts her back to town, too.

Jones pleads with Billy to take up his guns again. He has Billy's gun belt and pistols, which he says he has been using in his sermons (he took them off Billy's grave). This is Billy's chance to work for a good cause, but he won't break his word to Garrett. "I've been a disappointment to you ever since I was a little kid," he says. Besides, he's sick to death of killing and running, and this is not his fight. He set out to kill the man who killed the best friend he ever had, and earned a reputation that had all the top guns hunting him. He's not fighting any more.

Come Sunday, Billy attends the parson's sermon. So does Colonel Morgan, who is abused by Jones. Morgan signals his men to wreck the tent and the newspaper office. Lieutenant Nash is helpless to do anything about it, but he has declared martial law (and he still can't arrest Morgan and his henchmen?). Morgan isn't impressed, but when one of his killers, Piute, starts to knife the Army officer in his back, Morgan stops him. "You can't fight the Army," he says.

"My cousin, War Eagle," Piute says, "would."

Which gives Morgan an idea. "Get ahold of him. Tell him I've got plenty of guns and firewater for his braves."

When Billy rides back to his cabin, he finds it in flames, and Tonya savagely beaten by Slade. When Slade rides back, Billy tells him he didn't have to burn the place, that he had already made up his mind to leave. That infuriates Tonya, who has overheard the parson's talk and knows Antrim is indeed Billy the Kid, but she figures the real Billy the Kid must be dead. Sickened by Antrim's cowardice, she rides back to town with Slade.

War Eagle's braves ambush Lieutenant Nash's Army patrol (stock footage, of course, in this cheap production), leaving Morgan's men to hang out by the polls in town and scare off any would-be voters.

Billy rides into town, telling them that Nash and his men are dead, killed by Indians, and everyone knows who tempted the Indians onto the warpath. Especially the Reverend Jones. He shows up packing Billy's guns and gets the drop on Morgan and his men. But Slade says if the preacher plans on shooting, he should cock his weapons first. When Jones looks down, Slade kills him. Jones falls against the hitching post and dies in a crucifixion pose.

His sobbing wife then announces that those pistols were taken from Billy the Kid's grave by her husband, but that Billy was not killed by Pat Garrett, and that now Billy has come to reclaim his weapons.

Fear enters the hearts of all of Morgan's men, even Slade, and, yep, Billy is wearing his guns. He calls out Slade and kills him. Then tells Morgan to go for his guns.

Morgan tells him not to act recklessly. He got the man who killed his best friend. Besides, it's five against one. But Billy won't back down.

Morgan draws, and is killed. The other bad guys fill Billy full of holes, but are all dead when Billy mounts his horse. Tonya runs to his side, saying she wants to go with him, but Billy slumps in the saddle. Tonya leads him out of town as the final scroll tells us:

"Some say Billy the Kid died by the blazing guns of Pat Garrett, others swear the story you have just seen is true. But all agree on one account. Billy the Kid was the fastest man with a gun that ever lived."

The History

The one clergyman involved in Billy the Kid's life that we know of is Taylor Filmore Ealy. Born in 1848 in Schellsburg, Pennsylvania, Ealy was both a Presbyterian minister and a doctor who had taught school for black children at Fort Arbuckle in present-day Oklahoma. In 1877, Ealy was asked to establish a mission and school in Lincoln, New Mexico Territory, and he set off with his family and an assistant early in 1878. He didn't conduct Billy the Kid's funeral, but two days after arriving in Lincoln, he had preached the sermon at John Tunstall's funeral.[158]

Ealy also left a humorous depiction of Lincoln: "They say it is very healthy here," he wrote. "None, scarcely, die a natural death. Because they do not get an opportunity. There is too much lead in the air."[159] After Lincoln, Ealy worked as a missionary in Zuni, New Mexico, before returning home to Schellsburg, where he died in 1915.[160]

If you believe Jack Potter's account—and as Mark Lee Gardner notes, Potter "seldom felt constrained by the truth"—the man preaching over Billy's corpse was "the Sanctified Texan," Hugh Leeper. Potter visited Lincoln three years after the Kid's death, interviewed residents of Fort Sumner, and wrote[161]:

> The Sanctified Texan, who believed in predestination, preached the funeral and said that Billy's time and certainly come at last.
> They told me he made remarks about Billy, "our beloved young citizen," and read from the 14th chapter of Job—"A man that is born of woman is of few days and is full of trouble—he fleeth like a shadow and continueth not." In closing, he said, "Billy cannot come back to us, but we can go to him and will see him again up yonder, Amen."[162]

Nearly everyone living in Fort Sumner attended the Kid's funeral, but Billy's guns weren't draped over his tombstone. In fact, there was no marker until the following day, when Pete Maxwell had a wooden picket pulled from a fence, sawed in half and nailed into a cross and placed at the head of the grave.[163]

By most accounts, Jack Slade was a man to fear, but he spent most of his time in Colorado, Wyoming, and Montana. Slade was "a matchless marksman with a navy revolver," Mark Twain wrote in *Roughing It*. "[I]n fights and brawls and various ways, *had taken the lives of twenty-six human beings,* or all men lied about him!"[164]

Joseph Alfred "Jack" Slade was born in 1824 and grew up in Illinois. He served in the

Mexican War, then went to work for the Overland California and Pike's Peak Express Company. In 1859, he killed a horse thief named Jules Reni. More shootouts followed. Slade did not, however, kill Cherokee Bill (Crawford "Cherokee Bill" Goldsby was sentenced to death by Judge Isaac Parker and was hanged in 1896 in Fort Smith, Arkansas) or John Wesley Hardin (shot to death in El Paso, Texas, by John Selman in 1895). After working as division superintendent for stage lines in Julesburg and Virginia Dale, Colorado, Slade drifted to Montana in 1863. "[H]e was a quarrelsome alcoholic with a murderous temper, and the residents of Virginia City feared him." The vigilance committee asked Slade to leave town. When he didn't, they hanged him. He screamed before he was lynched, "My God! My God! Must I die like this? Oh my poor wife!" He never sided with Billy the Kid, never went gunning for the Kid, never even knew Billy the Kid because Jack Slade was dead in 1864.[165]

The Four Corners area marks the region where the borders of Utah, Arizona, New Mexico, and Colorado meet, say more than three-hundred-fifty miles from the border of the Texas Panhandle. That would make things hard for Texas to annex that much country, but it's not as crazy as you might think.

In 1841, and two more times in 1843, Texas tried to take more than half of New Mexico's territory by force. Those attempts failed. Historian Don Bullis writes: "All of this was not just a land-grab by the Texas Republic; its government was broke and it desperately needed the revenue that would be gained by taxing trade over the Santa Fe Trail."[166]

Like Jack Slade, however, that was happening long before Billy the Kid was roaming the territory.

The Players

Shot under the working titles of *The Killer and 21 Men* and *Return of the Outlaw*, *The Parson and the Outlaw* was filmed on location at Melody Ranch near Newhall, California.[167]

Anthony Dexter had a brief career because he looked like Rudolph Valentino. He even played the title role in the biopic *Valentino* (1951). He might have looked like the "Latin Lover," but he couldn't act. Bosley Crowther ripped him in his review of *Valentino*: "Anthony Dexter struts and parades as stiffly as though he were lacquered (which he actually appears to be). A resemblance to Valentino is the one valid thing he presents."[168]

In *Western Movies*, Brian Garfield wrote that, after *Valentino*, every one of Dexter's half-dozen movies was a 'comeback' but he never made it." Dexter died in 2001.[169]

Sonny Tufts wasn't much of an actor, either. Tufts had appeared in *Cat Women of the Moon* (1953) with co-star Marie Windsor, who said, "Sonny was a nice big fellow who tried to be very friendly. I don't think he ever cared much about acting, though." He had minor run-ins with the California police. He died on June 5, 1970, at age fifty-nine.[170]

A musician and orchestra leader as well as an actor, Charles "Buddy" Rogers might be best remembered as the husband of "America's Sweetheart," Mary Pickford. Pickford chose the Olathe, Kansas, native to play the leading man in *My Best Girl* (1927) after seeing him portray a young airman in the first Academy Award winner, *Wings* (1927). They were married in a small ceremony in 1937 after Pickford's divorce from Douglas Fairbanks. At age thirty-seven, Rogers joined the Navy in 1942 and he remained in the Naval Reserve until 1949. *The Parson and the Outlaw* (which he also produced) was his last film role, although he worked in radio and television. Rogers died in 1999 at age ninety-four.[171]

Marie Windsor, on the other hand, could deliver dynamic performances. A "Queen of the Bs," she played memorable tough-as-nails characters in *Force of Evil* (1948), the underrated *Hellfire* (1949), *The Narrow Margin* (1952), and *The Killing* (1956), earning *Look* magazine's best supporting actress award for the latter. But she also appeared in minor — and forgettable — fare like *The Fighting Kentuckian* (1949), *Swamp Women* (1955) and *Abbott and Costello Meet the Mummy* (1955). "I think those films added to my luster," she later told the *Los Angeles Times*. "I think people said, 'She can even do that and survive.'" Somehow, Windsor survived this terrible performance in an awful movie. Windsor died in 2000 at age eighty.[172]

Playing Ben the printer was a bonus for Joe Sodja, who had played guitar in Buddy Rogers's orchestra years earlier. When Rogers, as producer, decided on guitar music for the film score, he turned to Sodja to write it, then offered him the role in the movie.[173]

Since his run as movie star had ended, former PRC "Billy the Kid" Bob Steele had moved to supporting roles. He would continue those small jobs for the rest of his career in films like *Rio Bravo* (1959), *Requiem for a Gunfighter* (1965), *Hang 'Em High* (1968), *Rio Lobo* (1970) and *something big* [sic] (1971) as well as playing Trooper Duffy on TV's *F Troop*. His name was misspelled "Steel" in the *Parson and the Outlaw* credits but, considering how bad the movie is, maybe that was intentional. Steele died of heart failure in Burbank, California, in 1988. He was eighty-two.[174]

Analysis

In his review in *The Encyclopedia of Western Movies* (1984), Phil Hardy pointed out: "In the company of Westerns like *Forty Guns, The Tall T* and *The Tin Star* (all 1957), *The Parson and the Outlaw* looks as old-fashioned as it sounds."

Actually, it's more than just old-fashioned. It's awful.

A weak production all the way around, *The Parson and the Outlaw* is pretentious, preachy, pathetic. There's no history, and nothing memorable, and the acting is atrocious. Even considering the abysmal *Billy the Kid vs. Dracula, The Parson and the Outla*w might hold the distinction of being the worst Billy the Kid movie.

***

Variety (September 4, 1957): "They fail to put much wallop in the old west…"

The Left Handed Gun

(Warner Bros., May 1958, 101 minutes) CREDITS: Director: Arthur Penn. Producer: Fred Coe. Screenplay: Leslie Stevens. CAST: Paul Newman (Billy the Kid); Lita Milan (Celsa); John Dehner (Pat Garrett); Hurd Hatfield (Moultrie); James Congdon (Charlie Boudre); James Best (Tom Folliard); Colin Keith-Johnston (Tunstall); John Dierkes (McSween); Bob Anderson (Hill); Wally Brown (Moon); Ainslie Pryor (Joe Grant); Martin Garralaga (Saval); Denver Pyle (Ollinger); Paul Smith (Bell); Nestor Paiva (Maxwell); Jo Summers (Garrett's Wife); Robert Foulk (Sheriff Brady); Anne Barton (Mrs. Hill); Robert E. Griffin (Morton); Dan Sheridan (Bucky); Eve McVeagh (Mrs. McSween).

Synopsis

Billy the Kid is a juvenile delinquent!

Having lost his horse, Billy is walking across the New Mexico plains, carrying his saddle, when Tom Folliard finds him. Folliard's a cowhand for Mr. Tunstall, an Englishman (whose accent sounds more Scottish) and "the only rancher hardheaded enough" to drive a herd of cattle to Lincoln and break the stronghold a man named Morton has there.

Folliard and other riders, including a storekeeper named McSween, are suspicious of Billy. After all, the boy who calls himself William Bonney wears his left-handed holster in the tie-down fashion of a gunman. They think he might be working for Morton, but Mr. Tunstall has a trusting nature. "He's with us till he shows he's against us," he says.

Although taciturn and moody, Billy manages to befriend Folliard and another young cowboy, Charlie Boudre. Other, older riders aren't as trusting. Billy says he comes from Kansas City, but another man remembers him as a young boy in El Paso who stabbed a man to death for insulting his mother. Billy, who can't read (although he often lies that he can), grows to like Tunstall, who gives the Kid a Bible.

When Tunstall decides to ride into Lincoln to meet with the Army quartermaster and set a price for his cattle, Billy wants to go with him, arguing that Tunstall will need a gun to protect him from Morton's men. Tunstall, who never wears and doesn't like guns, is adamant: He won't be backed with a gun, and he rides to town unarmed.

Morton has ordered Sheriff Brady to stop Tunstall, so a posse waits in ambush. As Tunstall rides through, he is shot dead. Hearing the gunshots, Billy hurries to the scene of violence, discovers Tunstall's body, and sees the killers riding away.

He feels responsible, even has them load Tunstall's body on his horse, and they ride to Lincoln for the funeral. "I've got to do something," Billy tells McSween, who argues that

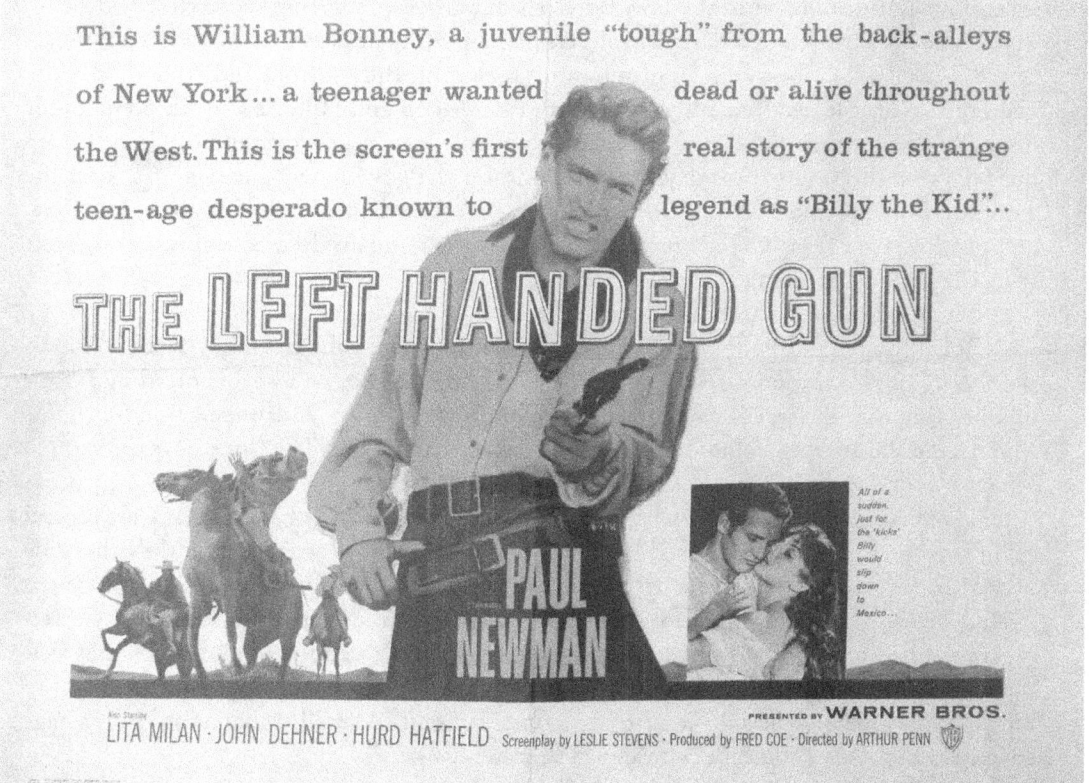

Half-sheet poster for *The Left Handed Gun* (1958).

Billy didn't even know Tunstall. "I knew him," Billy says. When McSween realizes that Billy plans to avenge Tunstall's death, he warns him that murder goes "against God."

After Tunstall's funeral, Billy's mood seems to be lifted. He's goofing around, befriending (as best as he can) a young drifter named Moultrie who becomes infatuated with the Kid. Billy even meets Pat Garrett. But when the laughing teenager heads upstairs to meet with Boudre and Folliard, he isn't that happy-go-lucky boy.

Holding four bullets, he announces his plan to kill the men who murdered Tunstall: Morton, Brady, Moon and Hill. Persuading those two cowboys to join him takes some doing. "They shot Mr. Tunstall," he says of the killers. "Nobody hangs them." Folliard soon agrees, and Billy formulates a plan.

Billy and Folliard meet Morton and Brady on the street, and when Brady draws, Billy kills both men. Folliard rides out of town, but the Kid runs to McSween's house, warning the store owner that they must get out of town because townsmen are coming for them. (Why would they come after McSween, who has been minding his own business?)

Furious, McSween lashes out at the Kid. When the lynch mob sets fire to his home, he loses all reason. Billy tries to save McSween, but the flames run through the place like it's a tinderbox. Bullets are flying. Billy is badly burned, but manages to escape. McSween dies in the inferno, and most people of Lincoln believe that the Kid died too.

Instead, the badly burned killer manages to stumble onto Folliard, and insists on being taken Saval, to a gunsmith in Madeiro. Saval's wife, Celsa, nurses Billy back to health, and Billy will eventually seduce her. Pat Garrett also lives in Madeiro, but he likes the Kid and isn't about to turn him in to the law. Boudre soon arrives, reuniting the three cowboys.

Once Billy has recovered, Army soldiers begin posting notices that Governor Lew Wallace has declared amnesty, freeing outlaws — including Billy — from indictment. Boudre and Folliard are pleased, but Billy still plans to kill Moon and Hill. As Garrett prepares for his wedding, gunman Joe Grant arrives in Madeiro. Grant's an old friend of Garrett from their days in Texas, but these days he's working for the government, keeping track on the amnesty. Billy provokes Grant into drawing on him, but the Kid has removed at least one, and possibly two, from Grant's revolver. Billy has the gunman dead to rights, but Garrett talks the Kid out of murder.

No one, however, can talk Billy out of finishing his vendetta.

Billy, Boudre and Folliard ride back to Lincoln, where Billy has a boy fetch Moon to the sheriff's office. Moon arrives, sees that he has been set up, and begins pleading for his life, begging that the war is over. Billy isn't certain what to do. A drunken Boudre shoots Moon dead, infuriating Folliard. The amnesty is now also dead. The three boys are wanted again.

That brings Hill to Madeiro, begging Garrett to take the sheriff's job, to at least protect Hill from the Kid. Garrett refuses. He's no lawman. In fact, he was once on the other side of that badge. Besides, he's getting married. On Garrett's wedding day, the three wanted killers show up, bringing gifts for both bride and groom. When Billy sees Hill, Garrett makes the Kid promise he won't kill him — not at Garrett's wedding — and the Kid agrees. Somehow, Billy holds his anger in check until he poses for a photograph, and Hill talks to him, telling him that he only wanted to arrest Tunstall. As Hill walks away, Billy's rage envelopes him. "Pat!" he calls out, and Hill draws his gun.

Lead flies. Folliard is wounded, and Hill, running away, is shot in the back and killed by Billy. That infuriates Garrett. Billy has broken his word, has ruined Garrett's wedding, frightened his new bride and all of their friends. Hill had come to him for help, but Garrett had declined. Well, that's over now. He vows to take that sheriff's job and bring in those three killers.

Back at their hideout, Folliard recovers enough to ride off. He has had his fill of an outlaw's life. When Folliard leaves, Billy, feeling bitter and betrayed, says, "That skinny dog ran off ... I don't want you."

Folliard doesn't get far. Acting against Garrett's orders, a deputy named Ollinger, who helped the lynch mob that killed McSween, blows Folliard out of the saddle with a shotgun. The posse surrounds the cabin and bombard it with bullets. One catches Boudre in his back, paralyzing him. The Kid helps him up and throws him out of the cabin, and Boudre is killed. The Kid surrenders and is taken back to Lincoln. Found guilty of murder, he is sentenced to hang.

While the Kid awaits execution, Ollinger torments his prisoner. Ollinger and a deputy named Bell guard the Kid, but on a privy break, the shackled prisoner knocks Bell to the ground and races back to the courthouse, upstairs, and breaks into the armory. He doesn't want to kill Bell, but the deputy gives him no choice.

Ollinger is another story. Most townsmen think Bell has killed the Kid, so the deputy isn't worried. From the courthouse balcony, Billy calls out, "Hey, Bob," and, with Ollinger's own shotgun, blows Ollinger out of one boot.

That turns into one of the movie's most memorable, and shockingly savage, scenes. Ollinger's bloody body lies on the dirt, with one of his boots still upright. A girl runs over, points at the boot, and laughs. Her mother slaps her.

Pauline Kael noted: "It says that even children must learn that some things that look funny are not funny. It says that only idiots would laugh at pain and death. The slap is itself funny, and yet we suck in our breath; we don't dare to laugh."[175]

Garrett's back in pursuit.

"He'd never go back to Madeiro," a deputy tells Garrett, who says, "That's where we're going."

He knows Billy, and Billy indeed returns to Madeiro, where Moultrie sees him, even shows him the dime novels being published about the Kid, not to mention photographs of the dead bodies of Boudre and Folliard. Billy lashes out against Moultrie, who cries out, "You're not like the books. You're not him. You're not him."

When Garrett arrives, it is Moultrie who sells out his former hero. "He has to be stopped," he tells Garrett.

Billy hides out in the home of Saval, but when the man realizes that the Kid has been having an affair with Celsa, his heart breaks. Celsa goes to Saval, ordering Billy to leave.

"I lost Tom," Billy says. "I lost Charlie. I can't read."

"I got myself all killed. Saval, you help me." He hands his revolver to Saval, a plead for the gunsmith to kill him, to put him out of his misery.

Instead, Celsa says, "We don't want you."

He backs out of the doorway, where Garrett is waiting, warning the Kid not to move, that he doesn't want to kill him.

"Not by him," Billy whispers. "Please, Saval."

But Saval can't, so Billy spins around, moving his left hand as if drawing his pistol.

Garrett can't see the empty holster, and kills the Kid.

"I couldn't see," he tells his wife. Distraught, he walks away from Billy's body, being led home by his new bride.

The History

Once again, Billy the Kid wasn't left-handed, but give director Arthur Penn creative license. "The only extant accredited photograph of Billy the Kid is of him standing holding a rifle," Penn said. "Either the plate was flipped — the plate is inverted — so that the rifle is in his left hand, or it wasn't and Billy was in fact left-handed. I chose to call him 'the left-handed gun.'"[176]

Well, Billy certainly wasn't illiterate. The letters he wrote to Governor Lew Wallace displayed remarkable penmanship for the era, he attended school while his mother was alive, and he reportedly loved reading dime novels.[177]

The story of a young Billy defending his mother's honor, first reported in Pat Garrett's ghostwritten 1882 biography of the Kid, is repeated, only this time the incident is moved from Silver City, where Billy did live, to El Paso, where he would have spent little, if any, time.[178]

Billy faces down Sheriff Brady and Morton on a Lincoln Street, but actually, he — and several others (not just one companion) — killed Brady and George Hindman from ambush. Billy Morton was a member of the posse that killed Tunstall, but in *The Left Handed Gun* he is played more as a composite of Lawrence G. Murphy and James Dolan, leaders of Lincoln's anti–Tunstall faction. Morton and posse member Frank Baker were murdered by several Tunstall-supporting Regulators (the Kid was likely one of them) after being captured on March 9, 1878, on a "little-used trail" in the Capitan foothills. The Brady assassination happened on April 1, 1878.[179]

In this version, the less-than-a-day siege at the McSween house begins immediately after the murder of Brady, but what became known as the "Five-Day Battle" or the "Big Killing" did not happen until mid–July. And Alexander McSween — in this movie, Mrs. McSween calls him "Ben" — was not burned to death, but shot down after fleeing the burning home. As Robert M. Utley writes: "He died on his back doorstep, lighted by the flames of his burning home." And as pointed out, actor Colin Keith-Johnston's sounds more Scottish than English in *The Left Handed Gun*. Tunstall was an Englishman; McSween was a Scot.[180]

Penn had his own interpretation of Billy the Kid: "Billy was afflicted with a sense of justice that he never saw acted upon in his society. He had an almost psychopathic sense of what was just and unjust. And he appointed himself judge, jury, and hangman for those who violated his sense of justice."[181]

The deaths of Billy's companions and his capture (at Stinking Springs) are also condensed. Folliard (or O'Folliard) was mortally wounded while riding into Fort Sumner on the snowy night of December 19, 1880. A few days later, Garrett's posse surrounded the Kid and several others (not just Charlie Bowdre) at the Stinking Springs cabin. Bowdre was shot (by rifles, not one shotgun) and staggered back inside. From inside, Billy Wilson yelled at the posse that Bowdre was dying and wanted to come out. Before he left, Billy the Kid told his dying friend, "They have murdered you, Charlie, but you can get revenge. Kill some of the sons-of-bitches before you die." Bowdre didn't. He collapsed in Garrett's arms and died.[182]

Billy the Kid did not let Joe Grant live. While examining Grant's revolver at a Fort Sumner saloon on January 10, 1880, he noticed that three of the six chambers were empty, so he rotated the cylinder so that the hammer would fall on an empty chamber. He didn't remove two bullets. When Grant drew on the Kid and fired, he heard that empty click.

Billy shot him and didn't bother checking to make sure Grant was dead. "No fear," he said. "The corpse is there, sure, ready for the undertaker."[183]

The death of Billy by Garrett is more myth, and symbolism, than fact. And, of course, most of the action takes place in Madeiro. There is no Madeiro, New Mexico; Billy was killed in Fort Sumner.

Yet for all of this, Leslie Stevens's screenplay does get some facts right. Not only was Billy popular with most Hispanics, Pat Garrett indeed married a Hispanic woman. Four days after the killing of Grant, Garrett married Apolinaria Gutiérrez at the Catholic church in Anton Chico. She might have been the sister of Juanita Gutiérrez, whom Garrett might have married in 1877, but died, possibly of a miscarriage, shortly after the wedding. Garrett also is depicted as a saloon owner in Madeiro, and, indeed, he was known to be, at the least, a bartender. And while historians remain divided on where the Kid got the revolver that killed Deputy James Bell, this version of the Kid's escape from the Lincoln County Courthouse, including the death of Deputy Robert Olinger, is fairly accurate.[184]

Finally, James Best plays Tom Folliard. Most accounts call Billy's comrade O'Folliard, but Mark Lee Gardner makes a convincing argument that the name was, indeed, Folliard in *To Hell on a Fast Horse*.[185]

The Players

According to the opening credits, Leslie Stevens's screenplay was based on a "play" by Gore Vidal. Actually, it was a teleplay for NBC's *The Philco Television Playhouse* that aired on June 24, 1955.[186]

At the time, Newman was appearing on Broadway in *The Desperate Hours* at $700 a week, and taking television gigs. Playwright Tennessee Williams had introduced Newman to Vidal, and Newman landed the lead role in Vidal's "The Death of Billy the Kid." Robert Mulligan directed the cast, which also included Muriel Berkson as Celsa Guitterrez, Michael Conrad as Charles Bowdre, Harold J. Stone—who went on to play Newman's father in *Somebody Up There Likes Me* (1956)—as Saval Guitterrez, Jason Robards as Joe Grant, and Frank Overton as Pat Garrett.[187]

Newman's reviews were better than the overall production's, and he pitched the teleplay as a movie to follow his first feature film, *The Silver Chalice* (1954). Warner Bros. balked, however, until the script was cleaned up to the studio's liking. "At least one critic complained that Vidal and Newman's Billy 'traipsed about' too much, a thinly veiled innuendo about the homosexual implications in the script, which might explain Warner Bros.' trepidation," Newman biographer Shawn Levy writes.[188]

Although panned by many critics, "The Death of Billy the Kid" was a personal favorite of Vidal. "I was aiming, no doubt inaccurately, at tragedy and I wanted a massive effect, a passionless inevitability which I believe, all things considered, the play's production achieved," Vidal said. He worked with Newman to get a screenplay for Warner Bros., and even told the *New York Times* that he was writing the screenplay, promising that this version of Billy the Kid's life would not "be like the others."[189]

Executives at Warner Bros., however, didn't care for Vidal's script. Said Newman: "They think it ought to end happily. That's like filming the life of Lincoln and having it end happily; like having his wife come in and say, 'Abe dear, I forgot the tickets for the theater tonight. We'll have to stay home." But Warner Bros. wasn't the only ones unhappy.

Fred Coe, who had produced "The Death of Billy the Kid" for *Philco Television Playhouse* and was producing the movie version, didn't like it, either.[190]

By that time, Arthur Penn had been brought on as director because "they couldn't get anyone else to direct it." (Delbert Mann was unavailable.) Penn also had reservations about the script but agreed to direct "if I could get a friend of mine, Leslie Stevens, to help write it."[191]

Penn had begun his career as an actor while an infantryman in World War II and turned to directing for television in the early 1950s, earning an Emmy nomination for directing "The Miracle Worker" for CBS's *Playhouse 90*. He had also worked with Newman, directing him as a battered prizefighter in "The Battler" for NBC's *Playwrights '56*. It was a role James Dean was to play before his death on September 30, 1955.[192]

Stevens changed Vidal's story "quite considerably" for the big screen, but Penn had a say in the script, too. Penn said that the character of Hurd Hatfield, the young man infatuated with Billy the Kid who would help spread the myth, was his idea.[193]

Being cast aside irked Vidal, who complained to Coe: "In principal, there is certainly nothing wrong with you calling in another writer and probing him with my script, but I believe you should have done me the courtesy of telling me *before* you made this arrangement than after."[194]

Newman didn't care much for Stevens's screenplay, but he didn't see the final product until two weeks before shooting started in the summer of 1957. Warner Bros. refused to pay actors to rehearse, so the cast gathered at Penn's rented house.[195]

Dell comic book movie tie-in for the Paul Newman–starring *The Left Handed Gun*.

Cast opposite of Newman was veteran character actor John Dehner. Born John Forkum in Staten Island, New York, in 1914, Dehner had been educated in Norway, France, New York, and at the University of California, and served as a radio news editor during World War II. His Hollywood career began as an animator for Walt Disney—his father was an artist—working on *Fantasia* (1940) and *Bambi* (1942). By 1944, the 6-foot-3 versatile player with a deep baritone was acting on radio and in small roles on film. In 1952, he moved to television, where he would rack up more than 160 credits. "He was a true professional," director Earl Bellamy said. "A fine actor, old reliable—he could do comedy or heavy villains." Dehner moved back and forth easily from film to television, heavy to good guy during a long career before his death in 1992.[196]

Playing Celsa was Lita Milan, born Iris Menshell in New York City in 1933. It was another Latino role, despite the fact that Milan was of Hungarian descent. Her Hollywood career lasted only a few years; in 1960 she married Rafael Leonidas "Ramfis" Trujillo, the playboy son of a Dominican Republic dictator who had been linked to actresses including Zsa Zsa Gabor and Kim Novak. The marriage ended Milan's acting career. When Molina was assassinated in 1961, Ramfis took power, but the couple soon was forced into exile and settled in Madrid, Spain. Ramfis died of pneumonia after a head-on car collision in 1969. He was forty years old. Milan still lives in Madrid.[197]

Cast as Moultrie — a Ned Buntline–type of myth-maker who wasn't only attracted to Billy the Kid for profit, but sexually — was Hurd Hatfield, a New York–born and England-trained actor best known for *The Picture of Dorian Gray* (1945), a role he never could escape. "I have been haunted by *The Picture of Dorian Gray*," he said. "New York, London, anywhere I'm making a personal appearance, people will talk about other things but they always get back to *Dorian Gray*." He must have felt more at home on stage than in front of a movie camera, but gave yet another solid, creepy performance in *The Left Handed Gun*. Hatfield died at age eighty in 1998.[198]

The Production Code Administration objected to several parts of Stevens's script, including Moultrie's relationship with Billy as being sometimes "erotic and possible effeminate." That started a "back-and-forth" that continued until the film's release.[199]

Penn was given a $400,000 budget and a 23-day shooting schedule. When he arrived at Warner Bros. on the twenty-fourth day, "my parking place bore another name."[200] All of which might have led film historian Andrew Sarris to note that *The Left Handed Gun* was "a tribute to the director's gift of improvisation."[201]

Penn also had to deal with the studio system and Warners boss Jack Warner. "*The Left Handed Gun* was made under the auspices of the old studio system," Penn said. "I ran into 'That's the way we do it' rather frequently. Having just come from television which was a medium that we made up as we went along — because nobody had ever been there before — making a film in this way was really a congested experience for me."[202]

Penn was also discouraged when he was not allowed to edit the finished product. Even the final scene was changed. "We stayed on Moultrie and then from some of the houses women came out with little candles, but they were dressed in black. And that was it," Penn recalled. "In the extant version, Garrett's wife suddenly appears and tells her husband, 'You can come home now.' It doesn't make any sense at all, but that was [a] typical Warner Bros. ending for a movie."[203]

Reviewers were not overly kind. The *New York Times* opined: "The life and times of Billy Bonney, or Billy the Kid, may have been as dull as they were yesterday in *The Left Handed Gun*, but let's hope not.[204] Which shouldn't have come as a big surprise. Even Newman found problems with the script. "There were good scenes in it, but all of a sudden there would be a visual jar, or a story jar, and you'd sort of shake your head, and it would take you ten minutes to get with it again."[205]

Jack Warner dumped the movie — "Jack Warner wouldn't know what *Cahiers du cinéma* was if it bit him in the ass," said Penn, who bought his own ticket to *The Left Handed Gun* at Loew's Eighty-sixth Street Theatre. It was the second feature of the double bill.[206]

Penn's first experience in feature films turned into a disaster, and he refused to stay in filmmaking until "he had full artistic control." Which he got when he made *The Miracle Worker* (1962). That movie earned him an Oscar nomination, and won Academy Awards for actress Anne Bancroft (as Annie Sullivan) and supporting actress Patty Duke (as Helen Keller). *The Left Handed Gun* started Penn's love-hate relationship with Hollywood (and a career the *New York Times* said "was one of violent ups and downs"). He went on to direct a number of memorable films, *Bonnie and Clyde* (1967), *Little Big Man* (1970), and *Night Moves* (1975) among them. He died in 2010 at age eighty-eight.[207]

Screenwriter Stevens would also have a long career as writer, director and producer. He died in 1998 at age seventy-four.[208]

Newman, of course, would outshine them all. He made more than sixty-five movies, earning nine Academy Award nominations and winning the Oscar for *The Color of Money* (1987). "When a role is right for him, he's peerless," Pauline Kael wrote. "Newman is most comfortable in a role when it isn't scaled heroically; even when he plays a bastard, he's not a big bastard — only a callow, selfish one, like Hud. He can play what he's not — a dumb lout. But you don't believe it when he plays someone perverse or vicious, and the older he gets and the better you know him, the less you believe it. His likableness is infectious; nobody should ever be asked not to like Paul Newman."[209]

Newman died at his Westport, Connecticut, home in 2008. He was eighty-three.[210]

Analysis

"I suppose it was inevitable once the theatrical chroniclers of the Old West discovered that cowboys and gunslingers have psyches and syndromes that they would turn their Freudian feelers loose on Billy the Kid," *Los Angeles Times* entertainment editor Cecil Smith wrote.[211]

Penn said he "toyed" with the idea of an "anti–Western" while making *The Left Handed Gun*,[212] but the movie fell somewhere between anti–Western and those teen angst films that had spread from urban settings — *Rebel Without a Cause* (1955) — to the West — *The Young Guns* (1956), *The True Story of Jesse James* (1957), *Gunman's Walk* (1958).

The movie, however, never found solid footing, and Newman's performance came across as irritating. Dehner, on the other hand, gave a solid performance. Whether the blame fell on Stevens ("Somewhere along the line that whole thing fell apart," Newman said) or the editors ("They call themselves editors," Penn said, "but they're really just studio employees. They spend their lives editing in a little toilet out back of Warner Bros. with a pair of scissors. They're a hopeless lot..."), or with Newman or Penn, *The Left Handed Gun* failed as Western or anti–Western. It failed as history, and as entertainment.[213]

But it was only Newman's seventh film, after cutting his teeth in theater and on television. Newman would have better luck in the Western genre down the road, but his acting and screen persona had improved by the time *Hud* (1963), *Hombre* (1967) and *Butch Cassidy and the Sundance Kid* (1969) came along.

***

Los Angeles Times (May 8, 1958): "*The Left Handed Gun* is hardly for juveniles, delinquent or otherwise. Adults will find its erratic, uneven course agitating when it isn't irritating. It's certainly 'different.'"

CHAPTER EIGHT

Pat Garrett Rides Alone, 1948–1958

The man who killed Billy the Kid got a few starring turns in films that didn't feature Billy the Kid.

Pat Garrett starred in *Four Faces West* (1948), *Outcasts of the Trail* (1949), and *Badman's Country* (1958). Billy has already been killed in *Four Faces West* and *Badman's Country*, whereas *Outcasts of the Trail* is set before Garrett runs across the Kid.

Four Faces West

(Enterprise Studios-United Artists, May 1948, 90 minutes) CREDITS: Director: Alfred E. Green. Producer: Harry Sherman. Screenplay: C. Graham Baker and Teddi Sherman. Adaptation: William and Milarde Brent. CAST: Joel McCrea (Ross McEwen); Frances Dee (Fay Hollister); Charles Bickford (Pat Garrett); Joseph Calleia (Monte Marquez); William Conrad (Sheriff Egan); Martin Garralaga (Florencio); Raymond Largay (Dr. Eldredge); John Parrish (Frenger); Dan White (Clint Waters); Davison Clark (Burnett); Houseley Stevenson (Anderson); George McDonald (Winston); Eva Novak (Mrs. Winston); Sam Flint (Storekeeper); Forrest Taylor (Conductor No. 2).

Synopsis

As the New Mexico town of Santa Maria is welcoming U.S. Marshal Pat Garrett, who has agreed to work in the town, young cowhand Ross McEwen rides to the local bank to ask for a loan. Outside, Garrett, "the fellow that gave Billy the Kid what was coming to him," is speaking about being backed by an unbeatable force, "law and order and justice." Inside, McEwen is pulling a revolver on the banker, Frenger, and taking $2,000.

McEwen's not a bad guy. He hands back bills when Frenger gives him too much money, even leaves an I.O.U. for the money he's taking, signing the note "Jefferson Davis." He forces Frenger to ride out of town a ways with him, then leaves him horse-less and bootless to walk back to Santa Maria while McEwen begins his escape.

Reaching Garrett's office, Frenger chastises the marshal and announces that he's putting up a $3,000 reward for the capture of the bank robber, dead or alive. Garrett warns the excited posse members that he doesn't care much for this "dead or alive" deal, that it makes men trigger-happy, and if they kill the robber, there better not be any bullets in the bandit's back.

McEwen's luck soon sours. He plans on catching a train at a water stop, but while he's caching his saddle, a rattlesnake bites him. He cuts his arm, sucks out the poison, and runs to the train, which is rapidly pulling away from the water stop. Another passenger, a Mexican named Monte Marquez who runs a saloon and gambling hall in Alamogordo, helps him aboard.

The conductor finds McEwen in the washroom, sees his injury, and sends the railroad's new nurse to assist him. Bound for the railroad hospital in Alamogordo, lovely Fay Hollister hails from the east, and doesn't see much to like about this desert Southwest, but she's soon attracted to McEwen.

Garrett isn't called "the greatest manhunter of the Southwest" for nothing. His posse members don't think the bank robber would take the train, but Garrett decides he's dealing with one smart hombre, who might do what everyone thinks he couldn't do. He sends word to the next town, and lawmen there search the train for the robber.

McEwen's smart, though. It's late at night, and most passengers are sleeping when he spots the lawmen boarding the train. He sits beside the sleeping Fay, wraps a bag in a blanket, holds a milk bottle, and pretends to be sleeping, too. To the lawmen, McEwen and Fay look like a young married couple with a newborn. Monte Marquez sees everything McEwen has done, but keeps his mouth shut.

Upon reaching Albuquerque, passengers are told that a storm has washed out the track, so they'll have to take the mail hack to Gallup or wait till the rails are fixed. McEwen, Fay, Marquez and others leave early that morning for Gallup.

The first stop is near Inscription Rock, where Fay sees the rock at El Morro and the inscrip-

Joseph Calleia and Joel McCrea starred in the non-violent *Four Faces West* (1948).

tions left by conquistadors and other travelers bound for the unknown of the desert. They carved onto the rock, "Pasó por aquí"—"He passed this way"—and their names. Back at the station, wanted posters are left with the mail hack to deliver to Gallup, and Fay begins to think Ross McEwen might be involved. Monte Marquez, of course, knows Ross is the outlaw, but he discretely cuts the rope binding the posters behind the hack and lets the wind scatter them.

Back on the train, Fay tells McEwen that she'd like to help him, and he writes a note to his father, including the money he has stolen. Fay and McEwen disembark in Alamogordo, and McEwen embraces Fay in farewell. Only he can't leave. In love with Fay, he sticks around. Monte Marquez helps him get a job at a nearby ranch.

McEwen works cattle, courts Fay, and gives some of his pay to Monte Marquez, asking him to send it to a bank in Santa Maria with a note signed Jefferson Davis. But Garrett and his deputy, Clint, are hot on McEwen's trail. When the lawmen arrive in Alamogordo, McEwen knows he must flee. He places a ring on Fay's finger and rides off. Fay follows him, and won't leave him even after McEwen tells her he robbed that bank.

Garrett's not the only one after McEwen. Bounty hunters want him, too. Eventually, Fay and McEwen separate and elude the bounty men. Fay is captured by Garrett. She can't tell the law anything. She doesn't know where McEwen's going.

McEwen rides his horse until it is played out, then ropes a longhorn steer, saddles it, and rides it across the White Sands desert. When he reaches another homestead, he plans to take another horse, only to find that the Mexican family of four there is sick, likely dying, of diphtheria.

McEwen can't leave them to die. Day and night, he works, trying a home remedy, trying everything to save this family. Finally deciding that he needs a doctor, he builds a bonfire, which Garrett and Clint see. When the lawmen arrive at the homestead, they find McEwen half-dead from exhaustion. Garrett sends Clint to Alamogordo to fetch a doctor and nurse, then he stays to help McEwen care for the family.

The doctor returns not only with the doctor and Fay, but Marquez. Turns out, Marquez knows the family. The husband-father is his uncle.

With the family recovered—thanks to McEwen—Garrett rides off. Marquez tells McEwen that he'll leave supplies for him at Inscription Rock, and McEwen rides away. Garrett's waiting for him, but the lawman isn't wearing a gun. He tells McEwen that he can handle this two ways. Ride to the train station and Garrett will see him off. Or turn himself in, and Garrett will put in a strong word for leniency, which—considering everything McEwen has done—he's sure to get.

That's enough for McEwen. He tells Garrett that he must see someone first, and Garrett lets him go. McEwen gallops to Inscription Rock, where he meets Marquez and Fay. He tells Fay that he's giving himself up, that they'll have to be separated for a while, but not for long. Then he rides back to turn himself in to Garrett.

Marquez points to the rock, saying that Ross McEwen's name should be carved here too: "Ross McEwen, *un caballero valiente,* passed this way."

"Ross McEwen," Fay says, smiling, "valiant gentleman."

The History

No year is stated in the film, but we know it's after Billy the Kid was killed and that Pat Garrett is a U.S. marshal in Santa Maria, New Mexico Territory. Only ... there is no town called Santa Maria in New Mexico, and Pat Garrett was never a United States marshal.

After Garrett killed Billy the Kid, the *Albuquerque Journal* suggested that he be appointed U.S. marshal for the territory, and the *Kansas City Journal* noted that he'd be just the man to bring in Frank and Jesse James. Instead, Garrett came out with an 1882 book, ghostwritten by Ash Upson, *The Authentic Life of Billy, the Kid, the Noted Desperado of the Southwest, Whose Deeds of Daring and Blood Made His Name a Terror in New Mexico, Arizona and Northern Mexico*. He did not run for re-election as Lincoln County sheriff but instead sought a seat in the territorial council, only to lose the election.[1]

He went into ranching, became the Southwest Livestock Detective Agency's chief, tried farming, lost in a bid to be elected Chaves County sheriff, tried an irrigation ditch project, gambled, drank, and pretty much retired until he became sheriff (first as a special deputy sheriff) of Doña Ana County, New Mexico, in 1896 to investigate the disappearance of lawyer Albert Jennings Fountain and his young son. He served until 1900. He was a deputy U.S. marshal during this time, but never the U.S. marshal.[2]

In Eugene Manlove Rhodes's short novel (or long short story, depending on what you want to call it) *Pasó Por Aquí*, Garrett is sheriff of Doña Ana County, meaning that it's set between 1896 and 1900.

Rhodes's work of fiction mentions certain locations. It opens in Alamogordo, and McEwen robs the bank in Belen (a real town, south of Albuquerque), not the fictitious Santa Maria. McEwen crosses the White Sands (part of which are now a national monument near Alamogordo) and heads to Wildy's (sometimes called Wildy) Well, where Garrett would be involved in an 1898 shootout with accused Fountain murderers Oliver Lee and James Gililland. At Wildy's Well, McEwen catches the steer to ride across the desert. And it's at Rancho Perdido — the Lost Ranch, west of Luna's Wells, and once owned by Otero County Sheriff Jim Hunter — where McEwen finds the family sick with diphtheria, and where he uses a signal fire to attract Pat Garrett and his deputy.[3]

All of which makes sense. Rhodes knew, loved and often wrote about southern New Mexico. Although he mentions Inscription Rock in *Pasó Por Aquí*, neither McEwen or Garrett ever set foot in what is now part of El Morro National Monument southeast of Gallup in western New Mexico.

The path the movie takes is a bit more convoluted. After robbing the Santa Maria bank, McEwen takes the train to Albuquerque. From there, he uses the mail hack for the two-day trip to Gallup, roughly 140 miles west. Then he takes the train to Alamogordo. Considering that Alamogordo's approximately 325 miles from Gallup but only some 200 miles from Albuquerque, that seems a long way to get there.

The Players

The movie opens with a dedication:

> Eugene Manlove Rhodes. He grew to manhood in this valley. Most of the stories which helped build his fame as a writer had their setting in southern New Mexico. One of the best known, *Pasó Por Aquí* was based on an actual occurrence at the Little Choza which his friends set aside as a monument to his memory. This is the story of Pasó Por Aquí.

"The Bard of the Tularosa," Nebraska-born Rhodes lived and worked in southern New Mexico before he began writing about it. At age thirteen, he started cowboying in 1883.

"He was known throughout southern New Mexico as a reckless bronc buster, a fanatic ball player and a fiend for poker and a fight," recalled Mrs. Tom Charles of Alamogordo in 1963. Rhodes knew Pat Garrett and Oliver Lee, and would write about the land he loved in fourteen novels and novelettes and sixty short stories, plus some poetry and essays. According to C.L. "Doc" Sonnichsen, "While they were uneven in quality, sometimes sinking pretty low, they always rose to remarkable heights when there was occasion to bring in the characters and the talk and the happenings and the landscape of southern New Mexico as it was in Gene's rarely days." *The New York Times* noted, "All the Western novels of the late Eugene Manlove Rhodes ... have a distinctive quality that sets them apart from other Westerns. He chose incidents of historical verity in New Mexico in the gone years of the cattle trade, and it has been said that his stories are so true to fact that certain revengeful characters threatened to shoot him on sight."[4]

Rhodes eventually moved to New York and California. When he died of a heart attack at his Pacific Beach, California, home in 1934, his body was returned to New Mexico. Inscribed on his tombstone at Rhodes Pass in the San Andres Mountains was the title of his best-known work, *Pasó Por Aquí*.[5]

Boston native Harry "Pop" Sherman came to Hollywood in 1913, seeking movies to show in his theater. He met D.W. Griffith and wound up advancing the director money to finish a film called *The Birth of a Nation*. Thus, Sherman became a producer. He also produced *The Light of the Western Stars* (1916), the first movie based on a Zane Grey novel, and in 1935 formed his own company and began producing the first 54 *Hopalong Cassidy* Westerns, which were distributed by Paramount. Eventually, Sherman sold the *Hopalong Cassidy* rights to Boyd.[6]

"Pop Sherman was rugged-looking, with white hair," Frances Dee recalled. "An outdoor man, an athlete — he was in those long bicycle marathons. He always liked bicycle riding — even in later years. He was charming, strong-looking, tall, and couldn't have been nicer to work with. He included everyone in on things. He was a very expansive kind of man. His personality suited his appearance."[7]

By 1941, Sherman wasn't "entirely happy" with Paramount, so when United Artists, which needed product, signed a distribution deal with Paramount, Sherman was included to produce three minor A-budget Westerns starring Richard Dix: *The Kansan* and *American Empire* (both 1942) and *Buckskin Frontier* (1943) — that would be financed by Paramount. *American Empire* and *Buckskin Frontier* lost money, but Sherman thought they were good and that his next A or higher-budget Bs would turn that trend around.[8]

The Woman of the Town (1943) starring Claire Trevor, Albert Dekker, and Barry Sullivan would get an Oscar nomination for Best Music. Sherman's 20th Century-Fox release *Buffalo Bill* (1944), with Joel McCrea and Maureen O'Hara, might have been "sentimental," "corny," and "dull," but it had great color and some fight scenes later borrowed as stock footage in other movies.[9]

In 1947, Sherman cast Joel McCrea in a gritty *noir* Western, *Ramrod*, based on a Luke Short novel. McCrea disliked the movie and director Andre De Toth. De Toth didn't like McCrea, saying, "I wanted somebody like a [Gary] Cooper or somebody with a little more guts." But the movie got good reviews, with *Time* magazine noting: "The landscape and shacks have a remoteness seldom appreciated in films." Film historians George N. Fenin and William K. Everson say *Ramrod* is "an austere, violent, suspenseful story of a range war."[10]

The next Sherman-McCrea teaming would be the exact opposite in tone.

In May 1947, production began on *Four Faces West*, which had the working title *They Passed This Way*. The movie reunited McCrea and Frances Dee in films.

A Los Angeles native who had grown up in Chicago, Dee signed with Paramount after taking a job as a movie extra. She starred in *Playboy of Paris* (1930) with Maurice Chevalier, one of the first musicals, and *An American Tragedy* (1931). In 1933, Dee starred with McCrea in *The Silver Cord*. They married that October and co-starred again in McCrea's breakout Western, Cecil B. DeMille's *Wells Fargo* (1937). They remained married until McCrea's death in 1990. Dee died of a stroke in 2004.[11]

McCrea was born in 1904 in South Pasadena, California. He wanted to be a rancher, but began doing bit and doubling jobs in movies. DeMille cast him in *The Silver Horde* (1930), after which McCrea toiled for various studios in movies such as *Barbary Coast* (1935), *These Three* (1936), and *Dead End* (1937). By the 1940s, McCrea was an A-list star, appearing for noted directors Alfred Hitchcock in *Foreign Correspondent* (1940), George Stevens in *The More the Merrier* (1943) and Preston Sturges in *Sullivan's Travels* (1941) and *The Palm Beach Story* (1942).[12]

He was making money in suspense movies and comedies, but at heart he was still a rancher. He had bought his first ranch, in California's Santa Rosa Valley, in 1932, and later bought ranches in Nevada and New Mexico. Actor James Mitchell, who appeared twice in movies with McCrea, recalled that McCrea often arrived at work in a pickup truck wearing dung-covered boots. So it should not have come as any surprise when, after his career stalled after World War II, McCrea told his wife, "If I'm gonna do claptrap, I may as well do claptrap on horseback." After 1945, McCrea pretty much stuck to Westerns.[13]

It was director Alfred A. Green, not Harry Sherman, who wanted Dee in *Four Faces West*. (Green had directed Dee in the 1942 comedy *Meet the Stewarts*.)[14] Green's directing career lasted forty years, beginning in the silents. He worked with Mary Pickford, Wallace Reid, John Barrymore, and Barbara Stanwyck, and directed George Arliss in *Disraeli* (1929) and Bette Davis in *Dangerous* (1935) to Academy Awards. Green's career was on the decline when *Four Faces West* came along. After retiring from the big screen after *Top Banana* (1954), he continued in television until his death in 1960.[15]

As far as working with her husband, Dee said, "He didn't like working with me, although I enjoyed working with him.... Joel never gave me any ideas — he thought it should be left up to the actor."[16] Sherman might not have been Dee's biggest backer, but he "was high on Joel; they loved westerns...."[17]

Much of the movie was filmed in New Mexico, specifically near Gallup, which was becoming a little Hollywood. R.E. Griffith had built a hotel in Gallup, the El Rancho Hotel, which would become sleeping quarters for Hollywood's elite and remains open today. Movies, especially Westerns, became commonplace in the area: *The Bad Man* (1941), *Pursued* (1947), *Streets of Laredo* (1949), *Colorado Territory* (1949), *Ambush* (1950), *Rocky Mountain* (1950), *Fort Massacre* (1958), *The Hallelujah Trail* (1965).[18]

For two months, *Four Faces West* was filmed between Gallup and Grants, including at El Morro National Monument and the 200-foot-tall Inscription Rock. "'Paso Por Aqui' ... — that inscription was on that rock — it's shown in the film," Dee said.[19] Sherman also sent his crew to White Sands National Monument near Alamogordo, not far from where the first atomic bomb was detonated in 1945. "This is the first time a camera crew has invaded the White Sands National Monument locally, which was strictly guarded during the war years," a press release for the movie said.[20]

Other scenes were filmed in Hollywood, across the street from Paramount at California Studios, home of Sherman's office.[21]

Charles Bickford took the role as Garrett. Originally a burlesque performer, Bickford had moved to the serious stage after World War I, making his Broadway debut in 1919. In 1929, he began in films, immediately finding work as Greta Garbo's lover in *Anna Christie* and as a heroic badman in *Hell's Heroes*, the latter based on Peter B. Kyne's popular and oft-filmed novella *The Three Godfathers*. He later played character roles, which he continued until his death in 1967.[22]

The other actor playing one of those four faces west was Joseph Calleia, born Giuseppe Maria Spurrin-Calleja in 1897. His films included *My Little Chickadee* (1940), *The Jungle Book* (1942), *Gilda* (1946), *Touch of Evil* (1958) and *The Alamo* (1960). He also collaborated on the screenplay of *The Robin Hood of Eldorado* (1936), starring Warner Baxter as California outlaw Joaquin Murrieta. In 1963, Calleia returned to his native Malta, where he died in 1975.

Author Rhodes wasn't alive to see his greatest work reach the big screen, but Sherman invited Alamogordo resident Mrs. Tom Charles, "as an oldtimer and an early-day friend of Gene and May Rhodes," to be a guest during filming in Gallup.[23]

In May 1948, *Four Faces West* opened to critical acclaim. *Time* magazine called it a "modest, attractive picture of the Southwest"; *Boys' Life* found it "a good story of a manhunt in New Mexico," and *The New York Times* raved, "*Four Faces West* emerges not only as a surprising but as an adult and edifying film." The Writers Guild of America nominated screenwriters C. Graham Baker and Teddi Sherman for its Best Written American Western award.[24]

What the movie didn't do was find much of an audience. "Kids didn't care much for *Four Faces West*—the mushy love scenes turned them off, and there wasn't much action...." Robert Nott writes.[25]

Like *Ramrod*, it failed at the box office. "Both were Westerns that William S. Hart would have endorsed, but both proved to be unsuccessful with audiences that wanted *The Outlaw* and *Duel in the Sun*," Fenin and Everson note.[26]

It proved to be Harry Sherman's last movie. He died on September 25, 1952.[27]

Analysis

Guns are drawn in *Four Faces West*, but not one shot is ever fired. No one dies. That makes the movie unique.

As *Boston Globe* writer John Riley wrote: "Most Westerns depend on a din of shooting and hordes of vengeance-seeking cowboys riding over the plains to furnish drama and suspense. But most of them fall flat because it requires more than noise and speed to make entertainment as well as art."[28]

Four Faces West shows that a Western doesn't need violence. Characters you care about, a solid story that's hard to predict, and great cinematography can make a movie. *The New York Times* noted that *Four Faces West*, "presents a familiar theme but it is a picture that is easy on the eyes and ears."

It's the perfect Western for families.

For the most part, the script faithfully follows Rhodes's novella, and the New Mexico locations are excellent. McCrea and Dee made a great team (they should have starred in more films together), Bickford is solid as always, and Calleia gets a chance to shine as a nice guy for a change.

Billy the Kid's dead long before this movie opens, and Pat Garrett is just a supporting player. Still, many film historians have suggested that the character of Ross McEwen is loosely based on Billy. If that's the case, then you can make a strong argument that *Four Faces West* is easily the best movie about Billy the Kid. Certainly, it's the best Pat Garrett movie.

***

Chicago Daily Tribune (June 29, 1948): "An extremely unconventional western, *Four Faces West* is an earnest effort but also an unfortunately obvious one."

Outcasts of the Trail

(Republic, June 1949, 60 minutes) CREDITS: Director: Philip Ford. Associate Producer: Melville Tucker. Screenplay: Olive Cooper. CAST: Monte Hale (Pat Garrett); Jeff Donnell (Lavinia "Vinnie" White); Paul Hurst (Doc Meadowlark); Roy Barcroft (Jim Judd); John Gallaudet (Tom "Ivory" White); Milton Parsons (Elias Dunkenscold); Tommy Ivo (Chad White); Minerva Urecal (Mrs. Rysen); Ted Mapes (Fred Smith); George H. Lloyd (Horace Rysen); Steve Darrell (Sheriff Wilson); Hank Patterson (Hank Ferris); Howard Mitchell (Bald-headed Man).

Synopsis

In Twin Wells, Nevada, Lavinia "Vinnie" White and her kid brother Chad are scorned by townspeople because their father, Tom "Ivory" White, is doing time for robbing $100,000.

The White kids are poor, and that has prompted Vinnie to enter a buckboard race for the $500 prize. She talks her way into the race, but Fred Smith warns her upfront: "I want that money, miss, and I'm drivin' hard to win it."

Another contestant, Pat Garrett, is kinder but she snaps at him, "I'm not shaking hands with you." She has her reasons. After all, it was Garrett's testimony that sent Vinnie's father to prison.

"There ain't no particular rules to this race," Doc Meadowlark announces, and Fred Smith meant his warning to Vinnie. He plays rough, wrecking one wagon, then forcing Vinnie, who was leading the race, off the course. That means it's up to Garrett, and he wins the race.

Kindhearted soul that he is, Garrett hands his winnings over to wheelwright Jim Judd. After all, Vinnie would have won the race had Smith not wrecked her, but he knows she'll never accept any money from Garrett. Judd agrees, and once Garrett has left, he sniggers: "Easiest $500 I ever made."

Judd then pays a visit to Ivory in the pen. Ivory has always said he did the job alone, but Jim Judd was in on it with him. He thinks he deserves his share of that $100,000, but Ivory says he might just turn the money in. Judd threatens Ivory's kids.

Meanwhile, townsman Elias Dunkenscold — who is in cahoots with Judd — learns that a man named George Davis is bringing $100,000 to town. That's tempting for Judd, and he concocts a brilliant plan. He coerces Vinnie into taking part in the holdup with him, and bribes Fred Smith to delay Pat Garrett from meeting up with the stage hauling the loot.

The plan almost works, only George Davis turns out to be Tom "Ivory" Smith, who is returning the stolen money. Ivory recognizes Vinnie, despite her masked face, and Judd is forced to kill one of the guards. By then, Garrett, who foiled Smith's attack on him, comes in shooting. Judd and Vinnie get away, and Garrett stops the runaway stagecoach.

Times are hard for the Smith family. They can't get an extension on their mortgage, and the money is still in the express office. That gives Judd another idea. He robs the money, and tries to frame Ivory. Pat and Sheriff Wilson take off after the bandits, but Judd kills Wilson, who deputizes the young stagecoach driver and sends him after the bad guys before dying.

Pat captures Fred Smith, but Judd kills him with a rifle shot before he can squeal.

There's too much circumstantial evidence pointing at Ivory for Garrett to overlook, so Ivory is arrested. But Elias, who has planted a money bag on the ranch, is discovered in the barn by Vinnie. He shoots her in the back.

Judd and Elias kidnap young Chad to keep Vinnie from talking, but Garrett and Doc find enough clues that lead them to Judd. Judd and Elias try to make a getaway in a freight wagon, carrying not only Chad but dynamite. Garrett and Doc take after the fleeing badmen.

Elias is shot dead, Garrett jumps into the wagon to fight with Judd. A gunshot ignites the hay. Garrett and Chad leap out of the wagon just before it explodes, killing Judd.

Well, that's enough for Pat Garrett. He releases Ivory and everyone's happy. The townspeople now accept the entire family, and Mrs. Rysen even informs Vinnie that she'll "go far with Sheriff Pat Garrett" as a husband.

(From left) actress Jeff Donnell, Monte Hale (as Pat Garrett) and John Gallaudet in Republic's *Outcasts of the Trail* (1949).

The History

Hailing from Oklahoma, Monte Hale gives Garrett a Southern accent, which likely fits. Garrett was born in Chambers County, Alabama, in 1850, the son of a Southern planter, and grew up on a cotton plantation in Louisiana. On the other hand, as a adult, he farmed, cowboyed, hunted buffalo, tended bar, opened a butcher shop, and might have raised hogs, and partnered in a saloon and grocery before becoming sheriff of Lincoln County. There's no documentation that he ever drove a stagecoach.[29] And while historians put Garrett in several places, primarily Texas and New Mexico, he likely never set foot in Nevada. Garrett was also nicknamed "Big Casino." The first mention of that nickname probably came in Miguel Antonio Otero, Jr.'s, 1936 book *The Real Billy the Kid*, where he says Garrett and Billy the Kid were good friends. "They were on the most intimate terms, and around Fort Sumner were generally known as 'Big Casino' and 'Little Casino.'"[30]

Garrett was nicknamed "Juan Largo" (Long John) because of his height.[31]

But "Big Casino"? Says biographer Mark Lee Gardner: "I've always been skeptical of the 'Casino' nicknames, primarily because I've never been able to verify the story with accounts from the Fort Sumner old-timers. Paco Anaya doesn't mention it, nor does anyone interviewed by Walter Noble Burns. Various interviews with Jesus Silva, Frank Lobato, and others fail to mention those nicknames. So, it's a bit of a mystery."[32]

The Players

One of the last of the singing cowboys, Monte Hale began playing guitar while in his teens, and was discovered at a World War II bond rally. He hitchhiked to California to make a screen test, got a part in *The Big Bonanza* (1944) and signed with Republic Pictures. Although he was born in Ada, Oklahoma, he later claimed to come from San Angelo, Texas, "because it sounded good," he said. Even his obituaries said he was born in San Angelo.[33]

Hale had a few bit parts before Republic cast him in the lead in *Home on the Range* (1946), and he became a favorite of teenage fans. *Home on the Range* was shot in Magnacolor—"a poor man's version of Technicolor," Hale said—and his first eight films were color features (Trucolor beginning with 1946's *Out California Way*). After that, Hale's movies, including *Outcasts of the Trail*, were filmed in black and white, usually taking eight to nine days to shoot. "When they started shooting them in black and white," Hale said, "I knew it was just about over." After his contract ran out, Hale pretty much left movies, although George Stevens cast him in *Giant* (1956) as Rock Hudson's lawyer because "he liked the way I put on my hat." He also had a bit part in *The Chase* (1966), starring Marlon Brando and Robert Redford.[34]

In October 1948, Fawcett Publications released the first *Monte Hale Western* comic book; the comics continued through June 1953, so "Monte Hale lasted longer in comic books than he did on the movie screen." Those comics also were a financial success. Six Monte Hale series were published in twenty-seven languages.[35]

Hale's Westerns featured more action and fewer musical numbers than the Gene Autry or Roy Rogers programmers, but *Definitive Country: The Ultimate Encyclopedia of Country Music and Its Performers* noted that Hale "did sing as well and in a natural, appealing, downhome style." After his run as a movie star ended, he returned to singing in clubs and appearing in guest roles on TV Westerns. He also was instrumental in founding, with friend Gene Autry, what is now the Autry National Center of the American West in Los Angeles.[36]

"Monte was a big old guy with a wonderful smile," Roy Barcroft recalled. "He was one of the few actors who was bigger than me."[37] Hale, who died in 2009 at age eighty-nine, had nice things to say of Barcroft, too: "In person, Roy Barcroft was the most likable, kindly, and soft-spoken gentleman you ever crossed trails with. But when the cameras started rolling, he was the meanest, lowdown, orneriest son-of-a-gun on the face of this earth."[38]

Barcroft, of course, was no stranger to movies about Billy the Kid (or Pat Garrett, in this case), having already been in *Alias Billy the Kid* (1942) and appearing later in *Captive of Billy the Kid* (1952) and *Billy the Kid vs. Dracula* (1966).

Barcroft signed with Republic in 1943 and stayed with the studio until it shut down in the late 1950s. Almost always, he played the heavy. "I think I like the roles best where I could be the dirtiest, meanest, [most] unkempt individual possible," he said. In fact, Fox West Coast Theaters voted him the "most popular villain of 1947."[39]

He was born Howard Harold Ravenscroft in 1902. At 15 he lied about his age, enlisted in the Army and fought and was wounded in World War I. After his discharge, he wandered about the country, reenlisted in the Army, took up acting and landed a role in the Republic serial *SOS Coast Guard* (1937); he soon found a steady career playing bad guys. Barcroft died of kidney cancer in 1969. His final film, *Monte Walsh* (1970), was released after his death.[40]

Analysis

There's no history here, but *Outcasts of the Trail* is an easy-to-watch Western. One thing that makes this little Republic programmer interesting is that the townspeople have specific jobs. Jim Judd is a wheelwright, often shown at work, and a man devoted to his craft—not just crime. Hale's also easy to like, and his Oklahoma accent suits him well as a friendly Pat Garrett.

***

Anniston (Alabama) *Star* (February 5, 1950): "Crammed with action, suspense and comedy...."

Badman's Country

(Warner Bros., August 1958, 68 minutes) CREDITS: Director: Fred F. Sears. Producer: Robert E. Kent. Screenplay: Orville H. Hampton. CAST: George Montgomery (Pat Garrett); Neville Brand (Butch Cassidy); Buster Crabbe (Wyatt Earp); Karin Booth (Lorna Farrell); Gregory Walcott (Bat Masterson); Malcom Atterbury (Buffalo Bill Cody); Russell Johnson (Sundance); Richard Devon (Harvey Logan); Morris Ankrum (Mayor Coleman); Dan Riss (Marshal McAfee); William Bryant (Roy Pardee); Fred Graham (Black Jack Ketchum).

Synopsis

Pat Garrett is on his way to Abilene, Kansas, to marry his girl, Lorna, when he's ambushed by a friend of the late Billy the Kid. The bullet instead hits Garrett's traveling companion Roy. Garrett wounds the would-be assassin.

Poor Pat. Many think of him as a "killer with a badge," and as he tells Roy: "Takes an awful lot of ridin' to lose a reputation like that."

Pat gets Roy to Abilene, where his girl's father is the town doctor. It seems that the doc has opposed the marriage of Lorna and Pat in the past, but he promises not to stand in their way this time. Poor Pa. "The West is still a wild animal to him," Lorna tells Pat.

But trouble's brewing in Abilene, and the West is about to get wilder. When that wounded outlaw gets back to his partners, the Sundance Kid fears he's ruined a plan he and Butch Cassidy have concocted to rob a train carrying $500,000. Sundance knows the layout, but he needs Cassidy's forty men to help him pull of this raid. Garrett's too much trouble, so Sundance and four other outlaws, including Harvey Logan, Black Jack Ketchum and Ben Kilpatrick, ride to Abilene to kill him.

In Abilene, the outlaws are inside the saloon or standing on the boardwalk when Marshal McAfee warns Pat. Pat orders the marshal to take care of the two men on the boardwalk with a shotgun, while he sneaks inside to get the drop on Sundance. Turns out that Buffalo Bill Cody's in the hospital after a run-in with some buffalo, and the famed scout throws in his chips with Garrett and the law.

After a shootout, Sundance, Logan and Ketchum are captured and hauled to jail, and the marshal is wounded. "Cody," Sundance warns Buffalo Bill, "this wasn't your fight. Maybe we'll pay you back sometime."

The town mayor asks Garrett to take over as marshal, but Garrett instead sends for Bat Masterson and Wyatt Earp in Dodge City. All this trouble is plaguing Pat. He tells

Lobby card for *Badman's Country* (1958).

Lorna that he wants to marry her, but his reputation and badge might cause problems. He must go to California alone first. She agrees to wait for him.

Meanwhile, Earp and Masterson spot Butch Cassidy and his horde along the trail. The lawmen hurry to Abilene, but Pat's on his way to California. Cassidy gets the drop on him, takes him to the hideout and whips him to learn where Sundance is. Naturally, Pat won't tell the bad guys anything.

Abilene's surrounded by Cassidy's gang, and the Army is off chasing Indians. That means that Abilene is wide open. They can't get the three prisoners out of town, but Earp and Masterson do manage to sneak out, find the hideout, knock out two sentries, and run off the horses. Cassidy and the outlaws, thinking a mountain lion (in Kansas?) must have scared the horses, leave the cabin to find their mounts (but they don't seem to notice two guards are missing). That gives the Dodge City lawmen time to free Garrett and escape back to Abilene.

Pat, who has heard Cassidy mentioning that $500,000, makes the mayor reveal the truth. Cattlemen are bringing their herds to Abilene, and the money is being shipped from Kansas City by train.

About this time, Cassidy and his hoods enter a telegraph relay station and kill the telegrapher. One of the men is left there to work the telegraph and relay any news to Cassidy. Bad idea. The Abilene telegrapher mentions that the relay telegrapher must be having a bad day the way he's striking the key, and that arouses Pat's suspicion. He deduces that Cassidy's men are controlling the relay station, and decides to lure the outlaws into a trap by saying that the money is already in Abilene.

And get the town shot up? Abilene's mayor won't stand for that, and encourages the town citizens not to help the lawmen.

Pat's adamant. He orders the telegrapher to send the false message.

Well, the mayor has other plans. He orders the three jailed outlaws to be freed, making them promise to tell Cassidy that the money's not in town. "You're all right, mayor," Sundance says when he's freed. "You should be workin' for us."

All of this gets Doc Parnell's goat. He tells his daughter what's going on, and she tells Pat. The good guys meet the bad guys on the street. Lead flies. Ketchum, Logan, and Sundance are killed.

That has everyone in town rethinking their actions. They mayor is discredited, and all of the townsmen agree to help stop the Cassidy gang. Even Doc Farrell picks up a gun. "I don't know about this type of thing, Pat," he says, "but I have to help."

Cassidy and his men ride into town, and the trap is sprung. Most of his men are killed, and Pat captures Cassidy when he tries to get away.

After that, Garrett and Lorna take off on their honeymoon and to start a new life together. She has told her dad that "the three of them would be very happy." Cody knows what that means: Pat, Lorna, and Pat's badge.

The History

"Hampton's script treats history in a cavalier fashion," film historian Phil Hardy writes.[41]
No kidding.

Pat Garrett's wife was named Apolinaria, but she wasn't from Abilene, nor was her father a doctor. Instead, she was "a very refined lady, the daughter of a well-known New

Mexico freighter." Garrett might have first married Apolinaria's sister Juanita, who is said to have died within weeks or months of their marriage. Juanita wasn't from Abilene, either. In fact, it's highly doubtful that Garrett ever set foot in Abilene or California. Not only that, Abilene was finished as a cattle town a decade before Billy the Kid was killed.[42]

Which brings us to the other legendary Western heroes who show up in this movie.

In *Western Films*, Brian Garfield points out: "Now just for the record, when Cassidy was in his heyday, Garrett was dead, Buffalo Bill was touring his Wild West Show, Earp was prospecting in Alaska and Bat Masterson was newspapering in New York."[43]

That's not quite accurate since Garrett wasn't killed until 1908 — seven years after Cassidy's reported death in Bolivia — and Masterson didn't settle in New York City until 1902. But it's close.[44]

Wyatt Earp? Well, Earp did wear a star in Kansas, but not until the cattle trade had moved west and away from Abilene. He worked as a lawman in Wichita and Dodge City before earning his place in Western history after a 27-second gunfight near the O.K. Corral in Tombstone, Arizona Territory.[45]

Bat Masterson? He was a lawman in Kansas, too — even served as Ford County sheriff — as well as marshal in Trinidad, Colorado. There's no evidence that Masterson ever met Garrett, either, but at least there was a connection. In Kansas, Masterson approached stagecoach and train robber Dave Rudabaugh, offering him a deal that if he snitched on his associates, he could go free. Rudabaugh accepted. "It was this act that brought Rudabaugh to Las Vegas, New Mexico, hoping that he had outrun any vengeful comrades from Kansas. Eventually he joined up with Billy the Kid...." Rudabaugh was among the outlaws captured with Billy the Kid by Garrett at Stinking Springs in December 1880.[46]

Buffalo Bill Cody? Well, he lived in Kansas as a young boy, and even knew Wild Bill Hickok — who had served as a lawman in Abilene — but by the 1880s, Cody was either acting in melodramas on stage, working on his ranch in Nebraska, or busy with his Wild West shows. Understandably, he would have been much too busy to go tracking down Butch Cassidy.[47] Especially considering that Butch Cassidy was fifteen years old when Billy the Kid was killed: He was born Robert LeRoy Parker on April 13, 1866, in Beaver, Utah. Cassidy's first major crime was probably the robbery of a Telluride, Colorado, bank on June 24, 1889. Cassidy and the Hole in the Wall Gang were associated with robberies in Wyoming, Utah, Idaho, Colorado and Nevada — not Kansas.[48]

Most Western fans know that Harvey "Sundance Kid" Longabaugh rode with Butch Cassidy. And Ben "Tall Texan" Kilpatrick and Harvey "Kid Curry" Logan were also members of Cassidy's Wild Bunch. On March 12, 1912, Kilpatrick and an accomplice were killed trying to rob a train in West Texas. Harvey Logan is believed to have committed suicide after a June 7, 1904, train robbery at Parachute, Colorado, and Longabaugh might have died with Cassidy in a shootout with Bolivian soldiers in 1901. "[T]he problem of documenting the final fates of Harvey Logan and Harry Longabaugh continues to fascinate historians of the western frontier," historian Larry Pointer writes. "Perhaps even the answers to these puzzles will be located someday." But no one thinks that they died in a shootout with Pat Garrett and company in Abilene, Kansas.[49]

Thomas Edward "Black Jack" Ketchum most certainly didn't die there. He had his own train-robbing gang, and didn't work with Cassidy. While attempting to rob a New Mexico train on August 16, 1899, he was wounded by a shotgun blast fired by the conductor, captured, had his right arm amputated, convicted and sentenced to hang. Instead of being gunned down in Abilene, Ketchum's end was much more grisly. On April 26, 1901, his execution in Clovis, New Mexico, was so badly botched that he was decapitated.[50]

The Players

Warner Bros. distributed this cheapie, but it was produced by Peerless Productions. The movie's working title was *Gun Trap at Abilene*, and original reports cited Vogue Pictures as the production company. Veteran producer Edward Small, whose career started during the silent era in the late 1920s and continued until the 1970s, owned Vogue as well as Peerless, so he probably released the film under the latter label, although Robert E. Kent was credited as producer.[51]

Hired as director was Fred F. Sears, "King of the B Movie," who "was no great shakes with actors to begin with, but the action in his films came fast and furious." His biggest successes came with the crime story *Chicago Syndicate* (1955), the science fiction *Earth vs. the Flying Saucers* (1956) and the rock 'n' roller *Rock Around the Clock* (1956), but after that his films became, even by B standards, poor. He suffered a fatal heart attack at age forty-four in 1957, and his last five films — including *Badman's Country*— were released after his death.[52]

George Montgomery was a Westerner, born George Montgomery Letz in Montana on August 29, 1916. He dreamed of becoming an actor after watching a Harry Carey movie in 1922, and took off for Hollywood as a teenager. He landed a job as an extra and then stunt man in MGM's *Conquest* (1937), starring Greta Garbo and Charles Boyer. After some odd jobs — carpenter, "French dip and soft drink slinger," tree pruner — he wound up in B-Westerns. In 1938, he made a screen test at 20th Century–Fox. As Montgomery's hands "flopped about like a couple of sides of beef, the cameraman exclaimed, 'Christ! Where'd you get those meat hooks?' 'Pulling tits!' Montgomery answered, and demonstrated milking before the camera. When Darryl F. Zanuck saw that test, he said: 'Sign him. He's got personality.'" At Zanuck's suggestion, the young actor dropped his last name, and George Montgomery was born.[53]

He starred with actresses Ginger Rogers (*Roxie Hart*), Gene Tierney (*China Girl*), and Maureen O'Hara (*Ten Gentlemen from West Point*), all in 1942, and Betty Grable (*Coney Island*) in 1943, then served three years in the U.S. Army Air Corps during World War II. Back in Hollywood, Montgomery earned accolades as Philip Marlowe in *The Brasher Doubloon* (1947, based on Raymond Chandler's novel *The High Window*), but by the 1950s he was appearing in a string of low-budget Westerns: *Davy Crockett, Indian Scout* (1950), *Dakota Lil* (1950), *The Texas Rangers* (1951), *Jack McCall, Desperado* (1953), *Masterson of Kansas* (1955), and *Last of the Badmen* (1957), just to name a few.[54]

"I was making six to eight films a year," Montgomery recalled, "earning $15,000 to $25,000 a week. However, the filming lasted only two or three weeks at most."[55]

In 1955, he appeared in a *General Electric True Theater* production for TV, "The Return of Gentleman Jim," and got offered roles in TV Westerns, turning down *Wagon Train* and *Gunsmoke* ("How wrong can one be?" he said of declining *Gunsmoke*) but accepting the starring role in *Cimarron City*. He hated the relentless schedule of series television, and conceded that the late-night cast parties of then-wife Dinah Shore "didn't help my memory" when it came to his lines. He left after twenty-six episodes.[56] So along came roles in films like *Badman's Country*. He and Shore separated in 1961 and divorced two years later.

"Perhaps it is telling that once Mr. Montgomery began producing and directing his own films in the 1960s, he never once cast himself as a cowboy," Rick Lyman wrote in the *New York Times*. "Instead, he enjoyed setting the films, often World War II adventures, in exotic locations in Africa and Asia."[57]

He also found success in other avenues: building eleven homes, making handmade wooden furniture and turning to sculpture in the 1970s. He became a serious collector of Western art, while his own artwork found homes in galleries and museums. Montgomery died of heart failure on December 12, 2000. He was eighty-four.[58]

Buster Crabbe's career had also lagged since his days playing Flash Gordon, Buck Rogers and Billy the Kid. He found himself touring with an aquacade and starred in the TV series *Captain Gallant of the French Foreign Legion* 1955–57 with his son Cullen "Cuffy" Crabbe. After *Badman's Country*, Crabbe appeared in only three other released films, all Westerns. One of his last roles was as an aging astronaut on NBC's *Buck Rogers in the 25th Century* in 1979. Crabbe ran a boys' summer camp near Saranac Lake, New York, joined a New York stock firm, made the rounds on TV talk shows, wrote a fitness book (*Energetics*), was active in planning for the 1984 Olympic Games in Los Angeles, and was swimming two miles a day at age seventy-two. He died of a heart attack at his home on April 23, 1983, at age seventy-five.[59]

The only other actor of note in *Badman's Country* was Neville Brand, a veteran character actor whose "cruel but intelligent face made him one of Hollywood's leading heavies." Born in 1921, Brand was the fourth-most decorated serviceman in World War II. His first try at acting came in an Army Signal Corps film in 1946 alongside another wannabe actor, Charlton Heston. He studied drama in New York on the G.I. Bill and made his film debut in *D.O.A.* (1949). He won the Sylvania Award for playing Willie Stark in *All the King's Men* on television in 1958 and had memorable roles in *Kansas City Confidential* (1952), *Stalag 17* (1953), *Riot in Cell Block 11* (1954), *The Tin Star* (1957), *Birdman of Alcatraz* (1962) and *Cahill, U.S. Marshal* (1973). He might be best remembered for a starring turn in a TV Western, *Laredo* (1965–67), and for playing Al Capone in *The George Raft Story* (1961) and on the popular TV series *The Untouchables* (1959–1961). Brand died of emphysema in 1992 at age seventy-one.[60]

Analysis

Billy the Kid was probably glad he didn't appear in this one. The plot was ridiculous, the history even worse. Combine those factors with low-budget Peerless Productions and washed-up actors and you get a dismal, trite, forgettable B.

***

Film Daily (May 23, 1958): "A slam-bang climax...."

CHAPTER NINE

The 1960s: The Decline of Billy the Kid

After regularly riding the range during the 1940s and 1950s, Billy the Kid began slipping out of the limelight in the turbulent 1960s.

He appeared in only four American releases, and that's only if you include *A Bullet for Billy the Kid* (1963), in which producer Jerry Warren inserted footage into a Mexican film (covered in the appendix). Otherwise, Billy showed up in one cheap independent production, a Three Stooges comedy, and battled Dracula.

Deadwood '76

(Fairway Films, June 1965, 97 minutes) CREDITS: Director: James Landis. Producer: Nicholas Merriwether (pseudonym for Arch Hall Sr.). Screenplay: Arch Hall, Jr., William Watters (pseudonym for Arch Hall Sr.). CAST: Arch Hall, Jr. (Billy May); Jack Lester (Tennessee Thompson); Melissa Morgan (Poker Kate); William Watters (Boone May); Robert Dix (Wild Bill Hickok); LaDonna Cottier (Little Bird); Richard S. Cowl (Preacher Smith); David Reed (Fancy Poggin); Rex Marlow (Sam Bass); Gordon Schwenk (Spotted Snake); John Bryant (Hubert Steadman); Barbara Moore (Montana); Ray Zachary (Spec Greer); William Willingham (Deputy Harding); Hal Bizzy (Curt Aiken); Read Morgan (Ben Hayes); Joan Howard (Mrs. Steadman); John Cardos (Hawk Russell); Jack Little (Bear Creek); Bobby Means (Indian); Harvey B. Dunn (Bartender).

Synopsis

In 1876, a group of Lakota Indians stop a wagon being driven across the Badlands by a trader named Tennessee. He's bringing cats to sell in the mining town of Deadwood, Dakota Territory. Before the Indians can kill Tennessee, a two-pistol-lacking drifter named Billy May stops them. Tennessee wants to kill the Indians, but Billy lets them go. The two white men decide to travel together to Deadwood.

Deadwood is a lawless town. The deputy sheriff is incompetent, and shootings occur daily, much to the regret of Preacher Smith, who hopes to build a church in town. Wild Bill Hickok's coming to town, and rumor has it that so is Billy the Kid. And that's gonna be a shootout to remember. Bets are already being taken.

When Billy May guns down two of Sam Bass's boys who tried to steal one of Tennessee's cats, naturally he's mistaken for Billy the Kid. He lets them think that. To his way of thinking, it'll be safer that way.

A fifteen-year-old kid named Hubert Steadman is looking to make a name for himself. He decides if he kills Billy the Kid, he'll be known as the Badlands Kid, fastest gun in the West.

The deputy sells a claim he thinks worthless to Tennessee, and he and his partner light out for the *Paha Sapa*. "It's Injun country," Fancy says. "Prospectors don't last long there."

Well, Billy and Tennessee head out there anyway, and Billy tells his story. Like Tennessee, he served in the Confederate Army, but when he got home, he found the farm in ashes. "Ma never recovered. Pa never came back. Heard he was killed up at Shiloh. So I just took off and headed west. Kept on the move."

Fancy was right. Those Black Hills are full of Indians, and they capture Billy. A brave spares his life and he is taken back to the Lakota encampment. What luck. Turns out that the chief, Spotted Snake, is one of the Indians that Billy wouldn't let Tennessee kill, so Billy is protected in camp. Soon he and Spotted Snake's daughter, Little Bird, are making eyes at one another.

And then, who should Billy find in camp but his dad, who isn't about to forget what the Yankees did to his home. "No Yankee took my sword and they never will."

His plan is to turn the Lakota into a new army (borrowing a plot device used in 1964's *Rio Conchos*) wipe out Custer's command, force a treaty and turn the *Paha Sapa* into the new Confederacy. All Billy wants to do is go back to Deadwood and find gold. "Deadwood!" his father yells. "When I go to Deadwood, I'll take an army and burn it to the ground."

Still from *Deadwood '76* with Arch Hall, Jr., cast as a gunfighter mistaken for Billy the Kid.

Billy suggests his pa might be a little mad. "I am a madman," Boone May admits. "I got good cause to be."

Boone tries to get his son to join his cause, but Billy wants none of that. All he wants is to find enough gold to get him back to Georgia so that he can live in peace. That suits Spotted Snake: "Peace. All men should think peace." The chief sends him back to his claim with his blessing.

But when Billy gets there, he finds Tennessee gone. Then Little Bird shows up, saying she'll stay, but Billy won't let her. He sends her away, and at a river, two more of Sam Bass's boys find her and rape her.

When Billy discovers her, he takes her to a Deadwood doctor and goes looking for the dirty dogs that did it. One should be easily recognized because Little Bird scratched him deep.

He finds Tennessee in the saloon, collecting a check for $40,000 from a miner. Tennessee is telling everyone that Billy May isn't the real Billy the Kid, but that's not what Fancy and Poker Kate want to hear. Especially after Billy finds that raping scoundrel in Poker Kate's place, and kills him in cold blood. Then he kills the guy's accomplice (well, the latter did have a gun). Billy has now killed four of Sam Bass's boys.

Wild Bill finally arrives. He has no quarrel with Billy, but doesn't know the Kid on sight, so he can't take any chances.

Well, the next morning, Hickok's waiting, and Billy May walks down the streets. More bets. It's gonna be a showdown.

Only it isn't. Billy tells Hickok that he isn't the Kid, that he's not gunning for him, says his name is Billy May. That's enough for Hickok, who realizes Poker Kate and Fancy were just trying to get him to kill Billy so they could clean up on wagers. Hickok walks away.

Turns out, he knows Boone May. Used to hunt buffalo with him. His pa "used to be proud of you, Billy," Hickok tells the young gunman. "Keep it that way." And Wild Bill rides off.

Billy's leaving, too, but Hubert Steadman tries to gun him down, forcing Billy to kill him. Which is about when Sam Bass arrives in town. Deadwood hasn't had a hanging in quite a while, so Bass leads a mob to string up Billy May.

Billy sends Tennessee and Little Bird away, and they take off for the Indian camp. Meanwhile, Billy tries to escape. Bullets fly in an exciting shootout that runs from building to building, through a corral, and ends when a Deadwood citizen catches Billy with his shotgun. Let the lynching begin.

But not so fast. The Indians, led by Boone May, have found Tennessee and Little Bird, and they're riding to the rescue.

Plus Preacher Smith tries to stop the hanging, despite Sam Bass's instructions that if he doesn't get out of the way, he'll be dead, too.

Cut to rescue party.

Cut to lynch mob and Preacher Smith reciting Psalms.

Boone May and the Lakota arrive, but it's too late. Billy May is hanging from a limb, and Preacher Smith is dead. They load Billy's body in the back of Tennessee's wagon, and leave Deadwood Gulch.

Spotted Snake tells Boone May, "Son of Great White Leader will always live with us in *Paha Sapa.*"

The History

Among the Indians mentioned are Big Foot, Gall, and Little Crow, and all three were real people. Big Foot, of the Minneconjou Lakota, was killed in the Wounded Knee massacre in South Dakota in 1890. Gall, a Hunkpapa warrior, fought white forces at Killdeer Mountain in 1864 and the Little Big Horn in 1876, and became the first major Indian participant in the latter fight to tell the Indian side of the story. Little Crow, Mdewakanton Dakota leader, became "a symbol of Indian resistance" during the Dakota War of 1862 in Minnesota, "one of the bloodiest Indian wars in history," and was killed in 1863.[1]

And when Boone singles out Red Cloud while boasting that the Lakota have better generals than any white men, he certainly has the backing of some historians. In the late 1860s, Red Cloud's name "commanded instant recognition and respect from both whites and Indians," biographer Robert W. Larson writes of the Oglala Lakota leader.[2]

In the Black Hills of Dakota Territory, Deadwood was a boomtown in 1876, thanks to the discovery of gold in 1874. Some twenty-five thousand white settlers populated the town by 1876, including Wild Bill Hickok. It was located on the Great Sioux Indian Reservation as designated by the Laramie Treaty of 1868, making Deadwood an illegal settlement. The Black Hills, which the Lakota did call *Paha Sapa*, were sacred to the Indians, and the breaking of the treaty helped lead to the 1876 Indian war and the Battle of the Little Big Horn. Hickok left Cheyenne, Wyoming, for Deadwood in June 1876. On August 2, he was shot and killed by Jack McCall at the No. 10 Saloon. A miners' court acquitted McCall, but the federal court proved a bit more legal, and McCall wound up hanging for the murder of a Western legend.[3]

Preacher Smith was there in 1876, too. Methodist minister Henry (or Hiram) Weston Smith began preaching from atop a packing crate. When not preaching, he worked in a sawmill or on the Pioneer ditch. That August, while on his way to deliver a sermon at Crook City, Smith was killed by Indians.[4]

Texan Sam Bass also made it to Deadwood, but not until 1877, when he was rumored to have taken part in a series of stagecoach robberies. In September 1877, Bass took part in the robbery of a Union Pacific train in Nebraska. A year later, he was mortally wounded in a bank robbery attempt in Round Rock, Texas, dying on his twenty-seventh birthday on July 21, 1878.[5]

Billy the Kid, on the other hand, never made it as far north as South Dakota, and there are no reports of a Billy look-alike being lynched in 1876.

The Players

"One of those shoestring independents," Fairway Films was formed by Arch Hall Sr., a South Dakota cowboy who had played bad guys in B Westerns during the 1930s and 1940s. In 1959, Hall turned to producing films with *The Choppers*, casting his fifteen-year-old son, Arch Jr., to play the leader of a car-stripping gang. His companies, Rushmore Productions and Fairway Films, turned out exploitative movies with an eye toward teenagers at drive-ins—movies like *Wild Guitar* (1962) and *The Sadist* (1963).[6]

Hall decided he wanted to do a Western, an ambitious movie, and he wanted to do it back home, so *Deadwood '76* was sort of a homecoming. He was raised in the Quinn-Philip area. Director James Landis was born in Rapid City.[7]

Arch Hall, Jr., had little interest in becoming an actor. Born in 1943 in Van Nuys,

California, while his father was serving in the Army Air Corps, the younger Hall had moved around often across Southern California as a kid, and Hall had far more interest in pursuing a "slender young Native American girl" than following James Dean's path. He was attending Coachella Valley Union High School when his dad cast him in *Eegah* in the summer of 1961. Not long later, *Deadwood '76* came about.[8]

More than seventy percent of the movie was shot in South Dakota's Black Hills, Badlands and Custer State Park. The film also included shooting at Devils Tower, just across the border in Wyoming. Hall Sr. also took advantage of local talent. LaDonna Cottier was a South Dakota Lakota. Other local cast members included Gordon Schwenk, of the Pennington County probation office, and Bobby Means, the brother of Indian activist Russell Means. Instead of hiring "done-over whitemen" to play Indians, the production used Indians, most of whom came from the Pine Ridge reservation.[9]

Filming wasn't easy. The weather proved uncooperative. Cloudy skies delayed exterior shooting, so the crew took advantage and shot some interiors at Madison's Boots & Spurs Ranch near Rapid City instead of shooting on a Hollywood set as originally planned. Then it got really hot. The temperature reached 103 degrees — hottest in the nation for that day — and Sharon Hall, wife of Arch Hall, Jr., fainted and was rushed more than forty miles from Interior to a Kadoka doctor and then taken to Rapid City, where she was hospitalized.[10]

On the same day, an eighty-seven-year-old Indian and the teenage son of actor Jack Lester fell victim to the heat. Others in the cast wobbled." Hall Jr. hurt his leg during a fight scene. One horseback rider broke a collarbone; another was knocked unconscious.[11] Other near-misses happened. Arch Hall, Jr., recalled:

> My dad said, "You know, Arch, this is not *real* safe to do, it *is* sort of ... like ... dangerous ... but if you would like to ride your horse through that herd of buffalo over there, we'd like to shoot that. How do you feel about that?" Buffalo are very unpredictable and they can take a horse down in just a matter of a second. But I said, "... Sure. I'll try it," and I went over and did it. There was nobody around — if one or two of the buffalo *had* made an aggressive move towards me, there were no cowboys or wranglers or anybody who could have dispersed 'em. The horse was real scared — horses don't really feel right around buffalo either. Horses, I think, have an innate fear of the buffalo. You could feel it, the horse was getting really skittish and real nervous.[12]

Another scene, a knife fight with Bobby Means, left Hall with "the scars to prove it. There was a rubber knife used when we jumped on the ground, but on the ground when the camera was close-up, only a real knife would pass.... I got cut up pretty bad. He was a little over-aggressive."[13] The worst part about that deal? "[I]t doesn't even look that spectacular as a fight scene!" Hall said.[14]

Robert Dix took the role as Wild Bill Hickok because his father, Richard Dix had played Hickok in 1941's *Badlands of Dakota*. Robert even got the same wardrobe his father, who died in 1949, had worn in that movie. "The labels were still in the vest and the coat and all that," Dix said. "So I had a little private trip down Memory Lane by being able to wear Dad's very same costume."[15]

Hall Sr., of course, loved what he was doing, and Fairway Films helped "push-start" behind-the-camera crew members. "The pictures weren't blinding successes," Hall Jr. recalled, "but [Hall Sr.] still was totally involved and had the great times and had a great nucleus of people around him.... There was a genuine feeling of camaraderie at Fairway Films and my dad just loved being in the center of all the action." Some of them, as we have learned, went on to great things, some of them maybe petered out along the way."[16]

Case in point: Vilmos Zsigmond (credited on *Deadwood '76* as William Zsigmond) organized a camera club for factory workers in his native Hungary, and was sent to the Academy of Theatre and Film Art in Budapest to study cinematography. After he and a classmate filmed a battle between Budapest citizens and Russian troops and tanks, he fled to Austria in November 1956, processed the film, sold it to a producer, and fled to the United States as a political refugee in March 1957. Eventually he moved to Los Angeles and went to work on documentaries, commercials, and mostly forgettable low-budget features like *Deadwood '76*. Then Peter Fonda hired him for *The Hired Hand* (1971). "I got the idea of how to light *The Hired Hand* from the villages in Hungary where there was no electricity and they used kerosene lamps," Zsigmond later recalled. "Creating the mood is more important than making everything look beautiful." That same year, he was director of photography for Robert Altman's *McCabe and Mrs. Miller*. He'd go on to film *Deliverance* (1972), *Close Encounters of the Third Kind* (1977) and *The Deer Hunter* (1978), winning an Oscar for *Close Encounters* and picking up nominations three more times. He remains in demand today.[17]

Deadwood '76 opened to a "packed house" in Rapid City. Hall Jr. and co-star David Reed were on hand, as was LaDonna Cottier. War Eagle Dancers, a local group, danced and sang at the world premiere. But nationwide, the film flopped. "*Deadwood '76* was Fairway's biggest mistake," Hall Jr. said. "A tragic miscalculation. I think at that point my dad should have stayed in the genre of exploitation and not tried to go too 'legit.'"[18]

Deadwood '76 brought an end to Hall Sr.'s Fairway Productions, even though Hall, as his son put it, "kept pouring money down a rat hole." Hall's father kept dreaming of making more movies, kept writing, but, "my dad was not a businessman." He worked with Richard Kiel on projects, wrote stories, ideas, scripts, novels, but nothing ever saw commercial success. Most went unrealized. Arch Hall Sr. died in 1978.[19]

Analysis

As Arch Hall, Jr., said. "Low-budget Westerns weren't really hot then. Even big-budget Westerns were bombs at the box office Yes, sadly, *Deadwood '76* was ... ill-advised."[20]

Good intentions, of course, don't mean good movies, and *Deadwood '76* fell far short of good. The scenery's nice, but the story is slow-moving and pretentious.

It's not about Billy the Kid, either, just another one of those confounded look alikes.

***

The (Heron, South Dakota) *Daily Plainsman* (May 19, 1965): "Described by Fairway International as a Technicolor 'spectacular,' it was the photography and South Dakota scenery that justified the billing."

The Outlaws Is Coming!

(Columbia, January 1965, 88 minutes) CREDITS: Producer-Director: Norman Maurer. Screenplay: Elwood Ullman. CAST: Joe DeRita (Curly-Joe), Larry Fine (Larry), Moe Howard (Moe), Adam West (Kenneth Cabot), Nancy Kovack (Annie Oakley), Mort Mills (Trigger Mortis), Don Lamond (Rance Roden), Rex Holman (Sunstroke Kid), Emil Sitka (Mr. Abernathy/Witch Doctor/Cavalry Colonel), Henry Gibson

(Charlie Horse), Murray Alper (Crazy Horse), Tiny Brauer (Bartender), Sidney Marion (Hammond), Jeffrey Scott, billed as Jeffrey Alan (Kid), Marilyn Fox (Girl No. 1), Audrey Betz (Fat Squaw), Lloyd Kino (Japanese Moe), Joe Bolton (Bob Dalton), Bill Camfield (Wyatt Earp), Hal Fryar (Johnny Ringo), Johnny Ginger (Billy the Kid), Wayne Mack (Jesse James), Ed T. McDonnell (Bat Masterson), Bruce Sedley (Cole Younger), Paul Shannon (Wild Bill Hickok), Sally Starr (Belle Starr).

Synopsis

In 1871, Rance Roden rules Casper, Wyoming Territory; aided by his trusty gunman Trigger Mortis (who shoots up the opening credits) and Wyatt Earp, Bat Masterson, Wild Bill Hickok, Cole Younger, Bob Dalton, Jesse James, Johnny Ringo and Billy the Kid, he wants to take over the entire West. "Just how do you aim to go about that?" Billy asks. By slaughtering the buffalo, thus inciting the Indians to take to the warpath and wipe out the Army. This will leave the West open for Roden's.

Only here comes Kenneth Cabot, editor of Boston-based *Society for the Preservation of Wildlife* magazine, with orders to find out what's going on with the buffalo. His assistants — the Three Stooges, of course — tag along with him.

Cabot might be green, but he's a man of principle, not to mention handsome, and Annie Oakley is smitten by him. She saves him from Trigger, but Roden isn't afraid. As

The Three Stooges met up with some of the West's most famous gunfighters in *The Outlaws Is Coming!* (1965).

Casper's mayor, he appoints Cabot sheriff, and a badge "still warm from our last sheriff" is pinned on him. The Stooges become his deputies. The catch? Sheriffs last about one day in Casper.

But Annie Oakley has never backed a sheriff before.

She, and those bumbling Stooges, repeatedly save the unsuspecting Cabot from harm. When Trigger keeps failing, Roden sends for his A Team, which includes Belle Starr. Moe manages to glue the gunmen's pistols in their holsters, saving Cabot again. Well, Annie helps, too, beating up Belle in a fight. Those bad men are reformed, and Cabot and the Stooges ride to the Indians and stop a war. Cabot beats up Trigger and Roden, winning over Annie.

The buffalo are saved.

The History

Wild Bill Hickok is running Roden's organization in Abilene. Bat Masterson controls Dodge City. Wyatt Earp has the lid on Tombstone. Jesse James keeps Missouri in check. And Billy? He's running things in the Dakotas. The Dakotas? Elwood Ullman must have gotten a peek at the screenplay for *Deadwood '76*. Billy was a New Mexico boy, but Johnny Ringo was running Roden's outfit in New Mexico. (Although Ringo is most identified with Tombstone, he did, by the way, hang out in the southern New Mexico mining town of Shakespeare.)

But, what the heck. You don't expect history in a Three Stooges film. You expect pie fights and pokes in the eye.

The Players

Say what you will about the Three Stooges, but they were loyal to their family.

Don Lamond (who plays Rance Roden) was Larry Fine's son-in-law. Jeffrey Scott (Kid) was Moe Howard's grandson. Scott's father, Norman Maurer — Moe's son-in-law — directed. Edward Bernds, a frequent Stooges screenwriter and director, said of Maurer: "Norman was a very nice guy but his ideas about comedy were a little peculiar."[21]

The Stooges got their start in vaudeville in 1922. That's when Howard (born Moses Horwitz) and Ted Healy began performing on stage. The act eventually included Howard's brothers Jerome and Shemp. Moe Howard's sixty-six-year career included more than 250 films, including roughly 190 Three Stooges shorts. Howard's death in 1975 ended the long run of the Stooges.[22]

Howard was always part of the trio, but the Stooges went through several other performers.

Moe's brother Jerome "Curly" Howard, who had joined the group in 1932, was forced to retire after suffering a massive stroke during the filming of *Half-Wits Holiday* (1947). "Curly" died in 1952 at age forty-eight. His replacement Shemp Howard (another brother) died in 1955 of a heart attack. Joe Besser, who had appeared in several Abbott and Costello films, joined the Stooges in 1956 but quit two years later. He was replaced that year by Joe DeRita, who became the trio's Curly-Joe. After Moe Howard's death, DeRita retired, and died in 1993.[23]

Larry Fine was still around in 1964, when production on *The Outlaws Is Coming!* began.

Fine started in vaudeville in the early 1920s, joining Healy and Howard as a Stooge in 1925. A stroke while filming the television pilot *Kook's Tour* (1970) forced him to retire in 1970. Fine died in 1975.[24]

Stooges regular Emil Sitka, who appeared in thirty-five shorts, took on three parts in *The Outlaws Is Coming!* The only actor to appear with all six Stooges, he replaced Fine and become a Stooge himself after Fine's retirement. Sitka died in 1998.[25]

The Stooges had appeared in cameos in Stanley Kramer's *It's a Mad Mad Mad, Mad World* and the Frank Sinatra–Dean Martin Western comedy *4 for Texas* (both 1963), but profits on their latest starring film *The Three Stooges Go Around the World in a Daze* (1963) had slipped, and Columbia was not excited about producing another kiddie comedy with the trio. Maurer, however, enticed executives on signing off on his story, which Ullman would adapt into a screenplay originally titled *The Three Stooges Meet the Gunslingers*.[26]

Walla Walla, Washington-born Adam West was a relative unknown in 1965, but that all changed a year later when he starred as Bruce Wayne–Batman in ABC's campy hit *Batman*, which ran until 1968. He learned he had landed the Batman part while filming *The Outlaws Is Coming!* Recalled Johnny Ginger: "[H]e came jumping up: 'I got a series. I'm gonna be Batman!' Moe said: 'If I were you I'd think twice about that. You'll get typecast and never get offered another role again.'"[27]

To play the legendary outlaws, the Stooges selected hosts of kiddie shows. Wayne "The Great McNutt" Mack (New Orleans) played Jesse James. "Officer Joe" Bolton (New York City) played Rob Dalton. Bill "Icky Twerp" Camfield (Dallas–Fort Worth) played Wyatt Earp. Hal "Harlow Hickenlooper" Fryar (Indianapolis) played Johnny Ringo. Ed "Major Mudd" McDonnell (Boston) played Bat Masterson. Bruce Sedley (San Francisco) was Cole Younger. Paul Shannon (Pittsburgh) was Wild Bill Hickok. Sally Starr (Philadelphia) played Belle Starr. Harry "Captain 11" Fender (St. Louis) was scheduled to play Doc Holliday, but a scheduling conflict forced him to bow out.[28]

And for Billy the Kid, the Stooges picked Johnny Ginger, who was host of *Curtain Time Theater* and *The Johnny Ginger Show* in Detroit's WXYZ-TV (Channel 7) from 1957 through 1968. Born Galen Grindle, Ginger said he saw the Three Stooges live and on vaudeville when he was six years old. As a kiddie-show host, Ginger showed more Three Stooges shorts than cartoons, which is why he got the Billy the Kid role.[29]

Principal photography began on May 5, 1964, taking advantage of the bison herd and sixty-six thousand acres of the B-Bar-B Buffalo Ranch in Gillette, Wyoming.[30] "It was a fun shoot," Ginger told the *Detroit Free Press* years later. "Moe was very intelligent, very soft-spoken. Larry was the jokester on the set. One time, we were shooting in the hotel. The Stooges weren't in that scene, but they were on the set. Larry knew how much I liked my booze. All of us had whiskey bottles, and Larry had one of the stagehands put actual booze in my glass."

One scene stood out for Ginger: When Adam West's character shot at Billy, with bullets ricocheting but not hitting the Kid, "he was supposed to holler, 'You're gonna hear from me!' "We had done 11 takes, and I was screaming at the top of my lungs and nearly blew my vocal cords. So Moe leaves the set, gets driven off in his car and comes back with a little bag. I looked inside and found this tin box with throat lozenges and Chloraseptic spray.... To me, he was one hell of a nice man."[31]

The movie's title was changed to *The Outlaws Is Coming!* to parody the advertising slogan for director Alfred Hitchcock's *The Birds* (1963): "*The Birds* Is Coming."[32]

The Outlaws Is Coming!, which premiered in San Antonio, Texas, for area dignitaries on January 13, 1965, and opened nationwide the following day, was the Stooges' last completed film together. "We were set to do four more movies," Ginger recalled, "with titles like *The Pirates Is Coming, The Gangsters Is Coming, The Circus Is Coming*, but then Larry had a stroke ... so nothing ever came of them."[33]

On January 9, 1970, Fine suffered a stroke while filming a travelogue television pilot, *Kook's Tour*. Scenes were scrapped, and others were shot with a double for Fine. Although the movie was completed, it was never sold for television broadcast. "There was a reason for that," Fine's biographers Stephen Cox and Jim Terry write. "It was unfunny and, at times, pathetic. It was a sad swan song for this legendary team." Eventually, director Maurer had it released on the Super 8 home movie market in the 1970s, and it later appeared on video.[34]

Analysis

Well, if you're a boy ten years old or younger, you might enjoy this movie. Or if you're a Three Stooges fan.

"It proved to be a fitting swan song, with the famed comedy trio generating plenty of laughs as they expose the schemes of a dastardly gang boss ... and induce the notorious gunslingers of the Old West to mend their ways," Jeff Lenburg, Joan Howard Maurer and Greg Lenburg write in *The Three Stooges Scrapbook*. Of course, they're Stooges fans.[35]

On the other hand, film historians Robin L. Murray and Joseph K. Heumann saw something entirely different in the comedy: "[It] addresses and blatantly critiques the buffalo extermination from a comic perspective," they write in *Gunfight at the Eco-Corral: Western Cinema and the Environment.*[36]

I had to sit through this one twice, first for *Jesse James and the Movies*, and then for this book. My son laughed a lot both times. Then again, he was eight and ten years old.

***

Hollywood Reporter (January 8, 1965): "[T]he picture is quite above the usual cut of Stooges' antics, an attempt having been made to give the trio more of a story line to follow, which they do to the accompaniment of their usual sight gags."

Billy the Kid vs. Dracula

(Embassy, March 1966, 73 minutes) CREDITS: Director: William Beaudine. Producer: Carroll Case. Screenplay: Carl Hittleman. CAST: John Carradine (Dracula); Chuck Courtney (Billy the Kid); Melinda Plowman (Betty Bentley); Virginia Christine (Eva Oster); Walter Janovitz (Franz Oster); Bing Russell (Dan "Red" Thorpe); Lennie Geer (Yancy); Roy Barcroft (Sheriff Griffin); Olive Carey (Dr. Henrietta Hull); Hannie Landman (Lisa Oster); Marjorie Bennett (Ann Bentley); William Forrest (James Underhill); George Cisar (Joe Flake); Charlita (Nana); Harry Carey, Jr. (Ben Dooley).

Synopsis

Eva Oster, an immigrant from Eastern Europe, awakens in the middle of the night and, fearing vampires, places a crucifix in the hand of her sleeping, nubile daughter, Lisa. Lucky for them, because as soon as Eva's asleep, a bat wobbles down behind the covered wagon, and Count Dracula walks to Lisa. He begins to suck her blood, but when Lisa's hand relaxes, the shiny gold crucifix drives the count away. Eva and her husband awake, find those telltale puncture marks on Lisa's throat, and wail and wail and wail.

And the credits roll.

We pick up the story on a stagecoach carrying a drunken whiskey drummer, a talkative woman ranch owner and her brother, James Underhill, from Boston. The stage has just picked up another passenger, a strange, silent, creepy man in cape — Dracula — who shows little interest in anything until the woman, Mrs. Ann Bentley, asks if he'd like to see a picture of her daughter. Dracula perks up: "Eighteen and beautiful. Yes, I would like to see her." He's even more interested when he learns that the ranch also has an abandoned silver mine.

When the stage pulls into a stop, most passengers head to the station for supper. Dracula, however, finds his supper in the throat of an Indian maiden. Now, those Indians haven't caused any trouble in ten years, but when they find that girl dead the next day, they're irritated and figure white men did it.

The stage leaves. No one knows what happened to that strange hombre in the cape, but the company has a schedule to keep, and the stationmaster says if the guy shows up, he'll be put on the next stage.

Indians attack the stagecoach and kill everyone on board. Then that bat creeps back, and Dracula — who doesn't seem bothered by the sun — takes papers from the corpse of James Underhill.

Back at the Bentley ranch, Billy the Kid has become not only foreman, he has swept Betty Bentley off her feet. They plan on being married. That doesn't set well with cowhand Dan "Red" Thorpe, who had been foreman and had been courting Betty.

In town, Dracula identifies himself as James Underhill and asks for a room. When Billy arrives to meet the stage, the bartender tells him Underhill is already here. That's odd, Billy thinks, since Underhill was supposed to have been traveling with Mrs. Bentley. But in his room, Dracula explains: "The stagecoach is too slow for me ... I came on ahead."

About then, word arrives of the stagecoach massacre. In the saloon, those immigrants babble on about vampires. Young Lisa recognizes Dracula, but the count calms everyone down. Billy rides back to break the sad news to Betty about her mother, and the count stays behind to suck the life out of Lisa. Then he bats his way back to the ranch, telling Billy and Betty that he hired a man in town to drive him there.

Billy's suspicious, but Betty believes the count. After all, she has never seen her uncle before. When Billy rides back to town to find out exactly how that guy saying he's Underhill got to the ranch, he learns that Lisa is dead. Murdered. Puncture wounds in her throat. "My Lisa is dead," Eva says. "The marks of a vampire on her throat.... I think it is Mr. Underhill." Nice guy that he is, Billy invites Eva and Franz Oster to work at the ranch — and protect Betty.

Well, Betty likes the fact that Billy, who's not certain what he believes, is scared for her sake. "I never thought I'd live to see the day Billy the Kid was afraid of anything," she says.

She should be afraid. A lamb is found with its throat cut. Odd things are going on at the ranch, and this Underhill is creepy. Thorpe and Billy tangle, and Thorpe beats the stuffing out of the Kid. Billy has to go see Dr. Henrietta Hull in town, and she fills him in on some stuff she's read about vampires.

Dracula (John Carradine) gets the upper hand on Billy the Kid (Chuck Courtney) in *Billy the Kid versus Dracula* (1965).

When Billy keeps questioning people about Underhill/Dracula, the count sees red. Since Betty is his guardian until she turns twenty-one, it's Dracula — er, Underhill — who runs the ranch. He has Billy fired, and the Kid rides back to town to drink. Dracula also kicks the Osters out of the house and into the bunkhouse, and sends Thorpe to town to finish Billy the Kid.

That doesn't work out too well. The Kid kills Thorpe in a saloon shootout.

Dracula is preparing to make Betty his mate. When Eva finds Betty, and sees those wounds on her throat the next morning, Betty is rushed to Doc Hull's. That's where Billy is when the sheriff comes in to arrest him. Sure, the killing of Thorpe was self-defense, but he still must stand trial. Dracula visits the sheriff, who tells him that Betty is with Doc Hull, and the count hurries there. At her office, Doc Hull holds up a mirror and sees no reflection of the count. Dracula roars at her and whisks Betty to his cave.

That's enough for Doc Hull. She helps break Billy out of jail and hands him a scalpel to drive through the vampire's heart. Billy, however, believes in his six-shooter. "This will do," he says. He steals the sheriff's horse, and Doc Hull joins the sheriff as they ride off in a wagon in pursuit.

At the abandoned silver cave, Dracula is preparing to finish off Betty when the Kid arrives. He empties his gun at the count, but Dracula is unhurt. He gets the Kid in a choke-hold, drags him away, and the Kid passes out. The count's back over Betty when the sheriff and Doc Hull arrive. This time, the sheriff empties his gun. By that point, Billy has regained consciousness. He takes the sheriff's empty gun and hurls it at Dracula. The gun hits the count in the head, and knocks him out.

That's right. A dozen bullets can't harm Dracula, but he can be knocked out. Go figure.

Billy takes the proffered scalpel (as big as a stake) from the doctor and, using a stone, pounds it into Dracula's heart (which sounds like an anvil pounding iron). As the count's flesh dissolves, Betty awakes, good as new. The spell has been broken with Dracula's death.

"Come on, honey," Billy tells Betty as he scoops her into his arms. "We're going home."

The History

On *Late Night with David Letterman* in 1986, the talk-show host jokingly asked John Carradine about *Billy the Kid vs. Dracula*: "That was a true story though, right?" Carradine replied, "No, no, I don't think so."[37]

Well, if Billy the Kid never met up with Bill Doolin, the Younger Brothers and the Sundance Kid (remember *Return of the Bad Men?*), he certainly was never introduced to Count Dracula. While we're at it, let's point out that Jesse James never met Frankenstein's daughter, either. Actually, in *Jesse James Meets Frankenstein's Daughter*, *Billy the Kid vs. Dracula*'s double-feature partner, it wasn't the mad doctor's daughter but his granddaughter causing such a ruction in the Old West.

And for any vampire buffs, Tom Weaver makes this point in *John Carradine: The Films*: "Contrary to vampire lore, Carradine's Dracula moves about in broad daylight, drinks the blood of lambs, eats food and sleeps in a bed instead of a coffin. For some reason, we even get to see him making the bed in one scene."[38]

Gee, did this movie get anything right?

Actually, yes. Most Western movies have their own sense of justice. When a gunman kills another in a "fair" fight, all he has to do is have a witness say, "The other man drew first," and the lawman declares "Self-defense!" No inquest. No trial. Nothing. In actuality, justice on the frontier was often not so rudimentary. Wild Bill Hickok faced trials after the killing of David McCanles and company in Nebraska in 1861 and Davis Tutt in Missouri in 1865. Even the Earp brothers and Doc Holliday went through an inquest after the Gunfight at the O.K. Corral. So when Sheriff Griffin jails Billy for the killing of Thorpe, saying he must stand trial, that much is historically and legally accurate — unlike how it would have been depicted in most Westerns.[39]

The Players

Embassy Pictures signed with Circle Productions in June 1965 to film two movies to be shown as a drive-in double-feature dubbed "Shockorama" and "The NeWest in Terrortainment!": *Jesse James Meets Frankenstein's Daughter* and *Billy the Kid vs. Dracula*.[40] Both movies were produced by Carroll Case, written by Carl K. Hittleman, and directed by William Beaudine.

Beaudine, "a big, cheery man with a pointed mustache" who was seventy-three years old when production began, had been in movies since "the halcyon days of the silent screen." He worked for the Biograph Company, starting out as an actor, then moved to directing, beginning as an assistant. In 1967, he recalled that his first directing job was a one-reel comedy called *Minnie the Lion* from 1915. He spent most of his career directing programmers for Poverty Row studios and was known as "One-Shot Beaudine." One oft-quoted anecdote shows his disdain for most of his movies. Told that an East Side Kids quickie he was directing for Monogram had fallen behind schedule, Beaudine said, "You mean someone out there is actually waiting to see this shit?"[41]

In 1967 he told a newspaper interviewer:

> Long ago I quit thinking that every picture I did was going to be an Academy Award contender. I'm a commercial director; I know how to save money and get something on the screen. I let those arty guys shoot the scenes through chandeliers or from behind a wine glass. That's not me.
>
> I'd like to see a George Stevens or a William Wyler shoot a *Lassie* in three days, the way I do. Heck, they'd be three days trying to make up their minds about the first shot.[42]

Veteran producer A.C. Lyles remembered: "[Beaudine] also did a lot of [films] that maybe he should have turned down, but he didn't because they were for friends." Likewise, Beaudine was loyal to actors he had worked with and liked. "We had a good relationship," Harry Carey, Jr., said, "and when there was a part for me, he'd ask for me. And I wasn't the easiest guy in the world to cast back then. When I worked on *Billy the Kid versus Dracula*, I remember I only had a few lines, but I took the job anyway because it was work."[43]

Loyalty was not why John Carradine took the job. "I needed the money, to be honest," he said. "Actors have to live, too, you know."[44]

Each Shockorama feature was filmed in eight days at California's Red Rock Canyon, Corrigan Ranch, and Paramount Studios. Beaudine had a reputation for keeping his movies at or under budget and never going over his shooting schedule. "They were made as cheap as movies can be made," assistant to the producer Howard W. Koch, Jr., said.[45]

"They were made for fun," production supervisor Sam Manners said, but added: "Levine expected to clear more than $5 million on each film."[46]

Beaudine spent the rest of his career filming television. He estimated that he turned out 200 to 250 TV shows. On March 18, 1970, he died of uremic poisoning at a Canoga Park, California, hospital. He was seventy-eight. "He made it look so easy because he did it so easy," Lyles said of his friend's career, "and he created a wonderful niche for himself in this business. He was so good in that niche that he stayed there."[47]

The director of photography was Lothrop Worth, who had started in the business filming title cards for *The Ten Commandments* (1923) and helped develop 3-D technology in the 1950s. He moved to sound engineer when the talking pictures began, but soon was back behind the camera, as camera operator and then cinematographer. His films included *Gog* (1954), *I Was a Teenage Frankenstein* (1957), and *Hostile Guns* (1967).[48]

Worth first met John Carradine in 1929 "when he was known as Peter Richmond and trying to get work in Hollywood, doing the lead in a dramatic thing on stage with Philippe De Lacy called *Window Panes*." Fast-forward to 1965: In a car with Beaudine, Carradine and a young girl during *Billy the Kid vs. Dracula*, Worth said, "So tell me, Mr. Peter Richmond...." Carradine, Worth recalled, "just about jumped out of his seat that I remembered him from that far back."[49] Worth died in 2000 at age ninety-six.[50]

Cast as Billy the Kid was Chuck Courtney, who was raised on a California cattle ranch and spent most of his Hollywood career as a stuntman, earning "anywhere up to a thousand dollars a minute for riding bucking broncos and bulls, falling off horses, driving flaming automobiles, and being the 'fastest gun in the West.'" Courtney died in 2000 at age sixty-nine.[51]

Five-foot-two, 100-pound Melinda Plowman got her first leading lady role. "Melinda has the ability to look any age from fourteen up to her own [almost twenty-five when the film was released]," the pressbook noted. "And she has had a busy and successful film and television career playing such parts, but, as she says, 'a girl does like to grow up and get kissed, too.'" She had started out as a child actress in the late 1940s and spent most of her career in television, but was out of Hollywood by the late 1960s.[52]

The rest of the cast included longtime supporting actors Roy Barcroft and Olive Carey (Harry's mother). Kurt Russell's father Bing got the role as the villainous cowboy.

John Carradine, on the other hand, had a lengthy, successful career. Born in 1906 in Greenwich Village, New York, he made his stage debut in New Orleans in *Camille* in 1925, joined a Shakespearean stock company — "[H]e had a deep, rich voice and loved Shakespeare and acting," Worth recalled — and hitchhiked west in 1927. He started out in motion pictures in the early 1930s as John Peter Richmond, but by 1936 had changed his name to John Carradine. Although he would land lead roles in several Bs, his greatest successes came in supporting roles: *The Prisoner of Shark Island* (1936), *The Grapes of Wrath* (1940), *The Ten Commandments* (1956), *The Man Who Shot Liberty Valance* (1962), *The Shootist* (1976).... Carradine even played Dracula, in *House of Frankenstein* and *House of Dracula* (both 1945).[53]

And then there was *Billy the Kid vs. Dracula*.

Carradine's opinion remained consistent:

- "I have worked in a dozen of the greatest, and I have worked in a dozen of the worst. I only regret *Billy the Kid Versus Dracula*. Otherwise, I regret nothing."[54]
- "My worst film? That's easy, a thing called *Billy the Kid Versus Dracula*.... It was a bad film. I don't even remember it. I was absolutely numb!"[55]

Nicknamed "The Bard of the Boulevard," Carradine (in his earliest Hollywood days) was known to dress in a red-lined satin cape and wide-brimmed hat and walk the streets of Los Angeles and New York, reciting Shakespeare. Four of his sons — David, Robert, Keith, and Bruce — followed in his acting footsteps. Carradine died in Milan in 1988 at age eighty-two.[56]

Analysis

Borrowing a lot from The *Return of Dracula* (1958), the plot of this turkey wasn't all that original. Film historian Tom Weaver noted that *Billy the Kid vs. Dracula* might have at least earned "the semi-respectability of another vampire Western, *Curse of the Undead* (1959), if it was truer to vampire lore, if it didn't feature a 'name' outlaw like Billy the Kid, if the vampire in it weren't Dracula, and if Carradine's performance was much better. (That's a lot of ifs.)"[57]

Even when viewed for campiness, this movie truly is abysmal. The question is, of course, which film is worse: *Billy the Kid vs. Dracula* or *Jesse James Meets Frankenstein's Daughter*? Well, the biggest "name" in the latter production was Jim Davis (in a minor role, too). Considering the talent of John Carradine, this one should have been slightly better. So maybe it's the worse.

But both movies stink.

***

Hope (Arkansas) *Star* (January 18, 1967): "... some real different slapstick and hokum."

CHAPTER TEN

Billy Turns Violent, 1970–1973

The 1970s introduced the revisionist movement in Western filmmaking, bringing out a more graphically violent Billy the Kid.

Even when he appeared with old-school cowboy star John Wayne, the violence and language turned a whole lot rougher than during the days of Johnny Mack Brown and Robert Taylor.

And when Sam Peckinpah got a hold of the story...

Chisum

(Warner Bros., June 1970, 111 minutes) CREDITS: Director: Andrew V. McLaglen; Writer-Producer: Andrew J. Fenady. CAST: John Wayne (John Chisum); Forrest Tucker (Lawrence Murphy); Christopher George (Dan Nodeen); Ben Johnson (James Pepper); Glenn Corbett (Pat Garrett); Bruce Cabot (Sheriff Brady); Andrew Prine (Alex McSween); Patric Knowles (J. Henry Tunstall); Richard Jaeckel (Jess Evans); Geoffrey Deuel (Billy the Kid); Pamela McMyler (Sallie Chisum); Lynda Day (Sue McSween); John Agar (Amos Patton); Lloyd Battista (Neemo); Robert Donner (Morton); Ray Teal (Justice J.B. Wilson); Edward Faulkner (James Dolan); Ron Soble (Bowdre); John Mitchum (Baker): Glenn Langan (Colonel Nathan Dudley); Alan Baxter (Governor Sam Axtell); Alberto Morin (Delgado); William Bryant (Jeff); Pedro Armendáriz, Jr. (Ben); Christopher Mitchum (O'Folliard); John Pickard (Sergeant Braddock); Abraham Sofaer (White Buffalo); Gregg Palmer (Karl Riker); Hank Worden (Stationmaster Elwood); Pedro Gonzalez (Mexican Rancher); Jim Burke (Trace); Eddy Donno (Cass); Trinidad Villa (Blacksmith); William Conrad (Opening Credits Narration).

Synopsis

Cattle baron John Chisum rides to Lincoln, New Mexico Territory, to pick up his niece Sallie, who has invited herself from Baltimore to stay at his ranch. Lincoln is changing, and if you were to ask Chisum's foreman, James Pepper, it's not for the better. A newcomer, Lawrence G. Murphy, is putting his hands on everything he can touch. Including Chisum's horses.

The Murphy-pawn sheriff, William Brady, and a hired gun named Karl Riker have just paid a Mexican bandit Neemo, who leads his men in an attack on Chisum cowboys, killing some and stealing the remuda. When a rider alerts Chisum in town, the baron's response is simple: "Well, let's go get 'em back."

Along the way, Chisum meets his neighbor, the peaceful transplant from England, Henry Tunstall, and his cowboys, including William H. Bonney. Bonney asks Chisum if he needs any help — a request cut short by Tunstall — and Chisum rides off.

Pressbook for *Chisum* (1970).

"Mr. Tunstall," Billy tells his employer, "I know you don't believe in guns, but I have a feeling Mr. Chisum's gonna have need of his. Well...."

"Well, what?" Tunstall asks.

"Well..." Bonney grins. "He didn't say no."

With help from Billy and Tunstall's and Chisum's riders, Neemo and his men are quickly dispatched, the horses recovered, and Tunstall sends Chisum off to Lincoln to find his niece. Chisum invites Billy to the party he has planned for Sallie, and doesn't change his invitation upon learning that that youngster is Billy the Kid.

In town, Chisum finds his niece, who has invited two other newcomers, Alex and Sue McSween, to the party. Alex McSween is going to work for Murphy, which leads Pepper to remark: "They's sure gonna be some interesting people at that party."

Yep. Sallie meets Billy at that party, and becomes infatuated with the young killer.

Murphy isn't done, of course. He has sent for Jess Evans from Dodge City, a gunman who used to pal around with Billy. Evans and his gun crew ride to steal or stampede Chisum's cattle, knowing that that herd is bound for the U.S. Army to feed the Comanches penned up on the reservation.

A former buffalo hunter, Pat Garrett, alerts Chisum's crew that rustlers are making off with the herd. More bullets fly. Riker is wounded and hauled back to the Chisum ranch. Chisum has the gunman arrested for murder, and sends for federal Justice J.B. Wilson, but Murphy can fix that. He tells Brady to let his prisoner escape. Meanwhile, Chisum tries to deliver the cattle he can gather to the army, but the commanding officer, Nathan Dudley, is a Murphy man, and he has already made arrangements to buy the beef from Murphy.

A bounty hunter with a mean disposition and a gimpy leg, Dan Nodeen, arrives hauling Riker's dead carcass to collect the reward. "He gimps because of Billy the Kid," Sheriff Brady tells Murphy. "Bonney put a bullet in him about two years back." Murphy tries to hire Nodeen, but the killer is only interested in collecting bounties.

Murphy continues his stranglehold, but without help from McSween. He's an honest lawyer, and quits McSween. Tunstall and Chisum get him to stay by opening a store and bank — on Chisum's dime — to compete against Murphy.

Naturally, Murphy has his men ambush the wagon train carrying supplies for the Chisum store. The bad guys are driven off, but Evans shoots Billy, who is saved by Garrett.

The Chisum store and bank hurt Murphy where it counts most, his pocketbook. Murphy has Evans slap a Tunstall brand on a Murphy cattle, charges Tunstall with rustling, orders Tunstall arrested, and rides off to Santa Fe to see Governor Axtell. The sheriff sends two men after Tunstall. Instead of bringing him in alive, Deputy Morton kills him. Tunstall was unarmed. That ain't gonna set well with Chisum.

Or Billy.

At Tunstall's funeral, the Kid makes a vow: "It says in the Bible, 'The candle of the wicked shall be put out.'"

Good thing Justice Wilson has arrived. He empowers Chisum to bring in deputies Morton or Baker "dead or alive," and Chisum, Garrett, Pepper and other riders go after the killers. They find them, capture them, and bring them back to Lincoln.

Well, that was the plan. After Chisum leaves the posse for his ranch to fetch Justice Wilson, Billy rides down, clubs Garrett with his pistol, and shoots Morton and Baker out of their saddles. Then he rides into Lincoln and guns down Sheriff Brady.

That's enough for Murphy. He makes the governor revoke Wilson's powers and appoint Nodeen as sheriff. Nodeen offers a $200 reward for the Kid, and Murphy ups that ante to $1,200.

With his pals Bowdre and O'Folliard, Billy decides to ride into Lincoln, rob Murphy's safe, and kill Evans and Murphy. They'll need dynamite, but the Kid figures they can steal that from McSween's store. With extra men, they ride in that night. But Nodeen sees them, surrounds the store, and more bullets fly.

The next day, Murphy allows Sue McSween to leave the store, but Nodeen won't let her husband out. More gunshots, and Sue McSween rides off to summon Chisum. "Exactly," Murphy says. "We'll fight them on our own grounds." He orders the streets barricaded.

Meanwhile, as Billy's men keep getting picked off, McSween walks outside, unarmed, to talk to the law. Nodeen kills him. More bullets, and finally Nodeen tries to burn down the store.

Mrs. McSween has ridden to the Chisum ranch, and Chisum has had enough. He and his men ride into town, free some of Murphy's cattle in the pens, and stampede them through the barricade. Billy guns down Jess Evans.

Chisum spots Murphy in his office, rides through the door and leaps from the saddle as Murphy fires a shotgun. It's the fight James Pepper had predicted, "head to head and horn to horn, and one hell of a fight. But one of you's got to lose, and the winner walks out with the herd and the whole shebang." The winner, of course, is Chisum. The fight rages to the upstairs, onto the balcony, and both men fall into the street. Chisum lands on the ground. Murphy lands on a cattle horn that skewers him.

So Dan Nodeen quits. "No more paydays," he says, and rides off. Billy rides off alone, and peace returns to Lincoln County.

Pat Garrett has been appointed sheriff, Lew Wallace has replaced Axtell as governor and declared amnesty, and the Lincoln County War is over. John Chisum rides off to a hilltop to watch over his kingdom.

The History

Often mistaken for Jesse Chisholm, the trader whose trail became associated with the great cattle drives from Texas to Kansas, John Simpson Chisum was "The Cattle King of New Mexico." He was born in Madison County, Tennessee, on August 15, 1824, and moved to northeast Texas when he was thirteen. In the 1850s, he was ranching — backed by New York's Stephen K. Fowler for ten years — and had developed his Long Rail brand and the jinglebob (an ear-lopping technique). Both the brand and the jinglebob method moved with him to New Mexico shortly after the Civil War. With his brother Pitzer, he settled on the Bosque Redondo near Fort Sumner. In the spring of 1875, he moved his headquarters to the South Spring River southeast of Roswell. Chisum did enter a partnership with lawyer Alexander McSween and John Henry Tunstall. He died in Eureka Springs, Arkansas, of cancer on December 22, 1884, leaving behind an estate of roughly $500,000. But his cattle empire did not survive, either. Lawsuits plagued his brothers, and by 1891, the Jinglebob empire was gone.[1]

Yet John Chisum was not a rough-and-tumble John Wayne character. "My Uncle John was one of the best men that ever lived, big-hearted and generous," recalled his niece Sallie. "He was a plain bacon and frijoles sort of man — no frills."[2]

Although he might carry a Colt .45 when traveling on horseback or by buggy, he was not know to pack a revolver. "You carry the guns," he once told a cowboy. "I'll carry the brains."[3]

The daughter of John Chisum's brother Jim, pretty, flaxen-haired nineteen-year-old Sallie arrived at the Chisum ranch — from Texas, not Baltimore — in December 1877. She certainly knew Billy the Kid, who gave her presents of an "Indian tobacco sack" and "two candi hearts"— but no carved wooden cross that we know of. On January 26, 1880, Sallie married George William Robert in Anton Chico. In 1890, Mrs. Sallie Robert filed on a homestead between Roswell and Carlsbad. That fall, she sank an artesian well, only the second well in the valley, thus giving the town of Artesia its name. "She has lived to see a good town spring up here and has benefited by the rapid development of the district," George B. Anderson wrote in 1907.[4]

Many other historical figures show up in this Billy movie. William Brady, of course, was sheriff of Lincoln County, but when he tells Chisum, "I'm the new sheriff," that wasn't necessarily the case. Brady, who had been mustered out of the Army at Fort Craig in 1866, was first elected sheriff of Lincoln County in 1870, and again in 1877.[5]

Jessie/Jesse Evans was likely born in Missouri or Texas and wound up in New Mexico around 1872. "The details of Jessie's early life are meager," biographers Grady E. McCright and James H. Powell write. So are details about most of his life. What is known is that he wound up on the opposite side from Billy the Kid during the Lincoln County War. In fact, some believe that Evans fired the bullet that killed John Tunstall. In *Chisum*, Billy says that he used to run around with Jesse Evans and Clay Allison, but there's no documentation that either Evans or Billy even knew Allison. And Jesse Evans was not killed on the streets of Lincoln by Billy the Kid. Shortly after the Lincoln County War, he returned to his old Texas stamping grounds. After a robbery, he was convicted of second-degree murder in the shooting death of Texas Ranger George R. Bingham in 1880 and was sentenced to ten years at the Huntsville penitentiary. "Leased" out to a contractor — a standard practice in prisons at the time — he escaped on May 23, 1882, and disappeared from history.[6]

James Dolan was working for Lawrence G. Murphy, and Nathan Dudley was commanding the Army post at nearby Fort Stanton.[7] Samuel Beach Axtell was governor of New Mexico Territory during the Lincoln County War, and might have been, as Chisum says in this movie, "a gutless wonder." Mesilla Valley *Independent* editor Montague R. Leverson said the governor was "influenced more by weakness and want of intellect than by intentional criminality." An Ohioan by birth, Axtell was appointed governor of Utah by President Ulysses S. Grant in 1875, then transferred to New Mexico shortly afterward. After being replaced by Lew Wallace, Axtell became chief justice of the New Mexico Supreme Court from 1882 to 1885, then took a job as legal counselor to the Southern Pacific Railroad Company. He held that position until his death in 1891.[8]

John Bautista Wilson was not a district judge, but justice of the peace in Lincoln. After Tunstall's murder, Alexander McSween knew better than to try to obtain warrants from the district attorney, district judge or county sheriff— all Murphy-Dolan men — so he did a legal end-around and obtained warrants from Wilson. Dick Brewer was appointed "special constable" and organized a posse that included Billy the Kid, Charlie Bowdre, Fred Waite, Doc Scurlock, Henry Brown, John Middleton, Jim French, Frank McNab, Sam Smith, John Scroggins, Frank and George Coe and several Hispanics. Considering what happened next, Governor Axtell probably had sufficient cause to revoke the powers of J.B. Wilson.[9]

Chisum was not part of the posse that captured deputies Buck Morton and Frank

Baker. But Morton and Baker were definitely killed before they ever reached Lincoln. So was Morton's friend William McCloskey, who was allowed to accompany the posse to Lincoln. With prisoners in tow, the posse left Chisum's ranch on March 9. Morton, Baker, and McCloskey were later found dead, shot trying to escape if you believe the posse. Or murdered, if you believe everyone else. Billy the Kid later told George Coe, "I never meant to let them birds reach Lincoln alive." But he didn't do it alone. Morton had been shot nine times. Nor was the murder of Sheriff William Brady a solo act by Billy.[10]

On the other hand, Dan Nodeen and James Pepper are fictitious characters. The sheriff who replaced William Brady was John Copeland, appointed by county commissioners, but Axtell quickly replaced him with George W. Peppin, another member of the Murphy-Dolan group. And the Comanches would not have been on a reservation in New Mexico. By 1878, Comanches were on a reservation near Fort Sill in present-day Oklahoma. The Mescalero reservation was the nearest reservation to Lincoln.[11]

John Tunstall — called Henry this go-round, likely to avoid confusion with John Chisum — is once again played as an older father figure, but Billy the Kid could not swear on Tunstall's grave that he would avenge his employer's death. He was in jail, along with Fred Waite, after being arrested by Sheriff Brady.[12]

The five-day battle is condensed into a two-day affair, and when Sheriff Nodeen tells Alexander McSween that the Army has no jurisdiction in this "civil" matter, he might have been right. Historically, however, that didn't prevent Colonel Nathan Dudley from deciding — after a conference of officers — "that humanity demanded some form of military intervention." A small command arrived at Lincoln on July 19, to protect women and children, but when they brought out a Howitzer, two-thirds of the McSween forces fled. "[T]here was a more confident bunch inside the McSween house than was to be found outside it, until after the soldiers arrived," Jack Long recalled.[13]

On the other hand, when Jess Evans says the Tunstall store "is built like a fort," he's not far off. Historian Frederick Nolan writes:

> The building was constructed as if in anticipation of a siege. Although the three-foot-thick walls were proof against anything short of a Howitzer, Tunstall specified window shutters made with a double thickness of heavy wood sandwiching a steel plate. With these closed, the building would have been well-nigh impregnable: but against what, or whose, expected attack were these precautions taken?[14]

McSween was killed while trying to escape the burning house, but not in the streets. And Lawrence G. Murphy? He didn't wind up on the wrong end of a longhorn. In 1877, he had been diagnosed with terminal bowel cancer. "[F]rom that point onward he left the running of the business to his protege, James Dolan, and spent much of his time in an alcoholic stupor." Whether cancer or alcoholism killed him, Murphy died in Santa Fe on October 20, 1878, "all but destitute, his life's work in ruins."[15]

The script shows the introduction of Billy the Kid and Pat Garrett — even has Garrett saving the Kid's life — and trumpets the unsubstantiated Miguel Antonio Otero, Jr., story of the two having nicknames, Billy the Kid being called "Little Casino" and Garrett nicknamed "Big Casino." But at least this time, Billy's right-handed. For that you can thank screenwriter and producer Andrew J. Fenady. Fenady says he got lots of letters about Billy the Kid being left-handed, and the movie's pressbook noted that Fenady put up a $1,000 reward to anyone who could prove conclusively during the movie's production that Billy was left-handed. "No takers," Fenady recalled forty years later.[16]

The Players

A native of Toledo, Ohio, Andrew J. Fenady had broken out in Hollywood with a 1958 low-budget ($21,000) crime-drama released by Warner Bros., *Stakeout on Dope Street*, that he helped write and produce. At the time of *Chisum* he was no stranger to Westerns, having developed the TV series *The Rebel* and *Branded*. "My ambition for many years," he said, "was to write a film for the biggest man in motion pictures—John Wayne."[17]

Fenady had met and befriended Wayne's oldest son, Michael, when Fenady's Andrew J. Fenady Productions and Wayne's Batjac Productions produced a short-lived television series *Hondo*, based on the popular John Wayne movie from 1953. John Wayne's brother, Bob Morrison, kept encouraging Fenady to write a screenplay for the Duke, saying, "He needs a good picture." When *Chisum* went into production in October 1969, Wayne was causing a stir with his performance in *True Grit*. By the time *Chisum* opened on June 24, 1970, Wayne was an Academy Award winner.[18] Fenady approached Michael Wayne about *Chisum*, and eventually Wayne signed off on the movie.

When the moviemakers were trying to decide what actor should play Billy the Kid, Wayne suggested Ben Johnson. The room fell silent, and Wayne asked, "What did I do? Did I say something wrong?"

Michael broke the news to his dad: "Ben Johnson is much too old to play Billy the Kid. Hell, he's about fifty years old."

Which got Duke's dander up. "The hell he is. What are you talking about? When did he make *Three Godfathers*?" Then Wayne thought on it, and finally sighed, saying, "Guess he is too old for it...."[19] Johnson instead got the part of Chisum's sidekick Pepper.

The role of Billy was offered to Ryan O'Neal, but O'Neal decided that he wasn't right for it. Instead, O'Neal starred in *Love Story* with Ali McGraw, which became one of the season's biggest hits. "It worked out pretty good for Ryan," Fenady says.[20]

Geoffrey Deuel, a TV actor who was the brother of *Alias Smith and Jones* star Pete Duel, got his first big-screen role. "I was terrified during the first few days of shooting," Deuel said, "but 'Duke' was wonderful to me. I learned more from him in a few weeks than I have in my previous four years in the business."[21]

For instance, Wayne offered one bit of advice when Deuel "came on yelling as I was pointing a pistol at someone." Wayne said: "You don't have to yell when you've got a gun on a man."[22]

Other actors were also recruited from television, including Christopher George (*The Rat Patrol*, 1966–68) as Dan Nodeen; George's wife Lynda Day (commercials and TV guest shots) as Susan McSween; and Glenn Corbett (*Route 66* in 1963–64, replacing original star George Maharis) as Pat Garrett. Pamela McMyler, as Sallie Chisum, had also acted mostly on television, although she had also acted in *The Boston Strangler* (1968) and a few other films.

For his role as Tunstall, Patric Knowles picked for his wardrobe "a half-dozen ensembles" that Rex Harrison had worn in Warners' *My Fair Lady* (1964). He even copied the hat Harrison had worn in his Oscar-winning performance.[23]

Other actors were veteran players. Bruce Cabot had appeared with longtime friend Wayne in fifteen films. John Agar, Forrest Tucker and Richard Jaeckel had acted with Wayne on *Sands of Iwo Jima*, the 1949 film that earned Wayne an Academy Award nomination as Best Actor. Director Andrew V. McLaglen, son of frequent Wayne co-star Victor McLaglen, served as second assistant director to Allan Dwan on that film.[24] British-born and American-raised, McLaglen had cut his teeth in television after serving as assistant to directors Dwan John Ford, Budd Boetticher, and William Wellman. He first directed Wayne in *McLintock!* (1963), followed by *Hellfighters* (1968) and *The Undefeated* (1969), and would direct Wayne again in *Cahill: United States Marshal* (1973). McLaglen retired in 1989.[25]

William H. Clothier, who had worked on several Wayne movies, including *Fort Apache* (1948), *The Sea Chase* (1955), *Blood Alley* (1955), *The Comancheros* (1961) and *The War Wagon* (1967), and been nominated for Oscars for *The Alamo* (1960) and *Cheyenne Autumn* (1964) served as cinematographer, and would work on just three more movies, all John Wayne Westerns: *Rio Lobo* (1970), *Big Jake* (1971) and *The Train Robbers* (1973). After years of retirement, he died in 1996 at age ninety-two.[26]

Fenady and Dominic Frontiere wrote the title song, "Ballad of John Chisum," which actor William Conrad, about a year away from starring in the detective series *Cannon*, narrated. Another song, "Turn Me Around," written by Frontiere and Norman Gimbel, was sung by Merle Haggard. Haggard had sold more than three million records, had eleven No. 1 singles (including his hit "Okie from Muskogee") and seven No. 1 country albums, but this was his first movie assignment. He "interrupted a busy concert schedule" for a one-day appearance at Warner Bros. Studio to record the song before a small audience of technicians and executives.[27]

John Chisum (John Wayne) and Billy the Kid (Geoffrey Deuel) in *Chisum* (1970).

Wayne had one complaint during filming, that the sets were too small. He said, "[G]ive me some room." Ever accommodating, Fenady enlarged some of the sets.[28]

Fenady remained close friends with the Wayne family. After filming, the Duke told Fenady: This is the most pleasant picture I've ever made. Let's do another."

Fenady shot back: "Want to do it on sea like *Wake of the Red Witch* or on land like *Chisum*?"

"Both," Wayne replied.[29]

Fenady actually wrote another script with Wayne in mind, *Double Eagles*. "We were always going to do it," Fenady said, "and going to do it, but..." They never worked together again. On June 11, 1979, Wayne died of complications from cancer in Los Angeles. He was seventy-two. Fenady turned his screenplay into a novel, and in 2002, Leisure Books, an imprint of New York–based Dorchester Publishing, released *Double Eagles* as a mass-market paperback.[30]

Riding on the coattails of Wayne's Oscar, *Chisum* proved to be a major hit, Batjac's biggest at the time, and, as Fenady puts it, more than "*Rio Lobo* and all that shit [Wayne] did after."[31]

President Richard Nixon saw the film, mentioning it in a 1970 speech in Denver. "I said, 'Well, it was a very good western, John Wayne is a very fine actor and it was: a fine supporting cast. But it was just basically another western, far better than average movies, better than average westerns.'"[32]

Wayne had won an Oscar for *True Grit*, but 1969 also saw the release of what might be considered anti–Westerns: *Butch Cassidy and the Sundance Kid* and *The Wild Bunch*. *Chisum*, on the other hand, was, as *Chicago Sun-Times* film critic Roger Ebert put it: "a typical, average dependable John Wayne Western."[33]

With protests on just about every college campus — the shooting of students by the Ohio National Guard at Kent State University occurring just months before the movie's release — and Vietnam dividing the country, another anti–Western, *Little Big Man*, was one of the biggest box office hits of 1970. So were *Woodstock* and *MASH*, all having "counter-cultural youth appeal."[34]

Chisum was, in the words of the *New York Times*, "a conventional Western, not the kind that such directors as John Ford and Henry Hathaway have pulled up taut with sharp character components." Kevin Thomas of the *Los Angeles Times* said, "John Wayne's 201st movie [which it wasn't] is mighty like the previous 200."[35]

But audiences, if they didn't love it, liked it a whole lot.

"Perhaps it's because, in these chaotic times, western fans feel some instinctive need for order," Ebert wrote. "In a western at least you know where you stand."[36]

Analysis

"It may ramble," the *New York Times* noted, "but it does move."[37]

Chisum has always been a guilty pleasure. Of mine. And Roger Ebert's. "If I had revealed how much I'd really liked *Chisum*," Ebert wrote, "I undoubtedly would have sent someone off to the theater expecting *High Noon*, or *Rio Bravo* at the last. And *Chisum* is just another Wayne flick."[38]

It's old-fashioned, without much depth, predictable, but it somehow manages to keep you watching. And compared to most of the Wayne movies that would follow — notable exceptions being *The Cowboys* (1974) and *The Shootist* (1976), his last film — it certainly stands out.

Besides, Billy the Kid's right-handed.

***

New York Times (July 30, 1970): "Forget substance. Settle for color and commotion and you won't feel cheated."

The Last Movie

(Alta-Light/Universal, September 1971, 106 minutes) CREDITS: Director: Dennis Hopper. Producer: Paul Lewis. Screenplay: Stewart Stern. CAST: Dennis Hopper (Kansas); Julie Adams (Mrs. Anderson); Rod Cameron (Pat Garrett); Peter Fonda (Young Sheriff); Samuel Fuller (Sam, the American Director); Stella Garcia (Maria); Don Gordon (Neville Robey); Dean Stockwell (Billy the Kid); Roy Engel (Harry Anderson); Severn Darden (Mayor); Clint Kimbrough (Minister); Michelle Phillips (Banker's Daughter); Russ Tamblyn (Member of Billy's Gang); John Phillip Law (Little Brother).

Synopsis

Let's see if you can somehow manage to follow this convoluted plot: An American film crew has descended upon a small Central or South American village to film a Western about Billy the Kid, starring Dean Stockwell as Billy and Rod Cameron as Pat Garrett.

There's plenty of shooting. The natives are enthralled by the whole process.

Before filming the death of Billy, the cavalry hat–wearing director announces his instructions: "This is the death of Billy the Kid. Now I want it legitimate and different and better than it's ever been done before.... I want balls when you die."

Working as a "hired hand"— wrangler or stunt man — is a young American nicknamed Kansas, who grew up on a farm outside of Dodge City. Kansas falls for a Mexican prostitute named Maria. After the film crew returns to California, he stays behind, hoping more productions will come to the still-standing set.

The only ones coming to the set are the locals, who pretend to be shooting a movie using model equipment made from junk. The priest complains when his former parishioners fight each other. Kansas tries to show the locals, and the director, how to fake punches, but that does no good. Eventually, Maria returns to prostitution.

Kansas and his friend Neville Robey, who wants a grubstake to look for gold, are drinking in a bar when they hit on two bored American tourists. One happens to be the wife of an American broom manufacturer, so they all get together. Robey tries to persuade him to back his gold-mining venture, but Harry Anderson is basically a dirty old man. So they go to Maria's whorehouse, where two prostitutes stage a lesbian sex scene for the gringos.

Eventually, Neville and Kansas go looking for gold, and they find it — despite the fact that Neville's only knowledge of goldmining comes from the movies *The Treasure of the Sierra Madre* and *Lust for Gold*. Their claim proves too far from the roads to develop commercially, driving the despondent Neville to suicide.

After that, Kansas drinks heavily, and is captured by the village moviemakers. He's even wounded in the shoulder — or is that just some drug-induced hallucination?— by the wannabe actors. He hides in the jail that once housed Billy the Kid and other actors playing bad guys, fearing that the villagers will shoot him down for real. "They're going to kill me," he warns Maria, but she tells him it's just for fun.

Kansas (Dennis Hopper) reenacts Billy the Kid's death scene among villagers in *The Last Movie* (1971).

Fun? The priest suggests that real blood will show up better.

In the end, the worn-out Kansas recreates Billy's death scene, running, hitting his mark perfectly, "dying" as Billy has died, as the *faux* camera equipment is destroyed by fireworks during fiesta.

Or something like that.

The History

It's a movie about the making of a movie about Billy the Kid.

There's no history here.

Some might argue that there's no film here, either, at least, a film that makes sense.

The Players

Born and reared in Dodge City, Kansas — same as his character — Dennis Hopper said that one of his earliest memories was watching Errol Flynn lead a parade of Warner Bros. stars to promote *Dodge City*. Considering that movie came out in 1939, when Hopper was three years old, that's hard to believe. By the late 1940s, Hopper's family had moved to San Diego, where he studied at the Old Globe Theater, then signed with Warner Bros. and moved to Los Angeles. He earned recognition in the James Dean films *Rebel Without a Cause* (1955) and *Giant* (1956) and continued to act in television and in films such as *Gunfight at the O.K. Corral* (1957) and *Cool Hand Luke* (1967). In 1969, a movie he directed, starred in, and co-wrote with Terry Southern and co-star Peter Fonda became the smash hit of the counterculture movement: *Easy Rider*, selected best first film at the Cannes Film Festival, put Hopper in demand.[39]

Hopper had pull. He had dated Susan Stein, the daughter of Jules Stein, who had founded Music Corporation of America, a powerful agency that had acquired Universal Studios in 1958. He had been married to agent-producer Leland Hayward's daughter Brooke. Most importantly, *Easy Rider* had been a smashing success for Columbia. Jules Stein, MCA's chairman of the board, gave the instructions: "Give the kid whatever he wants."[40]

Which turned out to be a budget of $600,000 or $1 million, depending on the source.[41]

Hopper got the idea for what became *The Last Movie* from his experiences in Durango, Mexico, where demanding director Henry Hathaway had shot *The Sons of Katie Elder* (1965), a Western starring John Wayne. Hopper, who had previously worked with Hathaway in the Western *From Hell to Texas* (1958), had a small part in *Katie Elder*. Reportedly, Hopper asked Hathaway to play the director in *The Last Movie*. He also wanted John Wayne to appear as one of the actors (probably the one playing Pat Garrett). Despite a rumored feud between Hopper and Hathaway, the director agreed to take the part.[42]

He got neither Hathaway nor Wayne. Rod Cameron, a fading Western film star, wound up as the Pat Garrett actor, and Sam Fuller, a B-director whose cult films included *I Shot Jesse James* (1949), *The Steel Helmet* (1951) and *Shock Corridor* (1963), got the chance to parody himself. Fuller had made a walk-on appearance in Jean-Luc Godard's *Pierrot le Foc* (1965), so when Hopper called with the offer to play a "macho film director," Fuller accepted. "It sounded like fun, and there was some dough in it. Besides, I'd never been to Peru." *Rolling Stone* reported that Fuller even handled the direction of the fake Western-movie shootout scenes for *The Last Movie*.[43]

Why choose Billy the Kid as the subject? Well, Hopper had played the outlaw once, in the pilot episode for ABC's hit Western series *Sugarfoot* in 1957. Who knows?

Hopper wanted to film in Mexico, but the Mexican government didn't want "poverty" shown, so the cast and crew headed to a mountain village in Peru in April 1970 to begin filming.[44]

The lead role was offered to Jack Nicholson, who had given a memorable performance in *Easy Rider*, but Nicholson turned it down because he knew Hopper wanted to play that part.[45]

Hopper also invited several friends — Russ Tamblyn, *Easy Rider* co-star Peter Fonda (who would, after his bit part, head to New Mexico for his directing debut in the unheralded gem *The Hired Hand*), Dean Stockwell, and young singer-songwriter named Kris Kristofferson. Kristofferson — who sang his hit "Me and Bobby McGee" in the film — wound up playing Billy the Kid in Sam Peckinpah's *Pat Garrett and Billy the Kid* (1973). Michelle Phillips, part of the popular group The Mamas and the Papas, came down, too. Fonda arrived with an ivory-handled .44–40 that had once belonged to Tom Mix. Hopper fell for Michelle Phillips.[46]

Hopper felt enormous pressure, telling a reporter: "This is the big one. If I foul up now, they'll say *Easy Rider* was a fluke. But I've got to take chances to do what I want."[47] Yet when it came to directing, he had no discipline. The Billy the Kid shootout scene was improvised, so that when someone suggested they pit "old guys" against "young guys," Hopper said, "That's cool."[48]

Nor did he have discipline off the set. He was addicted to cocaine, and cocaine was cheap in Peru, where a packet that cost $70 in the States could be had for $7.[49] It was drugs (cocaine, marijuana, acid, peyote, speed), booze, whoring and mayhem. One actress took LSD and, "having a bummer," began screaming at 2 A.M.[50]

Hopper "was the most self-destructive guy I had ever seen!" Kristofferson recalled. "He got a priest defrocked because he got him involved in some kind of weird mass for James Dean. He antagonized the military and all the politicians. It was crazy."[51]

Fuller, on the other hand, likened his experience in Peru to "working in Hollywood in the thirties, like being in an old Tom Mix picture. I'd always treasure the experience."[52]

Yet the filming had problems on set, too.

A horse panicked in one scene after gunfire and fell off a twenty-five-foot wall, breaking its back. A crew member pulled out a .45-caliber pistol and killed the animal. Almost immediately, two Indians began butchering it. At least one cast member fainted. Others hit the bar. By nightfall, Hopper had broken down and was crying.[53]

Somehow, the film was finished on schedule.

Only then, Hopper told Universal officials that he would need a year, rather than three months, to edit. He went home to Taos, New Mexico, editing—when not partying ("Everybody was just blotto," Tom Mankiewicz recalled). He started with forty hours of film and cut it down to some six hours.[54]

High on drugs, he married Michelle Phillips, who filed for divorce after eight days. "Everybody had the same question," Phillips said in 2007. "'A divorce after eight days? What kind of tart are you?'"[55]

When Fuller saw Hopper's first cut, he thought Hopper "had let the film get away from the simplicity of the script's central clash of cultures. Dennis was undecided about his ending. Hell, you've got to know your ending before you start shooting a single frame of film. Otherwise, your picture is like a goddamned train without a final destination."[56]

Finally, Hopper got the film cut to a manageable length.

At a preview at the University of Iowa, the movie was not received well by either general filmgoers or studio executives, who watched with obvious displeasure. On stage, Hopper tried to explain the movie. One story, perhaps apocryphal, goes that a female student came to Hopper afterward and asked if he made the film. When he replied that he had, she belted him in the nose, yelling, "You sexist fucking pig!"[57]

At a press screening, the first and last reels of the film had been reversed, but it didn't matter. "[T]he film was so confusing anyway that the audience didn't know the difference," studio executive Lew Wasserman said.[58]

Although *The Last Movie* won the Critics' Prize at the Venice Film Festival, American critics and audiences were not receptive at all. Nor was Universal, which pulled the movie after only a few weeks. As *Time* magazine noted: "That sound you hear is of checkbooks closing all over Hollywood. Dennis Hopper has blown it."[59]

Hopper did not direct another film until *Out of the Blue*, a 1980 Canadian film. He didn't direct a U.S. film until *Colors* (1988).

He spiraled downhill. "I was doing half a gallon of rum with a fifth of rum on the side, 28 beers and three grams of cocaine a day—and that wasn't getting high, that was just to keep going, man," he said. "I was a nightmare. I finally just shorted out."[60]

In the 1980s, while filming in Mexico, he hit rock bottom, suffered a nervous breakdown and was found walking naked along a dirt road. "You either die or you change," he said. He wound up in a psychiatric hospital, joined Alcoholics Anonymous, and moved to Venice, California.[61]

Five years later, Hopper earned raves for his performances in *Blue Velvet* and *Hoosiers* (both 1986), earning an Academy Award nomination as a recovering alcoholic assistant basketball coach for the latter. Other highlights included *Apocalypse Now (1979), Red Rock West* (1993), *Speed* (1994), the famous flop *Waterworld* (1995), and the first season of the television series *24* (2002). Suffering from prostate character, Hopper died in 2010 at age seventy-four at his home.[62]

"We rode the highways of America and changed the way movies were made in Hollywood," Peter Fonda said at Hopper's funeral in Taos. "I was blessed by his passion and friendship."[63]

Analysis

Pauline Kael labeled *The Last Movie* "visually beautiful, but the editing is so self-destructive that it's as if Hopper had slashed his own canvases."[64] Calling it "a wasteland of cinematic wreckage," Roger Ebert added, "There are all sorts of things you can say about it, using easy critical words to describe it as undisciplined, incoherent, a structural mess. But mostly it's just plain pitiful."[65]

It's a psychedelic footnote in the Billy the Kid film world, a strange, incomprehensible mess of a movie. Said Universal vice-president Ned Tanen: "*The Last Movie* was crap...."[66]

"Did it damage my career?" Hopper said years later. "I'll tell you, man, it *ended* my career. But I've no regrets."[67]

***

Judith Crist, *New York Magazine* (October 11, 1971): "There are tidy moments provided by Sam Fuller as the Hollywood director, and Julie Adams as a rich American matron, but Hopper's sprawling attempts at spiritual significances prove only that he's better at busting broncos than mythologies."

Dirty Little Billy

(WGR/Dragoti Ltd./Jack L. Warner/Columbia Pictures, November 1972, 93 minutes) CREDITS: Director: Stan Dragoti. Producer: Jack L. Warner. Screenplay: Charles Moss, Stan Dragoti. CAST: Michael J. Pollard (Billy); Richard Evans (Goldie); Lee Purcell (Berle); Charles Aidman (Ben Antrim); Dran Hamilton (Catherine McCarty); Willard Sage (Henry McCarty); Mills Watson (Ed); Alex Wilson (Len); Ronny Graham (Charlie Niles); Josip Elic (Jawbone); Richard Stahl (Sheriff Lovitt); Gary Busey (Basil Crabtree); Dick Van Patten (Harry); Scott Walker (Stormy); Rosary Nix (Lou); Frank Welker (Punk); Craig Bovia (Buffalo Hunter); Severn Darden (Big Jim); Henry Proach (Lloyd); Len Lesser (Slits); Ed Lauter (Tyler); Doug Dirksen (Orville); Cherie Franklin (Gerta Schmidt); Nick Nolte (Town Gang Leader).

Synopsis

In muddy Coffeyville, Kansas, in the early 1870s, young Billy arrives by train from New York City with his mother Catherine McCarty and stepfather Henry McCarty. Kansas is bleak, and the farm Ben Antrim sells to the McCartys doesn't look like much. Coffeyville doesn't look like much, either, but Antrim tells a community assembly that if a neighboring town folds and the residents there come here, then Coffeyville could become a "third-class" city with a mayor and peace officer.

Billy hates farm life and despises his stepfather (the feeling is mutual). "You were a bum in New York," Henry McCarty tells Billy. "You're a bum here.... You're useless." Eventually, McCarty throws his stepson out, vowing to kill Billy if he ever returns.

Billy hops aboard an eastbound train but then reconsiders, jumps off, and walks through the mud back to town. He's in the middle of the street, being bullied, when gunfire erupts from a ramshackle saloon. A man falls runs out and falls dead. From inside the saloon, a pimp named Goldie asks Billy to fetch the knife out of the corpse and bring it back.

Inside the saloon, Billy finds Goldie, a young crook; his concubine, Berle, who supports them through prostitution; the proprietor; and a bartender-bouncer. Ben Antrim fetches Billy, but the boy steals bread and eggs from his farm and returns to the saloon. Berle wants nothing to do with Billy and throws him out, but he's soon back, and Goldie takes him under his wing.

Eventually, the neighboring town folds, and Coffeyville celebrates its pending promotion to "third-class" city. A gunfight erupts during a card game between the cheating Goldie and a buffalo hunter, but nobody is hit. Billy picks up the hunter's gun and, encouraged by Goldie, tries to shoot the hunter, but the pistol misfires. Then the buffalo hunter's woman and Berle get into a knife fight, resulting in Berle cutting the ear off the woman.

Goldie tries to teach Billy how to shoot. Billy says he almost killed a man in New York City, but his friends don't really believe him. And Berle is not Billy's friend. She says she'll cross her legs permanently because she's not supporting Goldie and Billy. When a customer

Dran Hamilton shakes hands with Charles Aidman in the funeral scene in *Dirty Little Billy* (1972). Star Michael J. Pollard sits with a bowler on his knee.

comes for Berle, Goldie beats her when she refuses to whore. When Billy intervenes, he is hit by Goldie, too. Berle winds up with the customer. Goldie apologizes to Billy and takes him to see Berle. He even kicks out the customer so Billy can have sex for the first time with Berle.

Catherine McCarty comes into the saloon, informing Billy that his stepfather is dead. After the funeral, Ben Antrim tries to persuade Billy to quit those no-accounts in the saloon and get a real job in town, but Billy won't listen.

Coffeyville has become a "third-class" city, and Antrim has hired a feared lawman named Earl Lovitt to get rid of Goldie. Ben visits the saloon, telling Goldie that he has arranged things so that Goldie can leave, alive, in the morning with a horse and provisions. If he doesn't leave, he'll be killed.

Goldie refuses until morning comes, then relents. On a bitter, windy day, he mounts the horse after saying goodbye to Billy and Jawbone. Berle walks beside him.

Antrim is not a man of his word. An ambush has been arranged. Goldie is wounded. Berle runs back to grab a weapon and help. Ben tries to keep Billy from joining in, but Billy hits him in the groin and runs outside. Berle is gunned down by the townsmen, but Billy and Goldie manage to escape.

Billy's despondent over Berle's death, but Goldie says they must move on, perhaps join up with a gang of ruffians led by Big Jim McDaniels. They find Big Jim's camp, but these are bad men, not boys like Billy and Goldie. They threaten the newcomers with robbery, sodomy, and death. Goldie's slapped down, but Billy draws his revolver, killing Big Jim's men with pistol shots. He then puts a bullet in Big Jim's forehead and brains him with the revolver.

Goldie's impressed with Billy's ability. The two murderers steal everything they can from the dead men and Billy, now armed to the teeth and the new leader, and Goldie ride west.

The History

Motion Picture Daily noted,

> In the continuing modern-day campaign to destroy or, at least, "correct" the record of the romantic myths about the Old West which Hollywood fostered so profitably since the days of its infancy, there are two major methods open to movie-makers. One is satire, as in *Cat Ballou*. The other is to present the "true story" of the people of the time and their achievements and failures as opposed to the legends....[68]

Yet the "true story" in *Dirty Little Billy* isn't true at all, relying on the legends created by Pat Garrett-Ash Upson and Walter Noble Burns, and letting screenwriters Charles Moss and Stan Dragoti make up their own myths.

In this prequel to Billy the Kid's adventures in New Mexico, Moss and Dragoti rely on the story that Billy the Kid arrived in Coffeyville, in 1862. Billy's family at that time, according to Garrett's *The Authentic Life of Billy, the Kid* (ghostwritten by Upson), included his mother, stepfather and a brother. Billy's brother Joe is not to be found in this movie. Following the Garrett-Upson legend, Burns wrote that Billy was three years old when the family settled in Coffeyville, but Burns gives the family name as Bonney, not McCarty, and calls Billy's baby brother Edward instead of Joe.[69]

Neither Garrett-Upson nor Burns was right.

Billy the Kid might have been born in New York. His father was likely named Michael McCarty, and by 1868 Billy, brother Joe, and their widowed mother Catherine McCarty were living in Anderson, Indiana. By 1871, the McCartys had moved to Kansas — not Coffeyville, but Wichita. William (not Ben) Antrim, who had likely met Catherine in Indiana, had settled there, too. As depicted in this film, Catherine and Antrim become involved (as they probably were in Indiana). They would move, possibly to Colorado in 1872, but definitely to New Mexico, where they were married in Santa Fe on March 1, 1873.[70]

Kansas statutes allow "third-class cities." According to Chapter 15, Article 1:

> All municipal corporations of the territory or state of Kansas, heretofore organized as cities, towns, or villages, containing not more than two thousand inhabitants (and not heretofore organized as cities of the second class), including cities of the third class organized in accordance with the provisions of the act of which this is amendatory, and including also all un-incorporated towns (without regard to their population) which may now or hereafter be constituted a county seat of any county, shall be cities of the third class, and shall be governed by the provisions of this act; and all rights and privileges accrued under and by virtue of, or provided by, any act of the legislature of the territory or of the state of Kansas, before the day on which this act shall take effect, to any such municipal corporation, are hereby confirmed and preserved to such corporation, and the citizens thereof, respectively.[71]

Coffeyville wasn't around in 1862. It developed in the late 1860s when James A. Coffey, from Illinois, built a trading post to barter with Osage Indians. By the summer of 1869, a town had been laid out. It was incorporated in 1871. Another fairly authentic depiction in *Dirty Little Billy* regards a town rivalry. Coffeyville's historic competition came first from a nearby settlement called Parker. Also, when Ben Antrim says the Galveston railroad is coming to Coffeyville, his history isn't far off. The Leavenworth, Lawrence and Galveston Railroad, which James Coffey had courted, arrived and caused more competition. The railroad had its own townsite in mind, but while Coffey's site, dubbed Old Town, and the railroad town competed for a while, they merged in 1873 to thwart competition from Parker.[72]

Eventually, Coffeyville was served by three railroads, and cattle came up from Texas to the rails. In that regard, Coffeyville was like many other cattle towns. Twelfth Street, called "Red Hot Street" because of its saloons, gambling houses and brothels, "qualified fully as the sin strip of Coffeyville." In 1870, a year before incorporation, there were at least twelve murders, and vigilantes hanged three men. Civilization came to Coffeyville, however, and the town prospered because of wheat, not cattle, and later natural gas drilling. The town is remembered among Old West enthusiasts not because Billy the Kid once lived there (since he never lived there), but because on October 5, 1892, the Dalton gang tried, and bloodily failed, to rob two banks simultaneously.[73]

The Players

In 1967, Jack L. Warner sold Warner Bros. to Seven Arts for $32 million and planned on retiring, but the studio chief who had produced *Casablanca* and plenty of other classics couldn't just walk away from pictures.[74]

"Why Jack Warner was attracted to *Dirty Little Billy* remains a puzzle," Bob Thomas writes. "It certainly wasn't like any western he or anyone else had made before. Perhaps that was its appeal to him. 'You gotta do pictures that are different,' he preached."[75]

Warner hadn't produced a film since *Camelot* (1967) and *Dirty Little Billy* would be his first since leaving Warner Bros.[76]

Dirty Little Billy came to Warner's attention through screenwriters Charles Moss and Stan Dragoti, and the first woman president of an advertising agency, Mary Wells Lawrence, who had founded Wells Rich Green in 1966. Moss, a former child actor, was the first writer Lawrence hired. Dragoti was directing television commercials for the firm.[77]

Lawrence had studied theater and drama, so she had an interest in film. When she brought the project to Warner's attention, however, Moss only had a title, *Dirty Little Billy*. Which proved enough for Warner. "I like that title!" Warner yelled (he was always yelling). "It's got blood and guts! That could be very good, very commercial! I'm in!"[78]

Lawrence created a subsidiary with Warner, WRG/Dragoti Ltd., and the movie was budgeted at less than $1 million. Dragoti was named creative director of WGR/Dragoti; Moss was president.[79] Warner, who would take an active part in all aspects of the production, liked the anti-genre aspect of *Dirty Little Billy*. Although he had despised the movie *Bonnie and Clyde* (1967), he didn't remember Michael J. Pollard being in that film, so he liked Pollard for the part of Billy. Mainly because he was told they could get Pollard cheap.[80]

Pollard's show-business debut came when he played one of the First Lord's cousins in a third-grade production of *H.M.S. Pinafore* in Passaic, New Jersey. Known on stage and film for goofy character parts, he had earned an Oscar nomination for his supporting role in *Bonnie and Clyde*, which led to bigger parts, such as a co-starring one with Robert Redford in *Little Fauss and Big Halsy* (1970).[81]

He told *Chicago Sun-Times* writer Roger Ebert that he was making a violent movie called *Goodbye, Jesse James*. That film was never made (or at least not released), but Pollard had no problems about violence in film. "Everybody's criticizing violence," he told Ebert. "In *Bonnie and Clyde,* they criticized the violence. That's dopey, man. Everybody's violent. They're criticizing themselves. Everybody will realize that in a year or so and start on something else. I don't know. Hey, maybe they'll start on humor in movies. Too much humor in movies. Children laughing too much."[82]

A good thing, considering the violence in *Dirty Little Billy*. No one could criticize the humor, of course, since there's no humor in *Dirty Little Billy*.

The movie was shot primarily in southern Arizona. It marked the film debut of a thirty-year-old actor named Nick Nolte, who had a small, uncredited role. Nolte's career was lifted in the miniseries *Rich Man, Poor Man* (1976) and he began finding bigger, better roles on the big screen, beginning with *Who'll Stop the Rain* (1978).[83]

The movie premiered at the San Francisco Film Festival on October 20, 1972, and opened nationwide the next month. And it earned some good reviews, with the *New York Times* citing it as "a realistically raw view of the beginnings of the Billy the Kid legend."[84]

Revisionist Westerns were strong in the early 1970s, but films like *The Hired Hand* (1971), *Bad Company* (1972), and *Ulzana's Raid* (1972) debunked the mythology of the West, not a historical figure. And certainly not a *young* historical figure like Billy the Kid.

Fritz Lang had once considered debunking Billy the Kid, but decided against it. I would have loved to make a picture about Billy the Kid. He told Peter Bogdanovich:

> I would have loved to make a picture about Billy the Kid. You know the original man. In the photos, he looked like a moron, which he probably was. And if I could have had the chance to make the first picture, I would have made a moron out of him, not Bob Taylor [star of the 1941 film *Billy the Kid*]. But motion pictures have spread the legend, and because an audience is educated, they know from the films that Billy the Kid was a hand-

some, dashing outlaw, and if somebody would make him today as he really was, it would probably be so much against the grain of an audience that it couldn't be a success."[85]

In 1972, the youth movement was strong. Vietnam protests were in full force. Four students had been killed by National Guard troops in 1970. Young, anti-establishment characters were popular with *young* filmgoers: Steve McQueen in *Bullitt* (1968), Paul Newman and Robert Redford in *Butch Cassidy and the Sundance Kid* (1969), Dustin Hoffman in *Little Big Man* (1970), Warren Beatty in *McCabe and Mrs. Miller* (1971). No one wanted to see a movie about a young punk.

"Since Billy [the Kid] was an anti-establishment figure," Paul Andrew Hutton writes, "he did not make a particularly good target for the debunkers, especially for the alienated youth audience of 1972. The film failed miserably at the box office."[86]

Pollard went go back to supporting roles. The movie's failure reduced Moss's "desire for artistic success," but Dragoti left the advertising agency in 1973 and continue directing, with films like *Love at First Bite* (1979) and *Mr. Mom* (1983).[87]

Jack Warner, on the other hand, never produced another movie. He died in 1978 at age eighty-six.[88]

Analysis

Dirty Little Billy has its admirers.

"The only later western to come close to [Robert] Wise's [*Blood on the Moon* (1948)] in terms of feel and look," Barry Gifford writes, "is Stan Dragoti's *Dirty Little Billy* (1972), with Michael J. Pollard as Billy the Kid in one of the slimiest, filthiest, muddiest movies of all time—a real little masterpiece...."[89]

The *New York Times* noted: "The look of an authentic period and place is captured in the dirt, sloppy roads, rickety buildings and tattered itinerants who never owned fancy ten-gallon hats, spurs or chaps. And the unremitting struggle for survival is also starkly spotlighted, especially in a couple of brutal fights staged without glorification of the principals."[90]

Violent, dark, savage, brutal, *Dirty Little Billy* is a movie most viewers will either love or despise.

Unlike another art-like Western that is either loved or despised, *The Assassination of Jesse James by the Coward Robert Ford* (2007), *Dirty Little Billy* was far from historically accurate. It might look authentic, or at least muddy, but its history falls far off the course.

Billy the Kid, it seems, had misfired again.

***

Washington Post (April 28, 1973): "The only thing to be said for *Dirty Little Billy* ... is that it's aptly titled. The leading players look as if they'd just come off a shift in the coal mines. To accentuate the effect, director Stan Dragoti sets about 75 percent of the action in a gloomy, claustrophobic frontier saloon."

Pat Garrett and Billy the Kid

(MGM, May 1973) CREDITS: Director: Sam Peckinpah. Producer: Gordon Carroll. Screenplay: Rudy Wurlitzer. CAST: James Coburn (Pat Garrett); Kris Kristofferson (Billy the Kid); Bob Dylan (Alias); Richard Jaeckel (Kip McKinney); Katy Jurado (Mrs. Baker); Chill Wills (Lemuel); Barry Sullivan (John Chisum);

Jason Robards (Governor Lew Wallace); R.G. Armstrong (Bob Ollinger); Luke Askew (Eno); John Beck (John W. Poe); Richard Bright (Holly); Matt Clark (J.W. Bell); Rita Coolidge (Maria); Jack Dodson (Howland); Jack Elam (Alamosa Bill Kermit); Emilio Fernandez (Paco); Paul Fix (Pete Maxwell); L.Q. Jones (Black Harris); Slim Pickens (Sheriff Cullen Baker); Jorge Russek (Silva); Charles Martin Smith (Bowdre); Harry Dean Stanton (Luke Harris); Claudia Bryar (Mrs. Horrell); John Chandler (Norris); Mike Mikler (Denver); Aurora Clavel (Ida Garrett); Rutanya Alda (Ruthie Lee); Walter Kelley (Rupert); Rudy Wurlitzer (O'Folliard); Elisha Cook, Jr. (Cody); Gene Evans (Mr. Horrell); Donnie Fritts (Beaver); Dub Taylor (Josh); Don Levy (Sackett); Sam Peckinpah (Will).

Synopsis

In 1909, Pat Garrett is riding to Las Cruces, arguing with a neighbor over sheep grazing on his land. Lurking in the distance is a man with a Winchester rifle, who opens fire on Garrett. So do his traveling partners. As Garrett hits the dirt and is riddled with bullets, he flashes back to 1881 Old Fort Sumner, New Mexico.

There, Billy the Kid and his pals are shooting the heads of chickens buried in the sand to their necks when Garrett arrives. Garrett and his friend Billy head into the saloon, briefly talking about old times before Garrett asks, "You want it straight?"

"If that's why you're here," Billy says.

"The electorate want you gone, out of the country," Garrett informs him.

"Are they telling me or are they asking me?"

"I'm asking you," Garrett says as he prepares to leave. "In five days, I'm making you." That's when Garrett takes over as sheriff of Lincoln County.

Billy's pards think Garrett, who once rode with them, has sold out to the Santa Fe Ring. They ask Billy why he just doesn't kill Garrett, but Billy's answer is easy. "He's my friend," he says.

And the credits roll.

Pressbook for *Pat Garrett and Billy the Kid* (1973).

On the day Garrett takes office, Billy, Bowdre, and O'Folliard are at a shack at Stinking Springs, preparing to go rustle some of John Chisum's beef, but Garrett and his posse are waiting. Bowdre steps outside and is gut-shot, stumbling back into the shack. Bullets whine. The outlaws try to make a run for it. Bowdre and O'Folliard are killed, and Billy dives back inside, finally agreeing to surrender.

"You're poor company, Pat," he says, hands up.

"Yeah," Garrett agrees. "I'm alive, though."

Billy smiles. "So am I."

Awaiting his execution in the Lincoln jail, Billy plays cards with Garrett and deputy J.W. Bell, and is tormented by the Bible-quoting bully of a deputy, Bob Ollinger. Garrett leaves for

White Oaks to collect taxes. Ollinger almost rams his shotgun down Billy's throat, demanding that the outlaw repent before Jesus Christ. Bell forces Ollinger to stop, and the befuddled deputy heads across the street for a drink. Billy asks to go to the outhouse, where he finds a hidden revolver.

He pulls the gun on Bell on the stairs inside the jail. He tells Bell he doesn't want to kill him, but Bell says he knows the Kid won't shoot him in the back. He turns around to head down the stairs, and Billy shoots him in the back, killing him. Shackled, Billy hops up the stairs, finds Bell's shotgun, and waits by the window. Ollinger runs across the street and is killed by Billy.

Back in Lincoln, Garrett deputizes a man-killer named Alamosa and sends him on a wide loop searching for the Kid. In Santa Fe, Garrett meets with Governor Lew Wallace and two members of the Santa Fe Ring. Garrett's pressured to bring in the Kid, if he wants to keep his job. He's offered a $1,000 reward, and one of the businessmen offers him $500 in advance, which Garrett refuses, telling him he can "take your money, shove it up your ass, and set fire to it." (That line would be modified and delivered by actor James Coburn years later when he played John Chisum in *Young Guns II*.)

In Fort Sumner, Billy reunites with the old gang and a young newcomer named Alias who knows how to handle a knife. They kill some cutthroats gunning for the Kid — "too soon for bounty hunters," Billy says — and decide to rustle some more of Chisum's beef.

On Billy's trail, Garrett recruits an old sheriff named Baker to help him. Some of Billy's gang, including Black Harris, are hanging out, ruining the town, so Garrett, Baker, and Baker's wife decide to clean out the town, and maybe learn where Billy's hiding out.

After the outlaws are killed and Baker is mortally wounded, Garrett rides on alone. Then he's joined by a Texan named John W. Poe, whom Governor Wallace (or the Santa Fe Ring) has appointed as Garrett's deputy. He won't answer to Garrett, only to the Santa Fe Ring.

They don't get along.

They visit John Chisum, whom the Kid claims owes him $500 in back wages. Chisum denies it. He says he hears that Billy the Kid is everywhere, including eating at his own bunkhouse.

Actually, Billy has been busy rustling beef, killing men trying to kill him, and hanging out with his pals. He meets up with a Mexican sheepherder named Paco and his daughter and, taking Paco's advice, decides to quit the country and head to Mexico, even though his friend Luke Harris says he'll be just another "drunken gringo" across the border.

Garrett sends Poe one way, agreeing to meet him in Roswell. He finds Alias and some of the old boys at a roughshod saloon run by an old cur named Lemuel. He forces Alias to pistolwhip one of Billy's cronies, then gets the other drunk — while Alias is made to read labels on cans on a shelf behind the bar — until Garrett kills the second man, too.

On his way to Mexico, Billy stops in at the Horrell Trading Post for a meal. Unfortunately, new deputy Alamosa Bill is eating there, too. They share a meal with the Horrell family, then Alamosa Bill and Billy step outside for a showdown. There's no way to avoid it, least ways Alamosa Bill can't figure out anything, so they back up against each other, agreeing to take ten paces, turn and fire. As Alamosa Bill begins counting the steps, Billy turns, gun already in hand. Alamosa Bill turns at eight, and is shot down by Billy.

"That wasn't ten, hoss," Billy tells the dying gunman.

"I never could count."

On his journey to Mexico, Billy finds Chisum's riders beating Paco and raping his daughter (or is that his wife?). Billy murders the brutes. After Paco dies, the Kid knows he can't just ride away. He heads back to Fort Sumner.

In Roswell, Garrett has a prostitute named Ruthie Lee come to his room — she's eventually joined by several others — and Garrett makes Ruthie tell him where Billy is. Later, he meets Poe and the town sheriff, Kip McKinney, in the bar. They agree to ride to Fort Sumner to find the Kid.

With his girlfriend Maria, the Kid visits Pete Maxwell's place and takes Maria to bed. Maxwell sits alone at the table, reminiscing about the old times. Garrett arrives, walking past a coffin maker named Will who tells him, "You finally figured it out, huh? ... Go on, get it over with." On the porch, Garrett hears the Kid and Maria making love and he sits on the swing, waiting.

When they are done, and Billy announces that he's hungry, Garrett rises from the swing and walks to Maxwell's room. Outside, McKinney and Poe see Billy. McKinney urges Poe to shoot him, but the deputy can't. Hearing the voices, Billy enters Maxwell's room, asking about the men outside. Then he sees Garrett and smiles, before Garrett kills the Kid with a single bullet to his heart. When Garrett sees his own reflection in a mirror, he shoots that, too.

Billy the Kid lies dead. When Poe tries to cut off the Kid's trigger finger, Garrett explodes, beating the deputy senseless with his pistol, then collapsing on the porch swing. He sits there all night, and at dawn draws his badge from his pocket, pins it on, and rides out of town. A boy follows him, throwing rocks at the lawman as he rides away.

That's the way Sam Peckinpah likely envisioned *Pat Garrett and Billy the Kid*, but that's not the film that wound up playing in theaters in 1973.

The History

The movie opens with Pat Garrett's murder in 1909. But Pat Garrett was killed in 1908. On Saturday, February 29, 1908, Garrett was traveling by buggy with Carl Adamson for Las Cruces. They met Wayne Brazel on the way. Adamson was related to James P. Miller (a gunman known as "Killin' Jim" and "Deacon Jim"), who wanted to buy Garrett's ranch. The deal faced a setback because Brazel was leasing Garrett's ranch for his goats, not sheep as depicted there. Near Alameda Arroyo, Adamson and Garrett, still arguing with Brazel, stepped down from the buggy to urinate. Garrett's back was to Brazel and Adamson when he was shot in the back of his head.[91]

Who killed Garrett remains a mystery. Wayne Brazel confessed and was acquitted of murder. Not everyone believed that Brazel had pulled the trigger. Other theories point to Print Rhode and James Miller.[92]

After the epilogue, *Pat Garrett and Billy the Kid* opens in 1881 with Garrett about to take office as Lincoln County sheriff. Actually, Garrett won the election in November 1880, and although he would not take office officially until January 1, incumbent sheriff George Kimbrell appointed him deputy.[93]

On the morning of December 23, 1880, Garrett and his posse were waiting for Billy and his pards at a stone shack at Stinking Springs. The movie has Billy traveling with Charles Bowdre and Tom O'Folliard. The latter, however, had been killed by Garrett's posse on December 19 while riding into Fort Sumner. At Stinking Springs, Billy was with Bowdre, Dave Rudabaugh, Billy Wilson and a scared cowboy-rustler named Tom Pickett.[94]

When Bowdre stepped outside that morning to feed the horses, he was wearing a Mexican sombrero with a green hat band — possibly Billy's hat. Riddled with bullets, he stumbled inside. "They have murdered you, Charley," the Kid told his pal, "but you can get revenge. Kill some of the sons-of-bitches before you die." After pulling Bowdre's gun belt around, putting the holstered revolver in easier reach, he shoved Bowdre back outside.[95]

Bowdre got no revenge. He staggered up to Garrett, muttering, "I wish ... I wish, I wish — I'm dying," and died in Garrett's arms.[96]

The posse is supposed to be bringing in Billy the Kid for the murder of Buckshot Roberts. "Hell," Billy says, "that was a year ago. I shot him straight up." Although the Kid was indicted for that crime, Andrew "Buckshot" Roberts had been killed in 1878 during the Lincoln County War, and Billy didn't kill him. Roberts was killed by Bowdre. In addition to Bowdre and the Kid, Regulators John Middleton, Stephen Stevens, John Scroggins, George Coe, Fred Waite, Doc Scurlock, and Henry Brown were also indicted for Roberts's murder.[97]

There are various versions on how the Kid came to get the revolver he used in his jailbreak on April 28, 1881. Some argue that he managed to get Bell's own gun, although historian Bob Boze Bell says, "This version was discredited by Judge Lucius Dills, whose investigation revealed that Bell's pistol was still in its holster, fully loaded, when his body was removed."[98]

Returning from the outhouse, Billy struck Bell with his handcuffs on the staircase and fired twice as the deputy staggered down the stairs. One bullet struck Bell in the back, and he walked outside and died in the arms of Godfrey Gauss, the courthouse caretaker.[99]

Racing upstairs, the Kid found Olinger's shotgun and waited. When Olinger appeared below the courthouse, he called down to the surprised guard, but he didn't say, "How's Jesus look to you now, Bob?" He did send the loads of both barrels into Olinger's body, killing him instantly.[100]

After that, the Kid made Gauss bring him a pickax. After knocking off the shackles from one of his legs, he gathered some weapons and told Gauss to fetch him a horse. Here's a detail the movie amazingly gets right: When the Kid mounted the horse, it bucked him off. However, the Kid did not get another horse, but remounted the horse that had pitched him, promising to send it back.[101]

Garrett's even given a Hispanic wife in this movie, but her name is Ida. Garrett had married Apolinaria Gutiérrez in 1880.[102]

Garrett was with deputies John W. Coe and Kip McKinney when he caught up with Billy at Pete Maxwell's home on July 14, 1881. The Kid, in fact, could have just finished making love to a sweetheart (Paulita Maxwell, perhaps, and not a girl named Maria). When Billy stepped into Pete Maxwell's bedroom, Garrett fired twice, hitting Billy with the first shot. His second shot wasn't aimed at his reflection in a mirror, but also at the Kid. That bullet missed, ricocheted off the wall, and lodged in the headboard of Maxwell's bed.[103]

At least, that's the story commonly accepted. Another version was reported by an Englishman named Frederick W. Grey, who said McKinney told him that Garrett and his posse went into the room of a Mexican girl who the Kid liked to visit. They tied her up, gagged her, and Garrett waited behind a sofa. When the Kid entered his sweetheart's room, Garrett killed him, or, as Bob Boze Bell succinctly puts it, "shot him down like a dog."[104]

The Players

Sam Peckinpah's first attempt at telling the story of Billy the Kid was in 1957 when he adapted Charles Neider's 1956 novel *The Authentic Death of Hendry Jones*. In that work of fiction, the names were changed (Billy the Kid was Hendry Jones; Pat Garrett was Dad Longworth) but it was definitely a story about Billy the Kid. By the time the movie went into production, Peckinpah was no longer attached to the project. The picture went through six directors, including Stanley Kubrick, before star Marlon Brando took over as director and star. That film, *One-Eyed Jacks*, was released in 1961.[105]

"Marlon screwed it up," Peckinpah said. "He's a hell of an actor, but in those days he had to end up as a hero and that's not the point of the story. Billy the Kid was no hero. He was a gunfighter, a real killer."[106]

Gordon Carroll, who had produced *How to Murder Your Wife* (1965), *Cool Hand Luke* (1967), and *The April Fools* (1969), wanted to make a new movie about Billy the Kid, and he hired a young novelist named Rudolph Wurlitzer to write the screenplay. Wurlitzer had just finished the screenplay for *Two-Lane Blacktop* (1971), which became a cult favorite that Peckinpah immensely enjoyed. The screenplay was pitched to MGM; they liked the idea but wanted a top director attached. Carroll sent the screenplay to Peckinpah, who quickly accepted.[107]

"That's the one time in his life that he was really hot, with the exception of *Ride the High Country* [1962]," recalled Max Evans, a novelist who did some under-the-table script doctoring for Peckinpah and even acted in *The Ballad of Cable Hogue* (1970) for his longtime friend. "I knew he was serious about *Pat Garrett and Billy the Kid* for one damned reason. He hated MGM. They had really, really abused him."[108]

Peckinpah had feuded with the studio over *Ride the High Country*, and had been fired by the studio as director of *The Cincinnati Kid* (1965), yet he also officed at the studio. On the other hand, Peckinpah had also feuded with Columbia Studios (over 1965'a *Major Dundee*), and everyone else, including his friends.[109] "The son of a bitch was as bad as Billy the Kid," Evans says with a laugh. "They should have teamed up."[110]

Evans was in Peckinpah's office, "bullshitting" with a few other people, when the telephone rang. Peckinpah answered the phone, spoke briefly, hung up and turned to his guests. "Well, gentlemen," he said, "we've got a picture."[111]

James Aubrey, MGM's head of production, offered Peckinpah $228,000 to direct, guaranteed even if the project was scrapped, plus a percentage of profits. The latter could have been rewarding for Peckinpah. Shortly after *Pat Garrett and Billy the Kid* went into production in November 1972, Peckinpah's *The Getaway* was released; it would gross more than $36 million.[112]

Peckinpah began tinkering with Wurlitzer's script, adding scenes, dialogue from *Hendry Jones*, turning the project into a sort of allegory reflecting Watergate and the Vietnam War's My Lai massacre to make it relevant to early 1970s audiences.[113]

Singer-songwriter Kris Kristofferson was cast as Billy the Kid. "I just sort of fell into acting in a place called *The Last Movie* [1971], which Dennis Hopper directed in Peru," Kristofferson said. "I was down there scoring the music for it when I wound up doing a bit. I found I had a feel for [acting]." He followed *The Last Movie* with *Cisco Pike* (1972) and *Blume in Love* (1973). "'Course none of it had a thing on Billy," Kristofferson said. "This is just about the toughest role I've had yet, but I'm hanging in there."[114]

James Coburn signed as Garrett, although he had reservations about working again for Aubrey after a bad experience on *The Carey Treatment* (1972). Coburn even warned Peckinpah: "Jesus, are you sure you want to make this film here? Aubrey will fuck you up, man, he's gonna go for you. He screws everybody."[115]

Coburn, however, loved the part, "the most interesting role of my career," and Peckinpah would say, "Coburn is so into the part I'm beginning to think he *is* Pat Garrett."[116]

Jason Robards, Richard Jaeckel, Jack Elam, Slim Pickens, and Barry Sullivan signed on for small roles. Singer-songwriter Bob Dylan agreed to make his film debut, playing Alias, and also would contributed original songs for the soundtrack.[117] The movie, budgeted at $3 million, was to be filmed in Durango, Mexico.[118]

For almost everyone involved, it would not be a pleasant experience.

"I would not say that the picture was anything but a battleground, from two to three weeks before we started shooting until thirteen weeks after we finished," Gordon Carroll said.[119]

Kristofferson drank two quarts of whiskey a day during filming, while Peckinpah and Coburn "had one thing in common," Evans said. "Cocaine." The shooting schedule was tight. MGM's labs reported "focus" problems on the first batches of film sent back to Hollywood. Peckinpah grew so enraged watching the first night's dailies, he urinated on the screen. Eventually, Peckinpah got so ill, he "was puking every day."[120]

Peckinpah, who was called "*El Jefe*" (Spanish for "The Chief") on the set, began every morning drinking a tumbler of vodka, arriving thirty to forty-five minutes late. "He was a genius for about four hours," Coburn said, "then it was all downhill."[121]

Kris Kristofferson (center) in one of the numerous gunfights in *Pat Garrett and Billy the Kid* (1973).

When L.Q. Jones arrived in Durango to film his scenes, he said his first impulse was to say, "My God, Sam, I didn't realize you'd died."[122]

Peckinpah rewrote the script, and although he said he didn't do enough revision for a screenwriting credit, Wurlitzer complained to a reporter, "There's *no* script left." When the reporter followed up, "Then it's not a Wurlitzer?," Wurlitzer said, "It's a *Peckinpah*...."[123]

During the shooting of the scene in which Bob Ollinger (played by R.G. Armstrong) almost kills Billy the Kid, Peckinpah tormented Armstrong, an actor who had worked with the director on the Peckinpah-created TV series *The Westerner* (1960) as well as on the movies *Ride the High Country* (1962), *Major Dundee* (1965), and *The Ballad of Cable Hogue* (1970). "Sam had always been a real gentleman to me and I to him," Armstrong told Evans years later. "I had total respect for him. And that little rascal antagonized me. He deliberately antagonized me. I was hurt. I couldn't believe he was doing this to me. Then I got into a rage, a killing rage. It only lasted ten seconds, but that was one of the best performances I ever gave. It's a wonder I didn't kill Kristofferson right there."[124]

In the scene in which Chisum's cowboys lash Paco and rape his daughter (or wife), Peckinpah and Emilio Fernandez, who had played the Mexican general in *The Wild Bunch*, were drunk when filming started and proceeded to get drunker and drunker. Peckinpah wanted more and more blood smeared on Fernandez's body. He later complained that the blood looked bad.[125]

Peckinpah argued with Coburn over the scene in which Coburn shoots his reflection in the mirror, an idea Coburn came up with (Peckinpah had once shot his own reflection in a mirror at his home). Composer Jerry Fielding argued with Dylan over the film score so much that Fielding wound up quitting. Peckinpah hated Dylan's songs for the movie.[126]

Somehow, Peckinpah completed filming in late January 1973, only twenty days and $1.6 million over budget. Then Aubrey informed Peckinpah and Carroll that MGM wanted to release the film on Memorial Day weekend, which would require a quick turnaround on the editing process. Six editors, plus assistants, went to work around the clock every day to get it ready.[127]

Peckinpah's first version came in between two hours, two minutes and two hours, six minutes, when it was previewed on March 13. Thinking it was Peckinpah's first cut, Aubrey liked it. When he found out this was what Peckinpah considered his final cut, Aubrey blew up. He argued that the movie was too long and incoherent. Peckinpah's contract allowed only two public screenings for his cut, and MGM was going to make those screenings available only at MGM. While those screenings were arranged, MGM edited the movie behind Peckinpah's back.[128] "Aubrey was ordering scenes cut for no other reason except that he knew Sam didn't want them cut," editor Roger Spottiswoode said.[129]

At a screening of the studio's cut, Slim Pickens turned to Max Evans during Pickens's death scene, saying, "Sam doesn't cut a film like that. There's something wrong."[130]

Coburn agreed. "The MGM cut really blew my mind, it was really fucking terrible. It made me sick...."[131]

"We were terribly disappointed when that film was over," Evans said. "I could tell that Slim's heart was broken. He had seen it with Sam in the way Sam had envisioned it.... We expected to sit there and see a slow, wonderful film, to absorb the land, absorb the film. [Peckinpah] loved Mexico and he loved the people, whether they were New Mexico or Old Mexico. That was part of his appeal to Billy the Kid. They both loved that relationship with the Hispanics."[132]

Later, Evans met with Peckinpah, who by then was so paranoid he told Evans that his office was "bugged by those goddamn producers." Quietly, Peckinpah said, "They fucked up this wonderful film on little Billy."[133]

When a *Los Angeles Times* reporter called Peckinpah to ask if MGM had taken his film away from him and re-edited it, Peckinpah said, "That's true. I'm glad I'm not armed."[134]

The MGM release, which came in at around 106 minutes, eliminated the prologue and deleted the scene between Garrett and his wife Ida, in which she says she hopes Billy gets away. The Barry Sullivan cameo as John Chisum was cut. So were the scenes with the Garrett and the prostitutes, and in Tuckerman's Hotel in which Poe learns of the Kid's whereabouts (the one scene in which neither Billy nor Garrett appears). Various bits of dialogue were deleted, too.[135]

The film earned mixed reviews. "There are half a dozen things wrong with Sam Peckinpah's *Pat Garrett and Billy the Kid*," the *New York Times* noted, singling out that "Bob Dylan's lyrics sound silly and a century out of place."

Variety also lambasted Dylan's performance: "His acting is limited to an embarrassing assortment of tics, smirks, shrugs, winks and smiles."[136]

Time's Jay Cocks, one of the few journalists allowed to see a copy of Peckinpah's cut, wrote: "Even in the maimed state in which it has been released, *Pat Garrett and Billy the Kid* is the richest, most exciting American film so far this year."[137]

James Coburn and Sam Peckinpah talk during the shooting of *Pat Garrett and Billy the Kid* (1973).

After the film's release, Daniel Melnick, MGM's production vice-president, approached Peckinpah about making a "proper version" of *Pat Garrett and Billy the Kid*. "The first thing on Peckinpah's list of priorities, in addition to putting the wife scene back, was revisiting the issue of Dylan's lyrics in the killing of the old sheriff," Seydor says. Peckinpah did not take Melnick's offer.[138]

Peckinpah sued MGM for breach of contract, unfair competition, invasion of privacy and false attribution, asking for $1.5 million in damages and expenses.[139] "Sure enough," Evans said. "[MGM] released it, and [Peckinpah] fought the studio, made more enemies. It didn't do him any good. His film was a failure."

By the end of 1973, *Pat Garrett and Billy the Kid* had grossed only $4,652,724.[140]

In October, Aubrey announced that the studio was withdrawing from theatrical distribution. Aubrey resigned, and the studio sold its library of films to United Artists.[141]

"Mr. Aubrey is now unemployed," Peckinpah said at the San Francisco Film Festival in 1974. "So maybe I've done something good for the world."[142]

When the movie played on television, it wasn't the same as what had appeared in theaters, with scenes cut because of violence, but others, cut from the theatrical version, added back in.[143]

Yet Peckinpah's movie, which some would call a masterpiece on the same level as his classic Westerns *Ride the High Country* (1962) and *The Wild Bunch* (1969), would find new life years later.

Peckinpah's preferred cut was shown at the University of Southern California in 1986, was released by Ted Turner on videotape and laser disc in 1988, and showed up on cable television's Z Channel in 1989. For some reason, that version of the movie deleted, perhaps by mistake, the scene in which Garrett argues with his wife.[144]

That version, which, technically, was not properly finished, also included an epilogue, cutting back to Garrett's murder, but the scene had come about after Peckinpah had left the movie. "Even when they got the idea of doing the prologue, the epilogue was never part of that," Paul Seydor says. "The epilogue was only something that was constructed much, much later in the editing room by Roger Spottiswoode, the editor."[145]

Another video version, called the "Special Edition," was issued by Warner Bros. in 2005. It restored the scene with Garrett's wife, but deleted the Tuckerman's Hotel scene and the epilogue. Seydor says he wishes Warner Bros. had labeled this version as the "augmented theatrical version."[146]

Technically, Peckinpah's "preview" version has never been shown publicly, and today the 1973 MGM theatrical release is unavailable on DVD.[147]

These "restored" versions of Peckinpah's film have drawn comparisons to European version of *The Wild Bunch*, which was different from the American release shown in theaters in 1969. But Seydor points out: "The case of *The Wild Bunch* and the case of *Pat Garrett and Billy the Kid* are very, very different. Peckinpah actually finished *The Wild Bunch* and he released the longer European version. So that's something he actually did. *Pat Garrett and Billy the Kid* he walked away from, and he was dictating changes the day he stopped working on it."[148]

Today, viewers can watch either the preview version or the "augmented" theatrical release on video.

Yet it would come too late for the "Picasso of Violence." In December 1984, doctors in Puerto Vallarta, Mexico, discovered a blood clot in one of Peckinpah's lungs. He was flown to Los Angeles for surgery. On December 28, Peckinpah, who had a pacemaker and a history of heart problems, "had a cardiac arrest and didn't come out of it," his brother, Denver Peckinpah, told the *New York Times*. Sam Peckinpah was dead at age fifty-nine.[149]

Analysis

Unlike most Billy the Kid movies, *Pat Garrett and Billy the Kid* covers only the last few months of the Kid's life. Many regard it as a neo-classic. Others, of course, consider it a misfire.

The same can be said for its version of history: deadly accurate in places, and wildly Hollywood malarkey in others.

Some images stay with you, however, and despite any shortcomings — Dylan's performance, some disjointed vignettes that don't always make sense — it remains incredibly powerful.

"Train wreck" or "masterpiece," *Pat Garrett and Billy the Kid* is easily — unless you count *Four Faces West* as a Billy the Kid movie (a stretch, since Billy's not in it) — the best Billy the Kid film to date.

***

Chicago Sun-Times (May 23, 1973): "Sam Peckinpah attempted to have his name removed from *Pat Garrett and Billy the Kid*. I sympathized with him. If this wasn't entirely his work, he shouldn't have had to take the blame. And even if it was, the less said the better. It's a movie that exists almost entirely on one note — a low, melancholy one — and achieves what I thought would have been impossible for him Peckinpah: he's boring."

Chapter Eleven

The 1980s and Beyond: Young Actors, *Young Guns*

Critics kept announcing that the Western genre was dead in the 1980s, but Billy the Kid would help revive it. Two *Young Guns* movies brought the Kid back into the limelight, and the Kid even tagged along with Bill and Ted on their most excellent adventure.

Young Guns

(Morgan Creek/20th Century–Fox, August 1988, 107 minutes) CREDITS: Director: Christopher Cain. Producers: Joe Roth, Christopher Cain. Screenplay: John Fusco. CAST: Emilio Estevez (William H. Bonney); Kiefer Sutherland (Doc Scurlock); Lou Diamond Phillips (Chavez Y Chavez); Charlie Sheen (Dick Brewer); Dermot Mulroney (Dirty Steve Stephens); Casey Siemaszko (Charley Bowdre); Terence Stamp (John Tunstall); Jack Palance (Lawrence G. Murphy); Terry O'Quinn (Alex McSween); Sharon Thomas (Susan McSween); Geoffrey Blake (J. McCloskey); Alice Carter (Yen Sun); Brian Keith (Buckshot Roberts); Thomas Callaway (Texas Joe Grant); Patrick Wayne (Pat Garrett).

Synopsis

John Tunstall and Doc Scurlock rescue a young runaway, William Bonney, from a mob in Lincoln, New Mexico, and bring him to Tunstall's ranch. His ranch hands, called "Regulators," are pretty much the "flotsam and jetsam of frontier society"—"runaway, scud-bottom vagrants," Dirty Steve Stephens says. They're all young boys, and all pretty handy with guns. They need to be, to protect Tunstall's interests from Lawrence G. Murphy and his henchmen.

An Irishman, Murphy doesn't like competition from Englishman Tunstall threatens his store and his cattle enterprises. Murphy also happens to own the law, and the territorial governor's behind him, too. So is the powerful Santa Fe Ring, which includes major political officers throughout the territory. "Get ready," Murphy warns Tunstall, "for hell."

Tunstall doesn't just keep these boys around for his protection. He teaches them table manners, proper language, and how to read. Billy proves to be an excellent reader. A former Murphy employee named McCloskey—fired after calling his boss "a fat sow"—joins Tunstall's crew.

At a New Year's Eve dance, Doc Scurlock is drawn to a Chinese girl who calls Murphy her guardian. Turns out, Tunstall's lawyer and friend Alexander McSween says, that girl was taken by Murphy as payment after a laundress ruined a shirt. Nice guy, this Murphy.

On the way back to the ranch the next morning, the boys ride after wild pheasants. Billy stays behind until Tunstall encourages him to go with them. "Boys will be boys," he says, and Billy rides off, turning around to see Murphy's men come up behind Tunstall and shoot him dead.

After Tunstall foreman Dick Brewer reads over Tunstall's grave, McSween persuades Justice of the Peace J.P. Wilson to swear in Tunstall's "Regulators" as lawmen to bring in the killers. Sheriff Brady won't. He's a Murphy man, and half the possemen killed Tunstall work for Brady-Murphy. Wilson is opposed to the idea, arguing that Tunstall's riders aren't older than twenty-one, but he concedes. Warrants in hand, Brewer leads the Regulators out for justice.

Billy draws first blood. Brewer sends him to a saloon to see if one of Tunstall's murderers is there. Billy spots the killer and waits for him in the ambush. He shoots him dead, then sticks the warrant in the corpse's mouth.

Newspapers embellish the story, calling the Kid left-hander (he's right-handed), brave, daring, a veritable Robin Hood.

Before long, the Regulators have captured two other men, Morton and Baker. When McCloskey suggests they take another way to bring the prisoners to Lincoln, Billy suspects

Young guns — Casey Siemaszko, Charlie Sheen, Kiefer Sutherland, Emilio Estevez, Lou Diamond Phillips and Dermot Mulroney — in the 1988 film of the same name.

that McCloskey is as a spy, and shoots him dead. The two prisoners make a run for it, and are cut down.

They hide for a while. Chavez Y Chavez, who is part Navajo, introduces them to peyote, and all but Brewer get stoned. Then they head down to Blazer's Mill and are eating — Brewer and Billy come close to shooting each other — when along comes Buckshot Roberts, who "has killed more men than smallpox."

The Regulators have a warrant for Roberts, but he doesn't care. He says he has quit the Murphy bunch. He's simply after the $150 reward on the Kid (the others are only worth $110, but that'll do). "Let's dance," Roberts says, smiling, and begins shooting, despite the odds.

Chavez Y Chavez and Scurlock are wounded. Roberts takes shelter in a shed, which is peppered with lead from the Regulators. When Brewer walks forward, thinking Roberts is dead, the gunman blows him away, and the Regulators retreat.

Brewer's death means Billy has taken over the gang, and he's after Brady. Chavez Y Chavez wants no part of that even though Murphy has helped slaughter his people. Billy changes Chavez's mind by calling the Regulators Chavez's tribe. "You walk away from us," he says, "you break our sacred hoop."

Doc has visited Yen Sun in Lincoln, but she won't run away with him, so he rejoins the gang in time to ambush Brady and his deputies on Lincoln's main street.

That act not only infuriates McSween, it leads to the governor revoking the Regulators' commissions as peace officers. They're wanted for murder now, and a murdering, Murphy-backed bounty hunter named John Kinney has replaced Brady as sheriff.

The boys visit a brothel (for Charley Bowdre's sake) and Billy overhears a braggart of a gunman named Texas Joe Grant saying he plans to kill the Kid. Billy walks up to him, saying he would like to hold the gun that killed Billy the Kid. Grant lets him have it and the Kid removes the shells, returns the pistol, and provokes Grant into a gunfight. Then kills him.

"How many does that make?" Billy asks Doc. "Twenty-five."

Doc tells him it's only five. The Kid smiles, saying, "Call it ten."

Pat Garrett, who met Billy at the New Year's Eve dance, visits the boys in Mexico and warns them that Murphy plans to ambush McSween at his home in Lincoln. The Kid and his pals ride to the McSween home, but it's a trap set by Murphy's men. When the Army arrives the next morning, Billy cheerfully declares, "I love these odds."

Yen Sun dashes across the street, rejoining Scurlock in the home, which is soon fired. As the fire rages, a trunk is tossed out of the second story. When it lands on the ground, Billy pops out, guns blazing. The final shootout is on. Others come out of the house, working their guns.

Scurlock's wounded, but manages to pull Yen Sun on the horse behind him and they ride out. Charley Bowdre is riddled with bullets, but kills John Kinney before he dies. Dirty Steve is shot dead and falls into the mud. McSween cheers the boys on, only to be cut down by the Army's Gatling gun.

As Billy rides out of town, with one remarkable pistol shot he puts a bullet in Murphy's brain. "Now it's over," Billy says, and joins his friends.

Scurlock's voice narrates the epilogue as they ride off, saying that Chavez Y Chavez left for California; Scurlock married Yen Sun and moved to New York with her mother and fourteen siblings; Mrs. McSween became a prominent cattlewoman; President Rutherford

B. Hayes ousted Governor Sam Axtell from office; the Santa Fe Ring collapsed with Murphy's death; and Pat Garrett killed Billy the Kid, who was unarmed at the time, in a darkened room. Billy was buried beside Bowdre. Some time later, someone chiseled on the headstone, "Pals."

The History

In some ways, John Fusco's screenplay had a grasp of the history around Billy the Kid and the Lincoln County War. But he also embellished much of that history. A lot.

John Tunstall was competing with Lawrence G. Murphy with his ranching and mercantile operations. Tunstall was an Englishman, and Murphy was born in Ireland. Yet once again, Tunstall is played as the benevolent, older gentleman. In fact, he was not quite twenty-five years old when he was killed — not on New Year's Day, but February, 18, 1878.[1]

Tunstall's horse was also killed by his murderers, as depicted here. His riders, including Billy the Kid and Dick Brewer, had ridden ahead chasing wild turkeys. Tunstall, however, wasn't driving a buckboard. They were driving horses through the rough wooded terrain above the Ruidoso Valley, when the posse came upon them. According to John Middleton, Tunstall was "on a good horse; he appeared to be very much excited and confused. I kept singing out to him, 'For God's sake, follow me.' His last words were, 'What, John? What, John?'" Tunstall's riders fled, never firing a shot. *Young Guns* got that part right.[2]

Lawyer Alexander McSween circumvented Sheriff William Brady's office by having Justice of the Peace John B. Wilson deputize a posse and obtain warrants. Dick Brewer became a "special constable" to lead the Regulators. That name might have been suggested by Billy the Kid, who was fond of the dime novels of the day, but the boys weren't called Regulators until after McSween's death. In addition to Billy and Brewer, the Regulators included Charlie Bowdre, Henry Brown, Jim French, Frank and George Coe, John Middleton, Frank McNab (sometimes spelled MacNab), Doc Scurlock, John Scroggins, Sam Smith, and Fred Waite. "The number of these active Regulators varied from as few as ten to as many as sixty, including Hispanics sympathetic to the cause," writes Michael Wallis, who says that about twelve Anglos formed the core of the group. They were bound not by the "sacred hoop" but by the "iron clad," which meant they'd keep their actions a secret and never testify against another Regulator.[3]

Among the Regulars depicted here:

José Chávez y Chávez had settled in Lincoln County in the late 1860s. In San Patricio, he had served as constable and justice of the peace. He didn't join the Regulators until after the Blazer's Mill fight, but he was with the bunch that defended the McSween house during the bloody fight in July in which McSween was killed. He later served as a Las Vegas, New Mexico, peace officer, but in 1895 he was convicted of murder and sentenced to hang. That death sentence was commuted to life and he entered the territorial penitentiary in 1897. He was paroled in 1909. He even said he had killed Sheriff Brady, and that he had killed Albert Fountain and his young son in 1896. Chávez y Chávez died in 1923. He likely was not Navajo, and the Red Sand Creek massacre he mentions in *Young Guns* is fiction. The Sand Creek Massacre, in Colorado in 1864, involved the butchery of Cheyenne and Arapaho Indians. Also, the "sacred hoop" reference Chávez y Chávez speaks of is a Lakota concept, not Navajo.[4]

Born in Mississippi in 1848, Charles Bowdre came with Doc Scurlock to Lincoln in

1875 and they bought a ranch on the Ruidoso River. When Bowdre married Manuela Herrera, they lived in the old Indian hospital at Fort Sumner. Bowdre wasn't killed during the fight at the McSween house, but by Pat Garrett's posse at Stinking Springs on December 21, 1880. When his body was brought back to Fort Sumner, Manuela "kicked and pummeled Garrett until she had to be pulled away," Jim East recalled. "As we started in with [Bowdre's body], she struck me over the head with a branding iron, and I had to drop Charlie at her feet.... I always regretted the death of Charlie Bowdre, for he was a brave man, and true to his friends to the last."[5]

Josiah Gordon "Doc" Scurlock is believed to have studied medicine in New Orleans, and was working for John Chisum by 1875. He did not marry a "Celestial" and move to New York, but married Antonia Miguela Herrera in 1876. After the Lincoln County War, Scurlock moved to Texas, where he died in 1929. Yet the character Kiefer Sutherland plays on screen has some elements right. Lincoln County historian Frederick Nolan says Scurlock "was a most unusual gunfighter: a doctor, farmer, poet, teacher, later a linguist and reader of the classics."[6]

Little is known about the "relatively obscure" Dirty Steve Stephens, but he was indicted for the murder of Buckshot Roberts and was on hand during the climax in Lincoln in July. Stephens (or Stevens) helped defend Isaac Ellis's store and house along with Bowdre, Scurlock, John Middleton and eight or ten others. He might have died in Denver, Colorado.[7]

Dick Brewer was a native of Vermont (Doc Scurlock even says he must write Dick's mother in Vermont in *Young Guns*). He wound up in Carthage, Missouri, then moved to New Mexico, settling in the Peñasco Valley before buying a ranch on the Ruidoso River in 1876. He befriended Tunstall, even served as the Englishman's foreman, and was killed at Blazer's Mill on April 4, 1878.[8]

Which brings us to the fight that ended Brewer's life.

Andrew L. "Buckshot" Roberts, a horse thief and Army deserter, had been with the posse that murdered Tunstall. Brewer did have a warrant for Roberts's arrest, but Roberts didn't come to Blazer's Mill looking for the Kid. At that time, there was no reward offered for Billy. Roberts, who might have come from Texas, was trying to sell his farm on the Ruidoso River and leave the territory. He came hoping to find a check from a potential buyer.[9]

Frank Coe stepped out of the building where Clara Godfroy served meals and took in lodgers, and he tried to talk Roberts into surrendering. Roberts said he couldn't because "The Kid is with you and will kill me on sight." Thirty minutes later, the Regulators were done waiting. Bowdre, Middleton, McNab, Brown, and George Coe stepped out and demanded that Roberts give up.

Instead, Roberts brought up his Winchester rifle. Bowdre and Roberts fired. Roberts was hit in the stomach as his bullet slammed into Bowdre's belt buckle, ricocheted, and hit George Coe's gun hand. Mortally wounded, Roberts put a bullet into Middleton's chest while another hit Scurlock's holster and burned his leg. Yet another round "shaved" the Kid's arm. "I never saw a man that could handle a Winchester as fast as he could," Frank Coe marveled.

The Regulators dived for cover. Roberts, his rifle empty, took shelter in a one-story adobe, where he used a mattress as a barricade and found a Springfield .45–70 single-shot rifle, loaded it, and waited.

Brewer was determined to finish Roberts. He ran to a log pile near the sawmill, aimed, and fired into the building. Roberts saw the smoke and waited. When Brewer raised his head again, Roberts fired. The bullet, Frank Coe said, "knocked the top of [Brewer's] head off at 125 steps away."

Just as depicted in the movie, the Regulators fled. "Yes, sir," Billy the Kid later said, "he licked our crowd to a finish."

Roberts died the following day and was buried next to Brewer.[10]

The gunfight at Blazer's Mill, however, happened after Sheriff William Brady was killed on April 1. On that morning, Brady and deputies George Hindman, Billy Mathews, John Long, and George Peppin were walking down Lincoln's main street. Billy the Kid wasn't marching along behind the lawmen, but was in the Tunstall corral with plenty of others, waiting. Several Regulators fired from ambush, killing Brady and Hindman.

When the shooting stopped, Billy and Jim French leaped over the wall and ran to Brady's body. The reason is unknown, perhaps to find warrants or, more than likely, the Kid sought to retrieve the rifle Brady had taken from him in February. Billy Mathews opened fire, wounding French, and possibly Billy, in the leg. The killers retreated back to the corral and escaped.[11]

The killing of "Texas" Joe Grant follows close to the legend, and the Regulators did kill prisoners William "Buck" Morton and Frank Baker on the way to Lincoln. In the latter incident, Dick Brewer promised Morton and Baker that they would not be murdered but taken to Lincoln. Billy, however, said, "My time will come." McCloskey had worked for Tunstall, and while he might not have been a spy for Murphy, he was one of Morton's friends. So when the posse entered Agua Negra Canyon, one version has it, Frank MacNab drew his revolver, pointed it at McCloskey and said, "You are the son of a bitch that's got to die before harm can come to these fellows, aren't you?" He shot McCloskey out of the saddle. Another version has McCloskey being killed by Henry Brown. Yet another, unlikely version, has Morton grabbing McCloskey's gun, killing him, and then making a break for freedom with Baker. No matter the version, Morton, Baker, and McCloskey were all killed. The three bodies were left where they fell.[12]

Young Guns' climax at the McSween house, however, became Hollywood nonsense.

McSween had been on the dodge from the Murphy-Dolan outfit and was tired of running. When he heard that Governor Axtell would be replaced, he decided to return to his home. But he wasn't a fool. He went back to Lincoln with plenty of men, including Billy the Kid. With nearly sixty men, McSween and his backers entered Lincoln on the night of Sunday, July 14, 1878.

George Peppin was sheriff, and James Dolan was running the Murphy-Dolan House since Murphy was drinking himself into oblivion while dying of cancer. Peppin and Dolan, who were in Lincoln, sent for the posse, and by the evening of July 15, sporadic firing and shouts had become the norm.

Peppin asked Colonel Nathan Dudley, commanding officer at nearby Fort Stanton, for help. It was a civilian matter, so the Army had no jurisdiction, but Dudley sent in troops, saying they were there to protect the noncombatant citizens. A Gatling gun and cannon were soon aimed at the McSween encampments.

McSween's home was finally burned, forcing Billy and the occupants out. Billy and Scurlock, Chávez y Chávez managed to escape. So did Bowdre and Stephens (they die violent deaths in this movie). Alexander McSween was killed, but by Murphy-Dolan men, not an Army-manned Gatling gun.[13]

John Kinney was not killed. An Army veteran who reportedly was born in Massachusetts, Kinney had been leading a rustling operation around Las Cruces and had briefly run a saloon in El Paso before heading to Lincoln as a mercenary fighting for the Murphy-Dolan cause. After the Lincoln County War, he was sentenced to five years in Leavenworth. After serving less than three, he wound up in Arizona, where he died in 1919 in Prescott.[14]

Billy didn't put a bullet in Murphy's brain. A destitute Murphy succumbed to cancer (or alcoholism) in Santa Fe on October 20, 1878.[15]

Scurlock's epilogue is a bit off history, too.

Samuel Axtell was removed as governor and replaced by Lew Wallace, and Susan McSween did become the "Cattle Queen of New Mexico."[16]

Murphy's death, however, did not collapse the Santa Fe Ring. In fact, Jon Tuska notes, "The Ring flourished, its leader [Thomas Catron, U.S. attorney for the territory during the Lincoln County War] becoming the first U.S. senator from New Mexico after statehood in 1912."[17]

Billy the Kid was killed by Pat Garrett and was buried next to Bowdre and another one of his pals, Tom O'Folliard/Folliard. The marble stone over their marker today in Fort Sumner indeed reads "Pals."

That bit of history would be rewritten by Fusco in the sequel, *Young Guns II*.

The Players

John Fusco's agents begged him not to shop his idea for a movie about Billy the Kid because, they said, the Western was dead. Instead, Fusco "defied common sense, went off and wrote it on spec."[18]

Fusco had gotten the idea to write about Billy the Kid from the famous tintype photograph of the Kid. "[W]hat hit me was that it didn't correspond at all with the legend of the noble bandit: Robert Taylor dressed in black, the left-hander who whistled sad ballads, the lady-killer. I looked at the young man in the photo and said, 'No, there's something else here. This is a ferret in a derby.'"[19]

Using Bon Jovi's song "Wanted Dead or Alive" as mood music, Fusco wrote *Young Guns*.[20] It was a gamble for him, and it was a gamble for producer Joe Roth. "Seven out of eight studio heads would say it's not going to make money," Roth said.[21]

Roth, Morgan Creek Productions, and 20th Century–Fox, however, saw something other producers and studios were overlooking: "We have six of the 12 best actors among that age group," Roth said.[22]

Young Guns. Young Actors. For a young moviegoing audience.

Emilio Estevez, son of actor Martin Sheen, had starred in *The Breakfast Club* (1885), *St. Elmo's Fire* (1985) and *Stakeout* (1988) and would be playing Billy the Kid. Estevez's younger brother, Charlie Sheen, had appeared in *Ferris Bueller's Day Off* (1986), *Platoon* (1986) and *Wall Street* (1987). The son of actor Donald Sutherland, Kiefer Sutherland's credits included *The Lost Boys* (1987), while Lou Diamond Phillips had made his mark as Ritchie Valens in *La Bamba* (1987). Rounding out the "young guns" were Casey Siemaszko of *Stand by Me* (1986) and *Biloxi Blues* (1988) fame and Dermot Mulroney from *Sunset* (1988). All these actors were still in their twenties.

Yet it wasn't just young actors. Old Western hands Brian Keith — *The Deadly Companions* (1961), *The Rare Breed* (1966) — and Jack Palance — *Shane* (1953) and *Monte Walsh* (1970) — came in, as did Patrick Wayne, one of legendary cowboy actor John Wayne's sons.

Terence Stamp, who had been nominated for an Oscar for *Billy Budd* (1963), took the part of Tunstall.

Christopher Cain, whose credits included *The Stone Boy* (1984) and *Where the River Runs Black* (1986), came to direct.

"I loved working with the 'Young Guns,'" Fusco said, "but it was the Old Guns, like Jack Palance, James Coburn [from *Young Guns II*] and Brian Keith, who made it a true Western experience."[23]

In February 1988, the cast and crew came to New Mexico with an estimated $13 million budget to film a movie about events that happened in New Mexico. Cerrillos, a semi-ghost town near Santa Fe, was transformed into Lincoln. It was a physical shoot that required the stars to spend six weeks learning to ride horseback and getting in shape.[24]

The young actors had been dubbed the "Brat Pack"—a play off the old Frank Sinatra-Dean Martin-Sammy Davis, Jr.-etc. "Rat Pack"—and they lived up to their reputations.[25]

"Charlie Sheen was the only sane one," Fusco said. "He was always dragging us out of border bars and restoring order to bad situations. Not sure if he was just in character as the foreman Dick Brewer, but he would literally yell 'Regulators' and herd the guys out of trouble."[26]

Most actors had done their research, but Sutherland turned down Fusco's offer of books to research his role, preferring to rely on "imagination and take dramatic license rather than make a docu-drama.... There was a raw quality to life and to people's ideals back then. Basic values were cut and dried."[27]

Estevez did his research, but came always with more legend than fact. "Billy's Dad had died and he killed a man at age 12 or 13 for insulting his mother," he said. "Billy was an angry soul. He was abused as a child."[28]

Sheen learned that he didn't like horses. "My horse Blaze was a real piece of work. He didn't like me. It was kind of a hate-hate relationship.

"He was a great rehearsal horse. But the minute he heard the word action, which he understood, I was dead in the water. He blew more takes. I thought I had a good performance, good energy and the horse is off in the can."

By the end of March, shooting had finished, and the movie was turned around quickly for an August release. The buzz around Hollywood was: Can *Young Guns* resurrect the Western? In 1985, the last such attempts, *Silverado* and *Pale Rider*, had failed.

"If any movie can revive the Western," Paul Willistein wrote in the Allentown, Pennsylvania, *Morning Call*, "*Young Guns* might."

Emilio Estevez as Billy the Kid in *Young Guns* (1988).

Young Guns opened in August. Reviews were mixed. The *Los Angeles Times* proclaimed that it "Breathes Life into Old Genre," while the *Chicago Tribune* said it "falls short as a James Dean–style film."[29]

Audience response proved huge. The movie grossed more than $7 million on its opening weekend and went on to gross almost $47 million. It had — if only briefly — revitalized the genre, helping pave the way for the Academy Award–winning Best Pictures *Dances with Wolves* (1990) and *Unforgiven* (1992). It also likely inspired the ABC TV series *The Young Riders*, about young Pony Express riders, which led to Morgan Creek Productions suing MGM/Pathé for copyright infringement. The series kept its title, and *The Young Riders* ran for three seasons, 1989 through 1992.[30]

With a hit Western on his hand, Fusco got busy writing a sequel.

Analysis

Entertainment-wise, *Young Guns* is an odd movie, sometimes riveting, other times boring, often disjointed. Like Walter Hill's *The Long Riders*, a 1980 movie with the gimmick of casting the Keach (James, Stacy), Carradine (David, Keith, Robert), Quaid (Randy, Dennis) and Guest (Nicholas, Christopher) brothers as the James, Younger, Miller and Ford brothers, *Young Guns* had its Brat Pack gimmick. Sometimes it worked — Estevez is a fun psychotic killer — but more often it didn't.

The same is true when one regards the movie through a historical lens. *Young Guns* likely gets more of the Billy the Kid-Lincoln County War history right than any other theatrical release, but it also falls back to Hollywood-isms. Its ending, Paul Hutton notes, is "as wildly inaccurate" as the one in *Chisum*.[31]

What can't be overlooked, however, is the success of *Young Guns*. It proved that Westerns could appeal to younger viewers.

***

Washington Post (August 16, 1988): "The clubby atmosphere of Young Guns ... is so thick as to be almost suffocating. [It's] like a Western-style dress-up party for Hollywood kiddies, horses and guns included."

Bill & Ted's Excellent Adventure

(Interscope Communications/Soisson-Murphey Productions/Orion Pictures, February 1989, 89 minutes) CREDITS: Director: Stephen Herek. Producers: Scott Kroopf, Michael S. Murphey, Joel Soisson. Screenplay: Chris Matheson, Ed Solomon. CAST: Keanu Reeves (Ted Logan); Alex Winer (Bill Preston); George Carlin (Rufus); Terry Camilleri (Napoleon); Dan Shor (Billy the Kid); Tony Steedman (Socrates); Rod Loomis (Sigmund Freud); Al Leong (Genghis Khan); Jane Wiedlin (Joan of Arc); Robert Barron (Abraham Lincoln); Clifford David (Ludwig van Beethoven); Hal Landon, Jr. (Captain Logan); Bernie Casey (Mr. Ryan); Amy Stock-Poynton (Missy Preston); J. Patrick McNamara (Mr. Preston); Franzier Bain (Deacon Logan); Diane Franklin (Princess Joanna); Kimberley LaBelle (Princess Elizabeth).

Synopsis

Dudes, to put it mildly, Bill Logan and Ted Preston are total idiots who think Joan of Arc was Noah's wife. They're on the verge of failing history at San Dimas High School, which would be a bummer because Ted's dad will send him to military school in Alaska, meaning Bill and Ted's garage band will never get out of the garage, (which, seeing how they don't know how to play, wouldn't be a bad thing). On the other hand, that would be a calamity for history because in the year 2688, bowling scores are up and even the dirt is clean in San Dimas—thanks to Bill and Ted.

That's why "The Three Most Powerful People in the World" are sending Rufus back in time to help out our surfer-dude heroes. They have to ace their oral history report on what world figures from history think about San Dimas today. In his time-machine telephone booth, Rufus heads to 1988 San Dimas. The boys figure out the perfect way to ace that history project: bring people from history to San Dimas.

So after snagging Napoleon and leaving him with Ted's kid brother Deacon, the boys drop down in New Mexico in 1879—"just like Frontier Land"—and head to the nearest saloon. That's totally rocking because they can buy beer and not even get carded. Then Billy the Kid walks in, searching for two men, and Bill and Ted volunteer. "What I win, I keep," Billy tells them. "What you win, I keep." They sit down to play poker.

A fight breaks out when other card players suspect Billy, Ted, and Bill of cheating, but the boys save the Kid's life by whisking him away in the telephone booth and traveling to ancient Greece, where they meet Socrates. Next it's medieval England, where they meet some righteous looking babes but almost get their heads chopped off.

Eventually, they collect Genghis Khan, Joan of Arc, Sigmund Freud, Ludwig van Beethoven, and President Abraham Lincoln—it must be getting crowded in that phone booth—and head back to San Dimas. The historical figures run into all sorts of trouble at the mall (Billy has fun riding the escalator rail).

In the proverbial "fish out of water" sequences, Freud ruins Socrates's and Billy's chances of picking up chicks in the food court; Joan of Arc makes a scene at an aerobics workout; Beethoven jams at a music store; Genghis Khan destroys a sporting goods store mannequin with a baseball bat—and they all wind up in jail. They are rescued by smart-thinking Bill and Ted, who make it to school, in the nick of time, for their awesome history report.

Back in the garage, Bill and Ted figure out that maybe they should learn how to play their instruments, and Rufus is there to help. He brings back the two medieval English babes—who will play in the band—and sits in with a jam session.

The boys and girls try to play. "They do get better," Rufus tells the camera.

The History

Billy the Kid was a gambler, who excelled at cards. In the one substantiated photograph of Billy, he's even wearing a gambler's ring on his pinky finger. So when Billy sits down to play poker with Bill, Ted, and other cowboys, the history is correct. Even the playing cards are authentic replicas, without numbers. However, when Billy the Kid reveals his wanted poster, the reward is $1,200. Governor Lew Wallace had offered a $500 reward for the capture of Billy, which was printed in newspapers across the territory. That reward wasn't posted until November 1880, not in 1879, which is when Billy joins Bill and Ted.[32]

The Players

Scott Kroopf had co-produced only one movie, 1987's *Outrageous Fortune*, when he made *Bill & Ted's Excellent Adventure*, written by relative newcomers Ed Solomon and Chris

Bill (Alex Winter, left), Ted (Keanu Reeves, right), and Billy (Dan Shor) escape from the holding cell in *Bill & Ted's Excellent Adventure* (1989).

Matheson. Stephen Herek, who likewise had only one credit (1986's *Critters*), directed. There seemed nothing special about the project, and Warners put it in "turnaround," meaning the studio was no longer interested in it, leaving it available to be shopped to another studio.[33]

The cast included Keanu Reeves, a young actor of English-Chinese-Hawaiian descent who had trained as an actor in Canada and had appeared in a few Canadian and U.S. films. By the time *Excellent Adventure* was released, Reeves's credits included *River's Edge* (1987) and *Dangerous Liaisons* (1988). Alex Winter had studied at New York University, acted on Broadway, and had landed a role in the cult vampire film *The Lost Boys* (1987).[34]

For box office draw, standup comic George Carlin, whose "Seven Words You Can Never Say on Television" became a groundbreaking routine in the 1970s, took the role of Rufus. "The Three Most Important People in the World" were played by Clarence Clemons, star saxophonist for rocker Bruce Springsteen's E Street Band and the lead singers for The Motels (Martha Davis) and The Tubes (Fee Waybill). New York–born Dan Shor, who had appeared in several TV shows and films, landed the part of Billy the Kid.[35]

The movie was filmed in 1987 with an $8.5 million budget, and then Kroopf went shopping for a distributor.[36] He took it to Dino DeLaurentiis's DeLaurentiis Entertainment Group (DEG). "Dino had no idea what it was about," Kroopf said. "He didn't understand what dudes were..."[37]

DeLaurentiis had made a name for himself working with directors Federico Fellini and Roberto Rosellini in Italy before coming to America and producing the hits *Serpico* (1973), *Death Wish* (1974), *Conan the Barbarian* (1982), and *Dune* (1984). By the time *Excellent Adventure* was completed, however, his company was on the verge of bankruptcy. His past "successes," *Blue Velvet* and *Crimes of the Heart* (both 1986), had barely broken even. Yet DEG didn't even test Kroopf's film; "They just all looked at it in a screening room and decided it was no good." The film was in trouble. "Everybody's bailing out," Kroopf recalled. "I'm facing my baby being released on HBO."[38]

Kroopf went to see Rick Finkelstein, a former DeLaurentiis executive who had moved to Nelson Entertainment. Kroopf offered $1 million for the film and rights (DEG kept foreign rights). Interested, Nelson Entertainment tested the film. "They immediately realized that it tested great."[39]

In fact, it tested so well that in Los Angeles, Orion didn't believe the results and scheduled another preview in Secaucus, New Jersey. "The numbers were even higher," co-producer Michael Murphey said. "It appeals to ages 16 to 24."[40]

Still, the movie opened without fanfare in February 1989. Reviews weren't completely favorable—the *Washington Post* calling it "a dilapidated comedy"—but the box office draw was overwhelming. After four weeks, it had grossed $22 million and was fifth on the box office list. A sequel was planned. A soundtrack and two videos were released.[41] "We have literally hundreds of licensing offers to wade through," a Nelson executive said. "You can expect to see [Bill and Ted] on everything from lunch pails to T-shirts."[42] By midsummer, the movie had grossed almost $40 million.[43]

The sequel *Bill & Ted's Bogus Journey* was released in 1991, grossing more than $38 million in the United States, and by 2012 Solomon and Matheson had a script ready for *Bill & Ted 3*.[44]

Ironically, Bill and *Ted's Excellent Adventure* might have saved DeLaurentiis Entertainment Group, but by the time the movie was shattering expectations, DEG was bankrupt.[45]

Analysis

Now regarded as a cult favorite, *Bill & Ted's Excellent Adventure* didn't do much for Billy the Kid's cinematic legacy, but it did help boost another type of character's legend: the surfer dude.

Perhaps first lionized by Sean Penn in *Fast Times at Ridgemont High* (1982), that kind of character become a mainstay of 1980s-90s cinema, appearing in *Valley Girl* (1983, played by Nicolas Cage); *Wayne's World* (1992, played by Mike Myers, and based on a recurring *Saturday Night Life* skit); *True Romance* (1993, played by Brad Pitt); and *Dumb & Dumber* (1994, played by Jim Carrey)—and their sequels. Author Dave Gardetta even puts *The Big Lebowski* (1998, played by Jeff Bridges) on that list.[46]

The movie might have also inspired Michael J. Fox's character Marty McFly to head back to 1885 in *Back to the Future Part III* (1990), and security guard Larry Daley to run across Teddy Roosevelt (Robin Williams) in *Night at the Museum* (2006) and George Custer (Bill Hader) in *Night at the Museum: Battle at the Smithsonian* (2009).

***

Variety (February 22, 1989): "Reeves, with his beguilingly blank face and loose-limbed, happy-go-lucky physical vocabulary, and Winter, with his golden curls, gleefully good vibes and 'bodacious' vocabulary, propel this adventure as long as they can."

Young Guns II

(Morgan Creek/20th Century–Fox, August 1990, 104 minutes) CREDITS: Director: Geoff Murphy. Producers: Irby Smith, Paul Schiff, John Fusco. Screenplay: John Fusco. CAST: Emilio Estevez (William H. Bonney); Kiefer Sutherland (Doc Scurlock); Lou Diamond Phillips (Chavez Y Chavez); Christian Slater (Arkansas Dave Rudabaugh); William Peterson (Pat Garrett); Alan Ruck (Hendry William French); R.D. Call (District Attorney Rynerson); James Coburn (John Chisum); Balthazar Getty (Tom O'Folliard); Jack Kehoe (Ash Upson); Robert Knepper (Deputy James Carlyle); Tom Kurlander (J.W. Bell); Viggo Mortensen (John W. Poe); Leon Rippy (Bob Ollinger); Tracey Walter (Beaver Smith); Bradley Whitford (Charles Phalen); Scott Wilson (Governor Lew Wallace); Jenny Wright (Jane Greathouse); John Hammil (Pendleton).

Synopsis

On a desert highway, a lawyer arrives by car to meet with an old man who says he's dying and wants to be pardoned by the New Mexico governor. For what? The murder of twenty-one men. The old man says he's Billy the Kid. When the lawyer is skeptical, the man curses him, grabs the reins to his horse, and begins to walk back into the desert. The lawyer has second thoughts, and asks for proof of the man's identity, asks if he has any scars. Thus begins the flashback of "Brushy Bill" Roberts.

After the Lincoln County War, Billy the Kid was riding with Arkansas Dave Rudabaugh, a braggart who claims to have "killed sixty-five men, not counting Mexicans and Indians," and Pat Garrett. They rustle stock and kill the bounty hunters who are after the $500 reward offered for the Kid.

It's 1879, and the new governor, Lew Wallace, is determined to put a stop to the killing in Lincoln County. The district attorney, Rynerson, is having everyone involved rounded up and tossed into the dungeon of a Lincoln jail. They've even gone al the way to New York

City to capture Doc Scurlock, who had ridden with Billy during the late war, and hauled him back to jail. Another Billy rider, the half–Navajo Chavez Y Chavez, is also in jail.

Wallace has a new plan, however. If Billy agrees to turn state's evidence (can one turn *state's* evidence in a *territory*?) he can "hang your enemies." Billy agrees to meet with the governor, who says they'll fake his arrest — to keep him alive — and then he can testify and go free with a pardon for all his crimes.

It's a deal — until Rynerson lets the Kid know that the governor doesn't decide who testifies or who gets hanged. Rynerson plans to hang Billy. "The Irish politicians were still running Lincoln County," Brushy Bill lets us know. Double-crossed, Billy escapes.

He frees Scurlock and Chavez Y Chavez from the jail, and the old gang is running around again. It's not quite the same gang. A farmer named Hendry William French, who has only shot a sage hen, joins. A young teenager who idolizes Billy, Tom O'Folliard, keeps trying to join the gang. And Pat Garrett quits, a big disappointment to the Kid. Garrett plans on buying Beaver Smith's saloon and calling it "Garrett's Place."

Rynerson demands that the sheriff bring in the Kid dead, but Sheriff Kimbel tosses in his badge, saying, "I'd rather drunk turpentine and piss on a brush fire."

Billy tries to blackmail cattle baron John Chisum into giving him money, and then has his men kill two of Chisum's riders. This turns Chisum, who had backed the Tunstall-McSween faction during the Lincoln County War, against the Kid. In a meeting with Governor Wallace and Rynerson, Chisum suggests that they "hire a thief to catch one." That thief is Pat Garrett, who takes the job as Lincoln County sheriff.

Joining Garrett's posse is a member of a cattleman's association, John Poe, and a drunken newspaper editor, Ash Upson. Garrett wants Upson to write a book about the tracking down of Billy the Kid.

Billy leads his friends to a whorehouse in White Oaks. When the place is surrounded by a local posse, brothel owner Jane Greathouse is held outside while a deputy named James Carlyle enters the place to talk Billy into surrendering. Instead, the gang dresses Carlyle up to resemble Chavez Y Chavez and pushes him out through the front door. He is riddled with bullets.

When Garrett reaches White Oaks, he burns down the brothel. Jane Greathouse, in a last act of defiance, rides out of town like Lady Godiva.

Billy has been saying he's leading the boys on a trail to Mexico, but in reality, he has no intention of leaving New Mexico, where he's famous. That act gets Tom O'Folliard killed, and the gang takes shelter in an old hideout.

By this time, Doc Scurlock has had enough. He walks outside and is gut-shot by Poe. Dying, Scurlock decides to lead the gang out. It's a bloodbath. Scurlock is killed; Chavez Y Chavez is mortally wounded, but escapes with help from French; Rudabaugh manages to get away and make it all the way to Mexico. Billy, however, is left behind, captured, taken to Mesilla and sentenced to hang.

His guards back in the Lincoln jail are dimwitted James Bell and villainous Bob Ollinger, who threatens the Kid with his double-barreled shotgun. He has loaded the shells with $1.80 worth of dimes, and hopes to have the chance to blow the Kid away.

Jane Greathouse shows up and leaves a revolver in the outhouse. So while Ollinger is eating at a restaurant across the street, Bell takes Billy to the privy. Heading back upstairs, Billy draws the revolver. He doesn't want to kill Bell, but when the deputy aims his rifle, Billy guns him down, hobbles upstairs, fetches Ollinger's shotgun and waits.

The *Young Guns II* (1990) cast: from left, Balthazar Getty, Alan Ruck, Emilio Estevez, Kiefer Sutherland, Lou Diamond Phillips, and Christian Slater.

Ollinger thinks Bell has killed the Kid, until Billy breaks a pane in a second-story window and calls down, "Hello, Bob." He lets Ollinger have both barrels. "Goodbye, Bob! Best dollar-eighty I ever spent."

He grabs the keys to his shackles from Bell's body and, seeing the blood on his hands, writes on the wall, "Garrett's Place."

Back in Fort Sumner, Billy finds Chavez Y Chavez dying. (Let's see, Billy has been caught, tried, convicted, and escaped, while Chavez Y Chavez is still bleeding from a bullet wound.) French has had enough of being an outlaw.

Disillusioned, Billy walks into a darkened room where Pat Garrett's waiting. The outlaw's death is faked, and Billy steals Garrett's horse and rides out of history.

So, yeah, Billy tells the lawyer. He has scars.

The lawyer, it seems, believes that this "Brushy Bill" is indeed Billy the Kid.

The History

Screenwriter John Fusco's sequel to *Young Guns* gives Ollie "Brushy Bill" Roberts the limelight.

In August 1949, a Florida investigator named William V. Morrison met Brushy Bill Roberts, who said he was Billy the Kid, in Hico, Texas. On a road trip to New Mexico, Roberts often contradicted himself and history in his remembrances, but Morrison decided the old man was indeed Billy the Kid. By July 1950, Morrison was in El Paso, Texas, "to be near the records," and began working on getting Brushy Bill a pardon from New Mexico Governor Thomas Mabry.

On November 29, 1950, Mabry met with Morrison and Roberts in the governor's mansion in Santa Fe. Then the three met media, historians, and "interested parties" such as Pat Garrett's sons Oscar and Jarvis. When the interrogation ended, Mabry decided against pardoning Roberts because "I don't believe this man is Billy the Kid."

The disappointed Roberts returned to Hico, where he died of a heart attack on December 27.[47]

Roberts's story, *Alias Billy the Kid,* was published by the University of New Mexico Press in 1955, but almost every historian believes that Brushy Bill Roberts was a faker, the same way most dismiss J. Frank Dalton, who in the late 1940s claimed that he was really Jesse James. In Hico, on the other hand, many citizens "emotionally defend" Brushy Bill as being the real Billy the Kid.[48]

There is no documentation that Garrett and Billy ever rode together or rustled cattle together. Garrett did work in Beaver Smith's saloon, but he probably wasn't a bosom bud with Billy. "He minds his business," Garrett reportedly said, "and I attend to mine." And as far as a Billy the Kid gang, even the Kid said: "I wasn't the leader of any gang."[49]

Arkansas Dave Rudabaugh? Rudabaugh was likely born in Illinois and lived in Kansas before moving to New Mexico in the late 1870s. He tried to break a friend out of the Las Vegas, New Mexico, jail in April 1880, killing a guard, and then joined up with Billy the Kid. Rudabaugh was captured at Stinking Springs with the Kid, but later escaped from jail. One story does have him being decapitated by Mexicans — as *Young Guns II* suggests and notes in its epilogue — although another story has him dying in Oregon in 1928.[50]

Tom O'Folliard/Folliard, who was killed by Garrett's posse when Billy and his pals rode into Fort Sumner in December 1880, had joined up with Billy *during* the Lincoln County War. Billy and O'Folliard/Folliard would become great friends, but O'Folliard/Folliard wasn't the small fifteen-year-old kid depicted here. He was a big man, weighing around 180 pounds, and was likely the same age as Billy.[51]

Hendry William French must be a composite, because there was a Henry Brown and a Jim French who rode with Billy the Kid and the Regulators during the Lincoln County War, but no Hendry William French.[52]

Yet Fusco's script gets much right. Billy the Kid's large wrists but small hands made it easy for him to free himself from handcuffs. Wallace did promise the Kid a pardon in return for his testimony. The Lincoln County War was probably better described as a merchant war, as the Kid tells Wallace, and not a range war. William Rynerson was a district attorney and a member of the powerful and corrupt Santa Fe Ring, who wanted Billy the Kid dead.[53]

How brutal was Rynerson? In 1867, he shot and killed Chief Justice John P. Slough after an argument in a Santa Fe hotel. Pleading self-defense, he was acquitted.[54]

The Kid also feuded with cattle baron John Chisum, who had backed the Tunstall-McSween cause during the Lincoln County War. Billy seemed to believe that Chisum owed him wages. Although there were "crazy stories" about the Kid murdering three Chisum cowhands, that never happened, but the Kid did challenge Chisum in Fort Sumner in the spring of 1880.[55]

"Billy," Chisum said, "you know as well as I do that I never hired you to fight in the Lincoln County War. I always pay my honest debts. I don't owe you anything, and you can kill me but you won't knock me out of many years. I'm an old man now."

After a moment, Billy said, "Aw, you ain't worth killing."[56]

Chisum died of cancer in 1884.[57]

John W. Poe did ride with Garrett. Appointed a deputy U.S. marshal in Texas, he went after rustlers in the Texas Panhandle toward the end of the Lincoln County War. Once he arrived in New Mexico in 1881, he joined Garrett as a deputy and was with Garrett and Kip McKinney on the night of July 14, 1881, when Garrett killed the Kid in Pete Maxwell's bedroom. Poe succeeded Garrett as sheriff of Lincoln County (1883 to 1886) and then found success as a rancher and banker in Chaves County.[58]

One of the biggest changes comes in the form of prostitute Jane Greathouse and the death of James Carlyle. First, it wasn't "Jane" Greathouse, but "Whiskey Jim" or "Arkansas Jack" Greathouse, who fenced rustled cattle for Billy the Kid and other outlaws before he was killed in 1880. Greathouse's spread wasn't in White Oaks but on a ranch he owned with Fred Kuch on the Las Vegas–White Oaks road.[59]

On November 27, Carlyle, a blacksmith, was part of a posse from White Oaks and caught Billy and company at the Greathouse-Kuch ranch. After the gunfire died down, Carlyle volunteered to enter the house, unarmed, and negotiate the outlaws' surrender while the posse held Greathouse, at Greathouse's own request, hostage.

Negotiations got nowhere, but plenty of alcohol was consumed inside the house. That afternoon, a gun accidentally discharged and Carlyle panicked, leaping through a glass window into the snow. Carlyle was shot dead. The posse said the Kid had killed him. Billy argued that Carlyle had been shot by his own men.[60]

Doc Scurlock wasn't killed at Stinking Springs when Garrett's posse captured the Kid—Scurlock would die in Eastland, Texas, in 1929. Charlie Bowdre was the one shot when he stepped out of the stone house that cold morning, but since the Bowdre character was killed off in *Young Guns*, somebody else had to die. Likewise, the real José Chávez y Chávez would outlive the real Billy the Kid, too, reportedly dying in Milagro, New Mexico, in 1923.[61]

After his capture in December 1880, Billy the Kid was transported to Mesilla, New Mexico, where he was tried for murder. He first faced a federal indictment for the murder of Buckshot Roberts, but when that charge was dismissed on a technicality, he was tried in territorial court for the murder of Sheriff William Brady. That led to his conviction on April 9, 1881. Four days later, Judge Warren Bristol sentenced the Kid to die by hanging on May 13 in Lincoln. The Kid did not tell the judge that he could go to "hell, hell, hell," after hearing the sentence. He said nothing.[62]

Garrett did hire his friend Ash Upson, a former newspaper journalist, to ghostwrite his book about Billy the Kid, but not during the manhunt. After the death of Billy the Kid, Garrett was offered the chance to set the record straight—and make some cash. The book, *The Authentic Life of Billy, the Kid, the Noted Desperado of the Southwest, Whose Deeds of Daring and Blood Have Made His Name a Terror in New Mexico, Arizona and Northern Mexico, by Pat. F. Garrett, Sheriff of Lincoln County, N. Mex., by Whom He Was Finally Hunted Down and Captured by Killing Him*, was published in 1882. The epilogue of *Young Guns II* says Garrett was killed by a twenty-one-year-old, but Wayne Brazel, who said he killed Garrett but was acquitted of murder, was thirty-two when Garrett died. The epilogue is accurate, however, when it says the book was a failure. Publisher Charles Greene, who owned the Santa Fe New Mexican newspaper, lacked expertise in the book-selling and book-distribution business, and Garrett's book may not have sold more than a few hundred copies.[63]

Yet Garrett's book did succeed in one aspect.

It helped perpetuate the myth of Billy the Kid.

The Players

After the commercial success of *Young Guns* in 1988, John Fusco immediately went to work on a sequel, to be backed by Morgan Creek Productions and released by 20th Century–Fox. Morgan Creek head James Robinson even called Fusco, begging him to put Charlie Sheen, who played Dick Brewer in the original, in the sequel. "But Dick Brewer, his character, is dead," Fusco pointed out. "We had this shocking killing 20 minutes into the first movie."

Robinson countered: "Look, you're really into that Indian stuff. Isn't there some sort of mystical way you can revive him?"

"I don't think so," Fusco said.[64]

Sheen showed up on the set anyway, Fusco recalled, "just to see the guys, to see his brother [Estevez], getting into mischief with us, taking us all to Mexico for the weekend. It was that kind of movie. It just attracted people to the fun of doing a Western, and the whole spirit of the ensemble was contagious."[65]

To replace the other dead characters (Dermot Mulroney's Dirty Steve Stephens and Casey Siemaszko's Charley Bowdre), twenty-one-year-old Christian Slater was hired to play Dave Rudabaugh while thirty-something William Peterson (*Manhunter, To Live and Die in L.A.*) replaced fifty-something Patrick Wayne as Pat Garrett. Viggo Mortensen, who had made his big-screen debut in *Witness* (1985), was cast as John Poe. James Coburn, who had played Pat Garrett in Sam Peckinpah's *Pat Garrett and Billy the Kid*, came on as John Chisum.[66]

Young Guns had been filmed around Santa Fe, New Mexico. The sequel also filmed in New Mexico — including J.W. Eaves and Cook movie ranches near Santa Fe, Tent Rocks at Cochiti Pueblo, and White Sands National Monument near Alamogordo — but also shot in Arizona, primarily at Old Tucson Studios and in Bisbee. Filming began in January 1990 and wrapped by the end of March.[67]

Estevez wanted not only to reprise his role as the young Billy the Kid, he also wanted to play old Brushy Bill Roberts, but the studio had already hired an actor for the part. Estevez pleaded, but was turned down.

Undeterred, Estevez hired a makeup artist to make him look ancient, then went to a retirement home in Tucson. "I sat with a group of gentlemen — one of them was having his 90th birthday — and I was accepted into the fold," Estevez said. "When I told one of them that I'd just had my 83rd birthday, he just accepted it."[68]

Charlie Sheen videotaped his brother's real-life performance. When the studio heads saw the tape, they changed their minds.[69]

Makeup for the Brushy Bill part began at 3:30 A.M., but Estevez went beyond that to get into character. "He didn't want to go to bed," Fusco said. "He said, 'I need to have my eyes look good and bloodshot.' We went out and stayed up all night drinkin' tequila and he looked pretty weathered, pretty haggard. His voice was [hoarse]."[70]

The movie opened in August 1990, two years after *Young Guns* had premiered. The producers knew their audience. "Like the first film," the *Chicago Tribune* opined, "it's a movie that's meant only to flatter and cajole a teenage audience, using the trappings of a once great genre to cloak a fairly conventional appeal to adolescent self-pity and romantic fatalism."[71]

It was another hit, grossing more than $44 million. The franchise proved to be "a mil-

Director Geoff Murphy (front) with the stars of *Young Guns II* (1990): (from left) Lou Diamond Phillips, Kiefer Sutherland, Alan Ruck, Balthazar Getty and Emilio Estevez.

lion dollar idea for Fusco," who would continue to write in the Western genre: *Thunderheart* (1992), the animated *Spirit: Stallion of the Cimarron* (2002), and *Hidalgo* (2004).[72]

Yet the biggest winner might have been rocker Jon Bon Jovi.

Fusco had listened to Jon Bon Jovi's song "Wanted Dead or Alive" when he was working on the original *Young Guns* screenplay; he also approached the singer-songwriter, hoping to use it in the soundtrack. Instead, Bon Jovi agreed to write and sing a new song. "Blaze of Glory," used over the closing credits, would be nominated for an Academy Award as well as a Grammy and would win a Golden Globe Award.[73]

Analysis

Like the original, *Young Guns II* hits sometimes, misfires often. It has some semblance of history, only to fall back into Hollywood antics.

Brushy Bill Roberts says in the opening that he wants to be pardoned for the killing of twenty-one men, but he seems to kill at least that many over the course of this violent film. Yet Estevez seemed to have locked on something about the character of the real Billy the Kid. "He bought his own poster, as it were," the actor said. "He was enamored of his own celebrity, which was really part of his downfall. He would never leave New Mexico because he didn't want to be just another face in the crowd."[74]

The movie was a commercial success that "saved the Western,"[75] but it also did something else that alienated many historians. "Fusco resuscitated a dead idea [Brushy Bill] and gave it new life," Bob Boze Bell writes.[76]

A number of history books on the subject — *The Return of the Outlaw Billy the Kid, Billy the Kid's Pretenders: "Brushy Bill" & John Miller, Billy the Kid: The Lost Interviews*, and *Billy the Kid, His Real Name Was...*, to name a few — have been published since *Young Guns II*.

***

Philadelphia Daily News (August 1, 1990): "*Young Guns II*, in the tradition of *Young Guns*, is one of the silliest westerns ever made. Like the first, it pretends to explore the legend of Billy the Kid, but you can tell nobody was really serious about it. Least of all the screenwriter, who has all of the characters talking in corny metaphors as unending as the prairies themselves...."

Chapter Twelve

Billy in Foreign Films

As proof of Billy the Kid's worldwide popularity, one need look no further than the foreign countries that have produced movies about the outlaw.

Mexico did several (perhaps one more when you consider that 1963's *A Bullet for Billy the Kid* was originally a Mexican film re-edited with new American footage). Italy did one about Billy and another about Pat Garrett, and spaghetti Westerns rarely used historical figures.

Billy has shown up in Spain, France, even Japan, and his name has been used often in other movies in which he doesn't appear.

El Muchacho de Durango

(Radeant Films, September 1962, 90 minutes) CREDITS: Director: Arturo Martínez. Producer-Screenplay: Raúl de Anda. CAST: Rodolfo de Anda, Jaime Fernández, Sonia Infante, Tito Novaro, Óscar Pulido.

This was possibly the first of a Mexican series of movies about Billy the Kid starring Rodolfo de Anda as Billy the Kid and produced, written and sometimes directed by his father, Raúl de Anda. How many movies in this series actually existed is hard to determine, especially considering that de Anda appeared in a number of series, including "Dos Caballeros de Espada," "Los Hermanos Barragan," "El Hijo del Charro Negro," and "El Texano."

Alias El Alacrán
(Also released as *El Muchacho de Durango 2nda Parte*)

(Radeant Films, January 1963, 70 minutes) CREDITS: Director: Arturo Martínez Sr. CAST: Rodolfo de Anda, Jaime Fernández, Sonia Infante, Carlos López Moctezuma, Óscar Pulido.

In the Mexican sequel to *El Muchacho de Durango,* Billy sneaks across the border and poses as a ranch hand named El Venado, and protects the rancher's fiancée from a bandit known as El Alacrán.

El Solitario

(Estudios América/Radeant Films, July 1964, 87 minutes) CREDITS: Director: Arturo Martinez. Producer-Screenplay: Raúl de Anda. CAST: Rodolfo de Anda, Dagoberto Rodríguez, Fanny Cano, Rogelio Guerra, Sergio Barrios, Hortensia Santoveña.

Another entry in the Mexican film series with Rodolfo de Anda playing Billy the Kid.

Fuera de la Ley
(Also released as *Billy the Kid*)

(Carthago Coop. Cinematográfica, July 1964, 91 minutes) CREDITS: Director: León Klimovsky. Screenplay: Ángel del Castillo, S.G. Monner, Bob Sirens. CAST: George Martin, Jack Taylor, Luis Induni, Aldo Sambrell.

After his father is murdered and his home burned, Billy Carter swears revenge in this Euro Western produced by a small Spanish company. Klimovsky was an Argentine who moved to Spain and directed a number of spaghettis, including 1969's *Dos mil dólares por Coyote* (*Django, A Bullet for You*) and 1960's *Reverendo Colt* (*Reverend's Colt*), the latter starring Guy Madison.

French poster for the Spanish-produced *Fuera de la Ley*, or *Billy the Kid* (1964).

Duelo en el Desierto

(Estudios América/Radeant Films, August 1964, 85 minutes) CREDITS: Director: Arturo Martínez. Producer-Screenplay: Raúl de Anda. CAST: Rodolfo de Anda, Fanny Cano, Dagoberto Rodriguez, Carlos Lopez Moctezuma, Miguel Arenas, Armando Arriola, Sergio Barrios.

When Laura falls in love with and marries Billy, her brother frames him and sends him to jail and decides he should get rid of the Kid permanently. Another of de Anda's Mexican film series about Billy the Kid.

Le Pistole non Disctono
(Also released as *Bullets Don't Argue* and *Pistols Don't Argue*)

(Constantin Film Produktion/Jolly Film/Trío Films, October 1964, 92 minutes) CREDITS: Director: Mario Caiano. Producer: Fernando Rossi. Screenplay: Gianni Castellano, Pedro de Juan, Giuseppe Moccia. CAST: Rod Cameron, Horst Frank, Ángel Aranda, Vivi Bach, Luis Durán, Kai Fischer.

Pat Garrett's wedding day is interrupted when Billy Clanton and his brother George rob a bank, kill the banker, and flee to Mexico. Garrett crosses the border to bring them back. This Spanish-Italian-West German production, a fairly straightforward Western without the usual Italian touches, was filmed in Spain about the same time as Sergio Leone was directing Clint Eastwood in *A Fistful of Dollars*, whose success launched the spaghetti Western movement. Rod Cameron, who plays Garrett, was paid more than the combined cast of *Fistful*.[1]

El Hombre que Mató a Billy el Niño
(Also released as *I'll Kill Him and Return Alone* and *A Few Bullets More*)

(Aitor Films/Kinnesis Film, March 1967, 100 minutes) CREDITS: Director: Julio Buchs. Executive Producers: Silvio Battistini, Ricardo Sanz. Screenplay: Julio Buchs, Federico De Urrutia, Lucio Fulci. CAST: Peter Lee Lawrence (Billy the Kid), Fausto Tozzi, Dyanik Zurakowska, Gloria Milland, Carlos Casaravilla, Antonio Pica.

This Spanish-Italian spaghetti is a fairly conventional Western biopic, with Billy (Peter Lee Lawrence) forced into a life of crime after protecting his mother. His mother's friend Pat Garrett (Fausto Tozzi) is eventually forced to go hunting the young killer. Lawrence, born Karl Hirenbach, was a West German star whose blond hair doesn't quite fit the image of the real Billy. Suffering from a brain tumor, he died in 1974 at age twenty-nine.[2]

Su precio ... unos dólares

(Radeant Films, September 1970, 85 minutes) CREDITS: Director-Producer-Screenplay: Raúl de Anda. CAST: Rodolfo de Anda, Mario Almada, Pedro Armendáriz, Jr., Mario Cid, Sonio Furió.

In another Mexican production from the de Anda family, Billy helps others hold up a bank for $100,000, but then greed gets the better of everyone involved, leading to twists, turns and plenty of double-crosses.

Lobby card for *A Few Bullets More* (1967).

Une Aventure de Billy le Kid
(Also released as *A Girl Is a Gun*)

(Les Films Luc Moullet, 1971, 80 minutes) CREDITS: Director-Producer-Screenplay: Luc Moullet. CAST: Jean-Pierre Léaud (Billy the Kid), Rachel Kesterber, Michel Minaud, Luc Moullet.

This psychedelic Western was the first color film by France's *nouvelle vague* filmmaker Luc Moullet. It was not originally released in France, but played abroad in badly dubbed English. The dubbing was Moullet's idea, to pay tribute to what he considered the shabbiness of American genre movies. The plot has Billy (Jean-Pierre Léaud) walking to Mexico, picking up a girl, and falling in love.

Un Autre Homme, Une Autre Chance
(Also released as *Another Man, Another Chance*)

(Les Films 13, September 1977, 130 minutes) CREDITS: Director-Screenplay: Claude Lelouch. Producers: Georges Dancigers, Alexandre Mnouchkine. CAST: James Caan, Genevieve Bujold, Francis Huster, Susan Tyrrell, Jennifer Warren, Richard Farnsworth, Tony Crupi.

A French production filmed at Arizona's Old Tucson Studios. Veterinarian David Williams and immigrant Jeanne Leroy, an aspiring photographer, get together after their spouses are violently murdered. Billy the Kid is mentioned a lot in the film. Finding him is a lot harder. Tony Crupi is credited off-screen as Billy, but his scenes might have been deleted, as apparently were scenes including Jesse James (Christopher Lloyd).

Birî za Kiddo no Atarashii Yoake
(Also released as *New Morning of Billy the Kid*)

(Parco Co., August 1986, 109 minutes) CREDITS: Director-Screenplay: Naoto Yamakawa. Producer: Akira Morishige. CAST: Makoto Ayukawa, Yoshio Harada, Toshiyuki Hosokawa, Renji Ishibashi, Shin'ichirô Kurimoto, Hiroshi Mikami (Billy the Kid), Masayuki Shinoya.

This Japanese comedy, based on a novel by Genichirou Takahashi, has Billy the Kid (Hiroshi Mikami) walking out of a photo of Monument Valley that hangs in a Tokyo bar. He gets a job as a bouncer, joining a samurai, a World War II GI, a singer-songwriter and several others right out of history. They fend off mobsters and thugs.

Billy the Kid and the Green Baize Vampire

(Incorporated Television Company/Zenith Entertainment, April 1987, 121 minutes) CREDITS: Director: Alan Clarke; Producer: Simon Mallin; Screenplay: Trevor Preston. CAST: Phil Daniels (Billy the Kid), Alun Armstrong (Maxwell Randall), Bruce Payne, Louise Gold, Eve Ferret, Richard Ridings, Don Henderson, Zoot Money.

This British musical, which first ran on British television, is another movie that capitalizes on the Billy the Kid name. Billy the Kid (Phil Daniels) is a rising star in the snooker world who faces the legendary world snooker champion Maxwell Randall, aka the Green Baize Vampire (Alun Armstrong) in a seventeen-frame grudge match.

Lobby card for the British production *Billy the Kid and the Green Baize Vampire* (1987).

Revenge of Billy the Kid

(Montage Films, July 1992, 87 minutes) CREDITS: Director: Jim Gordon; Producer: Tim Dennison; Screenplay: Tim Dennison, Jim Groom, Richard Mathews. CAST: Michael Balfour, Samantha Perkins, Jackie D. Broad, Bryan Heeley, Trevor Beake.

Billy the Kid as a goat? Well, among the Hispanics, the original Billy the Kid was nicknamed "El Chivato," which means the young goat. This British comedy-horror film, however, has nothing to do with the historical Billy the Kid. Instead, farmer MacDonald fornicates with a goat, which gives birth to an offspring called Billy, which is tormented by the farmer's sons (but not the daughter). Naturally, Billy the Kid plots revenge. The financially plagued production reportedly took 3½ years to complete.[3]

Lola + Bilidikid
(Also released as *Lola and Billy the Kid*)

(Boje Buck Produktion/Westdeutscher Rundfunk/Zero Film GmbH, March 1999, 90 minutes) CREDITS: Director-Screenplay: Kutlug Ataman; Producers: Martin Hagemann, Zeynep Ozbatur Atakan, Martin Wiebel. CAST: Gandi Mukli, Baki Davrak, Erdal Yildiz, Inge Keller, Michael Gerber.

Another movie that uses the "Billy the Kid" name but isn't about the New Mexico outlaw. This German film is about a seventeen-year-old Turk living in Berlin who discovers his homosexuality. He meets Lola in a bar and makes Lola's man, Bilidikid, jealous.

Lucky Luke

(UCC YM, October 2009, 103 minutes) CREDITS: Director: James Huth. Producers: Said Ben Said, Yves Marmion, Sonja Shillito. Screenplay: James Huth, Sonja Shillito. CAST: Jean Dujardin, Michaël Youn (Billy the Kid), Sylvie Testud, Daniel Prévost, Alexandra Lamy, Melvil Poupaud.

A French comedy Western, first filmed in 1971 as the animated feature *Daisy Town*. Sends Lucky Luke returns to his hometown, Daisy Town, to bring back law and order. Daisy Town is being run by outlaws, including Billy the Kid (Michaël Youn), Jesse James, and Calamity Jane. It was based on the comic book series published by Belgium's Morris (aka Maurice De Bevere) from 1946 to 2001.

CHAPTER THIRTEEN

Billy in Made-for-TV Movies

While many documentaries have covered Billy the Kid's career, the outlaw has been a subject shied away from in made-for-television dramas.

Only one serious study has appeared on the small screen. Otherwise, Billy's appearances in made-for-TV original films is an odd mix.

Go West, Young Girl

(ABC, April 27, 1978, 90 minutes) CREDITS: Director: Alan J. Levi. Producer-Screenplay: George Yanok. CAST: Karen Valentine (Netty Booth); Sandra Will (Gilda Corin); Stuart Whitman (Deputy Shreeve); Richard Jaeckel (Billy the Kid); Michael Bell (Nestor); Cal Bellini (Chato).

A lighthearted pilot that wasn't picked up. A New England reporter (Will) and the widow of an Army officer (Valentine) head west in search of Billy the Kid. They have to outwit gamblers, bounty hunters and lawmen. Actor Richard Jaeckel was no stranger to the Billy the Kid story, having played Jess Evans in *Chisum* (1970), Kip McKinney in *Pat Garrett and Billy the Kid* (1973), and the Kid himself in a *Stories of the Century* TV episode. Only this time, it turns out he's not really Billy the Kid — after all, this movie's set in 1886 Arizona, five years after the real Billy was killed — but an impostor.

Billy the Kid

(TNT, May 10, 1989, 100 minutes) CREDITS: Director: William A. Graham. Executive Producers: Robert M. Sertner, Frank von Zerneck. Screenplay: Gore Vidal. CAST: Val Kilmer (William Bonney); Andrew Bicknell (Tunstall); Wilford Brimley (Governor Lew Wallace); Julie Carmen (Chelsa); Mike Casper (Ollinger); Jack Dunlap (Brady); Duncan Regehr (Pat Garrett).

Gore Vidal, still stewing over *The Left Handed Gun* (1958), which had been based on a 1955 Vidal teleplay, decided to tackle the Billy the Kid story again thirty years later.

Many regard this as the most accurate of all the Billy the Kid movies, which doesn't mean a whole lot. Besides, this one has Tunstall killed in 1879, instead of 1878, by Sheriff Brady (who wasn't there, and wasn't killed riding horseback down a country road) and omits Alexander McSween. And you won't find saguaro cacti (the movie was filmed in Arizona) in New Mexico. Wilford Brimley as Lew Wallace?! *Billy the Kid* was one of the first Western

Opposite: **Val Kilmer played Billy the Kid in the TNT movie *Billy the Kid* in 1989.**

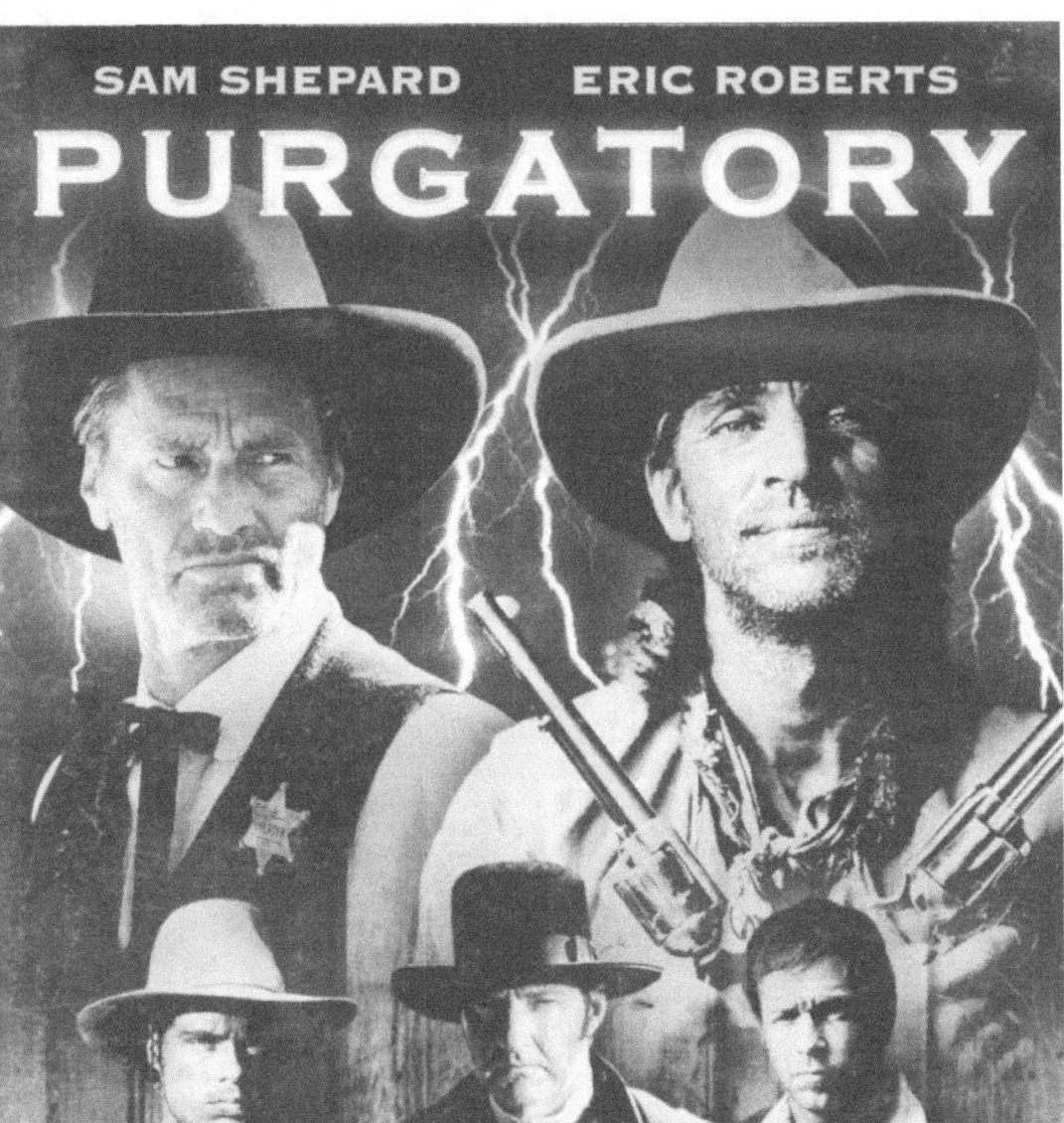

movies for Turner Network Television, the cable network that would go on to make *Conagher* (1991), *Riders of the Purple Sage* (1996), *Last Stand at Saber River* (1997), *King of Texas* (2002) and the epic miniseries *Into the West* (2005).

Purgatory

(TNT, January 10, 1999, 94 minutes) CREDITS: Director: Uli Edel. Producer: Daniel Schneider. Screenplay: Gordon T. Dawson. CAST: Sam Shepard (Sheriff Forrest/Wild Bill Hickok); Eric Roberts (Blackjack Britton); Randy Quaid (Doc Woods/Doc Holliday); Peter Stormare (Cavin Guthrie); Brad Rowe (Leo "Sonny" Dillard); Donnie Wahlberg (Deputy Glen/Billy the Kid); J.D. Souther (Brooks/Jesse James); Amelia Heinle (Rose/Betty McCullough); R.G. Armstrong (Coachman).

Fantasy-like Western puts bad guys in a small town where no one wears a gun or hardly ever sins. That's because the town of Refuge is actually Purgatory, where the lawman is really Wild Bill Hickok, the doctor really Billy the Kid, etc., etc., and they're trying to prove that they belong in Heaven. Sounds like *The Twilight Zone Meets Gunsmoke*.

Actually, the plot is vaguely similar to the 1972 *Night Gallery* segment "The Waiting Room," written by Rod Serling and starring Buddy Ebsen.

Copperhead

(Sci-Fi Channel, June 28, 2008, 90 minutes) CREDITS: Director: Todor Chapkanov. Producer: Jeffery Beach, Phillip J. Roth. Screenplay: Rafael Jordan. CAST: Brad Johnson (Wild Bill Longley); Keith Stone (Will Bonney); Brad Greenquist (Garrett); Wendy Carter (Jane); Gabriel Womack (Roscoe Burrell); Billy Drago (Jesse Evans).

This horror Western, set in New Mexico after the Civil War, finds Wild Bill Longley (an actual Texas gunman who was hanged in 1878) warning citizens about *La Serpienta Del Diablo*, some really, really mean, venomous snakes. Snakes attack the townsfolk, and then they have to deal with the mother of all snakes.

You'd think that, after going through an ordeal like this together, Pat Garrett, Jessie Evans, and Billy the Kid might have gotten along a little better than they did.

Opposite: DVD case for the 1999 TNT production *Purgatory*.

CHAPTER FOURTEEN

Billy in Continuing Television Series

Television series brought Billy the Kid to the small screen. Billy even had his own series, although he was a secondary character to Pat Garrett.

Starring Barry Sullivan as Pat Garrett (who indeed was a tall man) and Clu Gulager as Billy the Kid, *The Tall Man* debuted on NBC on September 10, 1960. The half-hour series was created by Samuel A. Peeples, with Nat Holt, no stranger to the Western genre, serving as an executive producer. All of the episodes put Garrett and Billy in fictional adventures. Pat was the older, wiser, stalwart lawman, and Billy the hotheaded, misguided youngster who usually did what Garrett suggested — and sometimes wound up saving Garrett's hide.

The series opened with Garrett being Lincoln County's new deputy sheriff under Sheriff Brady (Ford Rainey), who got murdered in episode five, allowing Garrett to become sheriff.

Ken Lynch played a mean rancher (a sort of Murphy-Dolan type) named Andy Gorman, and Jim Davis was Gorman's hardcase ramrod, Bob Orringer (instead of Olinger). They were gone after a handful of episodes.

There wasn't much history to it, and the series lacked the imagination and depth of *Gunsmoke* and *The Virginian*, although Gulager was fine as Billy.

The Tall Man lasted only seventy-five episodes over two

Barry Sullivan (left) was Pat Garrett and Clu Gulager played Billy the Kid in the short-lived TV series *The Tall Man*.

seasons, and, nope, Pat didn't shoot Billy in the last one. Billy, however, has had a long life in "guest" roles in TV series.

Omnibus
"Billy the Kid"

(CBS, November 8, 1953)

The Alistair Cooke–hosted series showed a range of subjects, from reenactments of Abraham Lincoln's life to a performance by the Benny Goodman Trio. This one was Aaron Copland's ballet, starring John Kriza as Billy and Scott Douglas as Pat Garrett.

Stories of the Century
"Billy the Kid"

(Syndicated, January 30, 1954)

Southwestern Railroad detective Matt Clark (Jim Davis) went after a number of historical outlaws in this Emmy-winning series. In the second episode from the first season, he gets the stuffing knocked out of him by Billy's boys. Since he's after Billy (Richard Jaeckel) for stealing a cattle herd from the railroad yards, he joins Pat Garrett (Richard Travis) in tracking down Billy. After Billy escapes from jail, blowing away Bob Olinger with a shotgun, Matt (instead of Kip McKinney) is in Fort Sumner with Garrett and John Poe when Garrett kills the Kid. Veteran William Witney directed this one.

Davis would also go after Belle Starr, the James brothers, Geronimo, the Daltons, Joaquin Murietta, Tom Horn ... pretty much every historical Western figure.

Buffalo Bill, Jr.
"Trail of the Killer"

(Syndicated, March 4, 1955)

Tricky, conniving and murderous Billy the Kid (Chuck Courtney) and Charlie Bowdre (Henry Rowland), on the run from the law, show up in Wileyville in this kiddie series starring Dickie Jones as Buffalo Bill, Jr. Buffalo Bill saves the life of Pat Garrett (Keith Richards) by getting the drop on Billy.

Stage 7
"Billy and the Bride"

(CBS, May 8, 1955)

Sweet, naive New Yorker Vanessa (Angela Lansbury) opens her home to a fellow who turns out to be Billy the Kid (Hugh O'Brian) while her husband (Dick Foran) is out with a posse hunting down the killer.

Four months later, O'Brian starred as another Western icon when *The Life and Legend of Wyatt Earp* debuted on ABC.

The Philco-Goodyear Television Playhouse "The Death of Billy the Kid"

(NBC, July 24, 1955)

Paul Newman played Billy in this Richard Mulligan–directed episode, written by Gore Vidal, in the seventh season of the series of live dramatic performances. Frank Overton played Pat Garrett, Matt Crowley played Lew Wallace, Michael Conrad was Charles Bowdre and Jason Robards was Joe Grant.

This is the teleplay that would lead to Newman's starring turn as Billy in *The Left Handed Gun* (1958).

Death Valley Days "Pat Garrett's Side of It"

(Syndicated, October 22, 1956)

When Billy the Kid refuses to accept a pardon from New Mexico's governor, Sheriff Pat Garrett is told to track him down.

Sugarfoot "Brannigan's Boots"

(ABC, September 17, 1957)

The pilot episode — inspired by the Warner Bros. Western film *The Boy from Oklahoma* (1954) — has Tom Brewster (Will Hutchins) appointed sheriff of Bluerock by the town's crooked politicians. Brewster aims to prove that he's capable of filling the boots worn by the late sheriff, the father of sharp-shooting Katie Brannigan (Merry Anders). Brewster's a timid soul who can't shoot worth a lick, but he takes his job seriously and won't back down — even when he's facing Billy the Kid (Dennis Hopper) in a saloon.

Tales of Wells Fargo "Billy the Kid"

(NBC, October 21, 1957)

Having already come up against Belle Starr and John Wesley Hardin in the second season, Jim Hardie (Dale Robertson), "a man from Wells Fargo," lands smack dab in the middle of the Lincoln County War. Turns out Billy the Kid (Robert Vaughn) has helped the lone survivor (Aline Towne) of the latest bloody stagecoach robbery. It's Hardie who delivers Governor Lew Wallace's amnesty proclamation to Billy. And it's Billy who saves Hardie's hide and helps put a stop to the bad guys robbing the stagecoaches.

Colt .45
"Amnesty"

(ABC, May 24, 1959)

Government agent Christopher Colt (Wayde Preston) is asked by Governor Lew Wallace (Willis Bouchey) to deliver an amnesty deal to Billy the Kid (Robert Conrad), and that really ticks off Sheriff Pat Garrett (Wayne Heffley).

Maverick
"Full House"

(ABC, October 25, 1959)

Itinerant gambler Bret Maverick (James Garner) is mistaken for Foxy Smith (Robert Lowery), the mastermind of a gang that includes Billy the Kid (Joel Grey), Belle Starr (Jean Willes), Cole Younger (Gregory Walcott) and Sam Bass (Kelly Thordsen). Can Bret come up with a heist plan that won't break the law or get him killed?

Bronco
"The Soft Answer"

(ABC, November 3, 1959)

It's cattlemen versus Quaker sheepherders, and Bronco Layne (Ty Hardin) is right in the middle, and allied with Billy the Kid (Ray Stricklyn).

The Deputy
"The Big Four"

(NBC, November 14, 1959)

Southern Arizona is being plagued by an outlaw gang busy robbing banks, trains and stagecoaches. Marshal Simon Fry (Henry Fonda) thinks Billy the Kid (Richard Bakalyan), Curly Bill Brocius (Gerald Milton), Ike Clanton (Charles E. Fredericks) and Johnny Ringo (Henry Brandon) might be responsible. Young deputy Clay McCord (Allen Case) tries to save the day with help from homing pigeons.

The Rebel
"Misfits"

(ABC, November 29, 1959)

Ex-Confederate Johnny Yuma (Nick Adams) tries to stop a teenage gang—Billy the Kid (Malcolm Cassell), Bull (Hampton Fancher) and Skinny (Hal Stalmaster)—from robbing a bank. This one actually gets the Kid's step-father's name right with Olan Soule playing William Antrim.

Bronco
"Death of an Outlaw"

(ABC, March 8, 1960)

Bronco (Ty Hardin) again crosses paths with Billy the Kid (this time the Kid's played by Stephen Joyce), as they fight cattle thieves, but then Bronco must bring the Kid in for murder. Rhodes Reason is Pat Garrett.

Cheyenne
"The Greater Glory"

(ABC, May 15, 1961)

Ray Stricklyn's back as Billy the Kid, this time joining tall Cheyenne Bodie to protect a Mormon woman (Mary Wiley) from a gang of bad hombres.

The Red Skelton Hour
"Frontier Coward"

(CBS, March 26, 1963)

Amanda Blake takes a break from *Gunsmoke* to play "the Widder Jenkins," who has replaced Sheriff Deadeye (Red Skelton). Who should turn up by Billy the Kid (Bobby Rydell), who performs a medley of "Hello Young Lovers," "Ciao Ciao Bambina" and "My Coloring Book."

The Great Adventure
"The Outlaw and the Nun"

(CBS, December 6, 1963)

Van Heflin narrated these one-hour productions of the short-lived series that featured stories about important events or figures from U.S. history. This episode has Andrew Prine as Billy the Kid and Marion Ross as Sister Marcella, who arrives in a Western town and discovers only two children in her classroom.

Death Valley Days
"The Kid from Hell's Kitchen"

(Syndicated, October 20, 1966)

Left-handed Billy the Kid (Robert Blake) rides for revenge after the murder of John Tunstall (John Alderson). Host Robert Taylor calls the Kid "a New York–born hoodlum," and he should know. He played the killer in MGM's *Billy the Kid* (1941). Another episode from 1969, "Biscuits and Billy the Kid," featured not the outlaw, but a blue-eyed goat.

The Time Tunnel
"Billy the Kid"

(February 10, 1967)

Time travelers Tony (James Darren) and Doug (Robert Colbert) wind up in Lincoln County in 1881 and run afoul of Billy the Kid (Robert Walker, Jr.), who wants to kill Doug. Allen Case is Pat Garrett.

Death Valley Days
"Lost Sheep in Trinidad"

(Syndicated, January 20, 1967)

This one's based on the legend of Sister Blandina (Mariette Hartley), who, the story goes, nursed Billy the Kid (Tom Heaton) back to health after he was injured.

The Monkees
"The Devil and Peter Tork"

(NBC, February 5, 1968)

After making a bad deal with the Devil (Monte Landis), Peter Tork goes on trial for his life in Hades. He must prove to criminals including Blackbeard (Ted de Corsia), Attila the Hun (Lee Kolima) and Billy the Kid (Peter Canon), that he can play the harp on his own, without the Devil's help.

Cade's County
"A Gun for Billy"

(CBS, November 28, 1971)

Sheriff Sam Cade (Glenn Ford) has his hands full as he tries to track down a psychotic ex-con (Bobby Darin) who thinks he's Billy the Kid and Cade is Pat Garrett.

The Ghost Busters
"They Went Thataway"

(CBS, January 1, 1975)

The ninth of only fifteen episodes of this unfunny comedy series starring Forrest Tucker and Larry Storch sends our ghost-hunting heroes and their pet gorilla Tracy (Bob Burns) against the spirits of Belle Starr (Brooke Tucker) and Billy the Kid (Marty Ingels).

Burns recalled that CBS censors wouldn't allow Ingels to carry a gun in the episode. "Not even a cap gun," Burns said. "Not even a *water* gun. No kind of gun. I asked, 'Can he have bananas in his holsters? Tracy could come up behind him and steal the bananas and eat 'em.' The censor said no, not even a banana — Billy the Kid couldn't have *anything* in his holsters! In fact, I'm not sure now whether the *holsters*, even though they were empty, were allowed!"[1]

Bret Maverick
"Anything for a Friend"

(NBC, December 15, 1981)

Tom Guthrie (Ed Bruce) hides his wounded friend Billy the Kid (Glenn Withrow) from a U.S. marshal (Lawrence Dobkin) at the ranch of Bret Maverick (James Garner). It's a long way from the hilarity and charm of ABC's *Maverick*, circa 1959.

Voyagers!
"Bully and Billy"

(NBC, October 24, 1982)

In another short-lived time-traveling series, ex-pirate Phineas Bogg (Jon-Erik Hexum) and twelve-year-old orphan Jeffrey Jones (Meeno Peluce) must stop Billy the Kid (Frank Koppala) from killing a young Theodore Roosevelt (Gregg Henry).

MacGyver
"MacGyver's Women"

(ABC, November 12, 1990)

Our hero (Richard Dean Anderson) falls asleep while watching a Western (how could that happen?) and dreams of mail-order brides, Jesse James (Wil Calhoun) and Billy the Kid (Russ Hamilton).

The Mask
"All Hallow's Eve"

(CBS, October 28, 1995)

A Halloween theme pops up in the animated Saturday morning series as "The Mask," Stanley Ipkiss (Rob Paulsen), runs across the reanimated corpses of Attila the Hun (Jim Cummings) and Billy the Kid (Kevin Michael Richardson).

Chapter Fifteen

Direct-to-Video Billies

In the 1980s, a new market exploded on the movie scene: direct-to-video. Low-budget horror movies, thrillers, romantic comedies, and Westerns — usually independents — were made and marketed to the home-viewing audience. Today, that market has expanded, covering studio films that don't make it to the theaters as well as sequels to studio films.[1]

"The audience is there, the market is there for broadcast, for features, for direct-to-DVD and cable, which is where all product ends up eventually," says filmmaker and film historian C. Courtney Joyner. "Westerns of all budgets and types find their audience when given the chance — from independents like [*Hatfields & McCoys:*] *Bad Blood* [2012] to studio 'disappointments' like *Cowboys and Aliens* [2011] — DVD is often that chance."[2]

Billy has made his way onto direct-to-DVD films.

Bad Jim

(Delaware Pictures, April 1990, 90 minutes) CREDITS: Director-Screenplay: Clyde Ware. CAST: James Brolin (B.D. Sweetman); Richard Roundtree (July); John Clark Gable (John T. Coleman); Harry Carey, Jr. (J.C. Lee); Rory Calhoun (Sam Harper); Ty Hardin (Tom Jefferd); Pepe Serna (Virgilio Segura).

Mexican bandit Virgilio Segura stumbles into the camp of three cowboys and trades the horse he's riding — which had belonged to his late partner, Billy the Kid — to young cowhand J.T. Coleman. As he rides that horse, J.T. becomes more and more like Billy the Kid, eventually persuading his pards, B.D. Sweetman and July, to begin a life of crime.

The son of legendary actor Clark Gable, John Clark Gable returned to America to open a car-repair business after finishing his education in Switzerland. He was married with two children when he decided to test the acting waters, and was cast in *Bad Jim*. James Brolin had starred as Clark Gable in *Gable and Lombard* (1976), which *New York* magazine called "a dismal throwback and throwaway, making you either cackle unhealthily (because feeling superior to garbage does not make for healthy laughter) or just quietly throw up." Richard Roundtree was almost twenty years past his *Shaft* prime. *Bad Jim* was filmed in Arizona in the spring of 1989, but was considered so bad — and it *is* wretched — that it went straight to video. Gable has rarely acted since.[3]

Still from *Bad Jim* (1990), starring James Brolin, John Clark Gable, and Richard Roundtree.

BloodRayne 2: Deliverance

(Brightlight Pictures, September 2007, 95 minutes) CREDITS: Director: Uwe Boll. Producer: Daniel Clarke, Shawn Williamson. Screenplay: Christopher Donaldson, Neil Every, Masaji Takei. CAST: Natassia Malthe (Rayne); Zack Ward (Billy the Kid); Michael Paré (Pat Garrett); Chris Coppola (Newton Piles); Chris Spencer (Bartender Bob); Brendan Fletcher (Muller); Sarah-Jane Redmond (Martha); Michael Teigen (Slime Bag Franson); Michael Eklund (The Preacher); John Novak (Sheriff Cogden).

This Canadian-German production, released theatrically overseas in 2008, is a sequel to the video game–inspired U.S.-German theatrical release *BloodRayne* (2005), which starred Kristanna Loken as the half-human half-vampire. A vampire army of gunmen led by Billy the Kid terrorizes the town of Deliverance, when who should ride in but Rayne. To beat the super-powerful Billy, she needs the assistance of Pat Garrett as well as a killer called Slime Bag Franson and a con-man preacher.

It was followed by *BloodRayne: The Third Reich* (2010) in which Rayne (again played by Malthe) fought Nazis.

Redemption

(Cas-Mor Productions/Gallery Films/Barnholtz Entertainment, February 2009, 90 minutes) CREDITS: Director-Screenplay: Robert Conway. Producers: Jerry L. Anderson, Robert Conway, Jason Mager. CAST: Dustin James (Frank Hardin); Tom Noga (The Apostle); Clint James (Till); Grady Hill (Black Feather); Candy Stanton (Jenny); Sanford Gibbons (Adams); Peter Sherayko (Sam); Isaac Farm (Olsen); Anthony Casanova (Sergeant Mathis); Jim Cegan (Renegade); Owen Conway (Billy the Kid); Miguel Corona (Miguel); Chad Grimes (Pat Garrett).

Brandon Thornton (center) is Billy the Kid, flanked by (from left) Chelsea Rae Bernier, Jason Zahodnik, Lance Leonhardt and Michael Hudson in *1313: Billy the Kid* (2012).

Ridiculously violent, allegorical Western about a young gunman (Leighton) who seeks redemption in the town of, well, Redemption. He's out to save a Mexican girl in a town divided by Southern and Northern renegades still fighting the Civil War. Also on his way to town is another gunman known as The Apostle. Billy the Kid and Pat Garrett make a cameo in a poker game; Pat decides to get out of town before The Apostle gets there, and Billy wisely follows. The plot's incomprehensible, but in the dimly lit saloon scene, Owen Conway probably comes closer to looking like the real Billy the Kid than any other actor in all the previous movies about the Kid.

1313: Billy the Kid

(Rapid Heart Pictures, June 2012, 80 minutes) CREDITS: Director: David DeCoteau. Producers: David DeCoteau, Marco Colombo. Screenplay: Moses Rutegar. CAST: Brandon Thornton (Billy the Kid); Chelsea Rae Bernier (Lottie); Michael Hudson (Rabanne); Kodi Baker (Uriel); Ryan Curry (Lloyd); Lance Leonhardt (Buck); Jason Zahodnik (Whitecastle); Ryan McIntyre (Doc Holliday).

This was another one of Roger Corman protégé David DeCoteau's cheap, trashy *1313* series (previous titles include *1313: Giant Killer Bees* and *1313: Bigfoot Island*). In this one, filmed in sepia tone, a wounded Billy the Kid, having escaped from the Lincoln County jail, winds up in Hell's Heart, where strange things are happening. Billy tells the town's lone girl, "I'm Billy the Kid, sweetheart, I ain't afraid of the bogeyman." But he should be. Because manitous (sort of vampire-zombies) rule this part of the West, where all of the male beefcakes, including Billy, run around in vests without shirts.

Appendix: Forgotten Billies

These two movies proved elusive. No reviews, no production notes, little in the way of any plot synopsis, and, most importantly, no copies of either film.

A Bullet for Billy the Kid

(Alameda Films/A.D.P. Pictures, November 1963, 61 minutes) CREDITS: Director: Rafael Baledón. Producers: Alfred Ripstein, Jerry Warren. Screenplay: Ramón Obón. CAST: Gaston Sands, Steve Brodie, Lloyd Nelson, Marla Blaine, Richard McIntyre, Gilbert Cramer, Rita Macdeo, Peter Gillon.

This movie is presumed lost. Producer Jerry Warren (1925–1988) regularly bought the rights to foreign films, re-cutting them and adding new American-shot footage in order to then release them to U.S. theaters. For *Terror in the Midnight Sun/Invasion of*

Gaston Sands in producer Jerry Warren's *A Bullet for Billy the Kid* (1963).

the Animal People (1959) and *Curse of the Stone Hand* (1964) he added footage with John Carradine. *Face of the Screaming Werewolf* (1964) combined footage from the Mexican-made *La Casa del Terror,* starring Lon Chaney Jr., and *La Momia Azteca.* The movies had one thing in common, filmmaker and historian C. Courtney Joyner points out: They were all awful. Taking that into consideration, *A Bullet for Billy the Kid* was likely originally a Mexican film for which Warren shot new footage with Steve Brodie and Lloyd Nelson.

The plot is said to follow Billy the Kid on a long journey to the ranch he owns with his sister while he is pursued by lawmen and gunfighters. It has no resemblance to Nelson C. Nye's novel *Pistols for Hire*, which was published in 1950 under the title *A Bullet for Billy the Kid*.

Poster for *The 1st Notch* (1977).

The 1st Notch

(Hi-Desert International/Clamil, May 1977) CREDITS: Screenplay-Director: Gil Ward. Producers: James Scobee, Gil Ward. CAST: Leo G. Willey, Jason Ward (young Billy the Kid), Joe Warder, Julie Ward, Eddie Mynatt, Cindy Rusler, Gail Carroll.

California-based Clamil Productions distributed mostly adult, horror and exploitation films in the 1970s. One possible exception might be *The 1st Notch*, a PG-rated Western about Billy the Kid that starred Jason Ward as "Young Billy the Kid" (as opposed to an *old* Billy the Kid?). Advertisements promoted the story as "The Beginning of a Legend." Gil Ward had composed the music for *Devil Rider!* (1970) and *Blood Freak* (1972), but directed, co-produced and wrote this Western. *The 1st Notch*, completed in 1974, was not released by Clamil until three years later, premiering in Los Angeles and then making its way to mostly drive-in theaters.

Chapter Notes

Introduction

1. *Los Angeles Times*, December 31, 2010.
2. David DeCoteau, email correspondence with author, January 27, 2012.
3. Robert M. Utley, *Billy the Kid: A Short and Violent Life* (Lincoln: University of Nebraska Press, 1989), photo caption on unnumbered page after page 110.
4. SuzAnne Barabas and Gabor Barabas, *Gunsmoke: A Complete History* (Jefferson, NC: McFarland, 1990), pp. 359–360.
5. Paul Andrew Hutton, "Dreamscape Desperado," *New Mexico Magazine* (June 1990), p. 57.

Chapter One

1. Information for this chapter is drawn from Bob Boze Bell, *The Illustrated Life and Times of Billy the Kid*, 2d ed (Phoenix: Tri Star, 1996); Joel Jacobsen, *Such Men as Billy the Kid: The Lincoln County War Reconsidered* (Lincoln: University of Nebraska Press, 1994); Mark Lee Gardner, *To Hell on a Fast Horse: Billy the Kid, Pat Garrett, and the Epic Chase to Justice in the Old West*, advanced reading copy (New York: William Morrow, 2010); Pat F. Garrett and Frederick Nolan, notes and commentary, *Pat F. Garrett's The Authentic Life of Billy, the Kid: An Annotated Edition* (Norman: University of Oklahoma Press, 2000); Leon C. Metz, *Pat Garrett: The Story of a Western Lawman* (Norman: University of Oklahoma Press, 1974); Robert N. Mullin, ed., *Maurice G. Fulton's History of the Lincoln County War* (Tucson: University of Arizona Press, 1980); Frederick Nolan, *The Lincoln County War: A Documentary History* (Norman: University of Oklahoma Press, 1992) and *The West of Billy the Kid* (Norman: University of Oklahoma Press, 1998); Miguel Antonio Otero, *The Real Billy the Kid* (Houston: Arte Público Press, 1998); Jon Tuska, *Billy the Kid: His Life and Times* (Albuquerque: University of New Mexico Press, 1994); Utley, *Billy the Kid*; Michael Wallis, *Billy the Kid: The Endless Ride* (New York: W.W. Norton, 2007).
2. *Logansport* (Indiana) *Journal*, May 19, 1881; (Albert Lea, Minnesota) *Freeborn County Standard*, June 9, 1881.
3. Otero, *The Real Billy the Kid*, p. 45.

Chapter Two

1. J.C. Dykes, *Billy the Kid: The Bibliography of a Legend* (Albuquerque: University of New Mexico Press, 1952), 12.
2. Walter Zvonchenko, Library of Congress (Washington, D.C.), email correspondence with author (October 20, 2011, and November 29, 2011); Garrett H. Leverton, *The Great Diamond Robbery & Other Recent Melodramas* (Princeton: Princeton University Press, 1940), p. xv.
3. *Atlanta Constitution*, May 2, 1913.
4. *Syracuse Post-Standard*, April 12, 1907.
5. Reprinted in Frederick Nolan, ed., *The Billy the Kid Reader* (Norman: University of Oklahoma Press, 2007), pp. 88–89.
6. Ibid.
7. Hutton, "Silver Screen Desperado," p. 153.
8. Stephen Tatum, *Inventing Billy the Kid* (Albuquerque: University of New Mexico Press, 1982), pp. 5, 7, 105–106, 143.

Chapter Three

1. Larry Langman, *A Guide to Silent Westerns* (New York: Greenwood, 1992), pp. 29, 102, 250.
2. Johnny D. Boggs, *Jesse James and the Movies* (Jefferson, NC: McFarland, 2011), p. 23.
3. *Iola Daily Register*, December 5, 1911.
4. Nancy Dowd and David Shepard, interviewers, *King Vidor* (A Directors Guild of America Oral History) (Metuchen, NJ: The Directors Guild of America and Scarecrow Press, 1988), pp. 111–112.
5. Paul Andrew Hutton and Jason Strykowski, comps., "Billy the Kid Filmography," *New Mexico Historical Review* (Spring 2007), 197.
6. *Sheboygan Journal*, September 1, 1911.
7. *Hamilton Evening Journal*, August 11, 1911.
8. *Mansfield News*, September 2, 1911.
9. Leverton, ed., *The Great Diamond Robbery & Other Recent Melodramas*, p. xv.
10. *Gettysburg Times*, September 7, 1910.
11. (Dunkirk, NY) *Evening Observer*, November 15, 1910.
12. Anthony Slide, *The Big V: A History of the Vitagraph Company* (Metuchen, NJ: Scarecrow Press, 1976), pp. 7–14; Richard Kioszarski, *Hollywood on the Hudson: Film and Television in New York from Griffith to Sarnoff* (New Brunswick: Rutgers University Press, 2008), p. 1,908.
13. Michael W. Robbins and Wendy Palitz, *Brooklyn: A State of Mind* (New York: Workman, 2001), p. 311; Slide, *The Big V*, pp. 55, 141.
14. *Gettysburg Times*, September 18, 1911.
15. *Sheboygan Journal*, September 1, 1911.
16. Denise Lowe, *An Encyclopedic Dictionary of Women in Early American Films, 1895–1930* (Binghamton, NY:

The Hawthorn Press, 2005), p. 500; Carolyn Lowery, *The First One Hundred Noted Men and Women of the Screen* (New York: Moffat, Yard, 1920), p. 174; www.imdb.com.

17. Ronald W. Lackman, *Women of the Western Frontier in Fact, Fiction, and Film* (Jefferson, NC: McFarland, 1997), p. 146.

18. Siobhan B. Somerville, "The Queer Career of Jim Crow: Racial and Sexual Transformation in *A Florida Enchantment*," reprinted in Jennifer M. Bean and Diane Negra, eds., *A Feminist Reader in Early Cinema* (Durham: Duke University Press, 2002), p. 259.

19. Langman, *A Guide to Silent Westerns*, p. 12.

20. Anthony Slide, *Silent Topics: Essays on Undocumented Areas of Silent Film* (Metuchen, NJ: Scarecrow Press, 2004), p. 53; Richard Abel, *Encyclopedia of Early Cinema* (New York: Routledge, 2010), p. 888.

21. Lowe, *An Encyclopedic Dictionary of Women in Early American Films, 1895–1930*, p. 500.

22. Lowery, *The First One Hundred Noted Men and Women of the Screen*, p. 174.

23. Bean and Negra, eds., *A Feminist Reader in Early Cinema*, p. 259.

24. Quoted in Bean and Negra, eds., *A Feminist Reader in Early Cinema*, p. 259.

25. Constance Severance, "Alone with a Mirror: The Exclusive Hobby of Edith Storey," *Photoplay Magazine* (May 1916), p. 85.

26. Lowe, *An Encyclopedic Dictionary of Women in Early American Films, 1895–1930*, p. 500; Bean and Negra, eds., *A Feminist Reader in Early Cinema*, p. 260; www.imdb.com.

27. *Hartford Herald*, October 9, 1901.

28. Peter Wade. "Tefft Johnson, of the Vitagraph Company," *The Motion Picture Story Magazine* (August 1912), p. 120.

29. *Huntingdon Daily News*, July 14, 1926.

30. Slide, *The Big V*, pp. 57, 69.

31. *Washington Post*, November 11, 1927, and May 10, 1930.

32. www.imdb.com.

33. Dykes, *Billy the Kid*, p. 14.

34. Although www.imdb.com—which can't always be trusted—and other sources credit Peggy Cartwright of *Our Gang* comedies in this movie, *Moving Picture World* listed Billy Mason and Peggy Custer in the film's credits. According to her obituary ([London] *Telegraph*, October 25, 2001), Cartwright was born in 1912 in British Columbia and did not move to Los Angeles until 1917. Cartwright said she made her film debut in *Face Value*, a 1917 Universal release. She went on to appear with Rudolph Valentino and Harold Lloyd before Hal Roach's *Our Gang* comedies, and even appeared in John Ford's epic Western *The Iron Horse* (1924). Peggy Custer, on the other hand, was appearing in silent shorts in 1916 and 1917, including films for Victor and University Film Manufacturing Company, which distributed *Billy, the Bandit*. A short article in *The Moving Picture World* (August 12, 1916) also listed Peggy Custer as part of the acting team to appear in a series of comedies starring Smiling Billy Mason and to be directed by John Steppling. My vote is for Peggy Custer and not Peggy Cartwright.

35. *Muscatine Journal*, January 29, 1917; *Indiana* (Pennsylvania) *Evening Gazette*, February 24, 1917. The *Journal* ad called it "a fine Victor comedy."

36. *Moving Picture World,* January 6, 1917, p. 102.

37. Dykes, *Billy the Kid*, pp. 11–12, 18.

38. www.imdb.com.

39. "John Steppling Again a Universalite," *The Moving Picture World*, August 12, 1916, p. 1090. Frontier had released a movie titled *Betty's Bandit* in 1913, according to Langman, *A Guide to Silent Westerns*, p. 28, as had Nestor in 1912, according to www.imdb.com.

40. www.imdb.com.

41. Dorothy Donnell, "'Smiling Billy' Mason, of the Essanay Company," *Motion Picture Story Magazine* (August 1913), p. 100; Hans J. Wollstein, *Strangers in Hollywood: The History of Scandinavian Actors in American Films from 1910 to World War II* (Metuchen, NJ: Scarecrow Press, 1994), p. 222.

42. Wollstein, *Strangers in Hollywood*, p. 222.

43. *New York Times*, January 26, 1941; Wollstein, *Strangers in Hollywood*, p. 222.

44. *Motion Picture Story Magazine* (August 1913); *New York Times*, January 26, 1941; www.imdb.com; Wollstein, *Strangers in Hollywood*, pp. 222, 225.

45. *New York Times*, January 26, 1941; Wollstein, *Strangers in Hollywood*, p. 226.

46. Mark Garrett Cooper, *Universal Women: Filmmaking and Institutional Change in Early Hollywood* (Champaign: University of Illinois Press, 2010), p. 73.

47. *Photoplay Magazine* (August 1917), p. 114.

48. *Frederick Post*, February 27, 1917.

49. *Moving Picture World*, January 6, 1917.

Chapter Four

1. Richard D. Jensen, *The Amazing Tom Mix: The Most Famous Cowboy of the Movies* Lincoln: iUniverse, 2005), p. 139; Paul E. Mix, *The Life and Legend of Tom Mix* (Cranbury, NJ: A.S. Barnes, 1972), pp. 140–142.

2. www.imdb.com; www.afi.com; A.J. Sharick, *Texas Bad Man* (New York: Engel van Wiseman, 1934); Lynton Wright Brent, *Gittin' in the Movies* (Hollywood: Moderncraft, 1936).

3. *Galveston Daily News*, February 28, 1933; (Massillon, Ohio) *Evening Independent*, September 29, 1932; (Burlington, North Carolina) *Daily Times-News*, November 15, 1932.

4. www.afi.com; www.imdb.com.

5. Gardner, *To Hell on a Fast Horse*, p. 273.

6. Utley, *Billy the Kid*, p. 6; Bell, *The Illustrated Life and Times of Billy the Kid*, 2d ed., p. 14.

7. Utley, *Billy the Kid*, pp. 33–34, 89.

8. Ibid., pp. 44–47; Gardner, *To Hell on a Fast Horse*, pp. 63–64.

9. Gardner, *To Hell on a Fast Horse*, pp. 66–69.

10. Wallis, *Billy the Kid*, pp. 68, 71–72.

11. Utley, *Billy the Kid*, p. 15.

12. Ibid., p. 136.

13. Wallis, *Billy the Kid*, p. 233.

14. Walter Noble Burns, *Saga of Billy the Kid* (Garden City, NY: Garden City, 1926), p. 139.

15. Ibid., pp. 139–140.

16. Wallis, *Billy the Kid*, p. 215.

17. Ibid.

18. Bell, *The Illustrated Life and Times of Billy the Kid*, 2d ed., pp. 82–84; Wallis, *Billy the Kid*, p. 225.

19. Bell, *The Illustrated Life and Times of Billy the Kid*, 2d ed., pp. 137–140.

20. Gardner, *To Hell on a Fast Horse*, pp. 139–144.

21. Burns, *Saga of Billy the Kid*, pp. 238–245; Gardner, *To Hell on a Fast Horse*, pp. 244–245; Bell, *The Illustrated Life and Times of Billy the Kid*, 2d ed., pp. 153–157; Utley, *Billy the Kid*, pp. 180–181.

22. Ibid.

23. Utley, *Billy the Kid*, pp. 181–182; Wallis, *Billy the Kid*, p. 244; Gardner, *To Hell on a Fast Horse*, pp. 146–148; Bell, *The Illustrated Life and Times of Billy the Kid*, 2d ed., pp. 155–157.

24. Ibid.

25. *Los Angeles Times*, August 24, 1930.
26. Hutton, "Silver Screen Desperado," pp. 152–153.
27. *Syracuse Herald*, January 30, 1928.
28. John Baxter, *King Vidor* (New York: Monarch, 1976), pp. 4–21.
29. *Los Angeles Times*, August 24, 1930.
30. *Syracuse Herald*, May 2, 1929; Dowd and Shepard, interviewers, *King Vidor*, p. 112; *Los Angeles Times*, August 24, 1930; John A. Rutherford, *From Pigskin to Saddle Leather: The Films of Johnny Mack Brown* (Waynesville, NC: The World of Yesterday, 1996), p. 14; www.afi.com; www.imdb.com.
31. Dowd and Shepard, *King Vidor*, p. 112.
32. Bobby J. Copeland, *Johnny Mack Brown: Up Close and Personal* (Madison, NC: Empire, 2005), pp. 10–26; Rutherford, *From Pigskin to Saddle Leather*, pp. 9–11.
33. Copeland, *Johnny Mack Brown*, p. 26; Rutherford, *From Pigskin to Saddle Leather*, p. 14.
34. Dowd and Shepard, *King Vidor*, p. 112.
35. Copeland, *Johnny Mack Brown*, p. 28.
36. Dowd and Shepard, *King Vidor*, p. 113.
37. Ibid.
38. Ephraim Katz, *The Film Encyclopedia*, rev. Fred Klein and Ronald Dean Nolen (New York: Harper Resource, 2001), p. 705; www.imdb.com.
39. Dowd and Shepard, *King Vidor*, pp. 113–114; Copeland, *Johnny Mack Brown*, p. 28; Rutherford, *From Pigskin to Saddle Leather*, p. 15.
40. Rutherford, *From Pigskin to Saddle Leather*, p. 15; Dowd and Shepard, *King Vidor*, p. 114.
41. *Los Angeles Times*, August 24, 1930; Dowd and Shepard, *King Vidor*, pp. 114–115.
42. *Los Angeles Times*, August 24, 1930.
43. Dowd and Shepard, *King Vidor*, p. 115.
44. Ibid., pp. 115–116.
45. Hutton, "Silver Screen Desperado," p. 155.
46. Dowd and Shepard, *King Vidor*, p. 116.
47. Ronald L. Davis, *William S. Hart: Projecting the American West* (Norman: University of Oklahoma Press, 2003), p. 220.
48. Ibid.
49. *Los Angeles Times*, August 24, 1930, and November 3, 1930; Clive Denton and Kingsley Canham, *The Hollywood Professionals: King Vidor, John Cromwell, Mervyn LeRoy* (London: Oak Tree, 1976), p. 22; John Douglas Eames, *The MGM Story: The Complete History of Over Fifty Roaring Years* (New York: Crown, 1976), p. 70; Hutton, "Silver Screen Desperado," p. 156.
50. Copeland, *Johnny Mack Brown*, pp. 40–41; Rutherford, *From Pigskin to Saddle Leather*, p. 16; Hutton, "Silver Screen Desperado," p. 156.
51. Copeland, *Johnny Mack Brown*, p. 44; Rutherford, *From Pigskin to Saddle Leather*, pp. 89–90.
52. Rutherford, *From Pigskin to Saddle Leather*, p. 90.
53. Dowd and Shepard, *King Vidor*, pp. 116–117; *New York Times*, November 2, 1982; www.imdb.com.
54. Dowd and Shepard, *King Vidor*, pp. 116–117.
55. Ibid., p. 112.
56. Tuska, *The Filming of the West*, p. 461; Boggs, *Jesse James and the Movies*, pp. 72–75.
57. Roy Rogers and Dale Evans, with Jane and Michael Stern, *Happy Trails: Our Life Story* (New York: Simon & Schuster, 1994), p. 105.
58. Wallis, *Billy the Kid*, pp. 15–17, 22–23, 35, 42, 63.
59. Ibid., p. 235; *New York Daily News*, June 26, 2011.
60. Johnny D. Boggs, "Mark Lee Gardner Trails Billy the Kid And Pat Garrett in New Dual Biography," *Wild West* (June 2010), p. 18.
61. Bell, *The Illustrated Life and Times of Billy the Kid*, 2d ed., p. 21; Jacobsen, *Such Men as Billy the Kid*, p. 15.
62. Wallis, *Billy the Kid*, pp. 74–75.
63. Bell, *The Illustrated Life and Times of Billy the Kid*, 2d ed., p. 21; Wallis, *Billy the Kid*, p. 74.
64. Tuska, *The Filming of the West*, p. 420; Barry Monush, *Screen World Presents the Encyclopedia of Hollywood Film Actors: From the Silent Era to 1965* (Montclair, NJ: Applause, 2003), p. 645; Chris Enss and Howard Kazanjian, *The Cowboy and the Senorita: A Biography of Roy Rogers and Dale Evans* (New York: Two Dot, 2005), pp. 64–65; Rogers and Evans, *Happy Trails*, p. 99.
65. *Dallas Morning News*, April 12, 1938.
66. David Quinlan, *Quinlan's Illustrated Guide to Film Directors* (London: B.T. Batsford, 1991), p.159; Katz, *The Film Encyclopedia*, p. 772.
67. Katz, *The Film Encyclopedia*, p. 772; Tuska, *The Filming of the West*, p. 420; www.afi.com.
68. Rogers and Evans, *Happy Trails*, p. 102.
69. William C. Cline, *In the Nick of Time: Motion Picture Sound Serials* (Jefferson, NC: McFarland, 1984), p. 137; *California and Californians, Volume 4* (Chicago: Lewis, 1926), p. 209; www.afi.com; www.imdb.com.
70. Rogers and Evans, *Happy Trails*, p. 108.
71. Paul Varner, *The A to Z of Westerns in Cinema* (Metuchen, NJ: Scarecrow Press, 2009), p. 109.
72. Rogers and Evans, *Happy Trails*, p. 108.
73. Varner, *The A to Z of Westerns in Cinema*, p. 109.
74. Rogers and Evans, *Happy Trails*, p. 106.
75. Ibid., p. 99.
76. Enss and Kazanjian, *The Cowboy and the Senorita*, p. 68; Katz, *The Film Encyclopedia*, pp. 429, 1173; www.royrogers.com; *New York Times*, July 7, 1998.

Chapter Five

1. Tuska, *The Filming of the West*, p. 200; Ted Okuda, *Grand National, Producers Releasing Corporation, and Screen Guild/Lippert: Complete Filmographies with Studio Histories* (Jefferson, NC: McFarland, 1989), p. 32.
2. Hutton, "Silver Screen Desperado," p. 161; Tuska, *The Filming of the West*, p. 200; Tuska. *Billy the Kid*, pp. 194–201.
3. Hutton, "Silver Screen Desperado," p. 161.
4. Okuda, *Grand National, Producers Releasing Corporation, and Screen Guild/Lippert*, p. 31.
5. Wallis, *Billy the Kid*, pp. 49, 159.
6. Bell, *The Illustrated Life and Times of Billy the Kid*, p. 26.
7. Gardner, *To Hell on a Fast Horse*, pp. 62–63.
8. Wallis, *Billy the Kid*, pp. 200, 222; Nolan, *The West of Billy the Kid*, p. 15.
9. Okuda, *Grand National, Producers Releasing Corporation, and Screen Guild/Lippert*, p. 32; Pitts, *Western Film Series of the Sound Era*, p. 22.
10. Ibid.
11. Katz, *The Film Encyclopedia*, p. 1,007; Quinlan, *Quinlan's Illustrated Guide to Film Directors*, p. 217; Pitts, *Western Film Series of the Sound Era*, p. 22.
12. Buck Rainey, *Heroes of the Range: Yesteryear's Saturday Matinee Movie Cowboys*. (Metuchen, NJ: Scarecrow Press, 1987), pp. 41–45; Jack Mathis, *Republic Confidential, Volume 2: The Players* (Barrington, IL: Jack Mathis Advertising, 1992), p. 141; Tuska, *The Filming of the West*, p. 199; George N. Fenin and William K. Everson, *The Western: From Silents to the Seventies: Revised Edition* (New York: Penguin Books, 1973), p. 157; Pitts, *Western Film Series of the Sound Era*, p. 22

13. Pitts, *Western Film Series of the Sound Era*, pp. 22–25, 342–366;
14. Pitts, *Western Film Series of the Sound Era*, p. 25.
15. *Variety*, November 26, 1941.
16. Tuska, *The American West in Film*, p. 157.
17. Don Miller, *Hollywood Corral: A Comprehensive B-Western Roundup* (Burbank, CA: Riverwood Press, 1993), p. 171.
18. Pitts, *Western Film Series of the Sound Era*, p. 22; Mario DeMarco, *Buster Crabbe: King of the Serial Aces and Western Action* (Self-published, no date or city given), p. 68.
19. Pitts, *Western Film Series of the Sound Era*, pp. 22–27.
20. *Variety*, November 26, 1941; Pitts, *Western Film Series of the Sound Era*, p. 26.
21. Jerry Vermilye, *Buster Crabbe: A Biofilmography* (Jefferson, NC: McFarland, 2008), p. 130; Katz. *The Film Encyclopedia*, pp. 699, 922–923.
22. Jim Driscoll, *Reflections of a "B"-Movie Junkie* (Bloomington, IN: Xlibris, 2008), p. 68.
23. Ibid.
24. Kalton C. Lahue, *Riders of the Range: The Sagebrush Heroes of the Sound Screen*. (Cranbury, NJ: A.S. Barnes and Co., 1973), p. 87.
25. Tuska, *Billy the Kid*, p. 201; Hutton, "Silver Screen Desperado," p. 161.
26. John C. Tibbetts and James M. Welsh, *American Classic Screen Interviews* (Lanham, MD: Scarecrow Press, 2010), p. 21.
27. Miller, *Hollywood Corral*, pp. 171–172; Fenin and Everson, *The Western*, p. 258.
28. Pitts, *Western Film Series of the Sound Era*, p. 16.
29. Okuda, *Grand National, Producers Releasing Corporation, and Screen Guild/Lippert*, p. 32.
30. Michael R. Pitts, *Hollywood and American History: A Filmography of Over 250 Motion Pictures Depicting U.S. History* (Jefferson, NC: McFarland, 1984), p. 61.

Chapter Six

1. *New York Times*, March 30, 1941.
2. Garrett, *The Authentic Life of Billy the Kid*, p. 7.
3. Otero, *The Real Billy the Kid*, p. 71; Metz, *Pat Garrett*, p. 306.
4. *Los Angeles Times*, June 12, 1941.
5. *Frederick Post*, December 11, 1940; Tuska, *The Filming of the West*, p. 200; Lawrence Quirk, *The Films of Robert Taylor* (Secaucus, NJ: Citadel Press, 1975), pp. 71–72; Boggs, *Jesse James and the Movies*, p. 55; Charles Tranberg, *Robert Taylor: A Biography* (Duncan, OK: Bear Manor Media, 2010), (Kindle), pp. 1,983–1,984.
6. Quirk, *The Films of Robert Taylor*, pp. 11–17; Tranberg, *Robert Taylor* (Kindle), p. x.
7. Tuska, *The Filming of the West*, p. 200.
8. *Hollywood Reporter*, January 13, 1941; Eames, *The MGM Story*, p. 168; Tranberg, *Robert Taylor* (Kindle), p. 1,983–1,987; *New York Times*, March 30, 1941; www.imdb.com.
9. Quinlan, *Quinlan's Illustrated Guide to Film Directors*, p 207; *New York Times*, March 30, 1941; www.imdb.com.
10. *New York Times*, December 19, 1940; March 6, 1987; June 11, 2009; Tranberg, *Robert Taylor* (Kindle), p. 1,987; www.afi.com; www.imdb.com.
11. Katz, *The Film Encyclopedia*, pp. 662–663.
12. *Los Angeles Times*, June 12, 1941; *New York Times*, April 6, 1972; *Variety*, May 28, 1941; Katz, *The Film Encyclopedia*, pp. 382–383.

13. *Sioux City Index*, May 16, 1941; *Frederick Post*, December 11, 1940; *New York Times*, March 30, 1941; Tuska, *The Filming of the West*, p. 200; Davis, *William S. Hart*, p. 224; Tranberg, *Robert Taylor* (Kindle), p. 1,988; "Billy the Kid: In Two Films about Him Hollywood Fakes History," *Life*, pp. 65–66, August 4, 1941.
14. Tranberg, *Robert Taylor* (Kindle), p. 1,988.
15. *New York Times*, March 30, 1941.
16. *Hollywood Reporter*, March 11, 1941; Otto Friedrich, *City of Nets: A Portrait of Hollywood in the 1940's* (Berkeley: University of California Press, 1997, pp. 124–125; Thomas Schatz, *Hollywood: Social Dimensions, Technology, Regulation and the Audience* (New York: Taylor and Francis, 2004), p. 160; "Billy the Kid: In Two Films about Him Hollywood Fakes History," *Life*, pp. 65–67, August 4, 1941; *New York Times*, March 30, 1941.
17. Quirk, *The Films of Robert Taylor*, p. 90.
18. *Los Angeles Times*, June 12, 1941.
19. *New York Times*, June 20, 1941.
20. *Life*, August 4, 1941.
21. *Variety*, May 28, 1941.
22. *Chicago Daily Tribune*, June 22, 1941.
23. *New York Times*, June 20, 1941.
24. Tranberg, *Robert Taylor* (Kindle), p. 1,989.
25. Quirk, *The Films of Robert Taylor*, p. 25; Tranberg, *Robert Taylor* (Kindle), p. 5.
26. *Frederick Post*, December 11, 1940.
27. Hitt, *The American West from Fiction (1823–1976) into Film (1909–1986)*, p. 198.
28. Utley, *Billy the Kid*, p. 201.
29. Bell, *The Illustrated Life and Times of Billy the Kid*, pp. 180–181; Gardner, *To Hell on a Fast Horse*, pp. 255–256; Utley, *Billy the Kid*, p. 201; Dale L. Walker, *Legends and Lies: Great Mysteries of the American West* (New York: Forge, 1997), p. 125.
30. *Hagerstown Morning Herald*, May 22, 1942.
31. Driscoll, *Reflections of a "B"-Movie Junkie*, p. 203; *New York Times*, March 26, 1986; Katz, *The Film Encyclopedia*, p. 1296; Pitts, *Western Film Series of the Sound Era*, pp. 64–67; *Doylestown Sunday Intelligencer*, December 21, 1986.
32. Michael G. Fitzgerald and Boyd Magers, *Ladies of the Western: Interviews with Fifty-one More Actresses from the Silent Era to the Television Westerns of the 1950s and 1960s* (Jefferson, NC: McFarland, 2006), p. 37.
33. Pitts, *Western Film Series of the Sound Era*, pp. 64–67; *Orange County Register*, February 12, 1986.
34. Rainey, *Heroes of the Range*, p. 247.
35. *Doylestown Sunday Intelligencer*, December 21, 1986; *Orange County Register*, February 12, 1986; *New York Times*, March 26, 1986.
36. Tuska, *Billy the Kid*, p. 199; Katz, *The Film Encyclopedia*, p. 606; *Hagerstown Morning Herald*, May 22, 1942; www.imdb.com.
37. Tuska, *Billy the Kid*, p. 200; www.imdb.com.
38. Karen Holliday Tanner, *Doc Holliday: A Family Portrait* (Norman: University of Oklahoma Press, 2001), pp. 124–125.
39. Utley, *Billy the Kid*, p. 35; George W. Coe, *Frontier Fighter: The Autobiography of George W. Coe, Who Fought and Rode with Billy the Kid* (Chicago: The Lakeside Press, 1984), p. 49.
40. Jeff Guinn, *The Last Gunfight: The Real Story of the Shootout at the O.K. Corral—and How It Changed the American West* (New York: Simon & Schuster, 2011), p. 300.
41. Guinn, *The Last Gunfight*, p. 1; Metz, *Pat Garrett*, pp. 98–100.
42. Thomas Doherty, *Hollywood's Censor: Joseph I. Breen & The Production Code Administration* (New York: Colum-

bia University Press, 2007), p. 252; Katz, *The Film Encyclopedia*, pp. 656–657.

43. Doherty, *Hollywood's Censor*, pp. 45–46, 61, 173; David Welky, *The Moguls and the Dictators: Hollywood and the Coming of World War II* (Baltimore: John Hopkins University Press, 2008), p. 9.

44. Tony Thomas, *Howard Hughes in Hollywood* (New York: Citadel Press, 1985), pp. 79–80.

45. Darwin Porter, *Howard Hughes: Hell's Angel* (Staten Island, NY: Blood Moon, 2010), p. 265.

46. Thomas, *Howard Hughes in Hollywood*, p. 80.

47. Ibid.

48. *New York Times*, March 30, 1941.

49. Charles Affron and Mirella Jona Affron, *Best Years: Going to the Movies, 1945–1946* (Piscataway, NJ: Rutgers University Press, 2009), p. 158.

50. Thomas, *Howard Hughes in Hollywood*, p. 80; Friedrich, *City of Nets: A Portrait of Hollywood in the 1940's*, p. 123.

51. Thomas, *Howard Hughes in Hollywood*, pp. 80–81; Friedrich, *City of Nets: A Portrait of Hollywood in the 1940's*, p. 123; Jane Russell, *Jane Russell: An Autobiography: My Path & Detours* (New York: Franklin Watts, 1985), pp. 9–11

52. Thomas, *Howard Hughes in Hollywood*, p. 81.

53. Friedrich, *City of Nets: A Portrait of Hollywood in the 1940's*, p. 123. Reports of how much Russell was paid vary, depending on the source, from $50 a week to $150 a week.

54. Katz, *The Film Encyclopedia*, pp. 558, 954.

55. Charles Higham, *Howard Hughes: The Secret Life* (New York: St. Martin's Griffin, 2004), p. 97.

56. Higham, *Howard Hughes*, p. 95; Thomas, *Howard Hughes in Hollywood*, p. 82.

57. Porter, *Howard Hughes*, p. 529.

58. Thomas, *Howard Hughes in Hollywood*, pp. 82–83; *New York Times*, December 11, 1940; December 15, 1940; Maurice Zolotow. *Shooting Star: A Biography of John Wayne* (New York: Pocket Books, 1975), p. 291; Russell, *Jane Russell*, p. 19.

59. Donald L. Bartlett and James B. Steele, *Howard Hughes: His Life & Madness* (New York: W.W. Norton, 2004), p. 107.

60. Tuska, *The Filming of the West*, p. 201.

61. Porter, *Howard Hughes*, p. 529.

62. Russell, *Jane Russell*, p. 56.

63. Russell, *Jane Russell*, p. 57.

64. Thomas, *Howard Hughes in Hollywood*, p. 84.

65. *New York Times*, March 30, 1941.

66. Thomas, *Howard Hughes in Hollywood*, p. 84; *New York Times*, March 30, 1941.

67. Thomas, *Howard Hughes in Hollywood*, p. 85.

68. Peter Harry Brown and Pat H. Broeske, *Howard Hughes: The Untold Story* (Chicago: Da Capo Press, 2004), p. 165.

69. Brown and Broeske, *Howard Hughes*, p. 165; Thomas, *Howard Hughes in Hollywood*, p. 85; *Daily Capital News*, February 2, 1972; www.afi.com.

70. Thomas, *Howard Hughes in Hollywood*, p. 86; *New York Times*, January 17, 1942; *Newsweek, Volume 21* (1943), p. 88; Russell, *Jane Russell*, p. 72.

71. Brown and Broeske, *Howard Hughes*, pp. 207–208; *Christian Science Monitor*, September 27, 1946; *Los Angeles Times*, April 4, 1946; Ronald Bergan, *The United Artists Story* (New York: Crown, 1986), p. 114; Gerald R. Butters, Jr., *Banned in Kansas: Motion Picture Censorship 1915–1966* (Columbia: University of Missouri Press, 2007), p. 233.

72. Boggs, *Jesse James and the Movies*, p. 135; *Los Angeles Times*, July 1, 1989; *New York Times*, February 28, 2011; *Variety*, February 28, 2011.

73. Richard B. Jewell with Veron Harbin, *The RKO Story: The Complete Studio History, with all of the 1,051 Films Described and Illustrated* (London: Octopus Books, 1982), p. 249; *New York Times*, October 10, 1949; www.afi.com.

74. *Hollywood Reporter*, June 26, 1968.

75. *Chicago Daily Tribune*, March 14, 1946.

76. *Daily Capital News*, February 3, 1972.

77. Boyd Magers and Michael Fitzgerald, *Westerns Women: Interviews with 50 Leading Ladies of Movie and Television Westerns from the 1930s to the 1960s* (Jefferson, NC: McFarland, 1999), p. 215; William C. Cline, *Serials-ly Speaking: Essays on Cliffhangers* (Jefferson, NC: McFarland, 2000), p. 41; Driscoll, *Reflections of a "B"-Movie Junkie*, p. 46; www.imdb.com.

78. Tuska, *The Filming of the West*, pp. 452, 462; Varner, *The A to Z of Westerns in Cinema*, p. 41; Mathis, *Republic Confidential 2*, p. 141; Katz, *The Film Encyclopedia*, p. 230; *Ironwood Daily Globe*, May 3, 1990; *Los Angeles Times*, May 3, 1990; www.imdb.com.

79. Fenin and Everson, *The Western: From Silents to the Seventies*, p. 257.

80. *Syracuse Post-Standard*, May 3, 1990; *Los Angeles Times*, May 3, 1990; Varner, *The A to Z of Westerns in Cinema*, p. 41; Fenin and Everson, *The Western*, p. 257; www.imdb.com.

81. Tuska, *The Filming of the West*, p. 426.

82. Robert Nott, *The Films of Randolph Scott* (Jefferson: McFarland, 2004), p. 142.

83. Marley Brant, *The Outlaw Youngers: A Confederate Brotherhood* (Lanham, MD: Madison Books, 1992), pp. 211–212, 246, 281–282, 289–290, 296–298, 314.

84. Paul Trachtman, *The Gunfighters* (Alexandria, VA: Time-Life Books, 1974), p. 84; Emmett Dalton, *When the Daltons Rode* (Gretna, LA: Pelican Books, 2012), ix–xix.

85. Trachtman, *The Gunfighters*, pp. 157–161.

86. Linda S. Watts, *Encyclopedia of American Folklore* (New York: Checkmark Books, 2007), p. 252.

87. Robert Barr Smith, *Daltons! The Raid on Coffeyville, Kansas* (Norman: University of Oklahoma Press, 1996), pp. 165–166.

88. *Las Vegas Daily Optic*, December 6, 1879; Henry F. Hoyt, *A Frontier Doctor* (Chicago: The Lakeside Press, 1979), pp. 183–184.

89. Arrell M. Gibson, *The History of Oklahoma* (Norman: University of Oklahoma Press, 1984), pp. 100–103.

90. Robert Nott, *Last of the Cowboy Heroes: The Westerns of Randolph Scott, Joel McCrea, and Audie Murphy* (Jefferson, NC: McFarland, 2000), pp. 16–17; Nott, *The Films of Randolph Scott*, pp. 128–129. Boggs, *Jesse James and the Movies*, p. 89.

91. Nott, *The Films of Randolph Scott*, p. 129.

92. Nott, *The Films of Randolph Scott*, p. 143; www.afi.com.

93. *Winnipeg Free Press*, April 23, 1947; *Joplin Globe*, July 1, 1947; www.imdb.com.

94. Nott, *The Films of Randolph Scott*, p. 144.

95. Nott, *The Films of Randolph Scott*, pp. 144–145; Quinlan, *Quinlan's Illustrated Guide to Film Directors*, p. 89.

96. Katz, *The Film Encyclopedia*, p. 699; Nott, *The Films of Randolph Scott*, p. 142.

97. *Hollywood Reporter*, April 29, 2006.

98. Nott, *The Films of Randolph Scott*, pp. 17–18, 225; *New York Times*, March 3, 1987; *Variety*, November 10, 2008; *Chicago Daily Tribune*, September 11, 1949.

99. Franklin Jarlett, *Robert Ryan: A Biography and Critical Filmography* (Jefferson, NC: McFarland, 1990), pp. 6–7, 193.

100. *New York Times*, August 5, 1948; *New York Herald-Tribune*, August 5, 1948.
101. *Time*, August 16, 1948.
102. Fitzgerald and Magers, *Ladies of the Western*, p. 111.
103. Jarlett, *Robert Ryan*, p. 193; *New York Times*, July 12, 1973.
104. *Denton Record-Chronicle*, September 25, 1949. The paper gave the movie a "fair" rating.
105. Walker, *Legends and Lies*, p. 125.
106. Utley, *Billy the Kid*, p. 192; Wallis, *Billy the Kid*, pp. 246–247; Gardner, *To Hell on a Fast Horse*, pp. 169–170.
107. Nolan, *The West of Billy the Kid*, p. 283.
108. *Son of Billy the Kid* press book, pp. 2–3; www.imdb.com.
109. Chuck Thorton and David Rothel, *Lash LaRue: King of the Bullwhip* (Madison, NC: Empire Publishing, 1988), pp. 13; *Cary News*, January 28, 1987. LaRue called comparisons to Bogart preposterous. "I have a lot more hair than Bogart had" (Thornton and Rothel, p. 38).
110. Thornton and Rothel. *Lash LaRue*, pp. 39, 42–43.
111. Tuska, *The Filming of the West*, p. 425.
112. Thornton and Rothel, *Lash LaRue*, pp. 14–17, 39, 42–43; Okuda, *Grand National, Producers Releasing Corporation, and Screen Guild/Lippert*, pp. 104, 111.
113. Okuda, *Grand National, Producers Releasing Corporation, and Screen Guild/Lippert*, p. 32.
114. Thornton and Rothel, *Lash LaRue*, pp. 17–18.
115. Thornton and Rothel, *Lash LaRue*, p. 45.
116. Ibid.
117. Thornton and Rothel, *Lash LaRue*, p. 51.
118. Tuska, *The Filming of the West*, pp. 425–426; *Baltimore Sun*, March 31, 1996.

Chapter Seven

1. Wallis, *Billy the Kid*, pp. 14–17, 52, 78; Garrett, *The Authentic Life of Billy the Kid*, p. 7.
2. Wallis, *Billy the Kid*, pp. 35, 63, 94–96.
3. Gardner, *To Hell on a Fast Horse*, pp. 63–64.
4. Wallis, *Billy the Kid*, pp. 199–204.
5. Ibid., p. 237.
6. Louis A. Garavaglia and Charles G. Worman, *Firearms of the American West, 1866–1894* (Niwot: University Press of Colorado, 1997), p. 220.
7. Bell, *The Illustrated Life and Times of Billy the Kid*, 2d ed., p. 95.
8. Sue Gossett, *Films and Career of Audie Murphy* (Madison, NC: Empire Publishing, 1996), p. 8.
9. Nott, *Last of the Cowboy Heroes*, pp. 42–43; Judy Alter, *Audie Murphy: War Hero and Movie Star* (Austin, TX: State House Press, 2007), pp. 20, 38; Gossett, *Films and Career of Audie Murphy*, pp. 8–9; Murphy, Audie, *To Hell and Back* (New York: Permabooks, 1955), pp. 8–9, 312.
10. *Los Angeles Times*, September 8, 1948; Bob Larkins and Boyd Magers, *The Films of Audie Murphy* (Jefferson, NC: McFarland, 2004), p. 35.
11. Nott, *Last of the Cowboy Heroes*, p. 45; Larkins and Magers, *The Films of Audie Murphy*, p. 35.
12. Gossett, *Films and Career of Audie Murphy*, p. 9; Nott, *Last of the Cowboy Heroes*, pp. 42–43; Murphy, *To Hell and Back*, copyright page.
13. Larkins and Magers, *The Films of Audie Murphy*, p. 32.
14. "The Role I Liked Best ...," *Saturday Evening Post* (January 13, 1951), p. 113.
15. Gossett, Sue, *Audie Murphy: Now Showing* (Madison, NC: Empire Publishing, 2002), p. 24; Larkins and Magers, *The Films of Audie Murphy*, p. 35.
16. Gossett, *Audie Murphy: Now Showing*, p. 24.
17. Nott, *Last of the Cowboy Heroes*, pp. 42–43.
18. Gossett, *Films and Career of Audie Murphy*, pp. 9–10; Nott, *Last of the Cowboy Heroes*, p. 45.
19. *La Crosse Tribune*, April 4, 1950.
20. Nott, *Last of the Cowboy Heroes*, pp. 45–46; *Hartford Courant*, April 13, 1950.
21. *La Crosse Tribune*, April 4, 1950.
22. Gossett, *Films and Career of Audie Murphy*, pp. 10–11. Nott, *Last of the Cowboy Heroes*, pp. 43, 46.
23. *Christian Science Monitor*, January 5, 1951.
24. *Long Beach Press Telegram*, October 27, 1950.
25. Ibid.
26. Gossett, *Films and Career of Audie Murphy*, p. 9; Nott, *Last of the Cowboy Heroes*, p. 164.
27. *Christian Science Monitor*, April 7, 1950.
28. Larry McMurtry, *The Last Picture Show* (New York: Penguin Books, 1985), p. 265.
29. Utley, *Billy the Kid*, pp. 96–99; Nolan, *The Lincoln County War*, pp. 329–331.
30. Utley, *Billy the Kid*, p. 97.
31. Robert M. Utley, *High Noon in Lincoln: Violence on the Western Frontier* (Albuquerque: University of New Mexico Press, 1987), p. 107.
32. Wallis, *Billy the Kid*, pp. 233–234.
33. Ibid., pp. 201–202.
34. Gardner, *To Hell on a Fast Horse*, pp. 85–102.
35. Wallis, *Billy the Kid*, pp. 225–227.
36. Utley, *Billy the Kid*, p. 174. Wallis, *Billy the Kid*, pp. 239–243.
37. Wallis, *Billy the Kid*, pp. 244–245.
38. Ibid., p. 238.
39. Gardner, *To Hell on a Fast Horse*, pp. 159, 171.
40. Ibid., p. 250.
41. Boggs, *Jesse James and the Movies*, pp. 114–115.
42. Fitzgerald and Magers, *Ladies of the Western*, p. 26.
43. Magers and Fitzgerald, *Westerns Women*, p. 26.
44. Tuska, *The Filming of the West*, p. 451.
45. Lahue, *Riders of the Range*, p. 52.
46. Nott, *The Films of Randolph Scott*, p. 193.
47. Boggs, *Jesse James and the Movies*, p. 101.
48. Magers and Fitzgerald, *Westerns Women*, p. 9.
49. Lahue, *Riders of the Range*, p. 52.
50. *Los Angeles Times*, July 18, 1980.
51. Mathis, *Republic Confidential*, p. 141; Driscoll, *Reflections of a "B"-Movie Junkie*, p. 105; Katz, *The Film Encyclopedia*, p. 785; Pitts, *Western Film Series of the Sound Era*, p. 271.
52. Driscoll, *Reflections of a "B"-Movie Junkie*, p. 105; Katz, *The Film Encyclopedia*, p. 785; Bobby J. Copeland, *Roy Barcroft: King of the Badmen* (Madison, NC: Empire Publishing, 2000), (Kindle) p. 65.
53. Driscoll, *Reflections of a "B"-Movie Junkie*, p. 105; *American Profile*, June 16, 2012.
54. Clayton Moore and Frank Thompson, *I Was That Masked Man* (Dallas: Taylor Trade Publishing, 1996), p. 130; *New York Times*, December 29, 1999.
55. Moore and Thompson, *I Was That Masked Man*, pp. 131–132, 138, 142, 254; *New York Times*, December 29, 1999.
56. *The Independent*, September 5, 1998; Katz, *The Film Encyclopedia*, p. 412.
57. Katz, *The Film Encyclopedia*, p. 1,476; www.imdb.com.
58. Katz, *The Film Encyclopedia*, p. 129.
59. Copeland, *Roy Barcroft* (Kindle), pp. 65, 815, 820–822.

60. Ibid., p. 822.
61. Utley, *Billy the Kid*, p. 127.
62. Ibid., p. 118.
63. Bell, *The Illustrated Life and Times of Billy the Kid*, 2d ed., pp. 14–16.
64. Ibid., pp. 16–18.
65. Ibid., p. 18.
66. Ibid., pp. 14–18, 26.
67. Nolan, *The West of Billy the Kid*, pp. 114–115; Mullin, *Maurice G. Fulton's History of the Lincoln County War*, pp. 137–141; Gardner, *To Hell on a Fast Horse*, pp. 65–70.
68. Wallis, *Billy the Kid*, p. 225.
69. Bell, *The Illustrated Life and Times of Billy the Kid*, 2d ed., pp. 133–135.
70. Ibid., p. 141.
71. Wallis, *Billy the Kid*, pp. 200–201, 243–244.
72. Wallis, *Billy the Kid*, p. 246; Gardner, *To Hell on a Fast Horse*, p. 160.
73. *New York Times*, September 25, 1950; April 18, 1985; *Los Angeles Times*, April 18, 1985; Monush, *Screen World Presents the Encyclopedia of Hollywood Film Actors*, p. 83; Tuska, *Billy the Kid*, p. 205.
74. Nott, Email correspondence with author, September 28, 2012.
75. *Nevada State Journal*, August 11, 1954.
76. Everett Aaker, *Television Western Players of the Fifties: A Biographical Encyclopedia of All Regular Cast Members in Western Series, 1949–1959* (Jefferson, NC: McFarland, 2007), p. 252.
77. Bernard Gordon, *The Gordon File: A Screenwriter Recalls Twenty Years of FBI Surveillance* (Austin: University of Texas Press, 2008), pp. 129–131; *New York Times*, May 14, 2007.
78. Gordon, *The Gordon File*, p. 131.
79. Ibid., pp. 121–125.
80. Gordon, *The Gordon File*, p. 131; Abraham Polonsky and John Schultheiss, *Odds against Tomorrow: The Critical Edition* (Canoga Park, CA: Sandanlaur Publications, 1999), p. 317; www.afi.com. Gordon wrote that the Stevenson play was unproduced, although a Philip Stevenson play, *Sure Fire, Episodes in the Life of Billy the Kid*, was presented in Santa Fe, New Mexico, in 1933. This might not have been, however, the play Gordon adapted for the screen.
81. Gordon, *The Gordon File*, p. 131.
82. Winston Dixon Wheeler, *Lost in the Fifties: Recovering Phantom Hollywood* (Carbondale: Southern Illinois University Press, 2005), p. 65. Another Gordon script written as Marcus was *Chicago Confidential* (1957), produced by Robert E. Kent and distributed by United Artists.
83. *Variety*, October 1, 1997.
84. Wheeler, *Lost in the Fifties*, p. 65.
85. Ibid.
86. Wheeler, *Lost in the Fifties*, p. 66; *New York Times*, May 14, 2007; www.imdb.com.
87. Wheeler, *Lost in the Fifties*, p. 66; *New York Times*, May 14, 2007; *Variety*, May 11, 2007.
88. Utley, *Billy the Kid*, pp. 12–13, 64–68, 77–78, 173–174.
89. Wallis, *Billy the Kid*, p. 7; Walker, *Legends and Lies*, p. 125.
90. Quinlan, *Quinlan's Illustrated Guide to Film Directors*, pp. 66–67.
91. *New York Times*, September 25, 1988.
92. James C. Robertson, *The Casablanca Man: The Cinema of Michael Curtiz* (New York: Routledge, 1993), p. 115; www.imdb.com.
93. Robertson, *The Casablanca Man*, p. 115.
94. Robertson, *The Casablanca Man*, p. 115; John Howard Reid, *Movie Westerns: Hollywood Films the Wild, Wild West* (Raleigh: Lulu, 2004), pp. 38–39.
95. Reid, *Movie Westerns*, p. 38; Douglas Brode, *Shooting Stars of the Small Screen: Encyclopedia of TV Western Actors, 1946-Present* (Austin: University of Texas Press, 2009, p. 281; "Westerners Who Changed America," *American Cowboy* (November-December 2004), p. 36; www.imdb.com.
96. Robert J. Conley, *A Cherokee Encyclopedia* (Albuquerque: University of New Mexico Press, 2007), p. 194; "Will Rogers' Boy: Humorist's son tries to imitate father for movies," *Life*, May 27, 1946; Arthur Frank Wertheim and Barbara Bair, eds, *The Papers of Will Rogers: From Vaudeville to Broadway: Volume Three: September 1909-August 1915* (Norman: University of Oklahoma Press, 2001), p. 441; www.imdb.com.
97. Conley, *A Cherokee Encyclopedia*, p. 194; "Will Rogers' Boy: Humorist's son tries to imitate father for movies," *Life* (May 27, 1946); Wertheim and Bair, *The Papers of Will Rogers*, p. 441–445; www.imdb.com.
98. *Boys' Life*, March 1954; Wertheim and Bair, *The Papers of Will Rogers*, p. 445–446. *The New York Times*, July 18, 1952, said *The Story of Will Rogers* "is not an important film. But it gives a tender reflection of a character that many people loved."
99. Wertheim and Bair, *The Papers of Will Rogers*, p. 445.
100. Ibid., p. 446.
101. Reid, *Movie Westerns*, p. 38; Brode, *Shooting Stars of the Small Screen*, p. 281; Wertheim and Bair, *The Papers of Will Rogers*, p. 446; www.imdb.com.
102. Hal Erickson *Encyclopedia of Television Law Shows*, pp. 254–255; Alvin H. Marill, *Television Westerns: Six Decades of Sagebrush Sheriffs, Scalawags, and Sidewinders* (Lanham, MD: Scarecrow Press, 2011), p. 57.
103. Reid, *Movie Westerns: Hollywood Films the Wild, Wild, West* p. 38;
104. Gardner, *To Hell on a Fast Horse*, pp. 13–17.
105. Lew Wallace, *Lew Wallace: An Autobiography* (New York: Harper & Brothers, 1906), p. 938.
106. Wallis, *Billy the Kid*, pp. 237, 241; George Thomas Kurian and James D. Smith III, eds, The *Encyclopedia of Christian Literature, Volume 1.* (Lanham, MD: Scarecrow Press, 2010), p. 622; Stewart Holbrook, "Gen. Wallace and Ben Hur," *Popular Culture* (August 6, 1944); James David Hart, *The Popular Novel: A History of America's Literary Taste* (Berkeley: University of California Press, 1950), p. 164.
107. John C. Cremony, *Life among the Apaches* (Lincoln: University of Nebraska Press, 1983), p. 257.
108. Sharon Nederman, *Explorer's Guide Santa Fe & Taos: A Great Destination* (Woodstock, VT: Countryman Press, 2006), pp. 33, 132.
109. William A. Keleher, *Turmoil in New Mexico, 1846–1868* (Santa Fe: Sunstone Press, 2007), p. 119.
110. Tom Philbin, *The Greatest 100 Greatest Inventions of All Time: A Ranking Past to Present* (New York: Citadel Press, 2003), pp. 118–119; George Ripley and Charles A. Dana, eds, *The New American Cyclopaedia: A Popular Dictionary of Knowledge, Vol. II* (New York: D. Appleton, 1867), p. 367.
111. Michael Troyan, *A Rose for Mrs. Miniver: The Life of Greer Garson* (Lexington: University Press of Kentucky, 1999), p. 148; Owen M. Lee, *The Best Films of Our Years*. (Bloomington, IN: Author House, 2007), p. 57; *New York Times*, June 5, 1942.
112. Troyan, *A Rose for Mrs. Miniver*, pp. 8, 96; *The Independent*, April 8, 1996; *New York Times*, April 7, 1996.
113. Troyan, *A Rose for Mrs. Miniver*, p. 260; *Albuquerque Journal*, June 10, 1955.

114. *New York Times,* September 14, 1987; Quinlan, *Quinlan's Illustrated Guide to Film Directors,* pp. 184–185.
115. Troyan, *A Rose for Mrs. Miniver,* pp. 121, 212–214, 225.
116. Troyan, *A Rose for Mrs. Miniver,* p. 261; www.imdb.com.
117. Troyan, *A Rose for Mrs. Miniver,* p. 262.
118. Ibid., pp. 262–263.
119. Carl Rollyson, *Hollywood Enigma: Dana Andrews* (Jackson: University Press of Mississippi, 2012), p. 244.
120. Rollyson, *Hollywood Enigma: Dana Andrews,* p. 292; James McKay, *Dana Andrews: The Face of Noir* (Jefferson, NC: McFarland, 2010), p. 22; *New York Times,* December 19, 1992.
121. Troyan, *A Rose for Mrs. Miniver,* p. 263; *New York Times,* May 15, 1949; July 9, 1994.
122. Troyan, *A Rose for Mrs. Miniver,* p. 266; *Los Angeles Times,* February 8, 1968; February 9, 1968; February 13, 1968; May 4, 1968; Mervyn LeRoy as told to Dick Kleiner, *Mervyn LeRoy: Take One* (New York: Hawthorn Books, 1974), pp. 198–1999.
123. *Los Angeles Times,* May 28, 1954; Troyan, *A Rose for Mrs. Miniver,* p. 263.
124. Troyan, *A Rose for Mrs. Miniver,* p. 263.
125. LeRoy, *Mervyn LeRoy,* p. 196.
126. Troyan, *A Rose for Mrs. Miniver,* pp. 264–265; *New York Times,* December 19, 1992; LeRoy, *Mervyn LeRoy,* p. 197.
127. LeRoy, *Mervyn LeRoy,* pp. 196–197.
128. Troyan, *A Rose for Mrs. Miniver,* p. 265; LeRoy, *Mervyn LeRoy,* pp. 196–197.
129. Troyan, *A Rose for Mrs. Miniver,* p. 265.
130. *Washington Post,* October 13, 1954; Troyan, *A Rose for Mrs. Miniver,* pp. 265–266.
131. LeRoy, *Mervyn LeRoy,* p. 197.
132. Troyan, *A Rose for Mrs. Miniver,* p. 266.
133. "D-B-H Biog Film Rights to 20th-Fox," *Billboard* (January 29, 1955), p. 24; Troyan, *A Rose for Mrs. Miniver,* p. 266–268.
134. *Los Angeles Times,* April 28, 1955; *New York Times,* May 21, 1955.
\135. Troyan, *A Rose for Mrs. Miniver,* p. 268.
136. *Albuquerque Journal,* June 10, 1955.
137. Troyan, *A Rose for Mrs. Miniver,* p. 330.
138. *New York Times,* April 7, 1996.
139. Ibid.
140. *Albuquerque Journal,* June 10, 1955.
141. Rollyson, *Hollywood Enigma,* p. 244.
142. Nolan, *The West of Billy the Kid,* pp. 281–287; Wallis, *Billy the Kid,* pp. 1–2, 246–247.
143. *Last of the Desperados* pressbook. Wallis, *Billy the Kid,* p. 246.
144. Nolan, *The West of Billy the Kid,* pp. 281–287; Wallis, *Billy the Kid,* pp. 1–2, 246–247.
145. Nolan, *The Lincoln County War,* pp. 482–483.
146. Utley, *Billy the Kid,* p. 195.
147. Wallis, *Billy the Kid,* p. 246.
148. Metz, *Pat Garrett,* pp. 126–127.
149. Ibid., p. 40.
150. Ibid., pp. 136–137, 145–146.
151. Dixon, *Lost in the Fifties,* p. 104.
152. Ibid.
153. Steven Ascher and Edward Pincus, *The Filmmaker's Handbook: A Comprehensive Guide for the Digital Age* (New York: Plume, 2007), p. 92; Jerry L. Schneider, *Corrigan Movie Ranch* (Raleigh: Lulu, 2007), p. 367. Donna Martel, telephone interview with author (May 1, 2002); Donna Martel recalled that the film was shot at Melody Ranch, but Jerry L. Schneider's book *Corrigan Movie Ranch* has it filmed there.
154. *New York Times,* April 27, 1981; Boyd Magers, Bob Nareau, and Bobby Copeland, *Best of the Badmen (Polecats, Varmints, and Desperadoes of Western Films)* (Madison, NC: Empire Publishing, 2005), (Kindle), pp. 2002–2020.
155. Karen Burroughs Hannsberry, *Bad Boys: The Actors of Film Noir* (Jefferson, NC: McFarland, 2008), pp. 162–166; David Bret, *Joan Crawford: Hollywood Martyr* (Chicago: Da Capo Pres, 2008), p. 147; Monush, *Screen World Presents the Encyclopedia of Hollywood Film Actors, Volume 1,* pp. 155–156.
156. Donna Martel interview.
157. Ibid.
158. Nolan, *The Lincoln County War,* p. 248. Wallis, *Billy the Kid,* p. 200.
159. Utley, *High Noon in Lincoln,* p. 65.
160. Nolan, *The Lincoln County War,* p. 248.
161. Nolan, *The Billy the Kid Reader,* pp. 338–341. Gardner, *To Hell on a Fast Horse,* p. 289.
162. Nolan, *The Billy the Kid Reader,* p. 341.
163. Nolan, *The Billy the Kid Reader,* pp. 341–342. Gardner, *To Hell on a Fast Horse,* pp. 175–176.
164. Mark Twain, *Roughing It* (New York: Signet, 1982), pp. 107, 110.
165. Richard Patterson, *Historical Atlas of the Outlaw West* (Boulder, CO: Johnson Books, 1985), pp. 98–99; Bill O'Neal, *Encyclopedia of Western Gunfighters* (Norman: University of Oklahoma Press, 1991), pp. 126–131, 286–287. Conley, *A Cherokee Encyclopedia,* pp. 104–105;
166. Don Bullis, "Wild Cowboys and Civilized Indians Dominate the Path to Statehood for New Mexico and Arizona," *Roundup Magazine* (April 2012), p. 11.
167. *Los Angeles Times,* February 10, 1956.
168. *New York Times,* April 20, 1951.
169. Brian Garfield, *Western Films: A Complete Guide* (New York: Rawson Associates, 1982), p. 256; www.imdb.com.
170. Fitzgerald and Magers, *Ladies of the Western,* p. 273; *New York Times,* April 26, 1950; September 4, 1957; June 6, 1970.
171. James E. Wise, Jr., and Anne Collier, *Stars in Blue: Movie Actors in America's Sea Services* (Annapolis: Naval Institute Press, 2007), pp. 225–226; *New York Times,* May 4, 1927; June 27, 1937; May 28, 1942; April 23, 1999.
172. *New York Times,* December 14, 2000.
173. *Variety,* February 23, 1956.
174. *Syracuse Post-Standard,* December 24, 1988.
175. Pauline Kael, *5001 Nights at the Movies: A Guide from A to Z* (New York: Holt, Rinehart & Winston, 1982), p. 323.
176. Michael Chaiken and Paul Cronin, eds., *Arthur Penn Interviews* (Jackson: University Press of Mississippi, 2008), p. 53.
177. Wallis. *Billy the Kid,* pp. 49, 66–68.
178. Garrett, *Authentic Life of Billy, the Kid,* pp. 10–11.
179. Utley, *Billy the Kid,* pp. 56–58, 64–65.
180. Utley, *High Noon in Lincoln,* pp. 1, 92; Gardner, *To Hell on a Fast Horse,* p. 75.
181. Eric Sherman and Martin Rubin, *The Director's Event: Interviews with Five American Film-Makers* (New York: Atheneum, 1970), p. 111.
182. Bell, *The Illustrated Life and Times of Billy the Kid,* 2d ed., pp. 133–138.
183. Gardner, *To Hell on a Fast Horse,* pp. 92–94.
184. Gardner, *To Hell on a Fast Horse,* p. 94; Bell, *The Illustrated Life and Times of Billy the Kid,* pp. 155–157; Wallis, *Billy the Kid,* pp. 234, 243–245; Metz, *Pat Garrett,* p. 40.

185. Gardner, *To Hell on a Fast Horse*, p. 277.
186. www.imdb.com.
187. Shawn Levy, *Paul Newman: A Life* (New York: Three Rivers Press, 2009), p. 105; www.imdb.com
188. Levy, *Paul Newman*, p. 106.
189. F.X. Feeney "Ben-Gore," *Los Angeles Review of Books* (August 1, 2012); Levy, *Paul Newman*, p. 123.
190. Levy, *Paul Newman*, p. 123.
191. Chaiken and Cronin, *Arthur Penn Interviews*, pp. 89, 119; Levy, *Paul Newman*, p. 123.
192. Quinlan, *Quinlan's Illustrated Guide to Film Directors*, pp. 229–230; *New York Times*, September 27, 2008; September 29, 2010; www.imdb.com.
193. Chaiken and Cronin, *Arthur Penn Interviews*, pp. 179, 205.
194. Nat Segaloff, *Arthur Penn: American Director* (Lexington: University Press of Kentucky, 2011), p. 63.
195. Levy, *Paul Newman*, p. 124; Segaloff, *Arthur Penn*, p. 64
196. Magers, Nareau and Copeland, *Best of the Badmen* (Kindle), pp. 2055–2082.
197. www.imdb.com; www.glamourgirlsofthesilverscreen.com; *St. Petersburg Times*, December 29, 1969; *Modesto Bee*, August 15, 1965; Lauren Derby, *The Dictator's Seduction: Politics and the Popular Imagination in the Era of Trujillo* (Durham: Duke University Press Books, 2009), p. 182.
198. *The Independent*, December 31, 1998.
199. Segaloff, *Arthur Penn*, p. 68.
200. Ibid., p. 60.
201. Andrew Sarris, *The American Cinema: Directors and Directions, 1929–1968* (Chicago: Da Capo Press, 1996), p. 136.
202. Chaiken and Cronin, *Arthur Penn Interviews*, p. 51.
203. Segaloff, *Arthur Penn*, p. 90.
204. *New York Times*, May 8, 1958.
205. Levy, *Paul Newman*, p. 124.
206. Segaloff, *Arthur Penn*, pp. 70–71; Levy, *Paul Newman*, p. 138.
207. *New York Times*, September 29, 2010; Scott Siegel and Barbara Siegel, *The Encyclopedia of Hollywood: An A-to-Z Guide to the Stars, Stories, and Secrets of Hollywood: Second Edition* (New York: Checkmark Books, 2004), p. 312.
208. *Los Angeles Times*, April 28, 1998.
209. *New York Times*, September 27, 2008; www.imdb.com.
210. Ibid.
211. *Los Angeles Times*, March 16, 1958.
212. Chaiken and Cronin, *Arthur Penn Interviews*, p. 108.
213. Levy, *Paul Newman*, p. 124; Chaiken and Cronin, *Arthur Penn Interviews*, p. 91.

Chapter Eight

1. Gardner, *To Hell on a Fast Horse*, pp. 178–188.
2. Gardner, *To Hell on a Fast Horse*, pp. 189–202; Don Bullis, *New Mexico Historical Biographies* (Los Ranchos, NM: Rio Grande Books, 2011), p. 275.
3. Metz, *Pat Garrett*, pp. 205–212; Eugene Manlove Rhodes, *Pasó por Aquí* (Alamogordo, NM: Alamogordo Printing Co., 1963), pp. 1–64.
4. C.L. Sonnichsen, *Tularosa: Last of the Frontier West* (Albuquerque: University of New Mexico Press, 1980), pp. 202–227; Rhodes, *Pasó por Aquí*, Forward; Bullis, *New Mexico Historical Biographies*, p. 601; *New York Times*, June 28, 1934; September 30, 1934; July 29, 1956.
5. Rhodes, *Pasó Por Aquí*, Forward; Bullis, *New Mexico Historical Biographies*, p. 601; *New York Times*, June 28, 1934.
6. Michael F. Blake, *Hollywood and the O.K. Corral: Portrayals of the Gunfight and Wyatt Earp* (Jefferson, NC: McFarland, 2007), p. 48.
7. Fitzgerald and Magers, *Ladies of the Western*, p. 48.
8. Blake, *Hollywood and the O.K. Corral*, p. 48; Tuska, *The Filming of the West*, pp. 481–483.
9. Nott, *Last of the Cowboy Heroes*, p. 30; Fenin and Everson, *The Western*, pp. 249, 257; www.imdb.com.
10. Nott, *Last of the Cowboy Heroes*, pp. 33–34; Fenin and Everson. *The Western*, p. 257
11. *Variety*, March 8, 2004; Nott, *Last of the Cowboy Heroes*, p. 30.
12. Nott, *Last of the Cowboy Heroes*, pp. 29–30.
13. Ibid., pp. 30–34.
14. Fitzgerald and Magers, *Ladies of the Western*, p. 47.
15. Quinlan, *Quinlan's Illustrated Guide to Film Directors*, p. 117.
16. Fitzgerald and Magers, *Ladies of the Western*, pp. 46–47.
17. Ibid., p. 47.
18. Leslie King, Karl Samson, and Shane Christensen, *Frommer's American Southwest* (Hoboken, NJ: Wiley, 2004), p. 257; Robert Nott, "Birth of a Film Nation," *Roundup Magazine* (April 2012), pp. 14–17; www.imdb.com.
19. Fitzgerald and Magers, *Ladies of the Western*, p. 47; *Council Bluffs Nonpareil*, November 7, 1948.
20. *Council Bluffs Nonpareil*, November 7, 1948.
21. Fitzgerald and Magers, *Ladies of the Western*, p. 47.
22. Katz, *The Film Encyclopedia*, p. 130.
23. Rhodes, *Pasó Por Aquí*, Forword.
24. "Cinema: Current & Choice," *Time* (July 12, 1948); *Boys' Life* (May 1948); *New York Times*, August 4, 1948; www.imdb.com.
25. Nott, *Last of the Cowboy Heroes*, p. 34.
26. Fenin and Everson. *The Western*, p. 256.
27. www.afi.com.
28. *Boston Globe*, October 7, 1948.
29. Wallis, *Billy the Kid*, p.234; Gardner, *To Hell on a Fast Horse*, pp. 26–35.
30. Otero, *The Real Billy the Kid*, p. 71.
31. Metz, *Pat Garrett*, p. 39.
32. Gardner, Email correspondence with the author, January 17, 2012.
33. *New York Times*, April 2, 2009; Copeland. *Roy Barcroft* (Kindle), p. 40; *Los Angeles Times*, March 31, 2009.
34. Copeland, *Roy Barcroft* (Kindle), pp. 53–55; *Stillwell Democrat*, January 19, 1950; *New York Times*, April 2, 2009; *Los Angeles Times*, March 31, 2009.
35. Copeland, *Roy Barcroft* (Kindle), p. 91; *Los Angeles Times*, March 31, 2009.
36. *Los Angeles Times*, March 32, 2009.
37. Copeland, *Roy Barcroft* (Kindle), pp. 373–374.
38. Ibid., p. 24.
39. Ibid., pp. 135, 160.
40. Magers, Nareau and Copeland. *Best of the Badmen* (Kindle), pp. 577–648.
41. Phil Hardy, *The Encyclopedia of Western Movies* (Minneapolis: Woodbury Press, 1984), p. 161.
42. Metz, *Pat Garrett*, p. 40; Wayne Gard, *The Chisholm Trail* (Norman: University of Oklahoma Press, 1979), p. 180.
43. Garfield, *Western Films*, p. 109.
44. Robert K. DeArment, *Bat Masterson: The Man and the Legend* (Norman: University of Oklahoma Press, 1989), pp. 367–368; Metz, *Pat Garrett*, p. 291; Trachtman, *The Gunfighters*, p. 93.

45. Guinn, *The Last Gunfight*, pp. 35–37; C.K. Crigger, "Celebrating Centennials," *Roundup Magazine* (October 2012).
46. Nyle H. Miller and Joseph W. Snell, *Great Gunfighters of the Kansas Cowtowns, 1867–1886* (Lincoln: University of Nebraska Press, 1987), pp. 193–214; Metz, *Pat Garrett*, pp. 76–79, 83.
47. Louis S. Warren, *Buffalo Bill's America: William Cody and the Wild West Show* (New York: Knopf, 2005), pp. 8, 62–65, 184–206.
48. Larry Pointer, *In Search of Butch Cassidy* (Norman: University of Oklahoma Press, 1988), pp. 42, 50; Eugene Cunningham, *Triggernometry: A Gallery of Gunfighters* (Norman: University of Oklahoma Press, 1996), pp. 332–349; Trachtman, *The Gunfighters*, pp. 90–93.
49. Pointer, *In Search of Butch Cassidy*, pp. xii, 255–256; Trachtman, *The Gunfighters*, p. 93.
50. Bullis, *New Mexico Historical Biographies*, p. 392.
51. *Hollywood Reporter*, October 18, 1957; November 1, 1957; www.afi.com;
52. Quinlan, *Quinlan's Illustrated Guide to Film Directors*, p. 267; www.afi.com; www.imdb.com.
53. George Montgomery and Jeffrey Millet, *The Years of George Montgomery* (Los Angeles: Sagebrush, 1981), pp. 13–35.
54. *New York Times*, December 15, 2000; *Variety*, December 19, 2000; Montgomery and Millet, *The Years of George Montgomery*, 165–185.
55. Montgomery and Millet, *The Years of George Montgomery*, p. 89.
56. Ibid., pp. 114–117.
57. *New York Times*, December 15, 2000.
58. *New York Times*, December 14, 2000; *Variety*, December 19, 2000.
59. DeMarco. *Buster Crabbe*, pp. 54, 66, 100; Katz, *The Film Encyclopedia*, pp. 303–304; www.imdb.com.
60. Katz, *The Film Encyclopedia*, p. 1,967; *New York Times*, April 19, 1992; www.imdb.com.

Chapter Nine

1. Rex Alan Smith, *Moon of Popping Trees: The Tragedy at Wounded Knee and the End of the Indian Wars* (Lincoln: University of Nebraska Press, 1981), pp. 1, 4–7, 199; Robert W. Larson, *Gall: Lakota War Chief* (Norman: University of Oklahoma Press, 2009), p. xi; Gary C. Anderson, *Little Crow: Spokesman for the Sioux* (St. Paul: Minnesota Historical Society Press, 1986), pp. 1–4
2. Robert W. Larson, *Red Cloud: Warrior-Statesman of the Lakota Sioux* (Norman: University of Oklahoma Press, 1999), p. 3.
3. Johnny D. Boggs, *Great Murder Trials of the Old West* (Plano: Republic of Texas Press, 2002), pp. 33–46; Watson Parker, *Deadwood: The Golden Years* (Lincoln: University of Nebraska Press, 1981), pp. 8–17, 55
4. Parker, *Deadwood*, pp. 162–163.
5. Rick Miller, *Sam Bass & Gang* (Austin, TX: State House Press, 1999), pp. 44, 55, 62–72, 257–262; Parker, *Deadwood*, pp. 96, 98.
6. Tom Weaver, *Earth vs. the Sci-Fi Filmmakers: 20 Interviews* (Jefferson, NC: McFarland, 2005), pp. 76, 161.
7. *Rapid City Journal*, September 2, 1964; Weaver, *Earth vs. the Sci-fi Filmmakers*, p. 202.
8. Weaver, *Earth vs. the Sci-fi Filmmakers*, p. 162.
9. *Daily Plainsman*, May 19, 1965; *Rapid City Journal*, September 2, 1964.
10. *Rapid City Journal*, September 2, 1964.
11. Ibid.
12. Weaver, *Earth vs. the Sci-fi Filmmakers*, pp. 202–203.
13. Ibid., p. 202.
14. Ibid.
15. Ibid., pp. 75–76.
16. Ibid., pp. 206–207.
17. www.cinematographers.nl; *The Guardian*, November 12, 2009; www.imdb.com.
18. *Daily Plainsman*, May 19, 1965; Weaver, *Earth vs. the Sci-fi Filmmakers*, p. 202.
19. Weaver, *Earth vs. the Sci-fi Filmmakers*, pp. 203–206; www.imdb.com.
20. Weaver, *Earth vs. the Sci-fi Filmmakers*, p. 202.
21. Jeff Forrester and Tom Forrester, *The Three Stooges: The Triumphs and Tragedies of the Most Popular Comedy Team of All Time* (Los Angeles: Donaldson Books, 2004), p. 168; www.imdb.com.
22. www.imdb.com.
23. Ibid.
24. Ibid.
25. Ibid.
26. Jeff Lenburg, Joan Howard Maurer, and Greg Lenburg, *The Three Stooges Scrapbook* (Chicago: Chicago Review Press, 2012), p. 105.
27. *Detroit Free Press*, June 12, 2008; Lenburg, Maurer and Lenburg, *The Three Stooges Scrapbook*, p. 105.
28. Stephen Cox and Jim Terry, *One Fine Stooge: Larry Fine's Frizzy Life in Pictures* (Nashville, TN: Cumberland House, 2006), p. 121.
29. *Detroit Free Press*, June 12, 2008.
30. Lenburg, Maurer and Lenburg, *The Three Stooges Scrapbook*, p. 105.
31. *Detroit Free Press*, June 12, 2008.
32. Cox and Terry, *One Fine Stooge*, p. 140; *Hollywood Reporter*, January 8, 1965.
33. *Detroit Free Press*, June 12, 2008); Lenburg, Maurer and Lenburg, *The Three Stooges Scrapbook*, p. 105.
34. Cox and Terry, *One Find Stooge*, pp. 166–169; www.imdb.com.
35. Lenburg, Maurer and Lenburg, *The Three Stooges Scrapbook*, p. 105.
36. Robin L. Murray and Joseph K. Heumann, *Gunfight at the Eco-Corral: Western Cinema and the Environment* (Norman: University of Oklahoma Press, 2012), p. 161.
37. Tom Weaver, *John Carradine: The Films* (Jefferson, NC: McFarland, 2008), p. 262.
38. Ibid., p. 261.
39. Joseph G. Rosa, *They Called Him Wild Bill: The Life and Adventures of James Butler Hickok* (Norman: University of Oklahoma Press, 1979), pp. 50–51, 75–77; Guinn, *The Last Gunfight*, pp. 239–240.
40. *New York Times*, June 27, 1965; *Billy the Kid vs. Dracula-Jesse James Meets Frankenstein's Daughter* pressbook, cover.
41. *Billy the Kid vs. Dracula-Jesse James Meets Frankenstein's Daughter* pressbook, p. 7; www.imdb.com; *Corpus Christi Caller-Times*, April 30, 1967.
42. *Corpus Christi Caller-Times*, April 30, 1967.
43. Wendy L. Marshall, *William Beaudine: From Silents to Television* (Metuchen, NJ: Scarecrow Press, 2004), p. 280.
44. Weaver. *John Carradine: The Films*, p. 262.
45. Marshall, *William Beaudine*, p. 280; Weaver, *John Carradine*, p. 262; *Corpus Christi Caller-Times*, April 30, 1967; www.imdb.com; *Billy the Kid vs. Dracula-Jesse James Meets Frankenstein's Daughter* pressbook.
46. Marshall, *William Beaudine*, p. 280.
47. Marshall, *William Beaudine*, pp. 283–284; *Corpus Christi Caller-Times*, April 30, 1967.

48. *New York Times*, March 26, 2000.
49. Weaver, *John Carradine*, p. 262.
50. *New York Times*, March 26, 2000.
51. *Billy the Kid vs. Dracula-Jesse James Meets Frankenstein's Daughter* pressbook, p. 12; www.imdb.com.
52. Ibid.
53. Katz, *The Film Encyclopedia*, p. 227; Weaver, *John Carradine*, p. 262.
54. Weaver, *John Carradine*, p. 261.
55. Ibid.
56. *New York Times*, November 29, 1988.
57. Weaver, *John Carradine*, p. 261.

Chapter Ten

1. Nolan, *The West of Billy the Kid*, p. 70; Bullis, *New Mexico Historical Biographies*, pp. 150–151.
2. Clifford R. Caldwell, *John Simpson Chisum: The Cattle King of the Pecos Revisited* (Santa Fe: Sunstone Press, 2010), p. 22.
3. Caldwell, *John Simpson Chisum*, p. 23.
4. Nolan, *The West of Billy the Kid*, pp. 112, 171; George B. Anderson, *History of New Mexico: Its Resources and People, Volume 2* (Los Angeles: Pacific States Publishing, 1907), p. 776; Caldwell, *John Simpson Chisum*, p. 155–156; Wallis, *Billy the Kid*, p. 221.
5. Bullis, *New Mexico Historical Biographies*, p. 92; Nolan, *The West of Billy the Kid*, p. 118.
6. Bullis, *New Mexico Historical Biographies*, p. 240; Keleher, *Violence in Lincoln County*, pp. 107–108; Grady E. McCright and James H. Powell, *Jessie Evans: Lincoln County Badman* (College Station, TX: The Early West, 1983), p. 20.
7. Nolan, *The West of Billy the Kid*, pp. 125, 154; Keleher, *Violence in Lincoln County*, pp. 53–54, 202–203.
8. Bullis, *New Mexico Historical Biographies*, p. 41; Keleher, *Violence in Lincoln County*, pp. 28–30.
9. Nolan, *The West of Billy the Kid*, pp. 114–115; Mullin, *Maurice G. Fulton's History of the Lincoln County War*, pp. 137–141; Gardner, *To Hell on a Fast Horse*, pp. 65–70.
10. Ibid.
11. Mullin, *Maurice G. Fulton's History of the Lincoln County War*, pp. 227–229; Keleher, *Violence in Lincoln County*, pp. 66, 134–135; Ernest Wallace and E. Adamson Hoebel, *The Comanches: Lords of the South Plains* (Norman: University of Oklahoma Press, 1987), pp. 327–328.
12. Gardner, *To Hell on a Fast Horse*, p. 64.
13. Utley, *High Noon in Lincoln*, pp. 95–99.
14. Nolan, *The Lincoln County War*, pp. 135–136.
15. Nolan, *The West of Billy the Kid*, p. 41; Utley, *High Noon in Lincoln County*, pp. 163–164
16. *Chisum* pressbook, p. 2; Andrew J. Fenady, Telephone interview with author, September 22, 2012.
17. *Chisum* pressbook, p. 3; *Toledo Blade*, October 3, 2007.
18. C. Courtney Joyner, *The Westerners* (Jefferson, NC: McFarland, 2009), pp. 223–224; *Chisum* pressbook, pp. 3–8; www.imdb.com.
19. Zolotow, *Shooting Star*, pp. 339–340.
20. Andrew J. Fenady interview.
21. *Chisum* pressbook, p. 3.
22. Ibid.
23. *Chisum* pressbook, p. 2.
24. Stephen B. Armstrong, *Andrew V. McLaglen: The Life and Hollywood Career*. (Jefferson, NC: McFarland, 2011), p. 10; *Chisum* pressbook, p. 3.
25. Armstrong, *Andrew V. McLaglen*, pp. 1, 194; Quinlan, *Quinlan's Illustrated Guide to Film Directors*, p. 203; www.imdb.com.
26. Armstrong, *Andrew V. McLaglen*, p.194; www.imdb.com.
27. *Coshocton Tribune*, June 9, 1970; www.imdb.com
28. *Toledo Blade*, October 3, 2007.
29. Andrew J. Fenady, *Double Eagles* (New York: Leisure, 2002), Introduction.
30. Joyner, *The Westerners*, p. 225.
31. Joyner, *The Westerners*, pp. 224–225; *New York Times*, June 12, 1979.
32. Armstrong, *Andrew V. McLaglen*, p. 195.
33. *Corpus Christi Caller-Times*, July 19, 1970.
34. Linda Ruth Williams and Michael Hammond, *Contemporary American Cinema* (Maidenhead, UK: Open University Press, 2006), p. 99.
35. *New York Times*, July 30, 1970; *Los Angeles Times*, August 20, 1970.
36. *Corpus Christi Caller-Times*, July 19, 1970.
37. *New York Times*, July 30, 1970.
38. *Corpus Christi Caller-Times*, July 19, 1970.
39. *New York Times*, May 29, 2010; John Andrew Gallagher, *Film Directors on Directing* (Westport, CT: Praeger, 1989), p. 127.
40. Dennis McDougal, The *Last Mogul: Lew Wasserman, MCA, and the Hidden History of Hollywood* (Chicago: Da Capo Press, 2001), p. 371.
41. *Variety*, November 6, 1969; McDougal, The *Last Mogul*, p. 371.
42. *Variety*, September 2, 1969, December 19, 1969; Judith Crist, "Uneasy Rider," *New York Magazine* (October 11, 1971); Brad Darrach, "The Easy Rider Runs Wild in the Andes," *Life* (June 19, 1970). Hopper told *Life* reporter Brad Darrach that after Hathaway shot one scene in *From Hell to Texas* eighty-six times, the director told him: "Kid, there's one thing I can promise you: you'll never work in this town again," and that he never worked at a major studio for eight years. That story has been repeated often, but one fact is often overlooked. Hathaway directed Hopper in *The Sons of Katie Elder* (1965) and again in *True Grit* (1969).
43. Samuel Fuller, *A Third Face* (New York: Alfred A. Knopf, 2002), p. 466; *Rolling Stone*, April 16, 1970.
44. *New York Times*, October 12, 1969.
45. *New York Times*, March 1, 1970.
46. Robert Sellers, *Hollywood Hellraisers: The Wild Lives and Fast Times of Marlon Brando, Dennis Hopper, Warren Beatty, and Jack Nicholson* (New York: Skyhorse Publishing, 2010), p. 126; Darrach, "The Easy Rider Runs Wild in the Andes," p. 54.
47. Darrach, "The Easy Rider Runs Wild in the Andes," p. 56.
48. Ibid.
49. McDougal, The *Last Mogul*, p. 371; Darrach, "The Easy Rider Runs Wild in the Andes," p. 54.
50. Sellers, *Hollywood Hellraisers*, p. 126–127; Margaret Moser, Michael Bertin, and Bill Crawford, *Movie Stars Do the Dumbest Things* (Los Angeles: Renaissance Books, 1999), p. 1,997; Darrach, "The Easy Rider Runs Wild in the Andes," p. 54–55.
51. Sellers, *Hollywood Hellraisers*, p. 126.
52. Fuller, *A Third Face*, p. 477.
53. Darrach, "The Easy Rider Runs Wild in the Andes," pp. 56–67
54. McDougal, The *Last Mogul*, p. 371; Sellers, *Hollywood Hellraisers*, p. 128.
55. Sellers, *Hollywood Hellraisers*, p. 126, 129.
56. Fuller, *A Third Face*, pp. 466–467.
57. Sellers, *Hollywood Hellraisers*, p. 129–130; David Morrell, interview with author, October 28, 2012.
58. Sellers, *Hollywood Hellraisers*, p. 129; Darrach, "The Easy Rider Runs Wild in the Andes," p. 59.

59. Sellers, *Hollywood Hellraisers*, p. 130.
60. *Los Angeles Times*, May 30, 2010.
61. Associated Press, "An Actor Prepares to Take His Bows," March 23, 1987, www.apnewsarchive.com.
62. Associated Press, "An Actor Prepares to Take His Bows"; *New York Times*, May 29, 2010.
63. *London Daily Mail*, June 3, 2010.
64. Kael, *5001 Nights at the Movies*, p. 409.
65. Roger Ebert, *I Hated, Hated, Hated This Movie* (New York: Andrews McMeel, 2000), p. 208
66. McDougal, The *Last Mogul*, p. 371.
67. Sellers, *Hollywood Hellraisers*, p. 130.
68. *Motion Picture Daily, Volume 10*, p. 33.
69. Garrett, *The Authentic Life of Billy, the Kid*, p. 8; Burns, *The Saga of Billy the Kid*, p. 70.
70. Garrett, *The Authentic Life of Billy, The Kid*, pp. 7–8; Bell, *The Illustrated Life and Times of Billy the Kid*, 2d ed., pp. 14–18.
71. www.kansasstatutes.lesterama.org.
72. Smith, *Daltons!*, pp. 14–15; Nolan, *The Authentic Life of Billy, the Kid*, p. 7.
73. Smith, *Daltons!*, pp. xii, xiii, 12–17.
74. Ronald Harver, *A Star is Born: The Making of the 1954 Movie and its 1983 Restoration* (New York: Applause, 2002), p. 225; Bob Thomas, *Clown Prince of Hollywood: The Antic Life and Times of Jack L. Warner* (New York: McGraw-Hill, 1990), p. 292.
75. Thomas, *Clown Prince of Hollywood*, p. 292.
76. Thomas, *Clown Prince of Hollywood*, p. 292. Warner also produced *1776*, which was filmed after, but released shortly before *Dirty Little Billy*; Harver, *A Star is Born*, p. 225; www.afi.com; www.imdb.com.
77. *New York Times*, May 19, 1973; May 16, 1990.
78. Mary Wells Lawrence, *A Big Life (in Advertising)* (New York: Touchstone, 2003), p. 132.
79. *Hollywood Reporter*, January 27, 1972; Lawrence, *A Big Life*, p. 133.
80. Thomas, *Clown Prince of Hollywood*, p. 293; Lawrence, *A Big Life*, p. 134.
81. *New York Times*, March 31, 1968; Katz, *The Film Encyclopedia*, p. 1,094.
82. *Chicago Sun-Times*, October 19, 1969.
83. Jeff Mayer, *Historical Dictionary of Crime Films* (Lanham, MD: Scarecrow Press, 2012), p. 292.
84. *New York Times*, May 19, 1973.
85. Peter Bogdanovich, *Who the Devil Made It* (New York: Alfred A. Knopf, 1997), p. 202.
86. Hutton, "Silver Screen Desperado," p. 180.
87. *New York Times*, May 16, 1990; Katz, *The Film Encyclopedia*, p. 1,094.
88. Segaloff, *Arthur Penn*, p. 270.
89. Barry Gifford, *Out of the Past: Adventures in Film Noir* (Jackson: University Press of Mississippi, 2000), p. 22.
90. *New York Times*, May 19, 1973.
91. Metz, *Pat Garrett*, pp. 287–291.
92. Metz, *Pat Garrett*, pp. 295–303; Gardner, *To Hell on a Fast Horse*, pp. 243–247.
93. Metz, *Pat Garrett*, pp. 57–58.
94. Bell, *The Illustrated Life and Times of Billy the Kid*, 2d ed., pp. 133–139; Utley, *Billy the Kid*, pp. 130–131, 157–160.
95. Utley, *Billy the Kid*, p. 158; Bell, *The Illustrated Life and Times of Billy the Kid*, 2d ed., pp. 137–138.
96. Utley, *Billy the Kid*, p. 159.
97. Utley, *Billy the Kid*, p. 72; Nolan, *The Lincoln County War*, p. 270.
98. Bell, *The Illustrated Life and Times of Billy the Kid*, 2d ed., p. 157.
99. Wallis, *Billy the Kid*, p. 244; Bell, *The Illustrated Life and Times of Billy the Kid*, 2d ed., p. 155.
100. Wallis, *Billy the Kid*, p. 244.
101. Ibid.
102. Metz, *Pat Garrett*, p. 40.
103. Utley, *Billy the Kid*, pp. 193–194.
104. Nolan, *The West of Billy the Kid*, p. 324; Bell, *The Illustrated Life and Times of Billy the Kid*, 2d ed., p. 164.
105. Paul Seydor, *Peckinpah: The Western Films* (Urbana: University of Illinois Press, 1980), pp. 183–184; Charles Neider, *The Authentic Life of Hendry Jones* (New York: Crest, 1960).
106. "*Playboy* Interview: Sam Peckinpah," *Playboy* (August 1972), p. 73.
107. David Weddle, "*If They Move ... Kill 'em!*": The Life and Times of Sam Peckinpah* (New York: Grove Press, 1994), pp. 453–455.
108. Max Evans, interview with author, October 11, 2011.
109. Weddle, "*If They Move ... Kill 'em!*," pp. 214–219, 254, 258–263.
110. Max Evans interview.
111. Ibid.
112. Weddle, "*If They Move ... Kill 'em!*," p. 455; www.imdb.com; www.afi.com.
113. Weddle, "*If They Move ... Kill 'em!*," pp. 458–459.
114. *Pat Garrett and Billy the Kid* Press/Campaign Book, p. 3.
115. Weddle, "*If They Move ... Kill 'em!*," p. 463; *Hartford Courant*, November 19, 1972.
116. *Pat Garrett and Billy the Kid* Press/Campaign Book, p. 2.
117. *Los Angeles Times*, December 5, 1972; *Hartford Courant*, December 3, 1972; December 31, 1972; January 14, 1973; January 21, 1973.
118. Weddle, "*If They Move ... Kill 'em!*," p. 464; Seydor, *Peckinpah*, p. 185.
119. Seydor, *Peckinpah*, p. 185.
120. Tuska, *Billy the Kid*, p. 212; Max Evans interview; Seydor, *Peckinpah*, pp. 186–187; Weddle, "*If They Move ... Kill 'em!*," p. 468.
121. Weddle, "*If They Move ... Kill 'em!*," pp. 471–472; *Pat Garrett and Billy the Kid Press*/Campaign Book, p. 5.
122. Weddle, "*If They Move ... Kill 'em!*," p. 472.
123. Seydor, *Peckinpah*, p. 190.
124. Max Evans interview.
125. Stephen Prince, "The Recutting of Pat Garrett and Billy the Kid: Ethical Problems in Film Restoration," from Michael Bliss, editor, *Peckinpah Today: New Essays on the Films of Sam Peckinpah* (Carbondale: Southern Illinois University Press, 2012), p. 108.
126. Seydor, *Peckinpah*, pp. 194–195; Weddle, "*If They Move ... Kill 'em!*," p. 479.
127. Seydor, *Peckinpah*, pp. 196–197; Weddle, "*If They Move ... Kill 'em!*," pp. 481, 490.
128. Seydor, *Peckinpah*, p. 197–198; Weddle, "*If They Move ... Kill 'em!*," p. 482–483. Stephen Prince says Peckinpah's preview version was two hours, four minutes long. (Prince, "The Recutting of Pat Garrett and Billy the Kid: Ethical Problems in Film Restoration." From Bliss, *Peckinpah Today*, p. 84).
129. Weddle, "*If They Move ... Kill 'em!*," p. 486.
130. Max Evans interview.
131. Weddle, "*If They Move ... Kill 'em!*," p. 487.
132. Max Evans interview.
133. Ibid.
134. *Los Angeles Times*, May 14, 1973.
135. Paul Seydor, telephone interview with author, October 28, 2012.

136. *Variety*, May 30, 1973.
137. *Newsweek* (June 11, 1973).
138. Paul Seydor interview.
139. Seydor, *Peckinpah: The Western Films*, p. 198.
140. Weddle, *"If They Move ... Kill 'em!,"* p. 498.
141. Ibid.
142. Ibid.
143. Paul Seydor interview.
144. Prince, "The Recutting of Pat Garrett and Billy the Kid: Ethical Problems in Film Restoration." From Bliss, *Peckinpah Today*, pp. 82–84; Paul Seydor interview.
145. Ibid.
146. Paul Seydor interview.
147. Prince, "The Recutting of Pat Garrett and Billy the Kid: Ethical Problems in Film Restoration." From Bliss, *Peckinpah Today*, pp. 84–85; Paul Seydor interview.
148. Paul Seydor interview.
149. *New York Times*, December 29, 1984.

Chapter Eleven

1. Nolan, *The West of Billy the Kid*, pp. 38, 41.
2. Bell, *The Illustrated Life and Times of Billy the Kid*, 2d ed., pp. 52–53; Gardner, *To Hell on a Fast Horse*, pp. 62–63.
3. Wallis, *Billy the Kid*, pp. 199–200.
4. Nolan, *The West of Billy the Kid*, p. 134; Wallis, *Billy the Kid*, pp. 204, 215; Tuska, *Billy the Kid*, p. 216. Patricia L. Faust, editor, *Historical Times Illustrated Encyclopedia of the Civil War* (New York: Harper & Row, 1986), p. 655.
5. Nolan, *The Lincoln County War*, 446–447; Nolan, *The West of Billy the Kid*, pp. 243, 248; James H. Earle, editor, *The Capture of Billy the Kid* (College Station, TX: The Early West, 1988), p. 86.
6. Nolan, *The Lincoln County War*, pp. 484–485.
7. Nolan, *The Lincoln County War*, pp. 254, 270, 312, 339, 363; Jacobsen, *Such Men as Billy the Kid*, p. 141; Clifford R. Caldwell, *Dead Right: The Lincoln County War* (No City Listed: Self-Published, 2008), p. 158.
8. Nolan, *The West of Billy the Kid*, p. 68; Wallis, *Billy the Kid*, p. 200.
9. Nolan, *The West of Billy the Kid*, p. 127; Nolan. *The Lincoln County War*, pp. 551–552.
10. The Blazer's Mill fight is recreated from: Nullin, *Maurice G. Fulton's History of the Lincoln County War*, pp. 172–177; and Nolan, *The West of Billy the Kid*, pp. 127–133.
11. The Brady assassination is recreated from: Wallis, *Billy the Kid*, pp. 201–202; and Gardner, *To Hell on a Fast Horse*, pp. 68–70.
12. Wallis, *Billy the Kid*, pp. 233–234; Gardner, *To Hell on a Fast Horse*, pp. 66–67; Bill O'Neal, *Henry Brown: The Outlaw-Marshal* (College Station, TX: The Early West, 1980), pp. 38–39.
13. Information regarding "The Big Killing" comes from: Wallis, *Billy the Kid*, pp. 209–216; Gardner, *To Hell on a Fast Horse*, pp. 75–82;
14. Nolan, *The Lincoln County War*, pp. 469–470; Wallis, *Billy the Kid*, p. 212.
15. Nolan, *The West of Billy the Kid*, p. 41.
16. Bullis, *New Mexico Historical Biographies*, pp. 41, 492.
17. Tuska, *Billy the Kid*, p. 218; Bullis, *New Mexico Historical Biographies*, pp. 131–132.
18. Fusco, John, "What History Has Taught Me," *True West* (April 2012), p. 128.
19. Hutton, "Silver Screen Desperado," p. 186.
20. Mandi Bierly, "Billy the Kid pardon debated on 20th anniversary of 'Young Guns II.' Coincidence?," *Entertainment Weekly* (August 6, 2010), www.popwatch.ew.com.
21. *Morning Call*, August 12, 1988.
22. Ibid.
23. Fusco, "What History Has Taught Me," p. 128.
24. www.imdb.com; *Morning Call*, August 12, 1988.
25. *Washington Post*, August 16, 1988; Lawrence Quirk and William Schoell, *The Rat Pack: Neon Nights with the Kings of Cool* (New York: HarperEntertainment, 2003), p. 1.
26. Fusco, "What History Has Taught Me," p. 128.
27. *Morning Call*, August 12, 1988.
28. Ibid.
29. *Los Angeles Times*, August 12, 1988; *Chicago Tribune*, August 12, 1988.
30. Hutton, "Silver Screen Desperado," p. 186; Tuska. *Billy the Kid*, p. 215; www.imdb.com.
31. Hutton, "Silver Screen Desperado," p. 186.
32. Wallis, *Billy the Kid*, pp. 87, 104; www.aboutbillythekid.com.
33. Luke Ford, *The Producers: Profiles in Frustration* (Lincoln, NE: iUniverse, 2004), p. 431.
34. Katz, *The Film Encyclopedia*, p. 1,138.
35. *New York Times*, June 24, 2008; June 18, 2011; www.imdb.com.
36. *Milwaukee Journal*, Marcy 17, 1989.
37. Ford, *The Producers*, p. 431.
38. Ford, *The Producers*, p. 431; Steven Priggé, *Movie Moguls Speak: Interviews with Top Film Producers* (Jefferson, NC: McFarland, 2004), p. 60.
39. *Chicago Tribune*, March 16, 1989; Ford, *The Producers*, p. 431.
40. *Chicago Tribune*, March 16, 1989.
41. *Milwaukee Journal*, Marcy 17, 1989; *Washington Post*, February 17, 1989.
42. *Los Angeles Times*, March 12, 1989.
43. *The Motion Picture Annual: 1990* (Kent, England: Cinebooks, 1990), p. 34; *Milwaukee Journal*, March 17, 1989.
44. *Hollywood Reporter*, August 13, 2012; www.imdb.com.
45. *Chicago Tribune*, March 16, 1989.
46. Dave Gardetta, "Desperately Seeking Spicoli," *Los Angeles Magazine* (February 2004).
47. Bell, *The Illustrated Life and Times of Billy the Kid*, 2d ed., pp. 180–181, 186.
48. Bell, *The Illustrated Life and Times of Billy the Kid*, 2d ed., pp. 180–181; Utley, *Billy the Kid*, p. 201.
49. Wallis, *Billy the Kid*, p. 234–235; Utley, *Billy the Kid*, p. 129; Boggs, "Mark Lee Gardner Trails Billy the Kid And Pat Garrett in New Dual Biography," p. 18.
50. Nolan, *The Lincoln County War*, pp. 482–483.
51. Nolan, *The West of Billy the Kid*, p. 164; Wallis, *Billy the Kid*, pp. 212, 238.
52. Wallis, *Billy the Kid*, p. 200.
53. Wilson, John P., ed., *Pat Garrett and Billy the Kid as I Knew Them: Reminiscences of John P. Meadows* (Albuquerque: University of New Mexico Press, 2004), p. 48; Ken Hundall and Sharon Hundall, *Spirits of the Border IV: The History and Mystery of New Mexico* (El Paso: Omega Press, 2005), p. 226; Wallis, *Billy the Kid*, pp. 228–229.
54. Wallis, *Billy the Kid*, p. 292.
55. Utley, *Billy the Kid*, p. 133; Gardner, *To Hell on a Fast Horse*, p. 159; Bullis, *New Mexico Historical Biographies*, pp. 150–151.
56. Utley, *Billy the Kid*, p. 133.
57. Bullis, *New Mexico Historical Biographies*, p. 151.

58. Ibid., pp. 582–583.
59. Nolan, *The Lincoln County War*, pp. 464–465; Wallis, *Billy the Kid*, p. 236.
60. The Carlyle affair is taken from: Bell, *The Illustrated Life and Times of Billy the Kid*, 2d ed., pp. 125–127; Wallis, *Billy the Kid*, p. 236.
61. Utley, *Billy the Kid*, pp. 158–159; Nolan, *The Lincoln County War*, pp. 452–453, 484–485.
62. Bell, *The Illustrated Life and Times of Billy the Kid*, 2d ed., pp. 148–151.
63. Garrett, *The Authentic Life of Billy, the Kid*, pp. ix–xii; Metz, *Pat Garrett*, pp. 292–295; Gardner, *To Hell on a Fast Horse*, p. 230.
64. Bierly, "Billy the Kid pardon debated on 20th anniversary of 'Young Guns II.' Coincidence?," *Entertainment Weekly*.
65. Ibid.
66. www.imdb.com.
67. www.imdb.com; Tuska, *Billy the Kid*, p. 218.
68. *Chicago Tribune*, August 9, 1990.
69. Ibid.
70. Bierly, "Billy the Kid pardon debated on 20th anniversary of 'Young Guns II.' Coincidence?," *Entertainment Weekly*.
71. *Chicago Tribune*, August 1, 1990.
72. Bell, *The Illustrated Life and Times of Billy the Kid*, p. 186.
73. Laura Jackson, *Jon Bon Jovi* (Secaucus, NJ: Citadel Press, 2005), p. 108; www.imdb.com.
74. *Chicago Tribune*, August 1, 1990.
75. Hutton, "Silver Screen Desperado," p. 188.
76. Bell, *The Illustrated Life and Times of Billy the Kid*, 2d ed., p. 186.

Chapter Twelve

1. Christopher Frayling, *Spaghetti Westerns: Cowboys and Europeans from Karl May to Sergio Leone* (London: I.B. Tauris, 2006), p. 147.
2. Peter Green, *Encyclopedia of Weird Westerns* (Jefferson, NC: McFarland, 2009), p. 82; Adrian Room, *Dictionary of Pseudonyms: 13,000 Assumed Names and Their Origins, 5th Edition* (Jefferson, NC: McFarland, 2010), p. 278.
3. "Breaking in as a Film Producer," Tweet with Tim Dennison, www.raindance.org; www.imdb.com.

Chapter Fourteen

1. Bob Burns and Tom Weaver, *Monster Ship Memories* (New York: Dinoship, 2003), p. 168.

Chapter Fifteen

1. C. Courtney Joyner, email correspondence with author, October 22, 2012.
2. Ibid.
3. David Bret, *Clark Gable: Tormented Star* (New York: Carroll & Graf, 2007),
pp. 257–258; John Simon, "Hack Work," *New York*, February 23, 1976; www.imdb.com.

Bibliography

Books

Aaker, Everett. *Television Western Players of the Fifties: A Biographical Encyclopedia of All Regular Cast Members in Western Series, 1949–1959.* Jefferson, NC: McFarland, 2007.

Abel, Richard. *Encyclopedia of Early Cinema.* New York: Routledge, 2010.

Affron, Charles, and Mirella Jona Affron. *Best Years: Going to the Movies, 1945–1946.* Piscataway, NJ: Rutgers University Press, 2009.

Alter, Judy. *Audie Murphy: War Hero and Movie Star.* Austin, TX: State House Press, 2007.

Anderson, Gary C. *Little Crow: Spokesman for the Sioux.* St. Paul: Minnesota Historical Society Press, 1986.

Anderson, George B. *History of New Mexico: Its Resources and People, Volume 2.* Los Angeles: Pacific States Publishing, 1907.

Armstrong, Stephen B. *Andrew V. McLaglen: The Life and Hollywood Career.* Jefferson, NC: McFarland, 2011.

Ascher, Steven, and Edward Pincus. *The Filmmaker's Handbook: A Comprehensive Guide for the Digital Age.* New York: Plume, 2007.

Barabas, SuzAnne, and Gabor Barabas. *Gunsmoke: A Complete History.* Jefferson, NC: McFarland, 1990.

Bartlett, Donald L., and James B. Steele. *Howard Hughes: His Life & Madness.* New York: W.W. Norton, 2004.

Baxter, John. *King Vidor.* New York: Monarch, 1976.

Bean, Jennifer M., and Diane Negra, eds. *A Feminist Reader in Early Cinema.* Durham: Duke University Press, 2002.

Bell, Bob Boze. *The Illustrated Life and Times of Billy the Kid*, 2d ed. Phoenix: Tri Star, 1996.

Benton, Lynton Wright. *Gittin' in the Movies.* Hollywood: Moderncraft Publishers, 1936.

Bergan, Ronald. *The United Artists Story.* New York: Crown, 1986.

Blake, Michael F. *Hollywood and the O.K. Corral: Portrayals of the Gunfight and Wyatt Earp.* Jefferson, NC: McFarland, 2007.

Bliss, Michael, ed. *Peckinpah Today: New Essays on the Films of Sam Peckinpah.* Carbondale: Southern Illinois University Press, 2012.

Bogdanovich, Peter. *Who the Devil Made It.* New York: Alfred A. Knopf, 1997.

Boggs, Johnny D. *Great Murder Trials of the Old West.* Plano: Republic of Texas Press, 2002.

_____. *Jesse James and the Movies.* Jefferson, NC: McFarland, 2011.

Brant, Marley. *The Outlaw Youngers: A Confederate Brotherhood.* Lanham, MD: Madison Books, 1992.

Brent, Lynton Wright. *Gittin' in the Movies.* Hollywood, CA: Moderncraft, 1936.

Bret, David. *Clark Gable: Tormented Star.* New York: Carroll & Graf, 2007.

_____. *Joan Crawford: Hollywood Martyr.* Chicago: Da Capo Press, 2008.

Brode, Douglas. *Shooting Stars of the Small Screen: Encyclopedia of TV Western Actors, 1946–Present.* Austin: University of Texas Press, 2009.

Brown, Peter Harry, and Pat H. Broeske. *Howard Hughes: The Untold Story.* Chicago: Da Capo Press, 2004.

Bullis, Don. *New Mexico Historical Biographies.* Los Ranchos, NM: Rio Grande Books, 2011.

Burns, Bob, and Tom Weaver. *Monster Kid Memories: Behind-the-Scenes, First-Hand Encounters with the Men who Made the Classic Movie Monsters!* New York: Dinoship, 2003.

Burns, Walter Noble. *The Saga of Billy the Kid.* Garden City, NY: Garden City, 1926.

Butters, Gerald R., Jr. *Banned in Kansas: Motion Picture Censorship 1915–1966.* Columbia: University of Missouri Press, 2007.

Caldwell, Clifford R. *Dead Right: The Lincoln County War.* No City Listed: Self-Published, 2008.

_____. *John Simpson Chisum: The Cattle King of the Pecos Revisited.* Santa Fe: Sunstone Press, 2010.

California and Californians, Volume 4. Chicago: Lewis, 1926.

Canham, Kingsley. *The Hollywood Professionals:*

Michael Curtiz, Raoul Walsh, Henry Hathaway. London: The Tantivy Press, 1973.

Catalogue of Copyright Entries, Volume 13, No. 9. Washington, D.C.: Government Printing Office, 1919.

Chaiken, Michael, and Paul Cronin, eds. *Arthur Penn Interviews.* Jackson: University Press of Mississippi, 2008.

Cline, William C. *In the Nick of Time: Motion Picture Sound Serials.* Jefferson, NC: McFarland, 1984.

_____. *Serials-ly Speaking: Essays on Cliffhangers.* Jefferson, NC: McFarland, 2000.

Coe, George W. *Frontier Fighter: The Autobiography of George W. Coe, Who Fought and Rode with Billy the Kid.* Chicago: The Lakeside Press, 1984.

Conley, Robert J. *A Cherokee Encyclopedia.* Albuquerque: University of New Mexico Press, 2007.

Cooper, Mark Garrett. *Universal Women: Filmmaking and Institutional Change in Early Hollywood.* Champaign: University of Illinois Press, 2010.

Copeland, Bobby J. *Johnny Mack Brown: Up Close and Personal.* Madison, NC: Empire, 2005.

_____. *Roy Barcroft: King of the Badmen.* Madison, NC: Empire Publishing, 2000.

Copeland, Bobby J., and Richard B. Smith III. *Gabby Hayes: King of the Cowboy Comics.* Madison, NC: Empire Publishing, 2008.

Cox, Stephen, and Jim Terry. *One Fine Stooge: Larry Fine's Frizzy Life in Pictures.* Nashville: Cumberland House, 2006.

Cremony, John C. *Life Among the Apaches.* Lincoln: University of Nebraska Press, 1983.

Cunningham, Eugene. *Triggernometry: A Gallery of Gunfighters.* Norman: University of Oklahoma Press, 1996.

Dalton, Emmett. *When the Daltons Rode.* Gretna, LA: Pelican Books, 2012.

Davis, Ronald L. *William S. Hart: Projecting the American West.* Norman: University of Oklahoma Press, 2003.

DeArment, Robert K. *Bat Masterson: The Man and the Legend.* Norman: University of Oklahoma Press, 1989.

DeMarco, Mario. *Buster Crabbe: King of the Serial Aces and Western Action.* Self-published, no city listed, n.d.

Denton, Clive, and Kingsley Canham. *The Hollywood Professionals: King Vidor, John Cromwell, Mervyn LeRoy.* London: Oak Tree, 1976.

Derby, Lauren. *The Dictator's Seduction: Politics and the Popular Imagination in the Era of Trujillo.* Durham: Duke University Press Books, 2009.

Doherty, Thomas. *Hollywood's Censor: Joseph I. Breen & The Production Code Administration.* New York: Columbia University Press, 2007.

Dowd, Nancy, and David Shepard, interviewers. *King Vidor* (A Directors Guild of America Oral History). Metuchen, NJ: The Directors Guild of America and Scarecrow Press, 1988.

Driscoll, Jim. *Reflections of a "B"-Movie Junkie.* Bloomington, IN: Xlibris, 2008.

Dykes, J.C. *Billy the Kid: The Bibliography of a Legend.* Albuquerque: University of New Mexico Press, 1952.

Eames, John Douglas. *The MGM Story: The Complete History of Over Fifty Roaring Years.* New York: Crown, 1976.

_____. *The Paramount Story.* New York: Crown, 1985.

Earle, James H., ed. *The Capture of Billy the Kid.* College Station, TX: The Early West, 1988.

Ebert, Roger. *I Hated, Hated, Hated This Movie.* New York: Andrews McMeel, 2000.

Enss, Chris, and Howard Kazanjian. *The Cowboy and the Senorita: A Biography of Roy Rogers and Dale Evans.* New York: Two Dot, 2005.

Erickson, Hal. *Encyclopedia of Television Law Shows: Factual and Fictional Series About Judges, Lawyers and the Courtroom, 1948–2008.* Jefferson, NC: McFarland, 2009.

Evans, Max. *Sam Peckinpah: Master of Violence.* Vermillion, SD: Dakota Press, 1972.

Everson, William K. *A Pictorial History of the Western Film.* New York: Citadel Press, 1969.

Fagen, Herb. *The Encyclopedia of Westerns.* New York: Checkmark Books, 2003.

Faust, Patricia L., ed. *Historical Times Illustrated Encyclopedia of the Civil War.* New York: Harper & Row, 1986.

Fenady, Andrew J. *Double Eagles.* New York: Leisure Books, 2002.

Fenin, George N., and William K. Everson. *The Western: From Silents to the Seventies: Revised Edition.* New York: Penguin Books, 1973.

Fitzgerald, Michael G., and Boyd Magers. *Ladies of the Western: Interviews with Fifty-one More Actresses from the Silent Era to the Television Westerns of the 1950s and 1960s.* Jefferson, NC: McFarland, 2006.

Ford, Luke. *The Producers: Profiles in Frustration.* Lincoln, NE: iUniverse, 2004.

Forrester, Jeff, and Tom Forrester. *The Three Stooges: The Triumphs and Tragedies of the Most Popular Comedy Team of All Time.* Los Angeles: Donaldson Books, 2004.

Frayling, Christopher. *Spaghetti Westerns: Cowboys and Europeans from Karl May to Sergio Leone.* London: I.B. Tauris, 2006.

Friedrich, Otto. *City of Nets: A Portrait of Hollywood in the 1940's.* Berkeley: University of California Press, 1997.

Fuller, Samuel. *A Third Face.* New York: Alfred A. Knopf, 2002.

Gallagher, John Andrew. *Film Directors on Directing.* Westport, CT: Praeger, 1989.

Garavaglia, Louis A., and Charles G. Worman.

Firearms of the American West, 1866–1894. Niwot: University Press of Colorado, 1997.

Gard, Wayne. *The Chisholm Trail.* Norman: University of Oklahoma Press, 1979.

Gardner, Mark Lee. *To Hell on a Fast Horse: Billy the Kid, Pat Garrett, and the Epic Chase to Justice in the Old West.* Advance Reading Copy. New York: William Morrow, 2010.

Garfield, Brian. *Western Films: A Complete Guide.* New York: Rawson Associates, 1982.

Garrett, Pat F., and Frederick Nolan, notes and commentary. *Pat F. Garrett's The Authentic Life of Billy, the Kid: An Annotated Edition.* Norman: University of Oklahoma Press, 2000.

Gibson, Arrell M. *The History of Oklahoma.* Norman: University of Oklahoma Press, 1984.

Gifford, Barry. *Out of the Past: Adventures in Film Noir.* Jackson: University Press of Mississippi, 2000.

Gordon, Bernard. *The Gordon File: A Screenwriter Recalls Twenty Years of FBI Surveillance.* Austin: University of Texas Press, 2008.

Gossett, Sue. *Audie Murphy: Now Showing.* Madison, NC: Empire Publishing, 2002.

_____. *Films and Career of Audie Murphy.* Madison, NC: Empire Publishing, 1996.

Graham, Don. *No Name on the Bullet: A Biography of Audie Murphy.* New York: Viking, 1989.

Green, Peter. *Encyclopedia of Weird Westerns.* Jefferson, NC: McFarland, 2009.

Guinn, Jeff. *The Last Gunfight: The Real Story of the Shootout at the O.K. Corral—and How It Changed the American West.* New York: Simon & Schuster, 2011.

Hannsberry, Karen Burroughs. *Bad Boys: The Actors of Film Noir.* Jefferson, NC: McFarland, 2008.

Hardy, Phil. *The Encyclopedia of Western Movies.* Minneapolis: Woodbury Press, 1984.

Hart, James David. *The Popular Novel: A History of America's Literary Taste.* Berkeley: University of California Press, 1950.

Harver, Ronald. *A Star Is Born: The Making of the 1954 Movie and Its 1983 Restoration.* New York: Applause, 2002.

Herzberg, Bob. *Savages and Saints: The Changing Image of American Indians in Westerns.* Jefferson, NC: McFarland, 2008.

_____. *Shooting Scripts: From Pulp Western to Film.* Jefferson, NC: McFarland, 2003.

Higham, Charles. *Howard Hughes: The Secret Life.* New York: St. Martin's Griffin, 2004.

Hirschhorn, Clive. *The Columbia Story.* London: Pyramid Books, 1989.

_____. *The Universal Story.* New York: Crown, 1983.

_____. *The Warner Bros. Story.* New York: Crown, 1982.

Hitt, Jim. *The American West from Fiction (1823–1976) into Film.* Jefferson, NC: McFarland, 1990.

Hoyt, Henry F. *A Frontier Doctor.* Chicago: The Lakeside Press, 1979.

Hundall, Ken, and Sharon Hundall. *Spirits of the Border IV: The History and Mystery of New Mexico.* El Paso: Omega Press, 2005.

Hunt, Rockwell Dennis, and Nellie Van de Grift Sanchez, eds. *California and Californians,* Vol. 4; Chicago: The Lewis Publishing Company, 1930.

Hurst, Richard Maurice. *Republic Studios: Between Poverty Row and the Majors.* Metuchen, NJ: Scarecrow Press, 1979.

Jackson, Laura. *Jon Bon Jovi.* Secaucus, NJ: Citadel Press, 2005.

Jacobsen, Joel. *Such Men as Billy the Kid: The Lincoln County War Reconsidered.* Lincoln: University of Nebraska Press, 1994.

Jarlett, Franklin. *Robert Ryan: A Biography and Critical Filmography.* Jefferson, NC: McFarland, 1990.

Jensen, Richard D. *The Amazing Tom Mix: The Most Famous Cowboy of the Movies.* Lincoln, NE: iUniverse, 2005.

Jewell, Richard B., with Veron Harbin. *The RKO Story: The Complete Studio History, with All of the 1,051 Films Described and Illustrated.* London: Octopus Books, 1982.

Joyner, C. Courtney. *The Westerners.* Jefferson, NC: McFarland, 2009.

Kadlec, Robert F., ed. *They "Knew" Billy the Kid: Interviews with Old-Time New Mexicans.* Santa Fe: Ancient City Press, 1987.

Kael, Pauline. *5,001 Nights at the Movies: A Guide from A to Z.* New York: Holt, Rinehart & Winston, 1982.

Katz, Ephraim. *The Film Encyclopedia: Fourth Edition,* rev. Fred Klein and Ronald Dean Nolen. New York: Harper Resource, 2001.

Kazanjian, Howard, and Chris Enns. *The Cowboy and the Senorita: A Biography of Roy Rogers and Dale Evans.* Guilford, CT, and Helena, MT: TwoDot, 2004.

Keleher, William A. *Turmoil in New Mexico, 1846–1868.* Santa Fe: Sunstone Press, 2007.

_____. *Violence in Lincoln County, 1869–1881.* Albuquerque: University of New Mexico Press, 1982.

King, Leslie, Karl Samson, and Shane Christensen. *Frommer's American Southwest.* Hoboken, NJ: Wiley, 2004.

Kioszarski, Richard. *Hollywood on the Hudson: Film and Television in New York from Griffith to Sarnoff.* New Brunswick, NJ: Rutgers University Press, 2008.

Kitses, Jim. *Horizons West.* Bloomington: Indiana University Press, 1970.

Kurian, George Thomas, and James D. Smith III, eds. The *Encyclopedia of Christian Literature, Volume 1.* Lanham, MD: Scarecrow Press, 2010.

Lackman, Ronald W. *Women of the Western Frontier*

in Fact, Fiction, and Film. Jefferson, NC: McFarland, 1997.
Lahue, Kalton C. *Riders of the Range: The Sagebrush Heroes of the Sound Screen.* Cranbury, NJ: A.S. Barnes and Co., 1973.
Langman, Larry. *A Guide to Silent Westerns.* New York: Greenwood, 1992.
Larkins, Bob, and Boyd Magers. *The Films of Audie Murphy.* Jefferson, NC: McFarland, 2004.
Larson Robert W. *Gall: Lakota War Chief.* Norman: University of Oklahoma Press, 2009.
_____. *Red Cloud. Warrior-Statesman of the Lakota Sioux.* Norman: University of Oklahoma Press, 1999.
Lawrence, Mary Wells. *A Big Life (in Advertising).* New York: Touchstone, 2003.
Lawton, Paul J. *Old Tucson Studios.* Charleston, SC: Arcadia, 2008.
Lee, M. Owen. *The Best Films of Our Years.* Bloomington, IN: Author House, 2007.
Lenburg, Jeff, Joan Howard Maurer, and Greg Lenburg. *The Three Stooges Scrapbook.* Chicago: Chicago Review Press, 2012.
Lentz Harris M., III. *Television Westerns Episode Guide: All United States Series, 1949–1996.* Jefferson, NC: McFarland, 2012.
LeRoy, Mervyn, as told to Dick Kleiner. *Mervyn LeRoy: Take One.* New York: Hawthorn Books, 1974.
Leverton, Garrett H., ed. *The Great Diamond Robbery & Other Recent Melodramas.* Princeton, NJ: Princeton University Press, 1940.
Levy, Shawn. *Paul Newman: A Life.* New York: Three Rivers Press, 2009.
Lowe, Denise. *An Encyclopedic Dictionary of Women in Early American Films, 1895–1930.* Binghamton, NY: The Hawthorn Press, 2005.
Lowery, Carolyn. *The First One Hundred Noted Men and Women of the Screen.* New York: Moffat, Yard, 1920.
McCright, Grady E., and James H. Powell. *Jessie Evans: Lincoln County Badman.* College Station, TX: The Early West, 1983.
McDougal, Dennis. *The Last Mogul: Lew Wasserman, MCA, and the Hidden History of Hollywood.* Chicago: Da Capo Press, 2001.
McKay, James. *Dana Andrews: The Face of Noir.* Jefferson, NC: McFarland, 2010.
McMurtry, Larry. *The Last Picture Show.* New York: Penguin Books, 1985.
Magers, Boyd, Bob Nareau, and Bobby Copeland. *Best of the Badmen (Polecats, Varmints, and Desperadoes of Western Films).* Madison, NC: Empire Publishing, 2005 (Kindle version).
Magers, Boyd, and Michael Fitzgerald. *Westerns Women: Interviews with 50 Leading Ladies of Movie and Television Westerns from the 1930s to the 1960s.* Jefferson, NC: McFarland, 1999.
Marill, Alvin H. *Television Westerns: Six Decades of Sagebrush Sheriffs, Scalawags, and Sidewinders.* Lanham, MD: Scarecrow Press, 2011.
Marshall, Wendy L. *William Beaudine: From Silents to Television.* Metuchen, NJ: Scarecrow Press, 2004.
Martin, Len D. *The Allied Artists Checklist: The Feature Films and Short Subjects, 1947–1978.* Jefferson, NC: McFarland, 1993.
_____. *The Columbia Checklist: The Feature Films, Serials, Cartoons and Short Subjects of Columbia Pictures Corporation, 1922–1988.* Jefferson, NC: McFarland, 1991.
_____. *The Republic Pictures Checklist: Features, Serials, Cartoons, Short Subjects and Training Films of Republic Pictures Corporation, 1935–1959.* Jefferson, NC: McFarland, 1998.
Mathis, Jack. *Republic Confidential, Volume 2: The Players.* Barrington, IL: Jack Mathis Advertising, 1992.
Mayer, Jeff. *Historical Dictionary of Crime Films.* Lanham, MD: Scarecrow Press, 2012.
Metz, Leon C. *Pat Garrett: The Story of a Western Lawman.* Norman: University of Oklahoma Press, 1974.
Miller, Don. *Hollywood Corral: A Comprehensive B-Western Roundup.* Burbank, CA: Riverwood Press, 1993.
Miller, Nyle H., and Joseph W. Snell. *Great Gunfighters of the Kansas Cowtowns, 1867–1886.* Lincoln: University of Nebraska Press, 1987.
Miller, Rick. *Sam Bass & Gang.* Austin, TX: State House Press, 1999.
Mix, Paul E. *The Life and Legend of Tom Mix.* Cranbury, NJ: A.S. Barnes, 1972.
Montgomery, George, and Jeffrey Millet. *The Years of George Montgomery.* Los Angeles: Sagebrush, 1981.
Monush, Barry. *Screen World Presents the Encyclopedia of Hollywood Film Actors: From the Silent Era to 1965.* Montclair, NJ: Applause, 2003.
Moore, Clayton, and Frank Thompson. *I Was That Masked Man.* Dallas: Taylor Trade Publishing, 1996.
Moser, Margaret, Michael Bertin and Bill Crawford. *Movie Stars Do the Dumbest Things.* Los Angeles: Renaissance Books, 1999.
Motion Picture Annual: 1990, The. Kent, UK: Cinebooks, 1990.
Motion Picture Daily, Volume 10. New York: Motion Picture Daily Inc., 1972.
Mullin, Robert N., ed. *Maurice G. Fulton's History of the Lincoln County War.* Tucson: University of Arizona Press, 1980.
Murphy, Audie. *To Hell and Back.* New York: Permabooks, 1955.
Murray, Robin L, and Joseph K. Heumann. *Gunfight at the Eco-Corral: Western Cinema and the Environment.* Norman: University of Oklahoma Press, 2012.

Nederman, Sharon. *Explorer's Guide: Santa Fe & Taos: A Great Destination.* Woodstock, VT: Countryman Press, 2006.

Neibaur, James L. *The RKO Features: Complete Filmography of the Feature Films Released or Produced by RKO Radio Pictures, 1929–1960.* Jefferson, NC: McFarland, 1994.

Neider, Charles. *The Authentic Death of Hendry Jones.* New York: Crest, 1960.

Newsweek, Volume 21. New York: Newsweek, 1944.

Nolan, Frederick, ed. *The Billy the Kid Reader.* Norman: University of Oklahoma Press, 2007.

_____. *The Lincoln County War: A Documentary History.* Norman: University of Oklahoma Press, 1992.

_____. *The West of Billy the Kid.* Norman: University of Oklahoma Press, 1998.

Nott, Robert. *The Films of Randolph Scott.* Jefferson: McFarland, 2004.

_____. *Last of the Cowboy Heroes: The Westerns of Randolph Scott, Joel McCrea, and Audie Murphy.* Jefferson, NC: McFarland, 2000.

Okuda, Ted. *Grand National, Producers Releasing Corporation, and Screen Guild/Lippert: Complete Filmographies with Studio Histories.* Jefferson, NC: McFarland, 1989.

O'Neal, Bill. *Encyclopedia of Western Gunfighters.* Norman: University of Oklahoma Press, 1991.

_____. *Henry Brown: The Outlaw-Marshal.* College Station, TX: The Early West, 1980.

Otero, Miguel Antonio. *The Real Billy the Kid.* Houston: Arte Público Press, 1998.

Parker, Watson. *Deadwood: The Golden Years.* Lincoln: University of Nebraska Press, 1981.

Patterson, Richard. *Historical Atlas of the Outlaw West.* Boulder, CO: Johnson Books, 1985.

Philbin, Tom. *The Greatest 100 Greatest Inventions of All Time: A Ranking Past to Present.* New York: Citadel Press, 2003.

Pitts, Michael R., compiler. *Hollywood and American History: A Filmography of Over 250 Motion Pictures Depicting U.S. History.* Jefferson, NC: McFarland, 1984.

_____. *Western Film Series of the Sound Era.* Jefferson, NC: McFarland, 2009.

Pointer, Larry. *In Search of Butch Cassidy.* Norman: University of Oklahoma Press, 1988.

Polonksy, Abraham, and John Schultheiss. *Odds Against Tomorrow: A Critical Edition.* Canoga Park, CA: Sandanlaur Publications, 1999.

Porter, Darwin. *Howard Hughes: Hell's Angel.* Staten Island, NY: Blood Moon, 2010.

Priggé, Steven. *Movie Moguls Speak: Interviews with Top Film Producers.* Jefferson, NC: McFarland, 2004.

Quinlan, David. *Quinlan's Illustrated Guide to Film Directors.* London: B.T. Batsford, 1991.

Quirk, Lawrence. *The Films of Robert Taylor.* Secaucus, NJ: Citadel Press, 1975.

Quirk, Lawrence, and William Schoell. *The Rat Pack: Neon Nights with the Kings of Cool.* New York: HarperEntertainment, 2003.

Rainey, Buck. *Heroes of the Range: Yesteryear's Saturday Matinee Movie Cowboys.* Metuchen, NJ: Scarecrow Press, 1987.

Reid, John Howard. *Movie Westerns: Hollywood Films the Wild, Wild West.* Raleigh: Lulu, 2004.

Rhodes, Eugene Manlove. *Pasó por Aquí.* Alamogordo, NM: Alamogordo Printing Co., 1963.

Ripley, George, and Charles A. Dana., eds. *New American Cyclopaedia: A Popular Dictionary of Knowledge, The, Vol. II.* New York: D. Appleton, 1867.

Robbins, Michael W., and Wendy Palitz. New York: *Brooklyn: A State of Mind.* New York: Workman, 2001.

Robertson, James C. *The Casablanca Man: The Cinema of Michael Curtiz.* New York: Routledge, 1993.

Rollins, Peter C., and John E. O'Connor. *Hollywood's West: The American Frontier in Film, Television, & History.* Lexington: University Press of Kentucky, 2009.

Rollyson, Carl. *Hollywood Enigma: Dana Andrews.* Jackson: University Press of Mississippi, 2012.

Rogers, Roy, and Dale Evans with Jane and Michael Stern. *Happy Trails: Our Life Story.* New York: Simon & Schuster, 1994.

Room, Adrian. *Dictionary of Pseudonyms: 13,000 Assumed Names and Their Origins, 5th Edition.* Jefferson, NC: McFarland, 2010.

Rosa, Joseph G. *They Called Him Wild Bill: The Life and Adventures of James Butler Hickok.* Norman: University of Oklahoma Press, 1979.

Russell, Jane. *Jane Russell: An Autobiography: My Path & Detours.* New York: Franklin Watts, 1985.

Rutherford, John A. *From Pigskin to Saddle Leather: The Films of Johnny Mack Brown.* Waynesville, NC: The World of Yesterday, 1996.

Sarris, Andrew. *The American Cinema: Directors and Directions, 1929–1968.* Chicago: Da Capo Press, 1996.

Schatz, Thomas. *Hollywood: Social Dimensions, Technology, Regulation and the Audience.* New York: Taylor and Francis, 2004.

Schneider, Jerry L. *Corrigan Movie Ranch.* Raleigh: Lulu, 2007.

Segaloff, Nat. *Arthur Penn: American Director.* Lexington: University Press of Kentucky, 2011.

Sellers, Robert. *Hollywood Hellraisers: The Wild Lives and Fast Times of Marlon Brando, Dennis Hopper, Warren Beatty, and Jack Nicholson.* New York: Skyhorse Publishing, 2010.

Seydor, Paul. *Peckinpah: The Western Films.* Urbana: University of Illinois Press, 1980.

Sharick, A.J. *Texas Bad Man.* New York: Engel van Wiseman, 1934.

Sherman, Eric, and Rubin, Martin. *The Director's*

Event: Interviews with Five American Film-Makers. New York: Atheneum, 1970.

Siegel, Scott, and Barbara Siegel. *The Encyclopedia of Hollywood: An A-to-Z Guide to the Stars, Stories, and Secrets of Hollywood: Second Edition.* New York: Checkmark Books, 2004.

Simpson, Paul. *The Rough Guide to Westerns.* London: Rough Guides, 2006.

Siringo, Charles A. *History of "Billy the Kid."* Albuquerque: University of New Mexico Press, 2000.

Slide, Anthony. *The Big V: A History of the Vitagraph Company.* Metuchen, NJ: Scarecrow Press, 1976.

_____. *Silent Topics: Essays on Undocumented Areas of Silent Film.* Metuchen, NJ: Scarecrow Press, 2004.

Smith, Rex Alan. *Moon of the Popping Trees: The Tragedy at Wounded Knee and the End of the Indian Wars.* Lincoln: University of Nebraska Press, 1981.

Smith, Robert Barr. *Daltons! The Raid on Coffeyville, Kansas.* Norman: University of Oklahoma Press, 1996.

Sonnichsen, C.L. *Tularosa: Last of the Frontier West.* Albuquerque: University of New Mexico Press, 1980.

Sperling, Cass Warner, Cork Millner and Jack Warner. *Hollywood Be Thy Name: The Warner Brothers Story.* Lexington: University Press of Kentucky, 1998.

Stiles, T.J. *Jesse James: Last Rebel of the Civil War.* New York: Vintage, 2003.

Tanner, Karen Holliday. *Doc Holliday: A Family Portrait.* Norman: University of Oklahoma Press, 2001.

Tatum, Stephen. *Inventing Billy the Kid: Visions of the Outlaw in America, 1881–1981.* Albuquerque: University of New Mexico Press, 1982.

Thomas, Bob. *Clown Prince of Hollywood: The Antic Life and Times of Jack L. Warner.* New York: McGraw-Hill, 1990.

Thomas, Tony. *Howard Hughes in Hollywood.* New York: Citadel Press, 1985.

Thomas, Tony, and Aubrey Solomon. *The Films of 20th Century–Fox.* Secaucus, NJ: Citadel Press, 1985.

Thompson, Frank. *The Star Film Ranch: Texas' First Picture Show.* Irving: Republic of Texas Press, 1996.

Thornton, Chuck, and David Rothel. *Lash LaRue: King of the Bullwhip.* Madison, NC: Empire Publishing, 1988.

Tibbetts, John C., and James M. Welsh, eds. *American Classic Screen Interviews.* Lanham, MD: Scarecrow Press, 2010.

Trachtman, Paul. *The Gunfighters.* Alexandria, VA: Time-Life Books, 1974.

Tranberg, Charles. *Robert Taylor: A Biography.* Duncan, OK: Bear Manor Media, 2010.

Troyan, Michael. *A Rose for Mrs. Miniver: The Life of Greer Garson.* Lexington: University Press of Kentucky, 1999.

Tuska, Jon. *The American West in Film: Critical Approaches to the Genre.* Lincoln: University of Nebraska Press, 1988.

_____. *Billy the Kid: His Life and Legend.* Albuquerque: University of New Mexico Press, 1994.

_____. *The Filming of the West.* Garden City, NY: Doubleday, 1976.

Twain, Mark. *Roughing It.* New York: Signet, 1962.

Utley, Robert M. *Billy the Kid: A Short and Violent Life.* Lincoln: University of Nebraska Press, 1989.

_____. *High Noon in Lincoln: Violence on the Western Frontier.* Albuquerque: University of New Mexico Press, 1987.

Varner, Paul. *The A to Z of Westerns in Cinema.* Metuchen, NJ: Scarecrow Press, 2009.

Vermilye, Jerry. *Buster Crabbe: A Biofilmography.* Jefferson, NC: McFarland, 2008.

Walker, Dale L. *Legends and Lies: Great Mysteries of the American West.* New York: Forge, 1997.

Wallace, Ernest, and E. Adamson Hoebel. *The Comanches: Lords of the South Plains.* Norman: University of Oklahoma Press, 1987.

Wallace, Lew. *Lew Wallace: An Autobiography.* New York: Harper & Brothers, 1906.

Wallis, Michael. *Billy the Kid: The Endless Ride.* New York: W.W. Norton, 2007.

Warren, Louis S. *Buffalo Bill's America: William Cody and the Wild West Show.* New York: Knopf, 2005.

Watts, Linda S. *Encyclopedia of American Folklore.* New York: Checkmark Books, 2007.

Weaver, Tom. *Earth vs. the Sci-Fi Filmmakers: 20 Interviews.* Jefferson, NC: McFarland, 2005.

_____. *John Carradine: The Films.* Jefferson, NC: McFarland, 2008.

Weddle, David. *"If They Move ... Kill 'em!": The Life and Times of Sam Peckinpah.* New York: Grove Press, 1994.

Welky, David. *The Moguls and the Dictators: Hollywood and the Coming of World War II.* Baltimore: John Hopkins University Press, 2008.

Wertheim, Arthur Frank, and Barbara Bair, eds. *The Papers of Will Rogers: From Vaudeville to Broadway: Volume Three: September 1909–August 1915.* Norman: University of Oklahoma Press, 2001.

Wheeler, Winston Dixon. *Lost in the Fifties: Recovering Phantom Hollywood.* Carbondale: Southern Illinois University Press, 2005.

Williams, Linda Ruth, and Michael Hammond. *Contemporary American Cinema.* Maidenhead, UK: Open University Press, 2006.

Wilson, John P., ed. *Pat Garrett and Billy the Kid as I Knew Them: Reminiscences of John P. Meadows.* Albuquerque: University of New Mexico Press, 2004.

Wise Jr., James E., and Anne Collier. *Stars in Blue: Movie Actors in America's Sea Services.* Annapolis: Naval Institute Press, 2007.

Wollstein, Hans J. *Strangers in Hollywood: The History of Scandinavian Actors in American Films from 1910 to World War II.* Metuchen, NJ: Scarecrow Press, 1994.

Zolotow, Maurice. *Shooting Star: A Biography of John Wayne.* New York: Pocket Books, 1975.

Articles

Associated Press. "An Actor Prepares to Take His Bows" (March 23, 1987), www.apnewsarchive.com.

Bierly, Mandi. "Billy the Kid Pardon Debated on 20th Anniversary of 'Young Guns II.' Coincidence?," *Entertainment Weekly* (August 6, 2010).

"Billy, the Bandit." *Moving Picture World* (January 6, 1917).

"Billy the Kid: In Two Films About Him Hollywood Fakes History." *Life* (August 4, 1941).

Boggs, Johnny D. "Mark Lee Gardner Trails Billy the Kid And Pat Garrett in New Dual Biography." *Wild West* (June 2010).

"The Boy from Oklahoma." *Boys' Life* (March 1954).

"Breaking in as a Film Producer," Tweet with Tim Dennison, www.raindance.org.

Bullis, Don. "Wild Cowboys and Civilized Indians Dominate the Path to Statehood for New Mexico and Arizona." *Roundup Magazine* (April 2012).

"Cinema: Current & Choice." *Time* (July 12, 1948), www.time.com.

Cocks, Jay. "Outlaw Blues." *Time* (June 11, 1973), www.time.com.

Crist, Judith. "Uneasy Rider," *New York Magazine* (October 11, 1971).

Crigger, C.K. "Celebrating Centennials." *Roundup Magazine* (October 2012).

Darrach, Brad. "The Easy Rider Runs Wild in the Andes," *Life* (June 19, 1970).

"D-B-H Biog Film Rights To 20th-Fox." *Billboard* (January 29, 1955).

Donnell, Dorothy. "'Smiling Billy' Mason, of the Essanay Company." *Motion Picture Story Magazine* (August 1913).

Fenny, F.X. "Ben-Gore." *Los Angeles Review of Books* (August 1, 2012).

"Four Faces West." *Boys' Life* (May 1948).

Fusco, John. "What History Has Taught Me," *True West* (April 2012).

Gardetta, Dave. "Desperately Seeking Spicoli," *Los Angeles Magazine* (February 2004).

Holbrook, Stewart. "Gen. Wallace and Ben Hur," *Popular Culture* (August 6, 1944).

Hutton, Paul Andrew. "Dreamscape Desperado." *New Mexico Magazine* (June 1990).

_____. "Silver Screen Desperado: Billy the Kid in the Movies." *New Mexico Historical Review* (Spring 2007).

Hutton, Paul Andrew, and Strykowski, Jason, comps. "Billy the Kid Filmography." *New Mexico Historical Review* (Spring 2007).

"John Steppling Again a Universalite." *The Moving Picture Story* (August 12, 1916).

Nott, Robert. "Birth of a Film Nation," *Roundup* (April 2012).

"*Playboy* Interview: Sam Peckinpah," *Playboy* (August 1972).

"The Role I Liked Best." *Saturday Evening Post* (January 13, 1951).

Severance, Constance. "Alone with a Mirror: The Exclusive Hobby of Edith Storey." *Photoplay Magazine* (May 1916).

Simon, John. "Hack Work," *New York* (February 23, 1976).

Spear, Ivan. "Anyone Who Hasn't Played Jesse James Please Step Up." Kansas City: *Boxoffice*, July 29, 1950.

Wade, Peter. "Tefft Johnson, of the Vitagraph Company." *The Motion Picture Story Magazine* (August 1912).

Warren, Holly George. "The Golden Age of the Western." Boulder: *American Cowboy*, March–April 2003.

"Westerners Who Changed America," *American Cowboy* (November–December 2004).

"Will Rogers' Boy: Humorist's son tries to imitate father for movies," *Life* (May 27, 1946).

Newspapers

(Albert Lea, Minnesota) *Freeborn County Standard*
Albuquerque (New Mexico) *Journal*
(Allentown, Pennsylvania) *Morning Call*
American Profile
Anniston (Alabama) *Star*
Atlanta Constitution
Baltimore Sun
Boston Globe
(Burlington, North Carolina) *Daily Times-News*
Cary (North Carolina) *News*
Chicago Sun-Times
Chicago Tribune
Christian Science Monitor
Corpus Christi (Texas) *Caller-Times*
Coshocton (Ohio) *Tribune*
Council Bluffs (Iowa) *Nonpareil*
Dallas Morning News
Denton (Texas) *Record-Chronicle*
Detroit Free Press
Doylestown (Pennsylvania) *Sunday Intelligencer*
(Dunkirk, New York) *Evening Observer*
Galveston (Texas) *Daily News*
The Guardian
Gettysburg (Pennsylvania) *Times*
Hagerstown (Maryland) *Morning Herald*
Hamilton (Ohio) *Evening Journal*
Hartford (Connecticut) *Courant*
Hartford (Connecticut) *Tribune*
Hartford (Kentucky) *Herald*
(Heron, South Dakota) *Daily Plainsman*

Hollywood Reporter
Hope (Arkansas) *Star*
(Hull, Iowa) *Sioux County Index*
Huntingdon (Pennsylvania) Daily NEws
Indiana (Pennsylvania) *Evening Gazette*
Iola (Kansas) *Daily Register*
(Jefferson City, Missouri) *Daily Capital News*
Joplin (Missouri) *Globe*
La Crosse (Wisconsin) *Tribune*
Las Vegas (New Mexico) *Daily Optic*
(Lebanon, Pennsylvania) *Daily News*
Logansport (Indiana) *Journal*
London Daily Mail
London Independent
Long Beach (California) *Press Telegram*
Los Angeles Times
Mansfield (Ohio) News
Mason City (Iowa) *Globe-Gazette*
(Massillon, Ohio) *Evening Independent*
Milwaukee Journal
Modesto (California) *Bee*
Muscatine (Iowa) *Journal*
New York Daily News
New York Herald-Tribune
New York Times
Orange County (California) *Register*
Rapid City (South Dakota) *Journal*
(Reno) *Nevada State Journal*
Rolling Stone
St. Petersburg (Florida) *Times*
Sheboygan (Wisconsin) *Journal*
Sioux City (Iowa) *Index*
Stillwell (Oklahoma) *Democrat*
Syracuse (New York) *Herald*
Syracuse (New York) *Post-Standard*
Toledo (Ohio) *Blade*
Variety
Washington Post
Winnipeg (Manitoba) *Free Press*
Zanesville (Ohio) *Times Recorder*

Movie Press/Campaign Books

A Few Bullets More. RAF Industries, 1967.
Billy the Kid vs. Dracula/Jesse James Meets Frankenstein's Daughter. Embassy, 1965.
Chisum. Warner Bros, 1970.
Last of the Desperados. Associated Film Releasing Corp., 1955.
The Parson and the Outlaw. Columbia, 1957.
Pat Garrett and Billy the Kid. MGM, 1973.
Son of Billy the Kid. Screen Guild, 1949.

Interviews, Letters

Cusic, Don. Nashville, Tennessee, email correspondence with author, November 30, 2011.
DeCoteau, David. Email correspondence with author, January 27, 2012.
Evans, Max. Albuquerque, New Mexico. Interview with author, October 20, 2011.
Fenady, Andrew J. Telephone interview with author, September 22, 2012.
Gardner, Mark Lee. Email correspondence with author, January 17, 2012.
Joyner, C. Courtney. Email correspondence with author, October 22, 2012.
Morrell, David. Santa Fe, New Mexico. Interview with author, October 28, 2012.
Nott, Robert. Email correspondence with author, September 28, 2012.
Seydor, Paul. Telephone interview with author, October 28, 2012.
Zvonchenko, Walter. Library of Congress (Washington, D.C.), email correspondence with author, October 20, 2011; November 29, 2011.

Internet Sources

About Billy the Kid, www.aboutbillythekid.com
American Film Institute Catalog, www.afi.com
Associated Press News Archive, www.apnewsarchive.com
Glamour Girls of the Silver Screen, www.glamourgirlsofthesilverscreen.com
Internet Encyclopedia of Cinematographers, www.cinematographers.nl
Internet Movie Database, www.imdb.com
Kansas Statutes, www.kansasstatutes.lesterama.org
The Official Roy Rogers & Dale Evans Website, www.royrogers.comThe Old Corral, www.b-westerns.com
Western Clippings, www.westernclippings.com

Index

Adams, Julie 109, 192, 195
Adams, Nick 124, 129, 245
Adamson, Carl 203
Agar, John 182, 188
Alias Billy the Kid (1946) 84–87, 161
Alias El Alacrán (1963) 231
Anderson, G.M. "Broncho Billy" 16
Andrews, Dana 124, 129, 131
Another Man, Another Chance (1977) see *Un Autre Homme, Une Autre Chance*
Antrim, Catherine see McCarty, Catherine
Antrim, Henry see Billy the Kid
Antrim, Joseph (Billy's brother) 5, 41, 121, 135, 197, 198
Antrim, William (Billy's stepfather) 5, 34, 101, 116, 198
Armstrong. R.G. 200, 207
Asher, Irving 64, 67–68
Aubrey, James 205, 206, 207, 209
Austin, Vivian 109
The Authentic Life of Billy, the Kid 12, 27, 66, 101, 197, 227
Un Autre Home, Une Autre Chance (1977) 235
Autry, Gene 35, 96, 160
Une Aventure de Billy le Kid (1971) 235
Axtell, Samuel B. 9, 26, 108, 186, 187, 216, 217

Bad Jim (1990) 249, 250
Badlands of Dakota (1941) 171
Badman's Country (1958) 110, 151, 161–166
Badman's Territory (1946) 90–91
Baker, Frank 8, 25, 102, 116, 146, 186–187, 216
Ball, Eve 24
Ballard, Lucien 81, 82
Barcroft, Roy 84, 110, 113, 114, 158, 161, 176, 181
Barry, Don 86, 98, 105, 108–109, 112
Bass, Sam 170
Bates, Sebrian 8
Beaudine, William 176, 179–180
Beckwith, Robert 8, 26, 107
Beery, Wallace 23, 29, 32
Bell, Bob Boze 24, 204, 229

Bell, James 10, 26, 27, 108, 126, 147, 204
Ben-Hur: A Tale of the Christ 9, 10, 126
Berke, William 105
Best, James 142, 147
Beutel, Jack 75, 80, 82, 83, 84
Bevans, Clem 110, 113
Bickford, Charles 103, 151, 157, 158
Big Foot 170
The Big Trail (1930) 28, 29, 30, 96
Bill & Ted's Excellent Adventure (1989), 219–223
Billy, the Bandit (1916) 19–21
Billy the Kid: aliases and nicknames 5, 66, 73, 160, 187; birth 5, 116, 198; death 3–5, 11, 27, 66, 95, 117, 134–135, 147, 204, 217, 227; education 35, 146; escapes Lincoln County Courthouse 10–11, 26–27, 108, 147, 204; murder trial 10, 227; relationship with Hispanics 25; tintype 4, 34
Billy the Kid (ballet) 13
Billy the Kid (1911) 15–19
Billy the Kid (1930) 22–32, 68, 79, 81
Billy the Kid (1941) 64–71, 81, 104, 199, 246
Billy the Kid (1989) 238, 239, 241
Billy the Kid (play) 12, 15, 16, 18
Billy the Kid and the Green Baize Vampire (1987) 235, 236
Billy the Kid in Santa Fe (1941) 46–47, 62
Billy the Kid in Texas (1940) 40–41
Billy the Kid Outlawed (1940) 38–40, 62
Billy the Kid Returns (1938) 32–37, 63, 68
Billy the Kid Trapped (1942) 50–51, 61
Billy the Kid vs. Dracula (1966) 142, 161, 176–181
Billy the Kid Wanted (1941) 47–48, 61
Billy the Kid's Fighting Pals (1941) 44–45
Billy the Kid's Gun Justice (1940) 42–43, 61

Billy the Kid's Range War (1941) 43, 61
Billy the Kid's Round Up (1941) 48–50
Billy the Kid's Smoking Guns (1942) 51–52, 61
Birî za Kiddo no Aarashii Yoake (1986) 235
Blazer's Mill 8, 214, 215–216
Blazing Frontier (1943) 58–59
BloodRayne 2: Deliverance (2007) 250
Bogart, Humphrey 96, 97
Bon Jovi, Jon 217, 229
Bonney, William H. see Billy the Kid
Borzage, Frank 68
Boteler, Wade 32, 36
Bowdre, Charles 5, 9, 10, 24, 101, 107, 117, 135, 146, 147, 186, 203, 204, 214, 215, 216, 217, 227, 228
The Boy from Oklahoma (1954) 119–123
Boyle, Andy 8, 107
Brady, Scott 98, 103, 114, 117
Brady, William 3, 6, 8, 9, 10, 25, 26, 73, 101, 102, 108, 116, 117, 121, 146, 186, 187, 214, 216, 227
Brand, Neville 161, 166
Brando, Marlon 205
Brazel, Wayne 203
Breen, Joseph I. 82
Brent, Lynton Wright 22
Bret Maverick (TV series) 248
Brewer, Dick 8, 24, 25, 101, 102, 116, 186, 214, 215, 216, 228
Bristol, Judge Warren 10, 227
Bronco (TV series) 1, 245, 246
Brown, Henry 186, 204, 214, 215, 216, 226
Brown, Johnny Mack 22, 27, 28–29, 30–31, 32, 68, 79–80, 182
Buffalo Bill, Jr. (TV series) 243
A Bullet for Billy the Kid (1963) 2, 167, 231, 253–254
Bullets Don't Argue (1964) see *Le Pistole non Disctono*
Burnette, Smiley 32, 35, 36, 37
Burns, Walter Noble 13, 15, 26, 27, 28, 32, 67, 70, 160, 197
Butler, Frank 124, 128, 129

277

Cabot, Bruce 182, 188
Cade's County (TV series) 247
Cagney, James 29, 66, 102, 108, 129
Cahill, "Windy" 6, 121
Cain, Christopher 211, 218
Calleia, Joseph 151, 157, 158
Cameron, Rod 191, 193, 233
Campbell, Bob 95
Captive of Billy the Kid (1952) 110–114, 161
Carey, Harry, Jr. 176, 180, 181
Carey, Olive 176, 181
Carlin, George 219, 222
Carlyle, James 227
Carr, Thomas 84, 87
Carradine, John 176, 179, 180, 181, 254
Carroll, Gordon 200, 205, 206, 207
Carroll, Virginia 109
Carson, Sunset 84, 86–87
Case, Carrol 179
Cassidy, Butch 164
Catron, Thomas 217
Cattle Stampede (1943) 57
Chapman, Huston 9
Chávez y Chávez, José 8, 214, 216, 227
Cheyenne (TV series) 1, 246
Chisholm, Jesse 185
Chisum (1970) 1, 182–191, 219, 238
Chisum, John 6, 9, 102, 185, 186, 208, 226, 228
Chisum, Sallie 185, 186, 188
Cline, William C. 36
Clothier, William 82, 189
Coburn, James 200, 206, 207, 208, 223, 228
Cody, William F. "Buffalo Bill" 12, 164
Coe, Frank 25, 79, 186, 214, 215, 216
Coe, Fred 142, 148
Coe, George 186, 187, 203, 214, 215
Coffeyville, Kansas 15, 66, 101, 197, 198
Colby, Marion 93, 96
Colt .45 (TV series) 245
Conrad, William 189
Copland, Aaron 13
Copperhead (2008) 241
Corbett, Glenn 182, 188
Courtney, Chuck 176, 180
Crabbe, Buster 38, 50, 51, 52, 53, 55, 56, 57, 58, 60, 61, 62, 161, 166
Craig, James 131, 136, 137
Crawford, Joan 29, 30, 68, 136
Crist, Judith 195
Curtiz, Michael 119, 121, 122, 123
Custer, Peggy 19, 20, 21

Dalton, Emmett 15, 89
Dalton, J. Frank 226
Dalton Gang 15, 89, 90, 198
Daughterty, Roy "Arkansas Tom" 90
Davis, Jim 131, 136, 181, 243

Day, Lynda 182, 188
Deadwood, South Dakota 170
Deadwood '76 (1965) 167–172
de Anda, Raúl 231, 233
de Anda, Rodolfo 231, 233
Death Valley Days (TV series) 1, 244, 246, 247
DeCoteau, David 1, 252
Dee, Frances 151, 155, 156, 157
Dehner, John 142, 148, 150
Dekker, Albert 98, 103
DeLaurentiis, Dino 222
DeMain, Gordon 71, 75
The Deputy (TV series) 245
DeRita, Joe 172, 174
Deuel, Geoffrey 188
Dexter, Anthony 137, 141, 155
Dirty Little Billy (1972) 195–200
Dix, Richard 74, 155
Dix, Robert 167, 171
Dolan, James 6, 9, 101, 146, 186, 187, 216, 217
Donlevy, Brian 64, 68
Doolin, Bill 89–90, 104, 179
Dragoti, Stan 195, 197, 199, 200
Dudley, Nathan 9, 102, 107, 186, 187, 216
Duelo en el Desierto (1964) 233
Durango Kid, 74
Dykes, J.C. 19
Dylan, Bob 200, 206, 208, 210

Ealy, Taylor Filmore 140
Earp, Wyatt 79, 164, 174, 179
East, Jim 215
Eastwood, Clint 233
Ebert, Roger 190, 195, 198
Edwards, Peggy 110, 113
Elam, Jack 200, 206
Ellis, Isaac 215
Enright, Ray 87, 91
Estevez, Emilio 211, 217, 218, 219, 223, 228, 229
Evans, Dale 37, 113
Evans, Jessie (Jesse) 186, 187, 238
Evans, Max 205, 206, 207, 208, 209
Everson, William K. 60, 86, 155, 157

Fenady, Andrew J. 182, 187, 188, 189, 190
Fenin, George N. 60, 86, 155, 157
Fergusson, Harvey 13, 27
Fernandez, Emilio 200, 207
Fessier, Michael 122
A Few Bullets More (1967) see *El Hombre que Mató a Billy el Niño*
Fine, Larry 172, 174, 175, 176
Finkelstein, Rick 222
The 1st Notch (1977) 2, 254
"Five-Day War" or "Five-Day Battle" 8, 9, 107, 146, 187, 216–217
Fogelson, Buddy 128, 131
Folliard, Tom 5, 8, 9, 24, 25, 101, 108, 116, 146, 147, 203, 217, 226
Fonda, Peter 191, 192, 193, 195
Ford, John 31, 67, 80, 130, 189, 190

Four Faces West (1948) 151–158, 210
The Fourth Horseman (1932) 22, 23
Fox, Michael J. 223
French, Jim 8, 186, 214, 216, 226
Frontier Outlaws (1944) 61
Fuera de la Ley (1964) 232
Fugitive of the Plains (1943) 56
Fuller, Sam 109, 191, 193, 194, 195
Fulton, Maurice G. 27
Fusco, John 211, 214, 217, 218, 219, 223, 225, 226, 228, 229

Gable, Clark 30–31, 129, 136, 249
Gable, John Clark 249, 250
Gall 170
Gallup, New Mexico 24, 30, 156, 157
Gardner, Mark Lee 35, 101, 140, 147, 160
Garfield, Brian 141, 163
Garrett, Apolinaria (Pat Garrett's wife) 135, 147, 163, 204, 208
Garrett, Pat 2, 3–4, 9–10, 11, 12, 25, 26, 27, 29, 30, 32, 34, 35, 36, 66, 73, 78, 80, 95, 101, 107, 108, 109, 117, 119, 126, 134, 135, 146, 147, 151, 158, 160, 161, 163, 164, 187, 188, 197, 203, 204, 205, 208, 215, 217, 226, 227, 231
Garson, Greer 124, 128, 130–131
Gauss, Godfrey 27
Gentlemen with Guns (1946) 61
George, Christopher 182, 188
Geronimo 126
The Ghost Busters (TV series) 247–248
Ginger, Johnny 173, 175
A Girl Is a Gun (1971) see *Une Aventure de Billy le Kid*
Go West, Young Girl (1978) 238
Godfroy, Clara 215
Gordon, Bernard 114, 116, 117, 118, 119
Grant, Joe 25, 108, 146, 147, 216
Gray, Gary 87, 91
The Great Adventure (TV series) 246
Greathouse, "Whiskey Jim" or "Arkansas Jack" 227
Green, Alfred E. 151, 156
Grey, Frederick W. 204
Griffith, James 114, 117, 119
Gulager, Clu 242
Gunsmoke 2, 246
Gutiérrez, Apolinaria *see* Apolinaria, Garrett
Gutiérrez, Celsa 3, 95, 147
Gutiérrez, Saval 95, 147

Haggard, Merle 189
Hale, Monte 158, 160–161
Hall, Arch, Jr. 167, 170–171, 172
Hall, Arch, Sr. 167, 170, 171, 172
Hampton, Orville 105, 109–110, 131, 137, 161
Hardy, Phil 114, 142, 163
Hargrove, Bob 25

Hart, William S. 30, 68, 96
Hatfield, Hurd 142, 148, 149
Hathaway, Henry 193
Hawks, Howard 69, 80, 81, 82, 83, 84, 105
Hayden, Russell 71, 74, 75, 109
Hayes, George "Gabby" 36, 87, 91
Hayes, Helen 29
Hayes, Rutherford B. 8, 26, 116
Hays, Will 79
Hays Code (Hays Office) 79, 82
Herek, Stephen 219, 222
Hickok, James Butler "Wild Bill" 164, 170, 174, 179
Hindman, George 8, 108, 146, 216
Hitt, Jim 70
Hittleman, Carl K. 179
Holliday, Doc 79, 80, 179
El Hombre que Mató a Billy el Niño (1967) 233, 234
Hopper, Dennis 191, 192, 193, 194, 195, 205, 244
Hough, Emerson 12, 108
Howard, Mary 64, 68
Howard, Moe 172, 174, 175
Hoyt, Henry F. 90
Hughes, Howard 64, 69, 75, 79, 80, 81, 82, 83, 84
Hunter, Ian 64, 68
Huston, Walter 75, 80–81, 82, 84
Hutton, Paul Andrew 1, 2, 30, 38, 200, 219

I Shot Billy the Kid (1950) 105–110, 137

Jaeckel, Richard 182, 188, 200, 206, 238, 243
James, Frank 15, 90
James, Jesse 2, 12, 14, 15, 22, 34, 70, 73, 90, 104, 174, 226
Jeffreys, Anne 50, 61, 87, 91, 92
Jesse James (1939) 22, 32, 64, 66, 67, 68, 69, 70, 81
Jesse James Meets Frankenstein's Daughter (1966) 179, 181
Johnson, Ben 188
Johnson, Kay 23, 29
Johnson, Tefft 15, 16, 17, 18
Jones, L.Q. 200, 207
Joyner, C. Courtney 1, 249, 254

Kael, Pauline 195
Kane, Joseph 32, 35
Katzman, Sam 114, 118
Keith-Johnston, Colin 142, 146
Ketchum, Thomas "Black Jack" 164–165
The Kid from Texas (1950) 98–105
The Kid Rides Again (1943) 55–56
Kieth, Brian 211, 217
Kilmer, Val 238
Kimbrell, George 108, 203
Kinney, John 26, 216–217
Knowles, Patric 182, 188
Kristofferson, Kris 193, 194, 200, 205, 207
Kroop, Scott 219, 220, 222

Lahue, Kalton C. 61, 109
Laine, Frankie 130
Landis, James 167, 170
Lane, Allan "Rocky" 98, 110, 112, 113, 114
Lang, Fritz 199–200
LaRue, Lash 75, 92, 96, 97
The Last Movie (1971) 191–195, 205
Last of the Desperados (1955) 110, 131–137
The Last Picture Show (1966 novel and 1973 film) 105
Law and Order (1942) 52–53
The Law vs. Billy the Kid (1954) 114–119
Lawrence, Mary Wells 199
Lease, Rex 42, 43, 61
The Left Handed Gun (1958) 1, 142–150, 238, 244
Leonard, Ira 9
LeRoy, Mervyn 124, 128, 129, 130
Lincoln County War 6–9, 24, 25, 40, 108
Lippert, Robert L. 109
Little Crow 170
Lobato, Francisco 95, 160
Lola + Bilidikid (1999) 236–237
Lola and Billy the Kid (1999) see *Lola + Bilidikid*
Long, John 216
The Long Riders (1980) 219
Longabaugh, Harry see Sundance Kid
Loring, Eugene 13
Lowery, Robert 105, 109, 137
Lucky Luke (2009) 237
Lyles, A.C. 31, 180

Mabry, Thomas J. 73, 225, 226
MacGyver (TV series) 248
MacNab, Frank see McNab, Frank
Martell, Donna 131, 136
The Mask (TV series) 248
Mason, "Smiling Billy" 19, 20, 21
Masterson, Bat 164, 174
Matheson, Chris 219, 220–222
Mathews, Billy 216
Maurer, Norman 172, 174
Maverick (TV series) 245
Maxwell, Deluvina 4, 135
Maxwell, Paulita 3–4, 95, 102, 108, 116, 117, 134, 135, 204
Maxwell, Pete 3–5, 95, 108, 134, 135, 140, 204, 227
Maynard, Ken 61, 87, 96
Maynard, Kermit 53, 56, 59, 61
McCall, Jack 170
McCarty, Catherine (Billy's mother) 5, 24, 101, 116, 117, 146, 198
McCarty, Henry see Billy the Kid
McCloskey, William 8, 116, 187, 216
McClure, Michael 13
McCrea, Joel 151, 155, 156, 157
McCubbin, Robert G 1
McKinney, Kip 3, 73, 134, 204, 227, 238
McLaglen, Andrew V. 182, 188–189

McLaglen, Victor 188
McMurtry, Larry 105
McMyer, Pamela 182, 188
McNab, Frank 186, 214, 215, 216
McSween, Alexander 6, 8, 13, 24, 25, 26, 32, 34, 101, 102, 105, 107, 146, 185, 186, 187, 214, 215, 216, 226
McSween, Susan 13, 102, 107, 188, 217
Means, Bobby 167, 171
Means, Russell 171
Melnick, Daniel 209
Middleton, John 40, 107, 186, 203, 214, 215
Milan, Lila 142, 148–149
Miller, David 64, 68
Miller, Don 61
Miller, James "Killin' Jim/Deacon Jim" 203
Miller, John 73, 95
Mitchell, Cameron 124, 129
Mitchell, Thomas 75, 78, 80, 82, 84
Mix, Tom 22, 96
The Monkees (TV series) 1, 247
Montgomery, George 161, 165–166
Moore, Clayton 110, 112
Morris, Harvey 8, 26
Morrison, William 73, 225, 226
Mortensen, Viggo 223, 228
Morton, William "Buck" 8, 25, 40, 102, 116, 146, 186–187, 216
Moss, Charles 195, 197, 19
El Mucacho de Durango (1962) 231
Mulroney, Dermot 211, 217, 228
Murphey, Michael 219, 222
Murphy, Audie 98, 101, 102, 103, 104
Murphy, Lawrence G. 6, 66, 101, 108, 146, 186, 187, 214, 216, 217
The Mysterious Rider (1942) 53–54, 61

Neufeld, Sigmund 38, 40, 42, 43, 44, 46, 47, 48, 50, 51, 52, 53, 55, 56, 57, 58, 60, 131
New Morning of Billy the Kid (1986) see *Birî za Kiddo no Aarashii Yoake*
Newfield, Joel (Joe; Joey) 47, 51, 61
Newfield, Sam 38, 40, 42, 43, 44, 46, 47, 48, 50, 51, 52, 53, 55, 56, 57, 58, 60, 61, 131, 135–136
Newman, Paul 98, 142, 147, 148, 150, 200, 244
Nixon, Richard 190
Nolan, Frederick 1, 134, 187, 215
Nolte, Nick 195, 199
Nott, Robert 89, 91, 117

O'Brien, Dave "Tex" 47, 51, 52, 53, 61
O'Folliard, Tom see Folliard, Tom
Olinger, Camelia 24
Olinger, Robert 10, 26, 27, 101, 102, 108, 117, 126, 147, 204
Omnibus (TV series) 243
Ondaatje, Michael 14

One-Eyed Jacks (1961) 205
O'Neal, Ryan 188
Ormond, Ron 92, 96
O'Sullivan, Maureen 68
Otero, Miguel Antonio 160, 187
Outcasts of the Trail (1949) 151, 158–161
The Outlaw (1943) 61, 64, 69, 75–84
The Outlaws Is Coming! (1965) 172–176
Outlaws of the Plains (1946) 61

Palance, Jack 211, 217
The Parson and the Outlaw (1957) 137–142
Parsons, Louella O. 123
Pasó por Aquí 154, 155, 157
Pat Garrett and Billy the Kid (1973), 193, 200–210, 228, 238
Peckinpah, Sam 92, 182, 193, 200, 205, 206, 207, 208, 209, 210, 228
Penn, Arthur 142, 146, 148, 149, 150
Penn, Sean 223
Peppin, George 107, 187, 216
Peterson, William 223, 228
The Philco Television Playhouse (also *Philco-Goodyear Television Playhouse*; TV series) 147, 148, 244
Phillips, Lou Diamond 211, 217, 223
Phillips, Michelle 191, 193, 194
Pickens, Slim 200, 206, 207
Pickett, Tom 9, 203
Pickford, Mary 141
Pierce, Milo 8
Le Pistole non Discutono (1964) 233
Pistols Don't Argue (1964) see *Le Pistole non Discutono*
Pitts, Michael R. 63
Plowman, Melinda 176, 181
Poe, John W. 3, 4, 30, 134, 208, 227, 228
Poe, Sophie 30
Pollard, Michael J. 195, 198, 200
Producers Releasing Corporation 22, 38, 60, 61, 62, 63, 64, 96
Purgatory (1999) 240, 241

Rainey, Buck 74
Reagan, Ronald 122
The Rebel (TV series) 188, 245
Red Cloud 170
The Red Skelton Hour (TV series) 246
Redemption (2009) 250–251
Reeves, Keanu 219, 222
The Renegade (1943) 58
The Return of Frank James (1940) 22, 69
Return of the Bad Men (1948) 61, 87–92, 179
Revenge of Billy the Kid (1992) 236
Rhode, Print 203
Rhodes, Eugene Manlove 154–155, 157
Richardson, Bill 1
Ringo, Johnny 174

Robards, Jason 200, 206, 244
Roberts, Andrew "Buckshot" 8, 9, 26, 102, 108, 203, 215, 215, 227
Roberts, Lynne 32, 36
Roberts, Ollie L. "Brushy Bill" 73, 95, 225, 226, 228, 229, 230
Robinson, James 228
Rogers, Charles "Buddy" 137, 141, 142
Rogers, Roy 32, 34, 35, 36, 37, 63, 87, 96, 109, 113, 160
Rogers, Will, Jr. 119, 121, 122–123
Romero, Vicente 8, 197
Roth, Joe 211, 217
Rudabaugh, Dave 9, 117, 135, 164, 203, 226, 228
Russell, Bing 176, 181
Russell, Jane 75, 80, 81, 82, 83, 84
Ryan, Robert 87, 92
Rynerson, William 9, 10, 226

The Saga of Billy the Kid 13, 15, 26, 27, 28
St. John, Al "Fuzzy" 38, 40, 42, 43, 44, 46, 47, 48, 50, 51, 52, 53, 55, 56, 57, 58, 61, 63, 92–93, 97
Salazar, Yginio 8, 107
Santa Fe Ring 6, 9, 226
Santley, Joseph 12, 16
Scott, Randolph 15, 87, 90, 91, 92, 123
Scroggins, John 186, 203, 214
Scurlock, Doc 25, 107, 186, 203, 204, 214, 215, 216, 217, 227
Sears, Fred. F. 161, 165
Seydor, Paul 209
Shawhan, Mary 22
Sheen, Charlie 211, 217, 218, 228
Sheen, Martin 217
Sheriff of Sage Valley (1942) 53
Sherman, Harry "Pop" 151, 155, 156
Shor, Dan 219, 222
Short, Paul 98, 102
Siemaszko, Casey 211, 217, 228
Silva, Jesús 95, 160
Silver City, New Mexico 5, 24, 34, 41, 66, 101, 146
Siringo, Charlie 12, 15
Sitka, Emil 172, 175
Skall, William V. 70
Slade, Jack 140–141
Slater, Christian 223, 228
Small, Edward 165
Smith, Beaver 107, 226
Smith, Leonard 70
Smith, Lois 124, 129
Smith, Preacher 170
Smith, Sam 186
Sodja, Joe 137–142
El Solitario (1964) 231–232
Solomon, Ed 219, 220, 222
Sombrero Jack 5–6
Son of Billy the Kid (1949) 75, 92–97
Spottiswoode, Roger 207, 209
Stage 7 (TV series) 243
Stamp, Terence 211, 218
Starr, Belle 90

Starrett, Charles 71, 74, 75
Steele, Bob 38, 40, 42, 43, 44, 46, 47, 48, 60, 62, 68, 131, 137, 142
Stephens (Stevens), "Dirty" Steve 215, 216, 228
Steppling, John 19–20
Stevens, Leslie 142, 147, 148, 149, 150, 203
Stewart, Peggy 84, 86
Stinking Springs, New Mexico 10, 26, 108, 116, 126, 146, 164, 203, 215, 226, 227
Stockwell, Dean 191
Storey, Edith 15, 17, 18, 19
Stories of the Century (TV series) 136, 238, 243
Storm, Gale 98, 103
The Story of Will Rogers (1952) 121
Strange, Glenn 47, 49, 50, 55, 56
Strange Lady in Town (1955) 124–131
Su precio ... unos dólares (1970) 233
Sugarfoot (1951) 123
Sugarfoot (TV series) 123, 193, 244
Sullivan, Barry 200, 206, 208, 242
Sundance Kid 90, 164, 179
Sutherland, Donald 217, 218, 223
Sutherland, Kiefer 211, 215, 217

Tales of Wells Fargo (TV series) 244
The Tall Man (TV series) 242–243
Tamblyn, Russ 191, 193
Tanen, Ned 195
Tascosa, Texas 41, 135
Taurog, Norman 68
Taylor, Ray 92, 96–97
Taylor, Robert 64, 66, 68, 69, 70, 81, 104, 182, 199, 217, 248
Terrors on Horseback (1946) 62
Thomas, Bob 198
The Three Stooges 173, 174, 175, 176
Tierney, Lawrence 117
The Time Tunnel (TV series) 247
Tufts, Sonny 137, 141
Tunstall, John 1, 6, 8, 9, 13, 24, 25, 40, 66, 101, 116, 140, 185, 214, 215, 218, 226
Tuska, Jon 60, 67, 87, 109, 217
Tyler, Tom 60

Un Autre Homme, Une Autre Chance (1977) 235
Upson, Ash 5, 11, 66, 101, 197, 227
Utley, Robert M. 25, 73, 95, 107, 146

Vernon, Wally 105, 109
Vidal, Gore 147, 238, 244
Vidor, King 13, 15, 22, 24, 27–28, 29, 30, 31, 32, 67, 79, 80
Vitagraph 16, 17
Voyagers! (TV series) 248

Waite, Fred 186, 187, 203, 214
Wallace, Lew 8, 9, 10, 11, 26, 34, 35, 66, 101, 102, 108, 116, 126, 146, 186, 217, 220

Index

Waller, Eddie 112
Wallis, Michael 1, 25, 214
Warner, Jack 122, 129, 130, 131, 149, 195, 198, 199, 200
Warren, Jerry 167, 253, 254
Washington, George 8
Wasserman, Lew 194
Wayne, John 28, 29, 30, 35, 60, 82, 182, 188, 189, 190, 191, 193, 217
Wayne, Michael 188
Wayne, Patrick 217, 228
Weaver, Tom 179, 181
West, Adam 172, 175
West of Tombstone (1942) 71–75, 97
Western Cyclone (1943) 56–57
When the Daltons Rode (1940) 15, 69, 91
White, Dean 87, 91
White, Jacqueline 87, 91, 92
Whitehill, Harvey 5–6, 101
Wichita, Kansas 5, 101, 116, 198
Wilson, Billy 9, 146, 203
Wilson, John B. "Squire" 8, 9, 41, 116, 186, 214
Windsor, Marie 137, 141–142
Winter, Alex 219, 222
Withers, Grant 110, 113
Wood, Natalie 129–130
Woods, Walter 12, 15, 16, 18
Worth, Lothrop 180
Wurlitzer, Rudy 200, 205, 207
Yates, Herbert J. 34, 86, 108
Young, Carleton 38, 40, 42, 43, 44, 61
Young Guns (1988) 1, 211–223, 228, 229, 230
Young Guns II (1990) 1, 217, 223–230
Younger, Bob 89, 179
Younger, Cole 15, 89, 179
Younger, Jim 89, 179

Zamora, Francisco 8, 107
Zozobra 126
Zsigmond, Vilmos 172

www.ingramcontent.com/pod-product-compliance
Lightning Source LLC
Chambersburg PA
CBHW081543300426
44116CB00015B/2736